RED RECKONING

RED RECKONING

THE COLD WAR AND THE TRANSFORMATION OF AMERICAN LIFE

EDITED BY **MARK BOULTON**
AND **TOBIAS T. GIBSON**

LOUISIANA STATE UNIVERSITY PRESS
BATON ROUGE

Published by Louisiana State University Press
lsupress.org

Copyright © 2023 by Louisiana State University Press
All rights reserved. Except in the case of brief quotations used in articles or reviews, no part of this publication may be reproduced or transmitted in any format or by any means without written permission of Louisiana State University Press.

LSU Press Paperback Original

DESIGNER: Michelle A. Neustrom
TYPEFACE: Whitman

Linda Weiss's essay is a condensed and abridged version of "Rise of the National Security State as a Technology Enterprise," in Linda Weiss, *America Inc.? Innovation and Enterprise in the National Security State* (Ithaca, NY: Cornell University Press, 2014), 21–50, copyright © 2014 Cornell University, and is used with permission of Cornell University Press.

Kurt Edward Kemper's essay is excerpted from *College Football and American Culture in the Cold War Era*. Copyright © 2009 by the Board of Trustees of the University of Illinois. Used with permission of the University of Illinois Press.

Tony Shaw's essay is an abridged version of chapter 1 of *Cinematic Cold War: The American and Soviet Struggle for Hearts and Minds*, by Tony Shaw and Denise J. Youngblood, published by the University Press of Kansas, © 2010. www.kansaspress.ku.edu. Used by permission of the publisher.

COVER ILLUSTRATION: *Doomtown VI*, by Doug Waterfield. Reproduced courtesy of the artist.

LIBRARY OF CONGRESS CATALOGING-IN-PUBLICATION DATA
Names: Boulton, Mark, 1973– editor. | Gibson, Tobias T., 1972– editor.
Title: Red reckoning : the Cold War and the transformation of American life / edited by Mark Boulton and Tobias T. Gibson.
Description: Baton Rouge : Louisiana State University Press, [2024] | Includes bibliographical references and index.
Identifiers: LCCN 2023012359 (print) | LCCN 2023012360 (ebook) | ISBN 978-0-8071-8008-2 (paperback) | ISBN 978-0-8071-8082-2 (pdf) | ISBN 978-0-8071-8081-5 (epub)
Subjects: LCSH: United States—Civilization—1945– | Cold War—Influence. | World politics—1945–1989.
Classification: LCC E169.12 .R4315 2024 (print) | LCC E169.12 (ebook) | DDC 973.92—dc23/eng/20230612
LC record available at https://lccn.loc.gov/2023012359
LC ebook record available at https://lccn.loc.gov/2023012360

CONTENTS

1   Introduction
MARK BOULTON AND TOBIAS T. GIBSON

11   **I. STRUCTURE AND SOCIETY**

19   Security against Democracy: The Legacy of the Cold War at Home
ELAINE TYLER MAY

44   From Subordinated to a Bedrock Principle: The Supreme Court on Free Speech during the Cold War
ERIC T. KASPER

62   Loyalty and Law: Cold War Conformity in the Legal Profession
MARY ELIZABETH BASILE CHOPAS

78   The Rise of the National Security State as a Technology Enterprise
LINDA WEISS

99   The Cold War and US Immigration Policy: The Legacy of Migrant Screening on Diaspora Communities in America
PETER J. VEROVŠEK

125   **II. CREATING A COLD WAR IDENTITY**

131   Race Relations and the Cold War
ANN V. COLLINS

146   Guns, Manhood, and the Cold War
ANGELA F. KEATON

162   No Substitute for Football: Cold War Culture and College Football
      KURT EDWARD KEMPER

182   Televangelism and the Transformation of American Christianity
      RANDI BARNES-COX AND CHARITY RAKESTRAW

202   A War of Colors: Cold War Food Advertising in US Newspapers and Magazines, 1946–1960
      FRANCESCO BUSCEMI

219   **III. CULTURE AND POPULAR ENTERTAINMENT**

225   Hollywood's Cold War: The Battle for Hearts and Minds on Film
      TONY SHAW

248   To Condense a Mockingbird: Harper Lee, *Reader's Digest*, and the Cold War
      KRISTEN POPHAM AND SIMON STOW

267   Playing by New Rules: Board Games and Cold War American Culture, 1945–1965
      MATT SPRENGELER

286   The Cops versus the Commies: Cold War Cuba and Chile in US Folk Music
      EUNICE ROJAS

304   Us and Them: The Eagle versus the Hammer and Sickle in the Cold War Sporting Arena
      KURT W. JEFFERSON

319   Contributors

325   Index

RED
RECKONING

INTRODUCTION

On May 1, 1950, communism came to America as an armed "combat team" overran the small town of Mosinee in the heart of Wisconsin.[1] The invading force marched on the homes of Mayor Ralph E. Kronenwetter and Police Chief Carl Gewiss and demanded that they submit to new Bolshevik rulers. From there, the team went on to seize the local paper mill and the library, and by midmorning the Soviet hammer and sickle flew over city hall. Other community leaders and church officials were soon rounded up and forced into concentration camps.

Throughout the remainder of the day, raiding parties inspected homes for anticommunist literature and confiscated sporting firearms. Every cherished aspect of American life was being dismantled. At downtown restaurants, traditional American fare gave way to beet-and-cabbage soup with rye bread on the side. Students ditched their springtime colors for drab Communist Youth uniforms. The candy store announced that only members of the Communist Youth could enjoy their treats. The movie theater removed reels of the anticommunist drama *Guilty of Treason* and replaced them with state-produced propaganda films.

The town's newspaper was renamed the *Red Star* and printed on pink paper. It abandoned local interest stories and declared itself "the new official publication of Mosinee's United Soviet States of America government." Alongside a hagiographic "History of Stalin Our Valiant Leader," the front page carried "Instructions to Citizens," which included turning all land, property, commercial enterprises, and resources over to the state. In addition to announcing the dissolution of all political parties, the paper concluded that "the Declaration of Independence, the Constitution of the United States and the Bill of Rights as instruments of bourgeois power and democracy are abolished and have no legal or moral force whatsoever in the country."

Less than three months earlier, Wisconsin senator Joseph McCarthy had foreshadowed these devastating events when, at a speech delivered to the Women's Republican Club of Wheeling, West Virginia, McCarthy asked his audience, "Can there be anyone tonight who is so blind as to say that the war is not on? Can there be anyone who fails to realize that the Communist world has said 'the time is now'—that this is the time for the showdown between the democratic Christian world and the communistic atheistic world?" He went on to claim that "known Communists" had infiltrated the State Department and were actively shaping policy at the highest levels of government. His speech ushered in an era of paranoia that bore his name and heightened concerns that communist subversion might undermine American society. The events unfolding in Mosinee seemed to confirm his worst fears.

But the "communist" takeover of a small corner of McCarthy's home state on that day in May was neither a fifth column nor the leading edge of an approaching Red storm. Instead, the Mosinee "Day under Communist Rule" was the idea of local American Legion leaders, led by World War II veteran Francis F. Schweinler. With McCarthy's words ringing in his ears, Schweinler wanted to show "what privileges and rights we would lose if communism took over." He implored the people of Mosinee to join with him so that they could give the world a "lesson in Americanism—by actually living for a day in the same manner that people are forced to live in communist-controlled land."[2]

The day's finale began just after sunset at Dessert Park, where the schedule of events called for the "'Communists' [to] cast aside their subversive roles and join in the raising of the American flag. Boy Scouts [will] burn all Communist banners, etc. in [a] huge bonfire. . . . Then [the] whole multitude will join in singing 'GOD BLESS AMERICA' and then start peacefully home thankful to God that they live in AMERICA." There was an unfortunate postscript to the day's events: Mayor Kronenwetter fell ill soon after being led from his house in his nightwear and died five days later, and one of the town's ministers suffered a fatal heart attack a week after his staged arrest.

The specter of global communism forced Americans to confront an existential threat to their very existence, and the "attack" on Mosinee captured many of the anxieties they felt throughout the Cold War. The event organizers wanted to highlight the need for constant vigilance against potential foes, foreign and domestic. With the ideological nature of the Cold War taking precedence over direct military confrontation, the victorious side would have to win hearts and minds as much as any battlefield victory. Therefore, the targets in the communist crosshairs in Mosinee included foundational tenets of American society such as representative democracy, religious freedom, civil liberties, gun ownership, consumer choice, tastes, and habits, and all forms of media and entertainment. As these things were challenged in Mosinee, so they were in America writ large. The most cherished aspects of society were either vigorously defended or mobilized throughout the Cold War in ways that altered the very fabric of American society. The following essays explore a cross section of just some of the ways in which the Cold War transformed American life.

This volume brings together interdisciplinary scholarship that illustrates how the Cold War challenged almost every facet of American life. The book is divided into three parts: "Structure and Society," "Creating a Cold War Identity," and "Culture and Popular Entertainment." The essays in part 1 analyze how basic societal structure adapted to the Cold War challenge. These adaptations included abandoning collective democratic norms in favor of individual security, the construction of a security state, restrictions on free speech, the manipulation of immigration laws, and conformity in professional life. Part 2 examines how the Cold War affected American identity in the areas of civil rights, gun culture, college football, religion, and consumerism. Part 3 explores the production and consumption of culture and popular entertainment such as movies, literature, music, sports, and leisure activities. Collectively, these essays reveal the multitude of anxieties and actions that led to a fundamental reordering of American life. They are relatively brief, provocative, and designed to generate discussion. While many of our authors allude to it, readers are encouraged to reflect further on the ways in which the world they live in today still bears the hallmarks of the Cold War.

* * *

The broad geopolitical contours of the Cold War are well known but are worth summarizing here to provide historical context for the essays that follow. By the eve of World War II, both the United States and the Soviet Union had fully developed and mutually incompatible systems of government based on their own historical experiences, and both nations aggressively sought to preserve and promote their ideology in the postwar world. For the United States, overthrowing the yoke of the British Empire had left a devotion to the Enlightenment values of political liberalism via parliamentary assemblies and constitutionally guaranteed individual freedoms, such as freedom of speech and worship, allied to a faith in the virtues of free market capitalism. In reality, these ideals were undermined by the system of chattel slavery up through the Civil War and the ongoing exclusion of many groups from the ideas enshrined in the nation's founding documents, but they remained aspirational and a key component of the image Americans sought to project abroad.

The Soviet Union adapted the ideals of Karl Marx, who, upon observing the inequalities and abuses wrought by the worst excesses of capitalism brought on by the Industrial Revolution, advocated a communal vision of global cooperation in which nations would no longer fight over resources and workers would be free to enjoy the fruits of their labor. Amid the chaos of Russia's decision to leave World War I, Vladimir Lenin's minority Bolshevik movement seized power and then consolidated it, following the Russian Civil War (1917–1922). This victory allowed the Bolsheviks to establish the first communist state, the Union of Soviet Socialist Republics. Instead of becoming the utopian society envisioned by Karl Marx, however, Lenin and—far more brutally—his eventual successor, Joseph Stalin, established a society in which equality of condition was coerced through strict government control of the economy and the curtailment of individual liberties. The establishment of the Communist International, or Comintern, in 1919, to promote bolshevism abroad, and Stalin's ruthless program of industrialization through a series of Five-Year Plans, made the Soviet Union a threatening presence to Western democratic societies.

Tensions between the communist East and capitalist West existed from the very inception of the Soviet Union. The United States was among a host of nations to send a small number of forces in a doomed attempt to prevent the Bolshevik victory during the Russian Civil War. Although the US government finally recognized the Soviet Union in 1933, relations were not helped by the Soviets' signing of a nonaggression pact with Nazi Germany in 1939. When the Nazis violated this pact by invading Russia in June 1941, the United States recognized the greater threat of Hitler's forces and sent supplies to aid the Soviet Union's defense through programs such as Lend-Lease. Following the Japanese attack on Pearl Harbor on December 7, 1941, and subsequent US entry into the war, the United States joined the Soviet Union and the United Kingdom in a "Grand Alliance" for the remainder of the conflict. Differences between the countries, however, simmered just below the surface. In particular, Soviet premier Joseph Stalin bristled at the perceived indifference of the British and Americans to opening a western front to alleviate pressure on his forces.

With Nazi Germany and imperial Japan vanquished in 1945, the division between the Allied nations became more acute. The West bristled at the Soviet Union's refusal to retreat from nations it had wrested from Nazi control. The Soviet desire to rebuild its economy and create a buffer zone to the West in the wake of World War II led it to install friendly regimes in Eastern Europe and to keep an iron grip on East Germany. Many Western observers were also alarmed by a speech Stalin gave to the Soviet Party Congress on February 9, 1946, in which he placed blame for World War II squarely on the West. Portending future conflict with his estranged allies, he claimed that "the development of world capitalism in our times does not proceed smoothly and evenly, but through crises and catastrophic wars."

Two weeks later, US diplomat George F. Kennan sent his influential "Long Telegram" from Moscow to the State Department. In it, he suggested that Soviet postwar goals would be to aggressively promote the "relative strength of USSR" while undermining the "strength and influence, collectively as well as individually, of capitalist powers." Soon thereafter, on March 5, 1946, former British prime minister Winston Churchill amplified these growing concerns in a speech at Westminster College in Fulton, Missouri. Accompanied by Harry S. Truman, Churchill warned of the events taking place behind the "Iron Curtain" in Eastern Europe and called for the forging of a special relationship between the United States and Great Britain to meet the threat of further communist expansion. Thereafter, relations between the United States and the Soviet Union deteriorated rapidly.

In 1947, in response to growing communist threats in Greece and Turkey, Truman committed the United States to "support free peoples who are resisting attempted subjugation by armed minorities or by outside pressures." His doctrine of "containment" of communism wherever it sought to spread established a policy of global military and covert intervention that gained bipartisan support throughout the duration of the Cold War. No longer would the nation retreat into the indolence of isolationism that had characterized its interwar foreign policy. Beginning in 1947, the Marshall Plan to rebuild Europe's economy further deepened divisions between Western and Eastern Europe while tying US foreign policy firmly to the vitality and security of the former. That same year, the National Security Act remade the US military, creating the Central Intelligence Agency and other components of the intelligence community to counter the growing communist threat.

A series of events at the end of the decade severed any remaining threads of goodwill. By 1948, the Soviet Union had blockaded Berlin, leading to the Berlin Airlift, and in 1949 the Soviets successfully tested their first nuclear weapon, ending the comforting security of a nuclear monopoly for Americans. Later that year, Mao Zedong's Chinese Communist Party triumphed in the Chinese Civil War, and from a US perspective, a billion people were "lost" overnight. The 1950 invasion of North Korea into the South gave fillip to concerns of communist expansion. At home, revelations of spying and the high-profile trial and execution of Julius and Ethel Rosenberg for passing nuclear secrets to the Soviets raised fears of domestic subversion.

With tensions rising and the World War II alliance now in ashes, both superpowers sought new security partners to whom they would provide economic and military support. The creation of the North Atlantic Treaty Organization (1949) and the Warsaw Pact (1955) solidified the division of the world into two opposing camps. This also led to both sides establishing military bases in friendly nations across the globe. Even those nations that remained formally nonaligned often favored one side over the other, depending on their own ideological, strategic, and economic interests.

Furthermore, both sides began to stockpile an enormous number of weapons. In April 1950, the US State Department's National Security Council Paper 68, or NSC-68, advocated massive military spending, which would continue for the duration of the conflict. The resulting arms race led to the rapid development of ever more powerful conventional and nuclear weaponry. The United States tested a hydrogen bomb in 1952, followed by the Soviets' test in 1955.

Meanwhile, sophisticated delivery systems (the nuclear triad of aircraft, submarines, and intercontinental ballistic missiles) threatened global annihilation, should war break out. The idea that any preemptive strike by either side would result in a retaliatory attack in which both sides would be destroyed created a fragile nuclear deterrent.

While this concept of mutually assured destruction helped to prevent the Cold War from turning hot, there were numerous indirect conflicts as both superpowers and their allies sent forces or lent material support to prevent the expansion of the other side's influence. This resulted in a series of proxy wars and flash points that punctuated the conflict. Oftentimes, these confrontations arose against the backdrop of decolonization, which accelerated during the decades following World War II. The vacuum created by the dismantling of empires provided opportunities for the two superpowers and their allies to support friendly governments in newly liberated countries. Leaders in those countries willingly accepted support from the power bloc that best served their nation's interests or their own ambitions.

Few areas of the globe were untouched by the conflict. In Europe, the Soviet crushing of liberation movements in Hungary in 1956 and during the Czechoslovakian Prague Spring of 1968 kept tensions high. The Berlin Wall served as a physical embodiment of the barriers between East and West, from its construction in 1961 through its demise in 1989. In Asia, the US pledge to prevent the spread of communism led to a massive military operation in South Korea and an even greater—if futile and costly—commitment to propping up South Vietnam. In the Middle East, the United States orchestrated the overthrow of the democratically elected Iranian leader, Mohammad Mosaddegh, in 1953. Compounded by its support of his repressive successor, Shah Mohammad Reza Pahlavi, this action led to intense anti-US sentiment, which culminated in the 1979 Islamic Revolution and which continues to this day.

That same year, the Soviet Union began a disastrous decade-long military commitment to propping up the socialist government in Afghanistan. In Africa, Egyptian leader Gamal Abdel Nasser's anti-imperialist policies received a significant boost of arms and support from communist nations. By contrast, when the Soviets supported Patrice Lumumba's efforts to lead the uranium-rich Congo out of Belgian control, the United States backed his pro-

Western opponent, Joseph-Désiré Mobutu. Lumumba was executed in the subsequent coup.

Closer to home, the United States was determined to prevent communism from taking hold in South and Central America. CIA-backed operations resulted in the overthrow of popular left-wing regimes in Guatemala (1953) and Chile (1973). Less successful was the calamitous Bay of Pigs attempt to oust Fidel Castro's communist regime from Cuba in 1961. The following year, the discovery of Soviet nuclear missiles on the island led to a standoff between President John F. Kennedy and Premier Nikita Khrushchev, which almost led to a direct confrontation. Kennedy's secretary of defense, Robert McNamara, recalled leaving a meeting during the crisis and fearing that he "might never live to see another Saturday night." Only last-minute diplomatic maneuverings averted disaster.

Beyond terrestrial confines, the boundaries of space also became a Cold War battleground. Space exploration represented the apotheosis of technological superiority and innovation. The Soviets' successful launch of the first satellite, Sputnik, in 1957, accelerated the US space program. And while the Soviets would go on to achieve notable firsts, such as the first animals in space, the first man and woman in space, the first spacewalk, and the first lunar probes, Americans took immense pride in sending the first man to the moon, in 1969. Lyndon Johnson even declared, in 1963, "I do not believe that this generation of Americans is willing to resign itself to going to bed each night by the light of a Communist moon." After an era of détente, ushered in by Richard Nixon's diplomatic overtures to the Soviet Union and China in the 1970s and a signing of arms limitation agreements (SALT I), the Cold War accelerated toward its denouement during the presidency of Ronald Reagan.

At the end of the 1970s, Jimmy Carter's presidency had seen a few notable diplomatic breakthroughs, including further arms reduction treaties (SALT II) and the promotion of human rights as a core foreign policy goal. But for the American electorate, these were overshadowed by the Soviet invasion of Afghanistan and the Iran hostage crisis, which followed the Islamic Revolution in 1979. Reagan came into office as an avowed anticommunist hawk, promising to restore a sense of American exceptionalism. His election coincided with the rising Solidarity anticommunist movement in Poland and unrest in other areas of Eastern Europe. Seeking to apply external pressure to these significant internal threats to the Soviet empire, Reagan recast the Cold War as a Manichean battle between good and evil, in which there could be no accommodation. He backed up his rhetoric with dramatically increased military spending and covert support of anticommunist forces known as Contras in Central America. He also touted the Strategic Defense Initiative, often referred to as "Star Wars," after the famed science fiction movie series, as a method of destroying incoming Soviet missiles. Although the technology was nowhere near advanced enough to create a viable system at the time, SDI threatened the balance of power created by the nuclear deterrent. Reagan's approach to the Soviets, however, was markedly different during his second term.

Mikhail Gorbachev's ascension to the Soviet leadership in 1985 proved to be the turning point in the Cold War. The young—certainly compared to his predecessors—Gorbachev ushered in seminal reforms in an attempt to ease widespread economic hardship and dissatisfaction. His policies of glasnost (openness) and perestroika (restructuring) unleashed pent-up frustrations, which brought down the Communist Party. Reagan's skill during this era was to reach out to Gorbachev and, in a series of high-profile summits, reach broad agreements on such issues as arms reduction. This easing of tensions allowed the Soviet Union to unravel from within. Across Eastern Europe, popular uprisings led to the rapid break-up of the USSR. The fall of the Berlin Wall—so long a symbol of division—on November 9, 1989, gave some of the most poignant images of the unfolding events.

A brief attempt by hard-line Communists to reverse Gorbachev's reforms led to his ouster, but the public backlash to this move finally ended the communist grip on the nation in 1991. In his State of the Union address on January 28, 1992, President George H. W. Bush proudly declared, "The biggest thing that has happened in the world in my life, in our lives, is this: by the grace of God, America won the Cold War." The war was over, but not without having fundamentally transformed American life.

NOTES

1. In this book, we use the lowercase form "communism" for general references to the system of thought and the uppercase form "Communist" only in reference to the political party.

2. The description of events in Mosinee is summarized from Carl R. Weinberg, "D-Day in Mosinee," *OAH Magazine of History* 24, no. 4 (October 2010), 3; Brett Rosenberg, "The Small, Midwestern Town Taken Over by Fake Communists," *New Republic*, October 22, 2020, https://newrepublic.com/article/159873/small-midwestern-town-taken-fake-communists; and the primary source documents "It Happened One Day in Mosinee, Schedule of Events, April 30–May 1, 1950," "The Red Star Mosinee Communist newspaper, May 1, 1950," and "American Legion: Letter to Citizens of Mosinee," undated.

STRUCTURE AND SOCIETY

The need for constant vigilance and security during the Cold War necessitated a physical transformation of the American landscape as well as the legal, economic, and professional frameworks in which Americans operated. These structures helped define what kind of a nation the United States became during the Cold War and beyond. Some of the most evident structural changes derived from the enormous military spending and preparedness that characterized the Cold War.

Before World War II, there was little need to maintain a large military, as Americans adopted their historic role of avoiding entangling alliances. Nonetheless, the nation's industrial might always held the potential to create a devastatingly powerful military. Even before Pearl Harbor, weapons development and military training had already begun, which would convert the nation into the world's preeminent military power. The rapid advent of the Cold War ensured that the nation's wartime footing barely abated. In 1947, the National Security Act created the National Security Council to provide rapid diplomatic and military advice to the president. It also created the Department of Defense to oversee the US Navy, Army, and newly created Air Force, and established the CIA. Following the recommendations of National Security Council Memorandum 68, in April 1950, the United States embarked on massive military spending on nuclear and conventional weaponry to counter the Soviet threat.

The reliance on a robust and technologically advanced military required that recruits in all branches be well trained, well equipped, and housed. As a result, there was an increase in the number, size, and geographic spread of domestic military bases. Due to the fear that a Soviet attack might come across the Arctic Circle, new Air Force facilities were built in northern border states, including Loring Air Force Base in Maine, which was opened in 1953 as the easternmost air base in the continental United States. North Dakota's Grand Forks Air Force Base housed fighters designed to intercept Soviet bombers, and the nearby Minot Air Force Base contained both inceptors and nuclear intercontinental ballistic missiles. Both opened in 1957. Even before its 1959 statehood, Alaska was a US focal point in the Cold War and contained forward operating bases out of which interceptor aircraft flew.

Across the forty-eight contiguous states, new bases were built for other branches of the military. The US Marines, for example, saw extensive expansion to their facilities. Camp Pendleton saw a $20 million expansion and renovation in 1950, which allowed it to train about 200,000 Marines for Korean War combat. In response to the perceived lack of preparedness of American forces in Korea, the Marines created the Cold Weather Battalion, renamed in 1963 as the Mountain Warfare Training Center.

Even the Interstate Highway System, which allowed enormous economic expansion, suburbanization, and greater mobility in American life, bore the influence of the Cold War. A national system of highways to boost economic development had been on the planning board for decades. The Cold War, however, gave these plans renewed impetus. The 1956 National Interstate and Defense Highways Act came to fruition in part due to the logistical lessons Eisenhower had learned while leading American forces in Europe. In contrast to the difficulties of moving military equipment using a patchwork of different quality roads and bridges, he noted the ease with which equipment could be moved on the German autobahn system of national highways and sought to replicate that system at home. For similar reasons, the Department of Defense supported the proposal. The often-repeated idea that interstates contain sections designed as emergency runways for military aircraft is, however, apocryphal.

The construction of nuclear fallout shelters further altered the American landscape. The threat of Soviet invasion or—more likely—a nuclear attack was consistently in the minds of many Americans. Schoolchildren were taught to "duck and cover" under their school desks to protect themselves from a nuclear fireball. At home, many families built fallout shelters to provide domestic protection. In 1961, President John F. Kennedy pushed the construction of private fallout shelters, and Americans complied, going from an estimated 60,000 to

200,000 by 1965. The cover story of *Life* magazine's September 15, 1961, edition was "How You Can Survive Fallout." The magazine contained an open letter from Kennedy advocating building more shelters and claimed that "97 of 100 people can be saved" by their construction.

Not only were the shelters themselves important, but so too was the sustenance (one hesitates to call it food) that stocked those shelters. Beginning in 1955, the Federal Civil Defense Administration advocated that every American have a seven-day supply of food and water. The need for long-lasting staples led the Department of Agriculture to develop a biscuit called the All-Purpose Survival Cracker. It was made of bulgur wheat and was selected because, as one civil defense leader suggested in congressional testimony, its "shelf life has been established by being edible after 3,000 years in an Egyptian pyramid." By 1964, more than 20 billion survival crackers had been made.

Other changes to American society went far beyond physical construction and impacted the social, legal, and professional frameworks of everyday life. From the very beginning of the Cold War, the government introduced security measures that challenged Americans' civil liberties. Just weeks after announcing his doctrine of communist "containment," Harry Truman implemented a form of domestic containment by introducing a loyalty program for federal employees via Executive Order 9835. The program authorized federal departments to set up review boards with the power to dismiss anyone whose activities were "reasonably" deemed a security risk. In the legislature, the House Un-American Activities Committee heard testimony from a succession of filmmakers and celebrities, including then actor Ronald Reagan, on the alleged influence of communism in the movie industry. Those who refused to comply with the commission faced either imprisonment, as in the case of the Hollywood Ten, or blacklisting from future employment in the industry which happened to hundreds more.

Events at the end of the 1940s and early 1950s seemed to confirm Americans' worst fears about the communist menace. The Soviet blockade of Berlin in 1948 and detonation of an atomic bomb in August 1949, the Communist victory in the Chinese Civil War in October 1949, the Communist advance into South Korea in 1950, and the uncovering of Communist spy rings in the United States and Great Britain engendered a sense of great unease that the nation was in peril. The politician whose name became synonymous with the resulting "Red Scare" was Wisconsin senator Joseph McCarthy.

At a speech in Wheeling, West Virginia, in February 1950, McCarthy held aloft a list of what he claimed were known Communists in the State Department. Despite remaining deliberately evasive about specific names or details of the alleged infiltration, McCarthy's accusations tapped into the growing paranoia. His charge that the Democrats had been soft on communism also gave Republicans a useful issue with which to regain the reins of government, which they had scarcely held since before the New Deal. In 1953, as chair of a Senate subcommittee, McCarthy began confronting numerous government officials and questioned their ties to communism in a series of contentious hearings.

It was clear that McCarthy reveled in the spotlight, but as his targets and his accusations grew increasingly outrageous, his crusade and his political career came to an ignominious end. In 1954, his aggressive questioning of army leaders at a televised hearing, which included the notorious retort from one army lawyer, who asked McCarthy, "Have you no sense of decency, sir?," soured the opinion of both the public and his Senate colleagues, who censured him for conduct unbecoming. Predictably, during the censure debate, McCarthy claimed that his accusers were cowards and communists conducting a "lynch party." Thereafter, McCarthy's influence quickly waned, and he died in 1957, most likely from the effects of alcoholism.

The McCarthy era elevated fears that communism had infiltrated all aspects of American life and gave rise to laws that challenged the limits of liberty. Among the most notable was the 1950 Internal Security Act, more commonly known as the McCarran Act, after its primary sponsor, Senator Pat McCarran (D-Nevada). The law focused on limiting communist reach in the United States and had three key provisions. First, it required communist organizations to register with the attorney general and it created the Subversive Activities Control Board, charged with investigating individuals with communist ties. Second, and perhaps more controversially, it also allowed the president to detain individuals who were thought to be plotting espionage or sabotage. Finally, the law allowed for the exclusion and deportation of communists and other suspected subversive persons—which severely limited the number of displaced Germans and Russians who were allowed to enter the United States. Congress passed the act over a veto by Harry Truman, who claimed that it went too far in compromising American liberties and that "it would help the communist propagandists throughout the world who are trying to undermine freedom by discrediting as hypocrisy the efforts of the United States on behalf of freedom." Although much of the act was eventually limited by Supreme Court cases in the 1960s, and the emergency detention was repealed under the Nixon administration, the Cold War continued to influence the government's approach to dissent among its own citizens.

By the mid-1960s, the domestic political environment had shifted, and radically so. After the assassination of President Kennedy, the US involvement in Vietnam, explicitly intended to push back communism from allied South Vietnam, became extremely controversial and served as a primer for a contested political environment. A bourgeoning antiwar movement, in tandem with an increasingly vocal and successful racial rights movement, changed the tenor of politics in the United States.

However, while much of the populace worked for increased civil rights and liberties, there were divergent responses by the institutions in the federal government. Congress passed laws recognizing the civil rights and voting rights of a wider section of American citizens, and the Supreme Court recognized broader rights in many areas, including free speech and civil rights based on race. The executive branch, however, responded by surveilling civil rights leaders such as Dr. Martin King Jr., antiwar activists, and even members of the Supreme Court. This reaction was justified by tying the antiwar and rights movements to the idea that leaders and participants were communists, or at least communist sympathizers. Elsewhere, the Cold War fueled the growth of federal power in more positive ways.

Education was another area of American life affected by the Cold War. The 1944 GI Bill helped World War II veterans go to college in record numbers. By 1956, about 8 million recipients had gone to college or trade school, leading to the opening of many universities and colleges across the country. The ongoing Cold War draft and the elevated personnel needs necessitated by involvement in the hot spots of Korea and Vietnam led to further GI Bills in 1952 and 1966. Although never as generous as the World War II GI Bill, these later versions enshrined the principle that the government would aid the reintegration of its veterans beyond the long-established bestowal of health care and pensions. Not all veterans benefited equally, it should be noted, as Black veterans often faced discrimination. Following World War II, for example, racist local administrators in the Deep South prevented the equal distribution of benefits, while during the Vietnam era, benefits were denied due to less-than-honorable discharges, which often were disproportionately given to Black soldiers.

The GI Bills elevated the importance of higher education, but they were just one part of increased federal investment in education fueled by Cold War concerns. The success of the Russian space program spurred calls for increased math and science education from kindergarten to university. The National Defense Education Act of 1958, which saw the first large-scale involvement of the federal government in education beyond the veteran population, came as a direct result of the Soviet lunch of Sputnik the previous year. Universities were also funded, in part, by components of the military. Programs such as the Reserve Officers' Training Corps (ROTC) and science education as part of the national security enterprise were tied directly to the rise of the Cold War university education. Additionally, public school homework increased because of the need for a scientifically literate, technologically advanced society to counter the threats posed by the Soviet space and nuclear programs.

Though science was a key part of the K-12 education and at universities and colleges, so too was civics. Understanding representative democracy and the economic hegemony of capitalism became key components of American education. At universities, Russian studies—covering history, culture, and language—were key to staffing the Cold War–era CIA and State Department with qualified diplomats and linguists.

The specter of communism was also used by those who wished to limit the expansion of the federal government. As Ronald Reagan transitioned from his acting career toward being an ardent anticommunist crusader in politics, he consistently used the threat of totalitarian government to oppose progressive measures and federal overreach. With his Hollywood career stalling, Reagan became a well-paid spokesperson for General Electric during the 1950s. He traveled the country, giving speeches to the company's workers in which he railed against government bureaucracy, organized labor, and high taxation while extolling the virtues of free market capitalism as the only antidote to what he saw as a dangerous slide toward a society that thwarted individualism and free enterprise.

His words also influenced the debate over universal health care, as in 1961 he spoke on an LP record on behalf of the American Medical Association, in opposition to Medicare. His/their reasoning was that any government control in health care, far from being an investment in the well-being of its citizens, would deny Americans individual choice and make them subject to further state control.

He carried this same theme that government programs represent dangerous steps on the road to totalitarian control into his successful run for the California governorship, and ultimately to the White House. In the Soviet Union, he had a perfect foil with which to contrast his antistatist policies. These ideas helped define the conservative movement, which far outlasted the end of the Cold War.

The essays in this section further elaborate on some of the ways in which the structure of American society evolved due to Cold War concerns. Elaine Tyler May's essay, "Security against Democracy: The Legacy of the Cold War at Home," describes the impact of the US "security obsession" as a challenge to democratic norms. Because American politicians and media highlighted the preeminence of individual security, the sanctity of the home, and consumer spending, May argues that there has been a subtle but continuous move away from the community ethic that defined the United States prior to the mid-twentieth century. Eric Kasper's essay, "From Subordinated to a Bedrock Principle: The Supreme Court on Free Speech during the Cold War," looks at how the Cold War directly impacted the court's views on free speech, which evolved from something that needed to be curtailed in the interests of security, early in the conflict, to something that needed to be reinforced, in the latter stages, as a fundamental indicator of the freedoms Americans enjoyed. In "Loyalty and Law: Cold War Conformity in the Legal Profession," Mary Elizabeth Basile Chopas details the impact of anticommunist loyalty oaths on lawyers and the practice of law and how the American Bar Association pushed back against some of the more egregious demands on the legal profession. Linda Weiss's "The Rise of the National Security State as a Technology Enterprise" describes the development of the national security state, its impact on the Cold War executive branch, its versatility in the face of national security threats, and how the national security state's reliance on technological development led to partnerships between the public and private sectors that drove technological advancements beneficial to both sectors. The final essay of this section, Peter J. Verovšek's "The Cold War and US Immigration Policy: The Legacy of Migrant Screening on Diaspora Communities in America," reveals how Cold War immigration policy was constructed to prevent communist sympathizers from relocating to the United States, while also allowing "extremist individuals with right-wing views from East-Central Europe" to immigrate, thereby affecting the political demographic of postwar America.

SECURITY AGAINST DEMOCRACY

The Legacy of the Cold War at Home

ELAINE TYLER MAY

The first decade of the twenty-first century was marked by the events of September 11, 2001, and the war on terror that followed. Since then, we have seen a dramatic preoccupation with security that sparked a wide range of antidemocratic policies, from torture to Guantanamo to the Patriot Act. We have become accustomed to orange alerts, metal detectors, and taking off our shoes at airports. But if we assume that all this started with 9/11, or that the trouble lies primarily with public policies, we miss the deeper roots of our national security obsession, which began more than half a century ago, permeating not just public life but private life as well.

The preoccupation with security emerged during the same decades that American democracy expanded to become more inclusive and more tolerant. As a result of what some have called the "rights revolution"—the civil rights, feminist, gay liberation, and disability rights movements—the United States came much closer to reaching its full democratic promise.

These two goals—to expand democracy and to achieve security—need not be in conflict. Democracy and security depend upon each other. In a thriving democracy, citizens engage with one another across differences, empowered to grapple with problems and address common concerns. Democracy fosters trust and a healthy public life. But when citizens retreat from public life, they are unable to achieve meaningful change on behalf of the common good. People are more likely to feel insecure and distrust each other, and democracy withers. Security also withers, shrinking to a negative concept that is little more than fear combined with force. Yet true security has more to do with trust and confidence than with boundaries, bunkers, and weapons.

In the United States since World War II, security and democracy have been on a collision course. Misguided ideas about security, along with an investment in private life at the expense of public life, have muted efforts to expand and strengthen democracy, resulting in a nation that is not as democratic, nor as secure, as it could be.

The reasons for this clash of national interests reach back far into American history. Citizens have long been willing to compromise their basic democratic rights to achieve national security, especially during wartime. But since World War II, that willingness to sacrifice rights for security has become chronic. The Cold War ushered in an uneasy era often described as "peacetime." In fact, however, the Cold War was more hot than cold, marked by more or less constant warfare. Despite all the talk of maintaining peace, war became a fixture of life. In the words of Michael Sherry, Americans have been living in the "shadow of war" since the 1930s.[1]

Antidemocratic policies, from the early Cold War purges of suspected communists and homosexuals to the erosion of individual rights in the war on terror, have received extensive attention from scholars. Less studied are the ways in which citizens, in their private lives, have adopted and internalized the preoccupation with security. I will argue that the undermining of democracy in the name of security has penetrated much deeper into American life than our public policies, right down to the level of daily life. In fact, the obsession with security at the personal level may be even more corrosive of democracy than the public policies promoted in the name of national security.

The Cold War laid the groundwork for this development. Cold War ideology wove several strands of American political culture into a tough fabric constructed to withstand the harsh postwar climate and to protect the American way of life. These strands included a belief in individual freedom, unfettered capitalism, and the sanctity of the home, and a suspicion of outsiders. Capitalism, grounded in private life and consumerism, defined the United States against the Soviet Union. When Vice President Richard Nixon traveled to Moscow in 1959 for the American National Exposition, in a discussion that came to be known as the Kitchen Debate, he articulated the American way of life in terms of domesticity and consumer goods.[2]

These historically rooted dimensions of Cold War ideology shaped how Americans responded to perceived dangers at home and abroad. For example, at the dawn of the atomic age, protection against external dangers took the form of a nuclear arsenal; protection against internal enemies took the form of a nuclear family. The two were profoundly connected. The United States vigorously opposed international control of nuclear weapons, insisting upon an accumulation of weapons, which led to a spiraling nuclear arms race. This reflected a turning away from the common good in favor of self-protection secured by an arsenal of atomic weapons. Rather than diffusing international tensions to achieve a safer world through democratic practices in the global arena, the nation's leaders chose preparedness in the face of danger.

A similar process unfolded at home. To avoid big government programs that might resemble socialism, policymakers rejected large-scale public civil defense efforts and instead encouraged citizens to plan for a possible attack by fortifying their homes.[3] The media did its part to keep citizens alert and insecure. For example, on July 26, 1950, the front page of the *Los Angeles Times* reported, "Experts Weighing A-Bomb Peril Here." To help readers figure out their own likelihood of being incinerated, the paper carried helpful illustrations. One map shows six hypothetical targets of atomic bombs dropped by the Soviet Union on Los Angeles. Another shows concentric circles from a potential ground zero, each one indicating various levels of blast, fire, damage, and destruction.[4] Civil defense officials, and enterprising businesses, offered homeowners tips on constructing basement shelters, backyard bunkers, or even the "all-concrete blast-resistant house . . . for the atomic age."[5]

There were good reasons for people to be worried. Atomic war was a real possibility. The United States had already waged it, and Americans had seen the results. Even those who opposed the proliferation of nuclear weapons fanned fears of an atomic catastrophe. To make their point, scientists who called for an end to the arms race pointed to the dire consequences of an atomic explosion, with the unintended consequence of heightening fears that could not be easily channeled into calls for peaceful coexistence. Americans became accustomed to the threat of nuclear annihilation, fueling a bunker mentality and a militarized society.[6]

Very few homeowners actually constructed shelters. But the message was clear: the world was dangerous, and citizens were responsible for their own safety. Americans adopted a framework for security based on self-defense bolstered by private enterprise rather than cooperative democratic efforts to ease international and domestic tensions. Over time, a domestic arms race developed parallel to the nuclear arms race: citizens responded to perceived threats by fortifying their homes and arming themselves. Soon Americans could boast that they had more missiles, and more pistols, than anyone else. The US nuclear stockpile consistently outnumbered that of the Soviet Union from 1964 to 1982. By the early 1990s, the percentage of American households with guns was far above that of other industrialized countries.[7]

It was not only the atomic age that made citizens fearful. Domestic dangers were also real. By the late 1960s, crime was rising and inner cities were exploding. There were also good reasons for citizens to distrust the government. In its investigative zeal, the government engaged in intrusive practices such as wiretapping and surveillance. In a 1970 Herblock political cartoon from the *Washington Post*, reprinted in *Time* magazine, a house is labeled "Individual Security." Two criminals breaking into the house are marked "Crime Increase," and two officials breaking into the house with them are marked "Administration" and "No Knock, Wiretapping, and Preventive Detention." The caption reads, "If you can't beat 'em, join 'em."[8] The cartoon suggests that government officials were no better than thugs and burglars. By the time the Watergate scandal unfolded a few years later, government officials had become the thugs and burglars. Trust in government dropped from 75 percent in 1963 to 25 percent in 1979.[9]

While dangers were real, citizens responded with exaggerated fear and distrust, much of it focused on crime. A 1974 study concluded, "The fear of crime in the US is a fundamental social problem which has not yet received attention in proportion to its severity and which may well prove to be more difficult to treat than criminality itself."[10] While it is difficult to quantify fear of crime, we do have poll data that indicate the level of fear in particular years. A poll taken in 1981 showed that while the chance of being murdered was a mere 1 in 10,000, and of becoming a victim of violent crime in general was just 6 in 1,000, fully 40 percent of Americans polled reported that they were "highly fearful" of assault. More than half said that they dress plainly to avoid attracting the attention of attackers. A majority reported that they kept a gun for protection.[11]

How did this happen? I will offer some examples to suggest that the legacy of the Cold War fed this irrational response to crime, encouraged citizens to retreat from public life, and worked against the democratizing momentum of the rights revolution. Although the Cold War was not the sole cause of this fear, the ideological premises embedded in the Cold War shaped the response to it.

Long before crime filled the headlines and the airwaves, there was the alleged communist threat. Anticommunism was "in the air," according to St. Paul native Patricia Hampl. In her memoir of her terror as a child in the 1950s, she writes that she was unable to sleep for fear of the "*Communists* who lurked in the dark." She did not know "whether to watch for man or beast, goblin or reptile, malicious intent or natural disaster, something large and looming or a thing so insidiously small that no degree of vigilance could assure safety: I didn't know, I didn't know." Noting the power of the new medium of television, she recalled watching TV shows, including the nightly news, which were filled with dire warnings about communism. Still, she wrote, "I could not concoct my Communists. . . . They remained, simply, dread."[12]

Such anxieties were not merely figments of an overly active imagination. Private enterprise did its part to whip up fear of communists. In 1953, for example, a public service ad in *Newsweek* for Norfolk and Western Railway pictured a frightened boy at home at night in a dark hallway, with the caption "You needn't be ashamed of being afraid in the dark, son. . . . The darkness is a hiding place for confusion, greed, conspiracy, treachery, socialism . . . and its uglier brother, communism. . . . In the USA you are free to become vigilant to see what's going on . . . If you ignore this responsibility . . . what you lose in the dark may be your freedom."[13]

Innocent children inside their homes appeared particularly vulnerable. Communists were not the only threat. The government was equally dangerous. A 1950 public service announcement in *US News and World Report* from the Electric Light and Power Companies warned of increasing government control and assured readers that the company was "battling this move toward a socialistic government." The ad pictured a small boy in front of a table holding four symbols of freedom: a key, a Bible, a pencil, and a ballot.[14] The Freedoms Foundation warned that "It Could Happen Here," with an ad of a father apologizing to his son for his lack of vigilance. Now the boy will have to grow up under communism.[15]

These public service advertisements used familial images to raise fears among citizens that they and their children were vulnerable. They portrayed big government as akin to socialism and communism. Companies called upon men to protect their families with do-it-yourself defense and to trust private enterprise, not the government, to keep them secure. This message was nowhere more explicit than in ads for the insurance industry, which promised "self-made security" for the "do-it-yourself American" who is "creating his own security."[16]

As these ads suggest, the home gradually shifted from the place that *provides* protection to the place that *needs* protection. An example of that shift appeared in *House Beautiful* magazine. One of the most outspoken advocates of privatized single-family dwellings was Elizabeth Gordon, editor in chief of *House Beautiful* from 1941 to 1964. Gordon articulated the intertwined Cold War themes of individualism, free enterprise, the sanctity of the home, and suspicion of outsiders. She railed against the International Style in the design of many postwar buildings, which she considered collectivist and un-American:

> We don't believe the International Style is simply a matter of taste; any more than we believe that Nazism or Communism are matters of taste, matters of opinion. . . . Either we choose the architecture that will encourage the development of individualism or we choose the architecture and design of collectivism and totalitarian control. . . . [The International Style] masses families together in one giant building so that relatively few, strategically placed, block leaders could check on all movements and conduct classes of ideological indoctrination. . . . [It is] a design for living that we associate with totalitarianism.[17]

According to Gordon, families flourished in privacy, fenced in and walled off from public gaze. Joseph Howland, the magazine's garden editor, agreed with Gordon:

> Good living is NOT public living. . . . Do the neighbors know your business? We consider [privacy] one of the cherished American rights, one of the privileges we fought a war to preserve. Freedom to live our own lives, the way we want to live them without being spied on or snooped around, is as American as pancakes and molasses . . . The very raison d'être of the separate house is

to get away from the living habits and cooking smells and inquisitive eyes of other people.[18]

By the early 1960s, the broad Cold War consensus was beginning to fracture. The excesses of McCarthyism had discredited the most vehement expressions of anticommunism. But fears of internal as well as external danger continued to permeate the country. Along with communism, criminality seemed to threaten individual security. In 1964, *House Beautiful* commented on the shift with a full-page illustration of a fortified house, with cannons, boarded-up doors and windows, alarms, guard dogs, locks, loudspeakers, and a large sign announcing, "Burglars Go Home."[19] *Ladies Home Journal* followed suit in 1968 with an article featuring several gadgets that could be purchased to make the home more secure against intruders.[20]

Companies that stood to profit from fear of crime did their best to whip up terror. In 1970, for example, General Telephone and Electronics took out a full two-page ad in *Time* magazine, promoting its new intercom system. One side of the ad was a full-page photo of a man wearing a trench coat, face obscured by a hat. The facing page said, in large bold letters, "Who's downstairs ringing your bell? A friend? Or the Boston Strangler?"[21] These rudimentary devices eventually gave way to elaborate security systems, alarms, and safe rooms. The private security business in the United States increased from $17 per capita in 1970 to $208 per capita in 1991—a total industry increase from $3.3 billion to $52 billion.[22] By the early twenty-first century, consumers could contemplate a custom-built "quantum sleeper," a bulletproof cocoon complete with CD and DVD player, microwave, and refrigerator.

The locks, gadgets, barricades, and warnings against dangerous strangers reflected a growing siege mentality that began to surface in the mid-1960s. It was not just about crime. Although crime was increasing, even at its peak in the last half of the twentieth century, the rate of violent crime barely exceeded its highest point in the first half. Throughout the twentieth century, the murder rate remained below eleven murders per 100,000 people. In the mid-1960s, the crime rate was relatively low, with violent crime affecting fewer than 2 people in 1,000. At its height, the rate of all violent crimes remained below 8 victims per 1,000 people. If we consider these numbers in terms of percentage of the population, the variations appear very slight. The murder rate remains consistently below 0.01 percent of the population. The number of people who were victims of all violent crimes remains consistently below 1 percent of the population.[23] But regardless of the slim likelihood of becoming a crime victim, crime came to stand in for the many upheavals at the time that disrupted the Cold War order, including political protests, urban riots, and the many challenges to the status quo and authority structures at the time.

The civil rights movement challenged racial hierarchies, and women were challenging domesticity by entering careers and public life. The counterculture, the antiwar movement, and the sexual revolution added to the sense that the tight-knit fabric of Cold War social order was coming apart. Urban riots across the country, along with a new militancy that accompanied the shift from civil rights to Black Power, heightened racial anxieties among white Americans. A backlash began immediately as an attempt to restore a sense of security and social order. Cold War ideology, with its emphasis on privatization, self-defense, and suspicion of both government and outsiders, gave shape to the backlash. Although the McCarthy era was over, anticommunism was still alive and well, fueling the "domino theory" that propelled the war in Vietnam as well as the suspicion of subversives within the country. In this atmosphere, it is not surprising that many people and government agencies, including the FBI, believed that "outside agitators" with communist sympathies were responsible for political protests, civil rights activism, and social disorder.

Politicians were quick to respond with a call for law and order. This was a new campaign issue. In the early Cold War years, from 1948 until 1964, candidates warned of the communist menace and promised to be tough on organized crime. But there was no mention of street crime in any presidential candidate's acceptance speech or in any inaugural address.[24] This changed dramatically in 1964. Law and order leaped into the center of political debates and stayed there for the rest of the century.

While the issue of crime was taking hold, in 1964 the Cold War still loomed large. Candidates argued about the greatest dangers facing citizens and who offered the best protection. Republican presidential candidate Barry Goldwater said that he would not rule out using tactical nuclear weapons in war. In response, Democratic incumbent Lyndon Johnson aired a powerful television ad suggesting that his opponent would unleash nuclear war. In the ad, a little girl counts as she pulls daisy petals in a field of flowers. As a freeze-frame captures her innocent face, a man's voice over begins an ominous countdown, followed by sounds of a blast and horrific scenes of a nuclear bomb exploding. Johnson speaks in an ominous voice-over: "These are the stakes: to make a world in which all of God's children can live, or to go into the darkness. We must either love each other, or we must die." The ad was so controversial that it only aired once. But it received tremendous attention. News programs aired the ad over and over in their coverage of the controversy. The "Daisy Girl" appeared on the cover of *Time* magazine, and two major networks did stories on her. Many analysts claimed that this ad ushered in a new era of television attack ad campaign advertising.[25]

Republican candidate Barry Goldwater responded with his own fear mongering, not about atomic war but about crime, political protest, and social chaos. Above scenes of crime, rioting youths, and jarring music are large bold words suggesting that Johnson was "soft" on the dangers facing the nation: "Graft! Swindle! Juvenile delinquency! Crime! Riots! Hear what Barry Goldwater has to say about our lack of moral leadership."[26]

Although Johnson easily won the election, Goldwater's message on crime and social chaos set the tone for later campaigns. In 1968, both Republican Richard Nixon and American Reform Party candidate George Wallace focused on law and order. Nixon had a well-earned reputation as a fierce anticommunist; in 1968, he turned his attention to street violence and political protest. Nixon ran a television ad that turned the tables on "civil rights," using the term to address law and order. Amid scenes of urban chaos and violence, with a soundtrack of snare drum and dissonant piano chords, Nixon says, "It is time for an honest look at the problem of order in the United States. Dissent is a necessary ingredient of change, but in a system of government that provides for peaceful change, there is no cause that justifies resort to violence. Let us recognize that the first civil right of every American is to be free from domestic violence. So, I pledge to you, we shall have order in the United States." Nixon drew no distinctions between crime, urban disturbances, and political demonstrations. In the ad, an eerie shot of an unclothed female mannequin torso tossed on the littered street underscored Nixon's pointed use of "domestic violence" to convey *public*, not *private* mayhem. His subtle use of language turned terms of the Black freedom struggle and the feminist movement—"civil rights" and "domestic violence"—against them.

The third-party candidate running for president that year, George Wallace, had a well-earned reputation as a segregationist. In one ad, he combined an anti-busing message with a warning that city streets were dangerous, especially for women. As a school bus drives off, the narrator says, "Why are more and more millions of Americans turning to Governor Wallace? Follow, as your children are bussed across town." Wallace responds, "As president, I shall—within the law—turn back the absolute control of the public school systems to the people of the respective states." The ad then cuts to a darkened street with a woman walking, only her feet and the hem of her skirt visible. The narrator says, "Why are more and more millions of Americans turning to Governor Wallace? Take a walk in your street or park tonight." The sounds of gunshots and breaking glass accompany the scene of a streetlight that is shot and then goes dark. Wallace says, "As president, I shall help make it possible for you and your families to walk the streets of our cities in safety."

Democratic candidate Hubert Humphrey was the only candidate to address crime as a social problem. In one ad he tells an assembled crowd, "You're not going to make this a better America just because you build more jails. What this country needs are more decent neighborhoods, more educated people, better homes. . . . I do not believe that repression alone builds a better society."

Humphrey, in 1968, was the last candidate of either party to articulate an approach to crime that addressed its underlying causes. Nixon and Wallace won a combined 57 percent of the votes. Although Humphrey's loss was in large measure due to his association with Johnson and the Vietnam War, the election results taught the Democrats a lesson. Four years later, Democratic candidate George McGovern embraced law and order and anticipated the war on drugs: "You're never going to get on top of crime in the United States until you get on top of drugs, because half of all the crime in this country is caused by the drug addict. They'll kill, they'll steal, they'll do anything to get that money to sustain that drug habit." From that time on, the rhetoric of law and order became a political necessity, embraced by both parties.

The framing of the crime issue reveals the escalating clash between security and democracy. The 1960s marked a shift in the Black freedom struggle, from civil rights to Black Power. While Black people were not the only targets of racial profiling, media coverage of groups like the Black Panthers and television images of urban riots fed a backlash that emphasized a Black/white binary. The rise of the feminist movement also intensified the backlash against women entering public life. Just at the time when African Americans and women were asserting their rights as citizens, the news media fused these two issues by reviving the age-old trope that Black men were dangerous and women—especially white women—were vulnerable.

The media contributed significantly to whipping up fear. By focusing on rare but heinous crimes to an extent far out of proportion to their frequency, television and newspapers contributed to exaggerated fears of random violence.[27] The popular press saturated readers with the message that attacks on city streets were practically inevitable. As early as 1963, *US News and World Report* exhorted women, "'First Scream, Then Scram.' . . . Muggings, rapes and assaults have become common"—which, of course, they had not. The *Washington Post* warned women not to "walk around alone at night," to keep all doors and windows locked, and to install burglar alarms.[28] By 1970, *Time* magazine asserted, "The universal fear of violent crime and vicious strangers . . . is a constant companion of the populous. It is the cold fear of dying at random in a brief spasm of senseless violence—for a few pennies, for nothing." Who were these vicious strangers? *Time* asserted that "the most crime-prone segment of the population—poor urban youths aged 15 to 24—will increase disproportionately at least until 1975. Sheer demography adds a racial factor: half the nation's blacks are under 21." *Time*'s warning was not subtle. Young Blacks were "crime prone," and their numbers were increasing. *Time* warned its white readers that "it is chiefly young black males who commit the most common interracial crime: armed robbery."[29]

Time gave the impression that the city streets were swarming with young Blacks eager to commit "interracial crime"—a term loaded with sexual associations. The police chief in Washington, DC, trained his officers "to treat blacks decently mainly as a matter of self-protection. A mistreated kid, for example, may hurt a cop when he gets big and dangerous." In other words, police should treat Blacks decently not because they deserve to be treated decently but because Black kids will get big and dangerous.

The term "Black militant" carried the most ominous weight, evoking power, violence, and danger. For example, *Time* quoted Julius Hobson, a critic of the city's leadership, and identified him simply as "a local black militant." *Time* failed to mention that Hobson was a longtime civil rights activist and World War II veteran who had attended Tuskegee, Columbia, and Howard Universities, held a master's degree in economics, was a member of the Washington, DC, school board, would soon be elected to the DC city council, and taught at three universities.

Like the reference to Hobson as a Black militant, these warnings twisted reality and exaggerated danger. The most likely victims of violent crime, then as now, were men of color. The least likely victims were white women. Moreover, women were much safer, statistically, on the city streets in the middle of the night than in their own homes, where most violence against women occurred. Nevertheless, the media focused on women who ventured out onto public streets as particularly vulnerable to attacks by strangers. Not surprisingly, public opinion polls showed that women were most likely to fear becoming a victim of crime, even though they were least likely to actually be victimized.[30]

Messages intended to scare women back into the home portrayed them as not only the most likely *victims* of crime but also the *cause* of crime. As increasing numbers of women with children entered the workforce, the media began to blame working mothers for leaving their homes unprotected and their children unsupervised and undisciplined. One article, noting an increase in crimes in the suburbs, explained, "As more and more husbands and wives hold down jobs, their unoccupied homes make tempting daytime targets for burglars. . . . The thieves are often the unattended sons of working couples who, say police, steal to keep up with the rising cost of marijuana."[31]

Meanwhile, as the backlash against feminism and civil rights intensified, so did the panic over crime. Calls for law and order led to harsher punishment for offenders. Although increasing numbers of European countries abolished the death penalty, and the United States followed suit with a moratorium on capital punishment in 1972, it lasted only until 1976, when state killing began again. Riding the wave of the backlash, Ronald Reagan became president in 1980 and breathed new life into the Cold War, calling for law and order, family values, and a "Star Wars" protective shield in outer space to keep the country safe from nuclear attack.

By this time, fear of crime had taken on a life of its own, which continued to escalate independently of the crime rate. According to a 1981 report, "A pervasive fear of robbery and mayhem threatens the way America lives.... The fear of crime is slowly paralyzing American society." Houston police chief B. K. Johnson lamented, "We have allowed ourselves to degenerate to the point where we're living like animals. We live behind burglar bars and throw a collection of door locks at night and set an alarm and lay down with a loaded shotgun beside the bed and then try to get some rest. It's ridiculous. Americans are arming themselves with guns as though they still lived in frontier days."[32]

But Chief Johnson himself kept several loaded guns in his own bedroom, and countless citizens did the same, arming themselves with guns, guard dogs, chemical mace, burglar alarms, karate classes, and target shooting practice. They emptied the streets, making the streets more dangerous. Officials warned that the worst was yet to come, basing their predictions on unfounded assumptions. The former director of the Bureau of Justice Statistics predicted that "within 4 or 5 years every household in the country will be hit by crime." In 1980, when the chance of becoming a murder victim was 1 in 10,000, an MIT study made the absurd claim that one out of every sixty-one babies born in New York City in that year would be a murder victim.[33]

Hollywood did its part to foster fear and encourage citizens to take crime control into their own hands, vigilante style. The popular *Death Wish* films, starring Charles Bronson, began in 1974 and continued into the mid-1990s. Undoubtedly inspired by the notorious grisly murders committed by Charles Manson and his hippie-styled followers in 1969, a unique crime that nevertheless convinced many that the counterculture had gone berserk, the plots of all five increasingly violent *Death Wish* movies follow the protagonist whose wife is murdered and daughter raped by a gang of thugs who break into their home. The villains in these films are usually portrayed as racial minorities and white hippies who commit Manson-style mayhem. The ineffectual police can do nothing. The main character, a New York City architect who had been a gentle, loving husband and father and "bleeding heart liberal," is transformed into a gun-toting vigilante out for revenge.[34]

Viewers reported that audiences in theaters stood and applauded when the hero shot the first mugger. At least one viewer boasted that he went out and bought a gun after seeing *Death Wish*. Many other popular movies carried similar themes, with violence providing the solution. During the Reagan era, the proportion of films ending in violence increased steadily, reaching 30 percent by 1990.[35]

Vigilante justice was not confined to movie screens. In December 1984, Bernhard Goetz, a white subway passenger, shot four Black youths when they tried to rob him, in a scenario much like one depicted in the first *Death Wish* movie ten years earlier. Goetz quickly became a folk hero. Although he was charged with attempted murder, assault, and several other crimes, a Manhattan jury acquitted him of all crimes except one count of illegal possession of a firearm. According to a *Newsweek* poll taken three months later, 57 percent of respondents approved of Goetz shooting the youths. Half said they had little or no confidence in the police to protect them against violent crime. *US News and World Report* was quick to comment, with a telling political cartoon depicting the inside of a crowded subway car. All the passengers are armed to the teeth, including elderly women, as one passenger reads a newspaper with the headline, "Muggings Down." The message was clear: the way to stop crime was for citizens to carry weapons, become vigilantes, and protect themselves, like Goetz.[36]

Racialized fear mongering intensified during the 1980s, reaching a new low in 1988 with the infamous Willie Horton ad by Republican presidential candidate George Bush, which featured a Black man who had failed to return after being released from prison on weekend furlough during the term of Governor Michael Dukakis. Horton later raped a woman and assaulted her fiancé. The Democratic candidate, Michael Dukakis, responded not with a condemnation of Bush's race baiting and fear mongering but with a Willie Horton ad of his own, "Furlough from the Truth," featuring a Latino parolee from a federal prison who had raped and murdered a woman during Bush's years at the helm of the CIA.[37] These messages had an impact. One study found that fear of crime increased among white viewers when criminals portrayed on television were minorities, but fear of crime did not increase when the criminals portrayed were white.[38]

In the 1990s, the clash between security and democracy reached a crescendo. It was a decade of small government and big business. A Democratic president presided over the end of the welfare program, a rapidly widening gap between rich and poor, and mergers of giant corporations into even more gigantic conglomerates with vast power. Citizens expressed distrust toward the government and toward one another. Although the crime rate declined in the 1990s, fear continued to rise. From 1989 to 1994, the percentage of those polled who said they were "truly desperate" about crime nearly doubled, from 32 percent to 62 percent. At the same time, the rate of violent crime declined, from .07 percent to .06 percent.[39]

As movies like *Death Wish* suggested, many people had little faith in government authorities and law enforcement. Because of a widespread belief that police could not be trusted to protect citizens and might not be around when needed, private security companies began patrolling neighborhoods.[40] From the 1970s onward, expenditures for private security exceeded expenditures for public law enforcement. A New Jersey security agency, for example, offered a Family Protection Plan that provided personal bodyguard service. Customers began hiring bodyguards to take them into New York City or to accompany them while shopping.[41] During the 1980s, the employment rate in the private security industry increased dramatically and far outstripped the rate in law enforcement, which declined.[42] By 1994, public perception of crime as the most important problem in America reached an all-time high.[43]

The Cold War was over, but the war on drugs took its place. Bringing atomic age fears full circle, a 1996 TV ad for Republican presidential candidate Bob Dole began with the footage of the little girl with a daisy, taken from the 1964 ad for Johnson. The female narrator says, "Thirty years ago, the biggest threat to her was nuclear war. Today the threat is drugs. Teenage drug use has doubled in the last four years. What's been done?" The ad continues with images of preadolescent children using various forms of drugs in a public park.

Dole's ad reflected the continuation of a trend that began with the 1950s' panic over juvenile delinquency. Children, while often portrayed as vulnerable, also appeared as threatening. Although the crime rate was declining rapidly in the 1990s, especially the rate of crimes committed by youths, polls revealed a vastly exaggerated sense of the danger. In 1994, juveniles committed only about 13 percent of all violent crimes, but Americans polled at the time believed that juveniles committed 43 percent of violent crimes—three times the actual proportion.⁴⁴ Not simply afraid *for* their children, Americans were becoming afraid *of* their children—especially Black children.

In 1996, Princeton political scientist John DiIulio made a startling prediction. Looking at demographic trends, he asserted that by 2005 the number of fourteen-to seventeen-year-old males would increase by 23 percent, and that the rate would rise faster among Black children than among white children. Assuming that Black boys would necessarily become violent teenage criminals, he coined the term "superpredator" and called the trend a "ticking time bomb" that would unleash "a storm of predatory criminality" on the nation.⁴⁵

Critics who called DiIulio's warnings alarmist, racist, and inaccurate were correct. The crime wave he warned about never happened. Crime was declining dramatically in the 1990s, just when DiIulio made his prediction, and within a decade violent crime by juveniles had dropped to its lowest point in twenty-five years. But DiIulio's claims about superpredators saturated the media. Michael Petit, deputy director of the Child Welfare League of America, said that superpredators were "literally being manufactured, programmed, hardwired to behave in a certain way." An editorial in the Omaha World Herald described these children as "killing machines."⁴⁶

False and frightening predictions like DiIulio's had an impact. Black people were incarcerated far out of proportion to their crimes. In the 1990s, white people comprised 70 percent of those arrested (in line with their percentage of the population) but only 30 percent of those who went to prison. The reverse was true for people of color, who comprised 30 percent of those arrested but 70 percent of prison inmates. By the end of the century, a quarter of young Black men were in jail, on parole, or on probation.

The overcrowding of prisons with nonviolent offenders guilty of crimes such as drug possession and immigration violations eventually brought private enterprise into the criminal justice system. For-profit prisons expanded across the country, with financial incentives to keep more people incarcerated for longer periods of time. Between the 1970s and the end of the century, the prison population grew tenfold, from 200,000 to more than 2 million. The rate of increase for prison costs was six times greater than the increase for higher education spending.⁴⁷

By the late twentieth century, it was not just criminals who lived behind bars and walls. Increasing numbers of unincarcerated Americans locked themselves up in fortified homes. Nowhere is this bunker mentality more obvious than in the rapid proliferation of gated communities across the nation's residential landscape. Gated communities have existed since the nineteenth century, but they were rare and reserved for the rich. In the 1960s, the numbers of gated communities began to grow, increasing in the 1970s and skyrocketing since the 1980s. By the turn of the twenty-first century, in the West, the South, and the Southeast, more than 40 percent of new residential developments were gated. In Southern California today, the majority of new housing units are in gated communities.[48]

Residents of gated communities often own their own streets, pay for their own services and utilities, and provide their own security guards. Homeowners pay significant fees for their infrastructure and security, which are independent of public funding and oversight. Some gated communities have actually incorporated as cities themselves, to enable homeowner associations to function as city councils and levy taxes. Some have built their own schools. Not surprisingly, residents of these communities often resent paying taxes to provide the same services for the general public. Even inside the gates and walls, as survey data demonstrated, there is little sense of community or concern for the common good.[49]

In many gated communities, freedom and security remain elusive. Homeowner associations develop policies that restrict residents' freedom to construct and decorate their homes as they wish, and enforce rigid behavioral codes as well.[50] Whether inhabited by the wealthy or those of modest means, gated communities sometimes actually heighten feelings of vulnerability. Residents often complain that security is lax and outsiders easily enter. An illusion of safety makes the wide streets more dangerous if cars speed and children play without the wariness they gain when living on public streets. In some cases, privatization actually makes these neighborhoods less safe. Police and fire emergency vehicles may have trouble entering these communities because access is restricted. Researchers report that children living in such communities may become fearful of strangers, especially strangers who look different from themselves.

A 1995 study found that most residents chose gated communities for security, with the vast majority saying that security was "very important" in their decision. High-income residents of gated communities believed there was less crime in their neighborhood than in ungated communities, and they felt that crime was lower *because of* the gates. They believed they were safer, but in fact they were not safer. There was actually no significant difference in crime rates between gated and ungated communities with residents of similar income levels.[51] Unfriendly warnings and barriers did little to keep out crime, in part because some of the residents who lived inside the gates committed crimes against their neighbors.

Perhaps the perfect symbol of the trend toward privatized protection is the sport utility vehicle. Although sales of SUVs have declined in recent years due to rising gas prices and the economic crisis, during the last two decades of the twentieth century they were the fastest-growing segment of the auto industry, outpacing the minivan with its comparable size and features. Families often purchased SUVs because they appeared to offer safety. But SUVs are more prone to rollovers and braking failures than cars. The National Highway Traffic Safety Administration reported that SUV occupants are 11 percent more likely to die in a traffic accident than those in cars. SUVs are also dangerous to other cars. In the event of a side impact collision with an SUV, car occupants are sixteen times more likely to die.[52]

Most SUV owners were men, but by 1989, women owned one-third of SUVs. SUVs carried a different appeal than the family-oriented minivan. A market research study that compared 4,500 SUV and minivan purchasers showed little demographic difference; typical owners of both vehicle types were affluent married couples in their forties with children. Yet consultants for the auto industry found that the buyers were quite different psychologically. SUV buyers were more restless, less social people with strong fears of crime. Minivan buyers were more self-confident and social, more involved with family and friends, more active in their communities. Minivan owners were more sexually satisfied; SUV drivers tended to be more sexually insecure.

These data suggest that minivan owners exhibited more democratic tendencies in terms of their sense of security and engagement with public life. SUV drivers, in contrast, exhibited more antidemocratic characteristics, insecurity, and a retreat from public life. One study concluded that the popularity of the SUV reflected American attitudes toward crime, random violence, and "the importance of defended personal space." Although advertised as rugged off-road vehicles, SUV owners almost never ventured off-road. Nonetheless, the large, intimidating vigilante vehicles offered the fantasy of escape, aggression, and conquest, even as their owners hunkered down. One researcher described SUVs as "weapons" and "armored cars for the battlefield."[53]

The last incarnation of the SUV was, in fact, a military vehicle: the Hummer, a civilian version of the Humvee used by the armed forces in the first Gulf War. Arnold Schwarzenegger urged automakers to develop the Hummer in the mid-1990s, bringing the aura of foreign military campaigns to the city streets. In 2001, the future governor of California promoted the new Hummer H2 at its unveiling in Times Square. Although at less than ten miles per gallon the Hummer did not survive the economic collapse, its presence on American streets at the turn of the twenty-first century was a symbol of the times.

By the end of the twentieth century, Americans had altered their way of life because of fear of crime. A study of eight major cities showed that nearly half of all Americans changed their lifestyles to avoid crime, whether by not going out alone or at night, by avoiding subways and downtown areas of major cities, or by avoiding contact with people who looked or seemed dangerous to them. Many parents, dubbed "helicopter parents," are so worried about their children's safety that they hover over them, refusing to let them out of their sight.[54]

Cities spend millions on surveillance cameras, but there is no sufficient evidence that these devices make public spaces safer. Cameras might help to identify and prosecute criminals after a crime takes place, but they do not often deter crime. Urban areas where security cameras outnumber people are not safe places.[55] Although women are less likely to be victims of crime, research shows that they are more fearful. Fear of crime inhibits their participation in activities perceived as being too dangerous for women, and it maintains gender hierarchies that limit women's power, rights, and achievements.[56]

The personal response to fears of crime mirrored the national response to the dangers of the atomic age: a heightening of alarm, a proliferation of arms, and a bunker mentality, rather than investment in the common good. The number of guns in the country has increased steadily, from 76 per 100 residents in 1994 to 90 per 100 residents in 2007. Per capita gun ownership in the United States is now far above that of other nations, including countries often described as lawless, such as Iraq, Mexico, and Colombia.[57]

A vigilante mentality permeates society, and forty states now allow citizens to carry concealed weapons. In Minnesota, for example, armed citizens can carry their guns into any building that does not post a sign at the door banning firearms. Progun groups now carry firearms openly, showing off their guns on their hips in places like Starbucks, a strategy they hope will intimidate the public into supporting concealed weapons laws. Firearms are now allowed in national parks. From 2008 to 2009, in just one year, the number of paramilitary militias tripled. The Supreme Court is currently considering striking down a Chicago law banning guns, an interpretation of the Second Amendment that would allow firearms everywhere in the country.[58]

So, as historians, how do we make sense of all this? I have suggested here that the Cold War was a factor in the obsession with security and the antidemocratic response to it, which has continued long after the Cold War ended. There are many outstanding studies of the domestic culture of the Cold War that point to several possible avenues for further exploration. We know that not all aspects of the Cold War were antidemocratic. After all, in an effort to eradicate inequalities and showcase to the world that the United States could live up to its ideals, national policies supported civil rights, women's rights, and the expansion of the welfare state in the Great Society programs. It is worth further study to examine why those liberal Cold War impulses were not powerful enough to prevent the antidemocratic tendencies that fostered the security obsession. It is also worth exploring the extent to which exaggerated concerns about security may have pushed the American political center to the right.

The principles of individualism and unfettered capitalism, of the sanctity of the home and a suspicion of outsiders, which gained salience in the early Cold War, era far outlived the Cold War itself. Those principles pushed back against the democratizing impulses of the rights revolution, fostered a bunkered, vigilante mentality, and inhibited citizens from acting on behalf of the common good. Although Americans have largely accepted the gains of civil rights and feminism, the security obsession has limited those achievements from reaching their full potential.

What, then, of security? Fear has made Americans feel less secure. As the twenty-first century unfolds, there is little evidence that Americans are safer, or more empowered, as a result of more weapons, more gated communities, and more muscular cars. But the security obsession has created an armed and bunkered citizenry. There are more guns on the streets and locks on the doors, walls around neighborhoods and along the nation's borders.

Hostility to government and lack of concern for the common good may have made the nation considerably *less* secure. While citizens were distracted by street crime that harms relatively few people, unregulated private enterprise fleeced the entire country. Locks on the doors did not protect families against losing their homes through mortgage foreclosure. Guns in their pockets did not prevent citizens from losing their shirts to Wall Street thugs.

And what about democracy? Democracy depends on citizens accepting their differences and trusting one another, at least to the extent that they understand themselves as belonging to a civic sphere as well as a private sphere. It requires investing in the common good and holding the government accountable as the institution that represents, and acts on behalf of, the citizenry. If, in the name of security, Americans distrust each other and the government and value private protection at the expense of the public good, then the basic social and political practices that ensure a healthy democracy cannot survive.

Understanding the way in which fear became a dominant force in American culture alongside the great achievements on behalf of democratic inclusiveness provides a historical perspective on the wisdom of Franklin Roosevelt, that if we believe in the democratic project, the only thing we have to fear is fear itself.[59] It is up to us as historians to figure out when and how democratic practices have expanded and flourished, and when and how they have withered.

NOTES

This essay was first published in the *Journal of American History* 97, no. 4 (March 2011): 939–57.

1. Michael Sherry, *In the Shadow of War: The United States since the 1930s* (New Haven, CT: Yale University Press, 1997).

2. See, for example, Elaine Tyler May, *Homeward Bound: American Families in the Cold War Era* (New York: Basic Books, 2008), 19–22.

3. See Laura McEnaney, *Civil Defense Begins at Home: Militarization Meets Everyday Life in the Fifties* (Princeton, NJ: Princeton University Press, 2000).

4. William S. Barton, "Experts Weighing A-Bomb Peril Here," *Los Angeles Times*, July 26, 1950, 1A.

5. Portland Cement Association, advertisement, in *Better Homes and Gardens* 33, no. 6 (June 1955): 3.

6. See Paul Boyer, *By the Bomb's Early Light* (Chapel Hill: University of North Carolina Press, 1994).

7. Gerald Segal, *The Simon & Schuster Guide to the World Today* (Simon & Schuster, 1987), 82. See also Edwin Bacon and Mark Sandle, eds., *Brezhnev Reconsidered* (Palgrave Macmillan, 2003). For comparative data on gun ownership, see E. G. Krug, K. E. Powell, and L. L. Dahlberg, "Firearm-Related Deaths in the United States and 35 other High- and Upper-Middle-Income Countries," *International Journal of Epidemiology* 27 (1998): 216; and "International Homicide Rate Table," GunCite, May 19, 2006, http://www.guncite.com/gun_control_gcgvinco.html.

8. The cartoon appeared in *Time* 96, no. 5 (August 3, 1970): 10.

9. Kevin Diaz, "Cynicism Is Out, Trust in Government Is In," *Minneapolis Star Tribune*, October 23, 2001, A11.

10. James Brooks, "The Fear of Crime in the United States," *Crime and Delinquency* 20, no. 3 (1974): 241–244, abstract.

11. "Crime: The Shape of Fear," *Economist*, November 29, 1980, 36. For crime and population, see Alexia Cooper and Erica L. Smith, *Homicide Trends in the United States, 1980–2008*, US Department of Justice Bureau of Justice Statistics, NCJ 236018, November 2011, https://bjs.ojp.gov/content/pub/pdf/htus8008.pdf, 2; and Michael R. Haines and Richard Sutch, "Population: 1790–2000 [Annual estimates]," table Aa6–8, in *Historical Statistics of the United States, Earliest Times to the Present: Millennial Edition*, ed. Susan B. Carter et al. (New York: Cambridge University Press, 2006). http://dx.doi.org/10.1017/ISBN-9780511132971.Aa1-109.

12. Patricia Hampl, *A Romantic Education* (Boston: Houghton Mifflin, 1981), 37–39.

13. Norfolk and Western Railway, advertisement, in *Newsweek* 42, no. 10 (September 7, 1953), 13.

14. Electric Light and Power Companies, advertisement, in *US News and World Report* 28 (May 12, 1950), 25.

15. Advertisement for the Freedoms Foundation, Valley Forge, Pennsylvania.

16. These quotes appeared on a number of insurance industry posters that have been collected by Caley Horan for her in-progress PhD dissertation on the insurance industry. I am grateful to her for allowing me to use these materials.

17. Elizabeth Gordon, "The Responsibility of an Editor," manuscript of speech delivered to the Press Club Luncheon of the American Furniture Mart, Chicago, June 22, 1953, 14–15, 21, quoted in Dianne Harris, "Making Your Private World: Modern Landscape Architecture and *House Beautiful*, 1945–1965," in *The Architecture of Landscape, 1940–1960*, ed. Marc Treib (Philadelphia: University of Pennsylvania Press, 2002), 182.

18. Joseph Howland, "Good Living is NOT Public Living," *House Beautiful*, January 1950, quoted in Harris, "Making Your Private World," 193.

19. *House Beautiful* 106, no. 7 (July 1964), 100.

20. "Making Your Home Safe Against Intruders," *Ladies Home Journal* 85, no. 7 (1968), 66.

21. General Telephone and Electronics, advertisement, in *Time* 96, no. 2 (July 13, 1970), 60–61.

22. William C. Cunningham, John J. Strauchs, and Clifford W. Van Meter, *Private Security*

Trends, 1970–2000: The Hallcrest Report II (Boston: Butterworth-Heinemann, 1990), 238. For population data, see Haines and Sutch, "Population: 1790–2000."

23. Federal Bureau of Investigation, *Uniform Crime Reports*, 1940–1960; Bureau of Justice Statistics, *Crime and Justice Data Online*; "Deaths by Homicide per 100,000 Resident Population in the US from 1950 to 2018, https://www.statista.com/statistics/187592/death-rate-from-homicide-in-the-us-since-1950; "United States Crime Rates 1960–2019," The Disaster Center, https://www.disastercenter.com/crime/uscrime.htm; Douglas Eckberg, "Reported Homicides and Homicide Rates, By Sex and Mode of Death: 1900–1997," Table Ec190–198, in Carter et al., *Historical Statistics of the United States*. For population, see United States Census Bureau, "Population Estimates," http://www.census.gov/popest/datasets.html; Haines and Sutch, "Population: 1790–2000."

24. The only mention of crime in any of these speeches referred to organized crime and political corruption. See Gregory Bush, ed., *Campaign Speeches of American Presidential Candidates, 1948–1984* (New York: Frederick Ungar, 1985); and Davis Newton Lott, *The Presidents Speak* (New York: Hold and Co., 1994).

25. Michael Carlson, "Obituary: Tony Schwartz: His Daisy Girl TV Ad Was a First, and Helped Put Lyndon Johnson in the White House," *Guardian*, June 28, 2008; Robert Mann, "How the 'Daisy' Ad Changed Everything About Political Advertising," *Smithsonian Magazine*, April 13, 2016, https://www.smithsonianmag.com/history/how-daisy-ad-changed-everything-about-political-advertising-180958741.

26. Quotes and descriptions of television ads are from "The Living Room Candidate: Presidential Campaign Commercials 1952–2020," Museum of the Moving Image, www.livingroomcandidate.org, which includes the ads themselves, the transcripts, and the voting outcomes of each election.

27. Robert Suro, "Driven by Fear: Crime and Its Amplified Echoes are Rearranging People's Lives," *New York Times*, February 9, 1992; Linda Heath, Jack Kavanagh, and Rae S. Thompson, "Perceived Vulnerability and Fear of Crime: Why Fear Stays High When Crime Rates Drop," *Journal of Offender Rehabilitation* 33, no. 2 (2001): 1–14.

28. "First Scream, Then Scram," *US News and World Report* 54.2, no. 13 (April 1, 1963), which included excerpts from the *Washington Post*, March 17, 1963.

29. "A Response to Fear," *Time* 96, no. 5 (August 3, 1970), 10.

30. Susan Douglas, *Where the Girls Are* (New York: Times Books, 1995), 209–211. On crime statistics, see Eric H. Monkkonen, *Murder in New York City* (Berkeley: University of California Press, 2001), especially chapter 3, which discusses the fact that most violent offenders as well as victims are men, and chapter 6, which discusses the fact that Black men are disproportionately victims of violent crime.

31. "The Curse of Violent Crime," *Time*, March 23, 1981.

32. Ibid.

33. Ibid.

34. See Paul Talbot, *Bronson's Loose! The Making of the "Death Wish" Films* (New York: iUniverse, 2006).

35. Data are from viewer response research collected by Lary May.

36. David M. Alpern, "A Newsweek Poll: 'Deadly Force,'" *Newsweek,* March 11, 1985, 53; "Behind Tough Public Stance on Criminals," *US News and World Report* 98, no. 2 (January 21, 1985), 60.

37. See "Living Room Candidate."

38. Sarah Eschholz, "Racial Composition of Television Offenders and Viewers' Fear of Crime," *Critical Criminology* 11, no. 1 (2002): 41–60.

39. Rorie Sherman, "Crime's Toll on the US: Fear, Despair and Guns," *National Law Journal,* April 18, 1994: A1, A19–20, in John J. Sullivan and Joseph L. Victor, eds., *Annual Editions: Criminal Justice 95/96* (Guilford, CT: Dushkin, 1995), 57–61. For crime statistics, see Matthew Friedman, Ames C. Grawert, and James Cullen, *Crime Trends, 1990–2016,* Brennan Center for Justice, New York University School of Law, 2017, https://www.brennancenter.org/our-work/research-reports/crime-trends-1990-2016, 7. Population data from United States Census Bureau, "Population Estimates"; and Haines and Sutch, "Population: 1790–2000."

40. Alpern, "Newsweek Poll."

41. Barry Meier, "Reality and Anxiety: Crime and the Fear of It," *New York Times,* February 18, 1993, A14.

42. Cunningham, Strauchs, and Van Meter, *Private Security Trends, 1970–2000,* 238.

43. Meier, "Reality and Anxiety."

44. Rorie Sherman, "Crime's Toll on the US: Fear, Despair, and Guns," in Sullivan and Victor, *Annual Editions: Criminal Justice 95/9,* 57.

45. John Dilulio, "Lock 'Em Up or Else: Huge Wave of Criminally Inclined Coming in Next 10 Years," *Lakeland Ledger,* March 23, 1996, A11; Joyce Purnick, "Youth Crime: Should Laws Be Tougher?," *New York Times,* May 9, 1996, B1.

46. Vincent Schiraldi, "Will the Real John Dilulio Please Stand Up," editorial, *Washington Post,* February 5, 2001, A19; "'Superpredators' Aren't Mere Kids," editorial, *Omaha World Herald,* May 16, 1997, 12.

47. See, for example, *State and Local Expenditures on Corrections and Education,* US Department of Education, Policy and Program Studies Service, July 2016, https://www2.ed.gov/rschstat/eval/other/expenditures-corrections-education/brief.pdf, which notes on page 1 that "From 1989–90 to 2012–13, 46 states reduced higher education appropriations per full-time equivalent (FTE) student. On average, state and local higher education funding per FTE student fell by 28 percent, while per capita spending on corrections increased by 44 percent." See also Ruth Wilson Gilmore, "Globalisation and US Prison Growth: From Military Keynesianism to Post-Keynesian Militarism," *Race & Class* 40, no. 2/3: 172–174.

48. Edward J. Blakely and Mary Gail Snyder, *Fortress America: Gated Communities in the United States* (Washington, DC: Brookings Institution Press, 1997), 7.

49. Georjeanna Wilson-Doenges, "An Exploration of Sense of Community and Fear of Crime in Gated Communities," *Environment and Behavior* 32, no. 5 (September 2000), 597–611.

50. Sharon Waxman, "Paradise Bought in Los Angeles," *New York Times,* July 2, 2006, Style section, 1.

51. Blakely and Snyder, *Fortress America,* 126–127.

52. See Keith Bradsher, *High and Mighty: SUVs—The World's Most Dangerous Vehicles and How They Got That Way* (New York: BBS Public Affairs, 2002); Josh Lauer, "Driven to Extremes: Fear of Crime and the Rise of the Sport Utility Vehicle in the United States," *Crime, Media, Culture* 1, no. 2: 149–168.

53. Keith Bradsher, "Delving into Psyche of SUV v. Minivan Buyers: Automakers' Research: Minivan Owners are Other-Oriented, SUV Owners Less Social," *Financial Post,* July 18, 2000, C03.

54. Esther Madriz, *Nothing Bad Happens to Good Girls: Fear of Crime in Women's Lives* (Berkeley: University of California Press, 1997).

55. Nikos Papanikolopoulos, "Camera Networks for Surveillance," Distinguished Faculty Lecture, University of Minnesota, February 17, 2010.

56. Madriz, *Nothing Bad Happens to Good Girls.*

57. Graduate Institute of International Studies (Geneva), *Small Arms Survey 2007: Guns and the City* (New York: Cambridge University Press, 2007), 47; *Small Arms Survey 2003: Development Denied* (Oxford: Oxford University Press, 2003), 4; Robert Hahn, Oleg O. Bilukha, Alex Crosby, Mindy Thompson Fullilove, Akiva Liberman, Eve K. Moscicki, Susan Snyder, Farris Tuma, and Peter Briss, "First Reports Evaluating the Effectiveness of Strategies for Preventing Violence: Firearms Laws," *Morbidity and Mortality Weekly Report,* Centers for Disease Control and Prevention, October 3, 2003, http://www.cdc.gov/mmwr/preview/mmwrhtml/rr5214a2.htm. For population, see United States Census Bureau, "Population Estimates"; Haines and Sutch, "Population: 1790–2000."

58. Ian Urbina, "Locked, Loaded, and Ready to Caffeinate," *New York Times,* March 8, 2010, A11; David G. Savage, "Justices May Rule for Gun Rights: A Pending Decision on Chicago's Ban has National Implications," *Los Angeles Times,* March 3, 2010, 1A.

59. I am grateful to Daniel May for this insight.

FROM SUBORDINATED TO A BEDROCK PRINCIPLE

The Supreme Court on Free Speech during the Cold War

ERIC T. KASPER

The First Amendment is a part of the US legal culture, representing the predominant thoughts and beliefs about what is legal.[1] Constitutional rights like the freedom of speech drive culture, defined as the values and norms embraced by the population at large.[2] Since the US Supreme Court decides the legal meaning of the First Amendment, it influences what Americans think about free speech.[3] Today in the United States, citizens enjoy what is characterized as the "emergence of free speech as constitutionally and culturally special."[4] Some First Amendment scholars have even explained that the United States goes beyond having a free speech *culture* to possessing a "First Amendment *magnetism*" (emphasis in original).[5] The court's evolving interpretation of the First Amendment during the Cold War helped fundamentally alter how American culture defines free speech, making it both special and magnetic today.

Although the freedom of expression is a core value in American culture and has been since before the country's founding, debates over what constitutes protected speech have erupted throughout American history.[6] This includes the passage of the Sedition Act of 1798, the suppression of antislavery speech in the antebellum South, and restrictions on antiwar speech during the Civil War.[7] The prevailing understanding of the freedom of speech prior to the twentieth century was narrow compared to today. Legally, until the end of World War I, "free speech" was understood to mean that the government could not engage in prior restraints, meaning the government was largely banned from halting speech or publication before the fact, but that the First Amendment put no restrictions on government power to punish expression after the fact. The court in the early twentieth century pushed the public understanding of the freedom of speech to encompass more than a prohibition on prior restraints.[8]

By the 1940s, the court led the nation in expanding this right, defining it as a preferred freedom. After World War II, however, the court—instead of teaching the country the value of expression—was gripped in Cold War paranoia; the justices in the late 1940s and the 1950s upheld prosecutions of those advocating for communism or similar ideas, fearing a Soviet-style revolution in America. The justices subordinated the freedom of speech to security concerns.

This retrenchment was not permanent, though. Just as the public finally saw the madness of Red Scare paranoia that enveloped the country through congressional hearings on communism, the justices rethought their understanding of free speech. In the 1960s, the court protected the freedom of expression to a much greater degree, even including the advocating of illegality. The court identified the freedom of speech as a right differentiating free from totalitarian societies.

At the end of the Cold War, in the same month that the Chinese government was cracking down on Tiananmen Square, the court held that the First Amendment protects the right of protestors to burn the American flag. This development of free speech doctrine during the Cold War has important implications today.

BEFORE THE COLD WAR: GROWING PROTECTIONS FOR FREE SPEECH

Before World War I, the Supreme Court construed freedom of speech narrowly, protecting relatively little of what is protected expression today. In the late nineteenth and early twentieth centuries, the court sustained the prosecution of a man preaching in a public park without a license, upheld a law punishing advocacy of anarchism, and ruled that states may require films to be approved by censorship boards before public showings.[9] Notably, in *Patterson v. Colorado* (1907), the court allowed the punishment of seditious libel (speech that is disloyal toward government or embarrassing to a public official), even if the speech was true. In *Patterson*, the court affirmed a conviction for criticizing a state supreme court, holding that the purpose of the Constitution's free speech protections "is to prevent all such previous restraints upon publications as had been practiced by other governments, and they do not prevent the subsequent punishment of such as may be deemed contrary to the public welfare."[10] Although labor groups sometimes successfully challenged protest injunctions in lower courts during these years, they were not victorious before the Supreme Court.[11]

Changes were soon forthcoming in the court's First Amendment doctrine. In *Schenck v. United States* (1919), the court upheld the conviction of Socialist Party secretary Charles Schenck for violating the Espionage Act, which prohibited attempting to cause insubordination or refusal of military duty, including when speaking truthfully.[12] Schenck distributed leaflets to draftees arguing that "conscription was despotism in its worst form and a monstrous wrong against humanity in the interest of Wall Street's chosen few." Justice Oliver Wendell Holmes, writing for the court, devised a new test for determining whether speech was protected by the First Amendment, asking "whether the words used are used in such circumstances and are of such a nature as to create a clear and present danger that they will bring about the substantive evils that Congress has a right to prevent."[13]

Although Holmes employed this test narrowly to the facts of *Schenck*—sustaining a prison sentence for distributing leaflets criticizing the government—the clear and present danger test was a much bolder protection of expression than the court had used previously.[14] Even this new test was rarely applied to free speech cases in the decade after *Schenck*, as the court upheld convictions for people convicted of advocating communism or anarchism through the first Red Scare of the 1920s.[15]

In the 1930s, the court started interpreting the First Amendment to protect the freedom of speech more within the spirit of *Schenck*'s clear and present danger test. In *Stromberg v. California* (1931), the court invalidated a conviction for displaying a communist flag. The court reasoned that the "maintenance of the opportunity for free political discussion to the end that government may be responsive to the will of the people and that changes may be obtained by lawful means, an opportunity essential to the security of the Republic, is a fundamental principle of our constitutional system."[16] In *United States v. Carolene Products* (1938), Justice Harlan Fiske Stone wrote that the court would defer to legislative regulation of commercial activities but that there "may be narrower scope for operation of the presumption of constitutionality when legislation appears on its face to be within a specific prohibition of the Constitution, such as those of the first ten amendments."[17] Since the freedom of speech is contained within the First Amendment, the court indicated it would apply more scrutiny to laws restricting expression.

This pro–free speech attitude of the court continued over the next several years, particularly in labor expression cases. In *Hague v. Committee for Industrial Organization* (1939), the court overturned a city's ban on public labor meetings and the distribution of labor information. The city denied a union's request on the grounds that labor unions were communist organizations. In *Hague*, the justices reasoned, "Citizenship of the United States would be little better than a name if it did not carry with it the right to discuss national legislation and the benefits, advantages, and opportunities to accrue to citizens therefrom."[18] The justices upheld labor picketers' rights in *Thornhill v. Alabama* (1940), with Justice Frank Murphy explaining that those "who won our independence had confidence in the power of free and fearless reasoning and communication of ideas to discover and spread political and economic truth. Noxious doctrines in those fields may be refuted and their evil averted by the courageous exercise of the right of free discussion."[19]

Although there were instances of the court upholding restrictions on expression during World War II, during this global conflict the justices also broadened the freedom of speech to an unprecedented degree.[20] In *West Virginia v. Barnette* (1943), the court found unconstitutional the expulsion of public school students who refused to salute the American flag during daily recitations of the Pledge of Allegiance. Justice Robert Jackson proclaimed for the court that the American idea of free speech condemns "attempts to compel coherence," such as with "Siberian exiles as a means to Russian unity" and "the fast failing efforts of our present totalitarian enemies" because "those who begin coercive elimination of dissent soon find themselves exterminating dissenters." Jackson concluded sweepingly: "If there is any fixed star in our constitutional constellation, it is that no official, high or petty, can prescribe what shall be orthodox in politics, nationalism, religion, or other matters of opinion or force citizens to confess by word or act their faith therein. If there are any circumstances which permit an exception, they do not now occur to us."[21] In *Thomas v. Collins* (1945), the court overturned the conviction of a man for not obtaining an organizer's card before addressing a union organizing meeting. Justice Wiley Rutledge spoke for the court of "the preferred place given in our scheme to the great, the indispensable democratic freedoms secured by the First Amendment" and how that "priority gives these liberties a sanctity and a sanction not permitting dubious intrusions."[22]

Constitutional protection for political and economic dissenters, including labor organizers and communists, was now well accepted on the court. Furthermore, the justices led public opinion: in a 1940 Gallup poll, only 22 percent of respondents answered yes to the question "Do you believe in [the freedom of speech] to the extent of allowing Fascists and Communists to hold meetings and express their views in this community?"[23] The beginning of the Cold War, however, drastically changed the court's outlook on the First Amendment.

THE EARLY COLD WAR: FREEDOM OF SPEECH IS "SUBORDINATED"

Winston Churchill's "Sinews of Peace" address at Westminster College in Fulton, Missouri, on March 5, 1946, provided the now famous "Iron Curtain" analogy that helped mark the emergence of the Cold War. Churchill called for a US–UK alliance opposing the Soviet Union, which he viewed as a danger to the free world.[24] Five days after Churchill's speech, George Orwell, in *The Observer*, made one of the first recorded uses of the term "cold war" to describe the emerging post–World War II order: "After the Moscow conference last December, Russia began to make a cold war on Britain and the British Empire."[25]

At the time of Churchill's speech and Orwell's newspaper article, Justice Jackson had taken leave from the Supreme Court to serve as an American prosecutor at Nuremberg. The author of the *Barnette* opinion was one of the court's most enthusiastic civil libertarians through World War II, but Jackson was affected by his observations at Nuremberg. While prosecuting war criminals, he reviewed how the Nazi Party rose to power by using rhetoric and paramilitary groups. He observed firsthand how Soviet leaders controlled their lawyers and judges at Nuremberg, demonstrating their organized strategies for exercising power. This experience changed Jackson's outlook on the freedom of speech when he returned to the court in 1946.[26]

Additionally, appointments in the later 1940s were creating a more closely divided court on the freedom of expression. Chief Justice Stone, who wrote in *Carolene Products* about how the court would scrutinize laws restricting fundamental freedoms, died in 1946 and was succeeded by Fred Vinson, who acceded to laws limiting expression. Justice Murphy, the author of the pro–free speech *Thornhill* decision, died in 1949; Tom Clark, a supporter of executive power, filled the vacancy.²⁷ Justice Rutledge, who penned the *Thomas* decision classifying freedom of expression as a preferred freedom, also died in 1949, and in his place was appointed Sherman Minton, who regularly upheld laws restricting radical speech.²⁸

The court's first move to limit freedom of speech occurred shortly before Murphy and Rutledge's deaths. In *Kovacs v. Cooper* (1949), the court deferred to New Jersey's legislature, which had prohibited sound trucks and similar devices that emitted "loud and raucous noises." The person claiming a constitutional violation was remarking on an ongoing local labor dispute, and there was no showing that he made any loud or raucous noises. Although the court cited *Thomas* and gave lip service to the "preferred position of freedom of speech in a society that cherishes liberty for all," the court emphasized the "permissible exercise of legislative discretion."²⁹

Justice Felix Frankfurter, a progressive before being appointed to the court but an advocate of judicial restraint as a justice (who also dissented in *Barnette*),³⁰ wrote an influential concurring opinion in *Kovacs*, referring to "the preferred position of freedom of speech" as "a mischievous phrase, if it carries the thought, which it may subtly imply, that any law touching communication is infected with presumptive invalidity." In a rebuke of the preferred freedoms approach to expression, Frankfurter demonstrated his commitment to judicial restraint: "These are matters for the legislative judgment controlled by public opinion. So long as a legislature does not prescribe what ideas may be noisily expressed and what may not be, nor discriminate among those who would make inroads upon the public peace, it is not for us to supervise the limits the legislature may impose in safeguarding the steadily narrowing opportunities for serenity and reflection."³¹ Frankfurter's denouncement of the "preferred freedoms" approach to expressive rights effectively buried the doctrine, as the phrase vanished from the court's jurisprudence after *Kovacs*.³²

Also in 1949, the justices decided *Terminiello v. Chicago*, the court's last significant pro–free speech case for years. A 5–4 court overturned a man's breach-of-the-peace conviction after he gave an inflammatory speech criticizing "various political and racial groups," which excited a crowd to the point of being "angry and turbulent." In what would become a fleeting sentiment on the court, Justice William Douglas wrote that "a function of free speech under our system of government is to invite dispute," which can be limited only if it is "likely to produce a clear and present danger of a serious substantive evil that rises far above public inconvenience, annoyance, or unrest." Vinson, Frankfurter, and Jackson dissented in *Terminiello*. Jackson emphasized how Terminiello's conviction should have been upheld because "fascist and communist groups . . . resort to these terror tactics to confuse, bully and discredit . . . freely chosen governments. Violent and noisy shows of strength discourage participation of moderates in discussions so fraught with violence, and real discussion dries up and disappears."[33] Jackson and other dissenters were becoming fearful of totalitarian groups (especially communists) using speeches to seize power.

The Cold War's stranglehold over the court's First Amendment doctrine expanded in *American Communications Association v. Douds* (1950), which upheld a federal law requiring labor leaders to take anticommunist oaths. For the court, Chief Justice Vinson underscored "the deference due the congressional judgment concerning the need for regulation of conduct affecting interstate commerce." Using strange logic, Vinson reasoned in *Douds* that "legitimate attempts to protect the public, not from the remote possible effects of noxious ideologies, but from present excesses of direct, active conduct, are not presumptively bad because they interfere with and, in some of its manifestations, restrain the exercise of First Amendment rights." The court's free speech jurisprudence had changed. In a partial concurrence, Justice Jackson showed how he was now willing to uphold viewpoint discrimination: "If the statute before us required labor union officers to forswear membership in the Republican Party, the Democratic Party or the Socialist Party, I suppose all agree that it would be unconstitutional . . . the Communist Party is something different in fact from any other substantial party we have known, and hence may constitutionally be treated as something different in law."[34]

The low point for free speech during the Cold War emerged in *Dennis v. United States* (1951). The court upheld the Smith Act, a peacetime antisedition law making it illegal "to knowingly or willfully advocate, abet, advise, or teach the duty, necessity, desirability, or propriety of overthrowing or destroying any government in the United States by force or violence."[35] In a reformulation of the clear and present danger test, Chief Justice Vinson wrote that the court would "ask whether the gravity of the 'evil,' discounted by its improbability, justifies such invasion of free speech as is necessary to avoid the danger."[36] Vinson asked not if danger was *present* but if it was *probable*, deferring to Congress on the restriction of expression. This reformulated test was much less protective of speech than the one announced by Justice Holmes in 1919.[37] Unlike the court's notion just a few years earlier that free speech was a "preferred freedom," the *Dennis* court announced that "the societal value of speech must, on occasion, be subordinated to other values and considerations."[38] By the early 1950s, that subordination was no longer occasional on the court; it was commonplace.

Concurring in *Dennis*, Justice Frankfurter emphasized judicial restraint again, noting how "courts are not representative bodies" and "primary responsibility for adjusting the interests which compete in the situation before us of necessity belongs to the Congress."[39] Even the once noted civil libertarian Justice Jackson joined the 6–2 majority in *Dennis*, arguing that "an individual cannot claim that the Constitution protects him in advocating or teaching overthrow of government by force or violence."[40] As explained in dissent by Justice Hugo Black, though, the *Dennis* defendants were punished simply for the ideas they expressed:

> These petitioners were not charged with an attempt to overthrow the Government. They were not charged with overt acts of any kind designed to overthrow the Government. They were not even charged with saying anything or writing anything designed to overthrow the Government. The charge was that they agreed to assemble and to talk and publish certain ideas at a later date . . . No matter how it is worded, this is a virulent form of prior censorship of speech and press, which I believe the First Amendment forbids.

Instead of leading the nation as it had in the 1940s, Justice Black spotlighted how the court was following anticommunist reactionary sentiment: "Public opinion being what it now is, few will protest the conviction of these Communist petitioners. There is hope, however, that in calmer times, when present pressures, passions and fears subside, this or some later court will restore the

First Amendment liberties to the high preferred place where they belong in a free society."[41] Justice Douglas also dissented, showing the justices in the majority their hypocrisy: "[Andrey] Vishinsky [sic] wrote in 1938 in *The Law of the Soviet State*, 'In our state, naturally, there is and can be no place for freedom of speech, press, and so on for the foes of socialism.' Our concern should be that we accept no such standard for the United States."[42]

Although years later the justices overturned some Smith Act convictions,[43] decisions like *Doud* and *Dennis* encouraged persecution of admitted and suspected communists. The House Un-American Activities Committee held hearings on communism in Hollywood, with the House finding ten uncooperative witness in contempt. Senator Joseph McCarthy alleged infiltration of communists in the State Department. With favorable court decisions, these efforts accelerated in the 1950s, resulting in more hearings, contempt citations, and backlisting, especially in the movie industry. Instead of citing the First Amendment to halt this hysteria, the court was emboldening it.[44]

Some films even championed this second Red Scare. *Big Jim McLain* (1952)—featuring John Wayne and James Arness—expressed support for the committee and its anticommunist efforts.[45] Many in the film industry, academia, government, and the private sector were forced to appear in front of congressional committees to testify about their affiliation with communism or knowledge of communist activities.[46] Although the court scrutinized some cases where it viewed congressional committees as merely exposing people or forcing them to "name names,"[47] even that effort collapsed in *Barenblatt v. United States* (1959).

Lloyd Barenblatt was convicted of contempt for refusing on First Amendment grounds to testify whether he had been a member of the Communist Party. The *Barenblatt* court held, "Where First Amendment rights are asserted to bar governmental interrogation, resolution of the issue always involves a balancing by the courts of the competing private and public interests at stake in the particular circumstances shown." The court reasoned, to "suggest that, because the Communist Party may also sponsor peaceable political reforms, the constitutional issues before us should now be judged as if that Party were just an ordinary political party from the standpoint of national security, is to ask this court to blind itself to world affairs which have determined the whole course of our national policy since the close of World War II." The court concluded that "the balance between the individual and the governmental interests here at stake must be struck in favor of the latter, and that, therefore, the provisions of the First Amendment have not been offended."[48] The Red Scare continued infecting the court's interpretation of the freedom of speech.

As the 1950s ended, the court had balanced away some of the First Amendment's protections due to Cold War concerns, reinterpreting the clear and present danger test. In the parlance of *Dennis*, free speech was "subordinated to other values and considerations." To Justice Black's point in *Dennis*, the court reflected public opinion of the time. In a 1953 Gallup poll, only 29 percent of respondents answered yes to this question: "Suppose a person known to favor Communism wanted to make a speech in this city . . . do you think he should be allowed to make the speech, or not?"[49] However, by the middle of the 1960s the court revisited the preferred freedoms promise it had made decades earlier.

MIDDLE AND LATTER COLD WAR: FREEDOM OF SPEECH AS A "BEDROCK PRINCIPLE"

The 1960s brought some of the Cold War's tensest moments: Soviets shot down a U-2 American spy plane, the Bay of Pigs invasion occurred in Cuba, the Berlin Wall was constructed, and the Cuban Missile Crisis brought the world to the brink of nuclear confrontation. Meanwhile, the tortured US mission to thwart communism in South Vietnam wrought intense social and political division. Domestically, though, public sentiment regarding the rights of dissenters was thawing: Hollywood ended the infamous blacklist, the civil rights movement was building, and Vietnam War protests were beginning.

During this time, the court began finding more protection for expression, particularly in cases involving civil rights protestors. In *Gibson v. Florida Legislative Investigation Committee* (1963), a 5–4 court ruled that a legislative committee's requirement that the National Association for the Advancement of Colored People produce a membership list violated the First Amendment. Limiting *Barenblatt*, Justice Arthur Goldberg wrote for the court that the "First and Fourteenth Amendment rights of free speech and free association are fundamental and highly prized, and need breathing space to survive." Nevertheless, the court still maintained in *Gibson* that "compelling such an organization, engaged in the exercise of First and Fourteenth Amendment rights, to disclose its membership presents . . . a question wholly different from compelling the Communist Party to disclose its own membership."[50] The court was bolder in *Watson v. Memphis* (1963), declaring that "constitutional rights may not be denied simply because of hostility to their assertion or exercise."[51]

New York Times v. Sullivan (1964) highlighted the court's evolving interpretation of free expression rights. Sullivan, a Montgomery police commissioner, sued the *New York Times* for an advertisement containing minor factual inaccuracies in describing a civil rights protest that had been quashed by the Montgomery police. The overall tenor of the ad was true. In overturning Sullivan's jury award, Justice William Brennan noted that, with regard to the First Amendment, the "constitutional protection does not turn upon the truth, popularity, or social utility of the ideas and beliefs which are offered." Brennan discussed the problems inherent in laws proscribing seditious libel, noting how "debate on public issues should be uninhibited, robust, and wide-open, and . . . may well include vehement, caustic, and sometimes unpleasantly sharp attacks on government and public officials."[52] This sentiment was quite different from the court's declaration in *Dennis*, where it upheld convictions and lengthy prison sentences for advocating communism.

Gibson, *Watson*, and *Sullivan* marked a point where the court was beginning to rethink First Amendment rights. This continued in *Cox v. Louisiana* (1965), where the justices ruled that a disturbing-the-peace statute was unconstitutionally vague when applied to peaceful protestors.[53] Although these cases all involved First Amendment rights of civil rights advocates, soon the court was also finding that the First Amendment protected communists. In *Elfbrandt v. Russell* (1966), a 5–4 court struck down a state law requiring loyalty oaths.[54] In *United States v. Robel* (1967), a 6–2 court held unconstitutional a ban on Communist Party members working in defense facilities.[55] While *Elfbrandt* and *Robel* centered on the freedom of association and did not directly touch on free speech, they signaled that the court was open to fundamentally reinterpreting the freedom of expression again.

The court's rethinking of the First Amendment in the 1960s correlated with changing public opinion and may have influenced it. Although support for dissidents' free speech rights in opinion polls conducted in the 1940s and 1950s was below 30 percent, that was shifting by the late 1960s. A 1967 National Opinion Research Center poll showed that 57 percent of respondents agreed that political and civil rights protests should be allowed. In a 1967 Harris poll, 61 percent of respondents agreed that "people have the right to conduct peaceful demonstrations against the war in Vietnam."[56]

Brandenburg v. Ohio (1969) demonstrated the court's profound rethinking of free speech. The case involved a Ku Klux Klan leader who gave a speech (including racial epithets and rhetoric) about taking "revengent" action against the president, members of Congress, and the Supreme Court. The court overturned a prosecution under the state's syndicalism law, passed in 1919 to prohibit advocating crime, violence, and other methods of industrial and political reform. Syndicalism laws like this were passed across the country to stop people and groups from advocating communism, and the court had previously upheld them. However, in *Brandenburg* the court unanimously sounded the death knell of these restrictions on political or economic advocacy, invoking a higher level of First Amendment protection: "The constitutional guarantees of free speech and free press do not permit a State to forbid or proscribe advocacy of the use of force or of law violation except where such advocacy is directed to inciting or producing imminent lawless action and is likely to incite or produce such action."[57] After *Brandenburg*, the government cannot decide that advocating certain political ideas—even communism and totalitarianism—is too hazardous for the American people to hear.[58] The strong language of *Brandenburg*'s imminent lawless action test protects more speech, more consistently, than the more malleable clear and present danger test did.[59]

Just as the United States and Soviet Union were entering détente in the 1970s, the court shifted its understanding of the freedom of speech, demonstrating that the First Amendment protects all forms of dissent. The court followed *Brandenburg* with decisions emphasizing the broad reach of free speech. In *Cohen v. California* (1971), the court found that even offensive speech is protected by the First Amendment, declaring that government may not "seize upon the censorship of particular words as a convenient guise for banning the expression of unpopular views."[60] In *Healy v. James* (1972), the court declared it unconstitutional for a public university to deny recognition to a chapter of the Students for a Democratic Society, a Leftist political organization. According to the justices, "state colleges and universities are not enclaves immune from the sweep of the First Amendment . . . The college classroom with its surrounding environs is peculiarly the 'marketplace of ideas.'"[61] The court was finding protection for the freedom of speech on a scale never seen before in American history.

This sentiment continued through the end of the Cold War. During the same year that the Berlin Wall fell, the court decided two cases demonstrating the lengths the justices had gone on free speech since the early days of the Cold War. In *Ward v. Rock Against Racism* (1989), the court, instead of emphasizing the dangers of advocating certain ideas as it had in *Dennis*, discussed how the freedom of expression was more protected in the United States than in the Soviet Union: "Music is one of the oldest forms of human expression. From Plato's discourse in the *Republic* to the totalitarian state in our own times, rulers have known its capacity to appeal to the intellect and to the emotions, and have censored musical compositions to serve the needs of the state."[62] The court majority now accepted Douglas's dissenting argument in *Dennis* that the American vision of free speech should not censor what are deemed "anti-American" views, lest the United States employ the same tactics as the Soviet Union.

Similarly, in *Texas v. Johnson* (1989) the court overturned a conviction for burning an American flag. In the same month that the Chinese government was using military force to crush the Tiananmen Square protests, Justice Brennan wrote for the court, "If there is a bedrock principle underlying the First Amendment, it is that the government may not prohibit the expression of an idea simply because society finds the idea itself offensive or disagreeable."[63] Brennan's words reflected Jackson's pre–Cold War sentiment in *Barnette*, where he explained that government may not "prescribe what shall be orthodox in politics, nationalism, religion, or other matters of opinion or force citizens to confess by word or act their faith therein."[64]

The court was protecting as much speech—and more—than was the case before the Cold War, interpreting the First Amendment to protect one's right to condemn even core American symbols. If these two American flag cases had been decided in the 1950s, the court likely would have upheld Barnette's suspension for refusing to salute the flag and Johnson's conviction for burning it. However, *Johnson* represented the court's return to zealously protecting the freedom of speech, ensuring that the American flag represents the freedom that is enshrined in the First Amendment.

Today the Supreme Court interprets the First Amendment's Free Speech Clause more expansively than it does just about any other constitutional right. In addition to the right to express unpopular views, described in cases like *Barnette, Brandenburg, Cohen,* and *Johnson,* the court in recent years has held that the First Amendment protects cross burning,[65] making corporate campaign expenditures,[66] depicting animal torture,[67] selling violent video games,[68] lying about having won military service medals,[69] protesting outside of abortion clinics,[70] and registering disparaging trademarks.[71] The court has found that the First Amendment "looks beyond written or spoken words as mediums of expression," including even expression that may not have a discernible message.[72] The court will overrule past First Amendment cases that afforded insufficient protection to expression: in *Janus v. AFSCME* (2018), the court acknowledged that "*stare decisis* applies with perhaps least force of all to decisions that wrongly denied First Amendment rights."[73] In alluding to Jackson's *Barnette* opinion, the *Janus* court proclaimed that it "has not hesitated to overrule decisions offensive to the First Amendment (a fixed star in our constitutional constellation, if there is one)."[74]

This overwhelming protection of expressive rights by the court today parallels strong support among the public. In a 2017 Pew poll, 79 percent of respondents thought that people should "have the right to nonviolent protest" and 74 percent agreed that the "rights of people with unpopular views" should be protected.[75] A 2021 Knight Foundation–Ipsos poll found that 81 percent of Americans agreed that a "group protest in a public space organized by a group with politically unpopular views" should be allowed.[76] This public support for the freedom of expression is higher than it was in similar polls in the 1960s, and it far outpaces responses to comparable poll questions from the 1940s or 1950s. Though it cannot be conclusively proven that the Supreme Court drove this American emphasis on free speech, there is clearly a correlation between the court's increased protection of free speech and the public's support for that right as the Cold War thawed and ended. The court's reinterpretation of the freedom of speech in the 1960s and thereafter is a part of America's changing free speech culture.

During the Cold War, the court backtracked on First Amendment protections. The court eventually changed course, but this was not guaranteed—nor is there a guarantee that freedom of speech will always be protected as much as it is now. Justice Jackson exemplifies how larger political forces can cause judges and other officials to deemphasize the freedom of expression in favor of other concerns. Although the Cold War ended more than three decades ago, significant threats to free expression exist around the globe today, including in Russia and China, and our current norm of placing a high value on this right in the United States has been under attack by government leaders and others in recent years.[77] Even some Supreme Court justices have recently questioned core First Amendment precedents, including *New York Times v. Sullivan*.[78]

The US experience during the Red Scare should be a cautionary tale about how the United States once fell far short of its commitment to protect the freedom of speech. In the words of Justice Douglas, we should "accept no such standard for the United States" and instead remain ever vigilant against threats to the freedom of expression, from wherever they may arise. Indeed, our nation's history since the 1960s has shown that freedom and security can coexist.

NOTES

1. Lawrence M. Friedman, "Law, Lawyers, and Popular Culture," *Yale Law Review* 98 (1989): 1579–1606, at 1579.

2. Ibid.; Eric T. Kasper and Quentin D. Vieregge, *The United States Constitution in Film* (Lanham, MD: Lexington Books, 2018), 7.

3. See *Marbury v. Madison*, 5 US 137 (1803); Eric T. Kasper and Troy A. Kozma, "Did Five Supreme Court Justices Go 'Completely Bonkers'? Saul Goodman, Legal Advertising, and the First Amendment Since *Bates v. State Bar of Arizona*," *Cardozo Arts and Entertainment Law Journal* 37 (2019): 337–371, at 350.

4. G. Edward White, "The First Amendment Comes of Age: The Emergence of Free Speech in Twentieth-Century America," *Michigan Law Review* 95 (1996): 299–392, at 308.

5. Frederick Schauer, "The Boundaries of the First Amendment: A Preliminary Exploration of Constitutional Salience," *Harvard Law Review* 117 (2004): 1765–1809, at 1789.

6. See Richard Kluger, Indelible Ink: The Trials of John Peter Zenger and the Birth of America's Free Press (New York: Norton, 2016), xi–xix.

7. Michael Kent Curtis, *Free Speech, the People's Darling Privilege: Struggles for Freedom of Expression in American History* (Durham, NC: Duke University Press, 2000), 3.

8. Thomas I. Emerson, "The Doctrine of Prior Restraint," *Law and Contemporary Problems* 20

(1955): 648–671, at 652; David M. Rabban, "The First Amendment in Its Forgotten Years," *Yale Law Journal* 90 (1981): 514–595, at 518.

9. *Davis v. Massachusetts*, 167 US 43 (1897); *Turner v. Williams*, 194 US 279 (1904); *Mutual Film Corporation v. Industrial Commission of Ohio*, 236 US 230 (1915).

10. *Patterson v. Colorado*, 205 US 454 (1907), 462.

11. Rabban, "First Amendment in Its Forgotten Years," 553–555.

12. *Schenck v. United States*, 249 US 47, 48–49 (1919); Sarah Sorial, *Sedition and the Advocacy of Violence: Free Speech and Counter-Terrorism* (New York: Routledge, 2012), 17.

13. *Schenck*, 249 US, at 49–52.

14. See Zechariah Chafee Jr., "Freedom of Speech in War Time," *Harvard Law Review* 32 (1919): 932–973, at 967–969.

15. See *Debs v. United States*, 249 US 211 (1919); *Abrams v. United States*, 250 US 616 (1919); *Gitlow v. New York*, 268 US 652 (1925); *Whitney v. California*, 274 US 357 (1927).

16. *Stromberg v. California*, 283 US 359 (1931), 369 (1931).

17. United States v. Carolene Products, 304 US 144, 152, note 4 (1938).

18. *Hague v. Committee for Industrial Organization*, 307 US 496, 501, 513 (1939).

19. *Thornhill v. Alabama*, 310 US 88, 95 (1940).

20. See *Chaplinsky v. New Hampshire*, 315 US 568 (1942), upholding a conviction for using offensive language toward police that was critical of the police's actions.

21. *West Virginia v. Barnette*, 319 US 624, 641–642 (1943).

22. *Thomas v. Collins*, 323 US 516, 530 (1945).

23. Hazel Erskine, "The Polls: Freedom of Speech," *Public Opinion Quarterly* 34 (1970): 483–496, at 486.

24. Erskine, "The Polls," 41.

25. "Was It Orwell's War?," *Irish Daily Mail*, March 8, 2013, 38.

26. Noah Feldman, *Scorpions: The Battles and Triumphs of FDR's Great Supreme Court Justices* (New York: Twelve, 2010), 349–350.

27. David Alistair Yalof, *Pursuit of Justices: Presidential Politics and the Selection of Supreme Court Nominees* (Chicago: University of Chicago Press, 1999), 35.

28. Linda C. Gugin, *Sherman Minton: New Deal Senator, Cold War Justice* (Indianapolis: Indiana Historical Society Press, 1997), 223.

29. *Kovacs v. Cooper*, 336 US 77, 78, 88–87, 98 (1949) (Black, J., dissenting).

30. Peter Irons, *A People's History of the Supreme Court: The Men and Women Whose Cases and Decisions Have Shaped Our Constitution* (New York: Penguin Books, 1999), 327–328; *Barnette*, 319 US at 646–671 (Frankfurter, J., dissenting).

31. *Kovacs*, 336 US at 90, 97 (Frankfurter, J., concurring).

32. White, "First Amendment Comes of Age," 340. The phrase would not be used as a Free Speech Clause test in a majority opinion by the court again.

33. *Terminiello v. Chicago*, 337 US 1, 3–4, 24 (1949) (Jackson, J., dissenting).

34. *American Communications Association v. Douds*, 339 US 382, 399, 411, 422–423 (1950) (Jackson., J, concurring and dissenting).

35. *Dennis v. United States*, 341 US 494, 496 (1951).

36. Ibid., 510 (quoting *United States v. Dennis*, 183 F.2d 201, 212 [2d Cir. 1950]).

37. Elizabeth J. Wallmeyer, "Filled Milk, Footnote Four and the First Amendment: An Analysis of the Preferred Position of Speech After the *Carolene Products* Decision," *Fordham Intellectual Property Media and Entertainment Law Journal* 13 (2003): 1019–1052, at 1042.

38. *Dennis*, 341 US, at 503.

39. Ibid., 525 (Frankfurter, J., concurring).

40. Ibid., 570 (Jackson, J., concurring).

41. Ibid., 579, 581 (Black, J., dissenting).

42. Ibid., 591 (Douglas, J., dissenting).

43. See *Yates v. United States*, 354 US 298 (1957).

44. Brian Neve, *Elia Kazan: The Cinema of an American Outsider* (New York: Taurus, 2009), 59–60.

45. Jeff Smith, *Film Criticism, the Cold War, and the Blacklist: Reading the Hollywood Reds* (Berkeley: University of California Press, 2014), 109.

46. Ted Morgan, *Reds: McCarthyism in Twentieth-Century America* (New York: Random House, 2003), 496, 518, 542.

47. See *Watkins v. United States*, 354 US 178 (1957).

48. *Barenblatt v. United States*, 360 US 109, 126, 128–129, 134 (1959).

49. Erskine, "The Polls," 489.

50. *Gibson v. Florida Legislative Investigation Committee*, 372 US 539, 544, 549 (1963) (internal quotation marks omitted).

51. *Watson v. Memphis*, 373 US 526, 535 (1963).

52. *New York Times v. Sullivan*, 376 US 254, 270–271 (1964) (internal quotation marks omitted).

53. *Cox v. Louisiana*, 379 US 536 (1965).

54. *Elfbrandt v. Russell*, 384 US 11 (1966).

55. *United States v. Robel*, 389 US 258 (1967).

56. See Erskine, "The Polls," 486, 489, 494, 491.

57. *Brandenburg v. Ohio*, 395 US 444, 444–447 (1969).

58. Steven G. Gey, "The Brandenburg Paradigm and Other First Amendments," *University of Pennsylvania Journal of Constitutional Law* 12 (2010): 971–1052, at 996.

59. See Bernard Schwartz (1995), "Holmes Versus Hand: Clear and Present Danger or Advocacy of Unlawful Action?," *Supreme Court Review* 1994 (1994): 209–245, at 239.

60. *Cohen v. California*, 403 US 15, 26 (1971). *Cohen* overturned an "offensive conduct" conviction for wearing a jacket bearing the words "Fuck the Draft."

61. *Healy v. James*, 408 US 169, 180–181 (1972).

62. *Ward v. Rock Against Racism*, 491 US 781, 790 (1989).

63. *Texas v. Johnson*, 491 US 397, 414 (1989).

64. *Barnette*, 319 US, at 642.

65. *RAV v. St. Paul*, 505 US 377 (1992).

66. *Citizens United v. FEC*, 558 US 310 (2010).
67. *United States v. Stevens*, 559 US 460 (2010).
68. *Brown v. Entertainment Merchants Association*, 564 US 786 (2011).
69. *United States v. Alvarez*, 567 US 709 (2012).
70. *McCullen v. Coakley*, 573 US 464 (2014).
71. *Matal v. Tam*, 582 US ___ (2017).
72. *Hurley v. Irish-American Gay, Lesbian and Bisexual Group of Boston*, 515 US 557, 569 (1995). See also Mark V. Tushnet, Alan K. Chen, and Joseph Blocher, *Free Speech beyond Words: The Surprising Reach of the First Amendment* (New York: New York University Press, 2017).
73. *Janus v. AFSCME*, 585 US ___, 2478 (2018).
74. Ibid., quoting *FEC v. Wisconsin Right to Life, Inc.*, 551 US 449, 500 (2007) (Scalia, J., concurring in part and concurring in judgment).
75. "Large Majorities See Checks and Balances, Right to Protest as Essential for Democracy," Pew Research Center, March 2, 2017, https://www.people-press.org/2017/03/02/large-majorities-see-checks-and-balances-right-to-protest-as-essential-for-democracy.
76. *Free Expression in America Post-2020*, Knight Foundation–Ipsos, 2022, https://knightfoundation.org/wp-content/uploads/2022/01/KF_Free_Expression_2022.pdf.
77. See *Freedom in the World 2022: The Global Expansion of Authoritarian Rule*, Freedom House, 14, 20–25, https://freedomhouse.org/sites/default/files/2022-02/FIW_2022_PDF_Booklet_Digital_Final_Web.pdf; *The Expression Agenda Report 2016/2017*, Article 19, 2017, https://www.article19.org/wp-content/uploads/2017/12/Expression-Agenda-Report-2017-for-web-_30.11.17.pdf. According to the Associated Press, "unauthorized protests are against the law" in Russia. Dasha Litvinova, "Hundreds Arrested as Shocked Russians Protest Ukraine Attack," Associated Press, February 24, 2022, https://apnews.com/article/russia-ukraine-vladimir-putin-europe-russia-moscow-9a3eab8c8cb047254c82f1839ef77b9f. On China, see *Freedom in the World 2022*, 3; *Freedom in the World 2019: Democracy in Retreat*, Freedom House, 20–22, https://freedomhouse.org/sites/default/files/Feb2019_FH_FITW_2019_Report_ForWeb-compressed.pdf.
78. Adam Liptak, "Two Justices Say Supreme Court Should Reconsider Landmark Libel Decision," *New York Times*, July 2, 2021, https://www.nytimes.com/2021/07/02/us/supreme-court-libel.html.

LOYALTY AND LAW

Cold War Conformity in the Legal Profession

MARY ELIZABETH BASILE CHOPAS

During the late 1940s and 1950s, many types of people were suspected by the US government of being communist sympathizers or members of organizations on the Attorney General's List of Subversive Organizations. The House Un-American Activities Committee (HUAC) issued charges of communism or fascism, often based on unsubstantiated or outdated information, which led to investigations into the associations and activities of diverse Americans. Groups and a broad range of individuals came under suspicion—workers in the maritime and shipping industry, prominent scientists, schoolteachers, professors, musicians, screenwriters, playwrights, broadcasters, and the attorneys who defended such individuals.[1]

As Michael Sherry suggests, "The boundaries between culture and politics were blurry and victims were found in many sectors of American life."[2] Members of many trades and professions and workers in all types of businesses were required to sign loyalty oaths stating that they would not advocate the overthrow of the US government and disavowing membership in any group that did so. Some individuals were more vulnerable to suspicion than others—political liberals and radicals, homosexuals working in the government or the military, foreign-born citizens and noncitizens, and sometimes actual Communists.

Anticommunist sentiment targeting the labor movement was evident in the passage of the 1947 Taft-Hartley Act, which among other things limited a union's ability to conduct boycotts or strikes deemed by the president to conflict with the national interest, and required union officials to sign affidavits saying they did not belong to the Communist Party or to any other "subversive" organization.[3] Likewise, universities were under pressure not to appoint as faculty people with communist leanings, and to fire those already on the faculty who were identified as Communists. Universities required faculty to sign exculpatory oaths stating that they had not in the past nor did they presently maintain memberships in subversive groups.[4] As a result of loyalty-security programs conducted by both private and public employers, thousands of people lost their jobs or security clearances.[5]

The Federal Bureau of Investigation infiltrated American society and created files on individuals suspected of communist leanings, which led to arrests, firings, and deportations of alleged subversives.[6] Because the FBI relied on secret informers, the people charged with disloyalty were not told who had made the accusations against them, and the panels reviewing the cases did not have any more specific information. The result was that proceedings under the loyalty-security programs, which were based on hearsay and vague charges, made it difficult for the accused to clear themselves of guilt even when innocent of communist activities.[7]

Lawyers practicing during the Red Scare had to be proficient in conflicting laws and rules of state and municipal governments that banned certain affiliations or activities that might be legal in other locales. But the biggest challenge for lawyers arguing on behalf of these individuals was that they often faced a court system that was reluctant to interfere with the decisions of political institutions.[8] For example, when in 1947 the "Hollywood Ten," a group of ten screenwriters, producers, and directors who had been or were still Communist Party members, refused to testify about themselves or other members of the film community and brought claims arguing the protection of the First Amendment, the federal courts sided with the government. HUAC's powers to conduct inquiries were upheld, and all ten were sentenced to prison for being in contempt of Congress. The result of these rulings was that many members of the film industry were blacklisted and unable to find employment unless they agreed to provide information on people whom they knew to have communist ties.[9]

Lawyers who defended or supported the causes of those suspected of communism could find themselves on a list of suspicious persons as well. This is exactly what happened when Zechariah Chafee Jr., a Harvard Law School professor and civil libertarian, criticized HUAC's methods and its 1947 Hollywood investigations. In early 1950, he joined an amicus brief of two American Civil Liberties Union lawyers asking the US Supreme Court to review the contempt convictions of two screenwriters who refused to answer HUAC's questions. The Supreme Court refused. Chafee also wrote a letter supporting Owen J. Lattimore, a Johns Hopkins University professor and former State Department employee whom Senator Joseph McCarthy labeled "the top Soviet agent in the United States." Two years later, Chafee's name was on a list compiled by Senator McCarthy of seven people who were "dangerous to America."[10] Lawyers representing suspected Communists were perceived as sharing their clients' unpopular views.

THE ATTORNEY LOYALTY OATH AND THE UNPOPULAR CLIENT

Historian Jerold Auerbach wrote that the politics of the Cold War "transformed" into subversive activities the New Deal legacy of attorneys' work with political reform, civil liberties, rights for minorities, and social justice. Auerbach wrote, "The professional elite, encouraged and abetted by two attorneys general, by the House Un-American Activities Committee, and by politicians eager to ride anti-Communism to political power, attempted to purge the profession of lawyers whose political and professional commitments deviated from the Cold War orthodoxy."[11] Amid the hysteria of the Red Scare, the American Bar Association (ABA) requested state bars to require each attorney to take an "anticommunist" oath and to file an affidavit stating whether they were or ever had been a member of the Communist Party or any organization advocating the overthrow of the United States government.[12] This stance was consistent with HUAC's attitude concerning attorneys identified as Communists. The committee asked, "How can a lawyer maintain his oath to uphold and defend the Constitution of the United States when he is an agent of a conspiratorial apparatus designed to destroy the Constitution?" HUAC questioned how such an attorney could be "an officer of the court . . . also an officer of the State, with an obligation to the public," when his loyalties were to the Communist Party.[13]

Legal scholars writing during the Cold War predicted a "sterility of the bar" as zeal in attorneys was interpreted by judges as an indication of communist or revolutionary inclinations, regardless of the political nature of the matter, a trend which they feared would eventually result in a softening of advocacy. Drawing on historical examples from as early as the reign of England's King Henry VIII (1509–1547), critics of the oaths predicted that if state bars were first to require anticommunist oaths of their members, then further disavowals of specific beliefs, doctrines or associations would follow, as dictated by the political necessities of the time.[14]

Attorneys practicing during times when loyalty oaths were imposed were often faced with the dilemma of defending the causes of their clients at the risk of having their own loyalty to the United States called into question. The bar elite, most effectively through the loyalty oath proposal, attempted "to intimidate lawyers for unpopular defendants and to discipline those whose beliefs or associations were adjudged subversive."[15] Auerbach argued that the Canons of Ethics did little to guide attorneys in their responsibilities to promote the administration of justice and equality under the law by failing to set useful parameters, since they "urged lawyers to defend the accused regardless of their personal opinion as to guilt" at the same time as "permitting lawyers to reject distasteful clients."[16] Loyalty oaths had the chilling effect of scaring attorneys from representing such clients, since they raised the specter that any time an attorney represented a Communist, he could lose his license.[17] Loyalty to country was prioritized over loyalty to client.

The late civil rights attorney and law professor Daniel H. Pollitt represented many individuals facing problems from loyalty-security programs in the 1950s—government officials accused of subversive activities, the United Auto Workers, Pullman railcar workers, the farm workers union, and the leaders of other labor unions. One of his most famous cases involved the defense of the playwright Lillian Hellman before HUAC, which sought information on people Ms. Hellman knew with communist ties. Pollitt represented at least ten individuals before HUAC at a time when most lawyers did not want any association with such controversial clients.[18] In a 1964 *Harper's* article, he reflected upon how during the height of McCarthyism in the early 1950s, local and national bar associations tacitly encouraged members to shun potential clients accused of communist sympathies as well as other unpopular clients. Pollitt recalled how "all too often, the public and the lawyers—who should know better—choose to believe that the lawyer who defends the right of free speech for Communists must himself be a Marxist."[19]

This blurring of a lawyer's professional obligation with their personal conviction left many defendants without counsel to defend them from government charges. And those attorneys who represented such clients suffered adverse publicity in the press as well as criticism from members of the bar and from their friends, resulting in serious harm to their practice.[20] It was a matter of professional integrity and adherence to the tenets of the US Constitution that guided an attorney's decision to take on the causes of unpopular clients.

The left-leaning National Lawyers Guild became a target for the government. The guild, in strong opposition to the loyalty program, had claimed that the program denied citizens their constitutional right to advocate for social, economic, and political change. HUAC issued a report in September 1950 entitled "The National Lawyers Guild: Legal Bulwark of the Communist Party," which recommended that the Department of Justice place the guild on its subversive organizations list and that its members be barred from obtaining federal jobs. HUAC also urged the ABA to consider whether membership in the guild was compatible with membership in the bar. Such attacks were devastating to the guild and its work in promoting the civil liberties of individuals. In Washington, DC, the number of government lawyers who were guild attorneys dropped from four hundred to zero. The guild could not recruit new members and had difficulty forming student chapters in law schools.[21]

The case of the progressive San Francisco law firm of Gladstein, Andersen, and Leonard illustrates how attorneys who took on Communists as clients came under attack themselves and faced rejection from the conservative ABA and society in general, regardless of their personal views. The FBI kept files on Richard Gladstein, George R. Andersen, and Norman Leonard, all of whom were National Lawyers Guild members. The FBI alleged that they were Communists, although only Andersen admitted to having once been a member. The allegation was likely the result of the firm's defense of clients accused of violating the 1940 Smith Act for advocating Marxist thought and principles. All three law partners represented the International Longshoreman's and Warehouseman's Union, its officer Archie Brown, who was a Communist Party member, and its president, Harry Bridges, whose FBI file was approximately thirty thousand pages. The attorneys were also involved with the Northern California Committee for the Protection of Foreign Born, an affiliate of the American Committee for the Protection of Foreign Born, which was on the Attorney General's List of Subversive Organizations.[22]

Gladstein's representation of the working class and foreign born caused him to be the subject of mail threats and to face possible disbarment. His defense of Communist Party leaders in New York resulted in a citation for contempt of court and a sentence to prison in 1949. FBI reports attributed his partner Andersen with having deep knowledge of Communist Party activities in the San Francisco area. In a mysterious incident occurring in 1948, Andersen was assaulted and shot in his law office; the police were never able to catch or identify the two unknown intruders, but there was speculation that the FBI was behind the assault. Although Leonard did not suffer consequences as dire as those of his partners, he too was the subject of accusations based on his representation of unpopular clients.[23] The experiences of these attorneys show how the choice of clients affected an attorney's treatment by both the judicial system and law enforcement. Defenders of communist sympathizers were treated like criminals rather than as officers of the court.

The case of *Dennis v. United States* illustrates the difficulty that leaders of the American Communist Party had in securing their desired legal representation, as well as the repercussions faced by the attorneys fearless enough to represent them.[24] In the New York trial, eleven Communist Party leaders were charged under the Smith Act with conspiracy to form an organization to teach and advocate a violent overthrow of the US government. Their efforts to hire attorneys of stature to counteract the public prejudice failed because high-profile attorneys feared loss of their reputation.[25] The defendants received a guilty verdict and the judge issued summary contempt charges against their attorneys. Five of the defense attorneys received a sentence of thirty days to six months in jail. Three had to undergo disciplinary proceedings and two were disbarred in state and federal courts.[26]

The lead counsel in the case, Harry Sacher and Abraham Isserman, were veteran attorneys who had devoted a substantial portion of their careers to cases involving civil liberties and labor defense. In addition to being jailed like their colleagues, both were disbarred—Sacher in New York and Isserman in New York and New Jersey. Although both were eventually readmitted in their respective states, their punishment was the beginning of a chapter in the legal profession of attorneys facing disciplinary proceedings for advocating the causes of unpopular clients. As Auerbach notes, "The Cold War represented an unprecedented episode of professional repression."[27]

THE AMERICAN BAR ASSOCIATION'S RESOLUTIONS SEEK ANTICOMMUNIST AVOWAL

In issues "involving the delicate balance of individual rights against national security," Pollitt argued, "the American Bar Association has allied itself with the state and against the individual."[28] Although this country would not experience any federally legislated requirement of loyalty oaths for attorneys as it had after the Civil War, national, state, and local bar organizations and state legislatures tried to accomplish the same thing.[29] In September 1950, after a favorable report by the Committee on Resolutions, the ABA Assembly and House of Delegates adopted resolutions holding that it was especially appropriate that all lawyers be required to take an anticommunist oath and requesting states to require each lawyer to file an affidavit regarding membership in the Communist Party.[30] The resolution requested of the states was that each member of the bar be required:

> within a reasonable time and periodically thereafter, to file an affidavit stating whether he is or ever has been a member of the Communist party, or affiliated therewith, and stating also whether he is or ever has been a member or supporter of any organization that espouses the overthrow, by force or by any illegal or unconstitutional means, of the United States Government, or the government of any of the states or territories of the United States; and in the event such affidavit reveals that he is or ever has been a member of said Communist Party, or of any such organization, that the appropriate authority promptly and thoroughly investigate the activities and conduct of said member of the Bar to determine his fitness for continuance as an attorney.[31]

The House of Delegates called for expulsion of Communists from the ABA and recommended that states disbar Communists.[32] The vote to adopt the resolution was taken without benefit of any debate, at the end of the session, after many delegates had left.[33] Those in favor of loyalty oaths expressed the concern that if there were no requirement of such an oath, there would be no plan in place for identifying Communists for disbarment.[34]

Opponents cited a host of constitutional issues raised by the proposed attorney loyalty oath. First, as the oath required a statement of past as well as present membership in the Communist Party, on which basis disbarment would result, it would violate the *Garland* doctrine making it unconstitutional to punish past conduct.[35] Second, its limitation on groups supported by an attorney, or the views they espoused, would run counter to the First Amendment's protection of the freedom of speech and equal protection of the law under the Fourteenth Amendment. Finally, in the sense that the oath could effectively condemn an attorney through their own words, it could violate the privilege against self-incrimination under the Fifth Amendment.[36] All of these arguments presumed that a loyalty oath would require avowals that went beyond that of the oath upon admission.

BACKLASH FROM STATE AND LOCAL BAR ASSOCIATIONS: THE CASE OF MASSACHUSETTS

Loyalty oaths during the 1950s incited anger among attorneys who perceived them as contradicting the duty that the profession owed to society. Rather than a testament to an attorney's beliefs in the principles of the Constitution and a guarantee of allegiance to the United States government, which oaths upon admission to the bar presumably already accomplished, the true aim of the loyalty oaths was to purge unpopular opinions or sympathies among members of the bar.[37]

Resistance to loyalty oaths on the part of various state and city bar organizations reflected the fierce independence of the legal profession. Among the groups of attorneys not intimidated by the ABA was the New York City Bar Association. On December 12, 1950, that group adopted a resolution opposing the requirement of any oath other than the traditional oath to support the Constitution.[38] A group of twenty-seven ABA members (eight from New York, two from Boston, and seventeen from other cities) issued a public statement opposing the requirement of an anticommunist oath as repetitious of the universally required professional oath upon admission. The group also felt that the requirement implied "widespread disloyalty and illegal acts on the part of lawyers generally," when there was no evidence of such.[39]

Despite the debate over the worth of oaths, the ABA House of Delegates voted on February 27, 1951, to affirm its stance on the anticommunist oath. It also voted not to adopt a resolution calling for a poll of members of the ABA regarding the question of membership in the Communist Party, which was expensive and useless, since members could choose to ignore it or not answer truthfully.[40] Apparently, the feeling was that an oath carried a significance that attorneys could not take lightly.

Some state bar associations not only were pitted against the ABA with respect to the oath initiative but also often found themselves opposing their own state legislature. In Massachusetts, a special committee of the legislature whose mission was "to curb communism" reached a majority decision to recommend adoption of legislation patterned after the Maryland "Ober" law, and another calling for an additional loyalty oath for attorneys.[41] Pursuant to "An Act to Require Attorneys-at-Law to Take an Oath of Loyalty to the Principles of the Constitution of the United States and the Commonwealth," the following oath was proposed:

> I, (insert name), do solemnly swear (or affirm) that I do not advocate, and have not advocated, nor am I a member of any political party or organization that advocates, the overthrow of the government of the United States or of this commonwealth by force or violence or by any other illegal or unconstitutional method; and that so long as I am an attorney, I will not advocate nor become a member of any political party or organization that advocates the overthrow of the government of the United States or of this commonwealth by force or violence or by any other illegal or unconstitutional method.[42]

Due process was provided in Section 39F of the proposed legislation, which gave attorneys the right to an evidentiary hearing before the board of bar examiners, with adequate time beforehand to prepare for a defense.

One Massachusetts legislator, Representative William E. Hays, spoke out against what he called "hasty legislation." He pointed out that there was "adequate Federal law to deal with any serious subversive activity," presumably referring to the Smith Act.[43] The argument that national security is the domain of Congress rather than the state board of bar examiners meant that the onus to determine seditious activity among the bar and to examine any charges against an attorney should be ultimately placed upon the courts. The procedural safeguards of a court trial, namely the formality of pleading requirements that call for careful formulation of charges, an opportunity to fully develop a defense, rules on admissibility of evidence, and the use of a jury as trier of fact, would make it a much fairer forum for the determination of the loyalty of attorneys. Hays not only considered the requirement of a loyalty oath unnecessary but also thought it would operate as an "affront to the legal profession," and he went so far as to term it "an inquisition." Further, he warned that the legislation could "lul[l] citizens into a false sense of security."[44] Certainly the level of sincerity of attorneys taking an oath would vary, but undoubtedly many would treat it simply as a necessary step to maintain their license to practice law, comparable to the payment of yearly fees.

In support of the Massachusetts Bar Association Executive Committee's stance against attorney loyalty oaths, Harvard law professor George K. Gardner went before the Massachusetts legislature at a hearing on the issue. Consistent with his position before the ABA House of Delegates in Chicago in February 1951, Professor Gardner argued that the attorney oath upon admission, which requires lawyers to swear to uphold both the federal and state constitutions, already operates as a "loyalty" oath and contains "a short code of professional ethics." To require the proposed loyalty oath in addition to the lawyer's oath would in effect make the latter "perfunctory in spirit and in fact." In a May 1, 1951, letter to the *Boston Herald*, Gardner further explained that the proposed oath was no more than an "oath of submission" and that the citizens of the Commonwealth do not want "submissive lawyers."[45]

There was not enough resistance from the members of the Boston Bar Association (BBA) to prevent that organization from adopting policies consistent with the ABA's resolutions. That association's Special Committee to Inquire into Communism Within the Bar put forth proposals, in response to the ABA, that included disbarment of members found after investigation and a hearing to advocate the overthrow of the governments of the United States or the Commonwealth; denial of admission to members of the Communist Party or adherents of Marxism–Leninism; and an additional attorney oath pledging loyalty to the federal and Massachusetts constitutions and opposing communism. The committee's recommendations were submitted for approval through a poll to members of the BBA.

In response to these proposals, a group of eleven Massachusetts lawyers, including Harvard Law Professors Paul A. Freund and Mark DeWolfe Howe, issued a protest to the BBA. Taking issue with the BBA's plea for lawyers "to forget for the moment that they are lawyers and accept the greater responsibility of citizens and patriots," the group explained:

> As members of the Massachusetts Bar we oppose the proposals precisely because we believe that our civic duty requires us to remember, and, not even momentarily, to forget, that we are lawyers. As lawyers we have been schooled by training and experience in the careful definition of ends and the skillful devising of means to attain those ends. . . .
>
> Let us content ourselves with the all-inclusive oath to support the Constitution, and not stimulate the invention of sub-loyalty oaths. For the rest, let us meet specific abuses within and without the profession by specific remedies, in the characteristic common-law way.

They acknowledged that the times presented problems of "internal security" but that the bar was responsible for disciplining attorneys only for violations of the professional code, not for matters of national loyalty. Moreover, it was the responsibility of the bar to provide "the voice of seasoned and constructive counsel" rather than perpetuate the anticommunist frenzy.[46]

Although the Massachusetts legislature did pass a law in 1951 making it a crime to be a Communist, the law requiring a loyalty oath of attorneys was not successful.[47] Ultimately, only a few states prescribed a loyalty oath for attorneys that included language that went beyond the promise to uphold state and national constitutions.[48]

THE FIFTH AMENDMENT AS A DEFENSE TO LOYALTY INQUIRIES

Erwin N. Griswold, dean of Harvard Law School, became an outspoken critic of the lack of procedural safeguards in loyalty inquiries before congressional bodies. His thoughts on the rights of the individual accused of communist ties to plead the Fifth Amendment address larger concerns about the role of the attorney in representing suspects during the Red Scare. In reaction to what he perceived as a dearth of response from the academic world to the impact of Senator McCarthy and his supporters on proceedings before legislative committees in which professors who refused to answer questions on Fifth Amendment grounds were deemed guilty, Griswold emerged as a proponent of an individual's right to invoke Fifth Amendment protections without any repercussions.[49]

Griswold first spoke on the topic of the Fifth Amendment upon invitation to the midwinter meeting of the Massachusetts Bar Association in Springfield on February 5, 1954.[50] He traced the long history of legal provisions against self-incrimination, beginning in twelfth-century England as a result of controversies between the king and bishops, through the establishment of the privilege against self-incrimination in the common law of English courts in the latter half of the seventeenth century, to the adoption of a provision in the Massachusetts constitution in 1780, which antedates that in the United States Constitution. He hailed the Fifth Amendment as a sound provision of both federal and state laws, pointing out that the establishment of the privilege against self-incrimination "is closely linked historically with the abolition of torture." He stated his position as follows: "If a man has done wrong, he should be punished. But the evidence against him should be produced, and evaluated by a proper court in a fair trial. Neither torture nor an oath nor the threat of punishment such as imprisonment for contempt should be used to compel him to provide the evidence to accuse or to convict himself."[51]

Griswold's implication was that current congressional procedures were infringing on the role of the courts. His ideas about the specific treatment of attorneys who pled the Fifth Amendment were expressed during a debate with Tracy E. Griffin, a Seattle attorney and member of the ABA Special Committee on Communist Tactics, Strategy and Objectives, at the 78th annual meeting of the ABA in Philadelphia in August of 1955. Griffin stated the position of the ABA committee to be that "any lawyer who pleads the Fifth Amendment should be immediately disbarred"; however, no such action had been taken against an attorney on that ground.[52] Griffin called for the yielding of individual rights in such circumstances because "obtaining the truth from a witness, establishing a fact material to the security of the United States, is more important to the general welfare and the public as a whole."[53]

Griswold strongly opposed automatic disbarment, which would cause an individual's freedom and right to dissent to yield to the concern for national security. He conceded that when the conduct of an attorney who invoked the Fifth Amendment raised a question of security, an investigation was in order, but one along the lines of a judicial inquiry rather than a congressional hearing.[54] Through their traditional processes of fair and deliberate consideration, courts were better equipped to determine whether there was a substantial basis for drawing a negative inference from an attorney's invocation of privilege under the Fifth Amendment.[55]

What distinguishes the experience of many lawyers during this time was that their claim of Fifth Amendment privilege alone was deemed evidence of the facts of sedition. There was a lack of evidence in congressional investigations, which in an ordinary criminal court case would result in a directed verdict in favor of the defendant.[56] Similarly, the loyalty review process in various government departments denied individuals the rights of "fair notice of the charges against them, the presumption of innocence, and an opportunity to confront their accusers."[57]

The climate of suspicion during the Cold War allowed the government to cast its net widely, relying upon group identity rather than individual conduct, thereby calling into question the activities of many innocent people. Individuals accused of communism faced difficulties in finding representation against government charges or after being fired from their jobs for failing a loyalty test or for refusing to take an oath. In turn, attorneys were challenged to explore their conscience, some choosing to hold steadfast to the ideals of the legal profession, particularly that every individual accused of a crime deserves zealous representation, no matter how unpopular the position. Those lawyers brave enough to take on the cases of people accused of being communist sympathizers risked both financial and reputational harm, since their practice was marked as un-American, and some even risked disbarment or imprisonment. Although they may have taken their duties as officers of the court seriously, these attorneys did not find support in professional organizations that imposed loyalty oaths or investigations for members and that ostracized some for their choice of clients. Consequently, most lawyers practicing during this period were forced to yield their independence in the profession to national security measures.

NOTES

This essay was adapted from Mary Elizabeth Basile, "Loyalty Testing for Attorneys: When Is it Necessary and Who Should Decide?," *Cardozo Law Review* 30, no. 5 (2009): 1843–1884. Material from the Erwin Griswold Papers is reproduced with permission of the Harvard Law School Library.

1. See Colin Wark and John F. Galliher, *Progressive Lawyers under Siege: Moral Panic during the McCarthy Years* (Lanham, MD: Lexington Books, 2015), 23–24.

2. Michael S. Sherry, *In the Shadow of War: The United States since the 1930s* (New Haven, CT: Yale University Press, 1995), 171.

3. John M. Murrin, Paul E. Johnson, James M. McPherson, Gary Gerstle, Emily S. Rosenberg, and Norman L. Rosenberg, *Liberty, Equality, Power: A History of the American People,* 2nd ed. (Fort Worth, TX: Harcourt College Publishers, 2001), 738.

4. Donald L. Smith, *Zechariah Chafee, Jr.: Defender of Liberty and Law* (Cambridge, MA: Harvard University Press, 1986), 258.

5. Ellen Schrecker, "'Mere Shadows': The Early Cold War," in *Security v. Liberty: Conflicts Between Civil Liberties and National Security in American History,* ed. Daniel Farber (New York: Russell Sage Foundation, 2008), 84.

6. Sherry, *In the Shadow of War,* 173.

7. Schrecker, "Mere Shadows," 85.

8. See Sherry, *In the Shadow of War,* 171, 173.

9. Murrin et al., *Liberty, Equality, Power,* 739.

10. Smith, *Zechariah Chafee, Jr.,* 261–262.

11. Jerold S. Auerbach, *Unequal Justice: Lawyers and Social Change in Modern America* (New York: Oxford University Press, 1976), 233.

12. "Proceedings of the House of Delegates," in American Bar Association, *Annotated Reports* 75 (1950), 148–149.

13. *Report on Communist Legal Subversion: The Role of the Communist Lawyer,* 86th Congress, House Committee on Un-American Activities (Washington, DC: US Government Printing Office, 1959), 2, 5.

14. Samuel M. Koenigsberg and Morton Stavis, "Test Oaths: Henry VIII to the American Bar Association," *Lawyers Guild Review* 11 (1951): 111, 125–126.

15. Auerbach, *Unequal Justice,* 240. See also James E. Moliterno, "Politically Motivated Bar Discipline," *Washington University Law Quarterly* 83 (2005): 725.

16. See Auerbach, *Unequal Justice,* 258, referring to American Bar Association, *Canons of Professional Ethics* (adopted on August 27, 1908), canon 15, "How Far a Lawyer May Go in Supporting a Client's Cause," and canon 44, "Withdrawal from Employment as Attorney or Counsel."

17. See Terence C. Halliday, "The Idiom of Legalism in Bar Politics: Lawyers, McCarthyism, and the Civil Rights Era," *American Bar Foundation Research Journal* 7 (1982): 911, 923–924.

18. John C. Boger, "Daniel H. Pollitt: In Memoriam," *North Carolina Law Review* 89 (2010): 9, 11.

19. Daniel H. Pollitt, "Timid Lawyers and Neglected Clients," *Harper's Magazine* 229, no. 1371 (August 1964): 81–82.

20. See Pollitt, "Timid Lawyers and Neglected Clients," 82–83.

21. Ann Fagan Ginger and Eugene M. Tobin, eds., *The National Lawyers Guild: From Roosevelt through Reagan* (Philadelphia: Temple University Press, 1988), 113, 117.

22. Wark and Galliher, *Progressive Lawyers under Siege*, 101–103.

23. Ibid., 63–64, 67–68, 76–77, 91–93.

24. Dennis v. United States, 341 US 494 (1951).

25. See Charles Grutzner, "Court Offers '2d Team' Reds 10 Lawyers to Defend Them," *New York Times*, August 9, 1951, 1.

26. Ginger and Tobin, *National Lawyers Guild*, 124.

27. Auerbach, *Unequal Justice*, 242, 244–246.

28. Pollitt, "Timid Lawyers and Neglected Clients," 84.

29. See William A. Russ Jr., "The Lawyer's Test Oath During Reconstruction," *Mississippi Law Journal* 10 (1937–1938): 154–155, note 3.

30. For a close analysis of the resolution adopting the requirement of loyalty oaths, see Zechariah Chafee Jr., *The Blessings of Liberty* (Philadelphia, PA: Lippincott, 1956), 161–176.

31. "Proceedings of the House of Delegates," 148–149.

32. "Proceedings of the House of Delegates: February 26–27, Chicago," *American Bar Association Journal* 37, no. 4 (April 1951): 309, 312.

33. "The Current American Swearing Epidemic," *Massachusetts Law Quarterly* 36, no. 1 (May 1951): 47, 56.

34. See comments of William C. Walsh of Maryland in "Proceedings of the House of Delegates: February 26–27, Chicago," 319.

35. "Constitutional Issues Raised by the Proposed Loyalty Oath for Lawyers," *Iowa Law Review* 36 (1950–1951): 529, 531–32. In *Ex parte Garland*, 71 US (4 Wall.) 333 (1866), the Supreme Court decided that the federal test oath for attorneys was unconstitutional, viewing it as punishment for past conduct.

36. "Constitutional Issues Raised," 532–535.

37. Zechariah Chafee Jr., "Purge Trials Are for Russian Lawyers, Not American Lawyers," *New Jersey Law Journal* 74 (1951): 169.

38. "The Lawyer's Loyalty Oath," *American Bar Association Journal* 37 (1951): 128.

39. "The Proposed Anti-Communist Oath: Opposition Expressed to Association's Policy," *American Bar Association Journal* 37 (1951): 123.

40. "Proceedings of the House of Delegates: February 26–27, Chicago," 320.

41. This statute, the Subversive Activities Act of 1949, MD Ann. Code, art. 85A, §15, which made membership in the Communist Party or any organization found to advocate the overthrow of the government a crime, served as a model for other state statutes. The Massachusetts version can be found in HR 2759, 157 Gen. Ct. (Mass. 1951).

42. HR 2323, 157 Gen. Ct. (Mass. 1951), Appendix C-II (proposed Mass. Gen. Laws, ch. 221, §39B).

43. "Supplementary Statement of Representative William E. Hays," in "The Current American Swearing Epidemic," 50; Smith Act (Alien Registration Act), 18 USC §2385.

44. "Supplementary Statement," 51.

45. Professor Gardner's May 1, 1951, letter to the *Boston Herald* is reprinted in "The Hearing," in "Current American Swearing Epidemic," 52–54.

46. "Record of the 40th Annual Meeting of the Massachusetts Bar Association at Plymouth, June 9, 1951," *Massachusetts Law Quarterly* (July 1951): 15–21.

47. S. Res. 774, 157 Gen. Ct. (Mass. 1951), "An act providing for the adjudication of certain organizations as subversive, and imposing penalties for membership in, or the furnishing of certain aid or assistance to subversive organizations," as amended, was approved by the governor on November 17 as chapter 805 of the Acts of 1951.

48. See Ralph S. Brown Jr. and John D. Fassett, "Loyalty Tests for Admission to the Bar," *University of Chicago Law Review* 20 (1952–1953): 480, 483–497.

49. See Erwin N. Griswold, *Ould Fields, New Corne: The Personal Memoirs of a Twentieth Century Lawyer* (St. Paul, MN: West Publishing, 1992), 192–193.

50. This was the first of a series of three speeches reproduced in Erwin N. Griswold, *The Fifth Amendment Today: Three Speeches* (Cambridge, MA: Harvard University Press, 1955).

51. "Dean Erwin N. Griswold's Speech on Fifth Amendment," *Legal Intelligencer* 130 (March 16, 1954), 335, 339, Papers of Erwin Griswold (Griswold Papers), Harvard Law School Library, box 88, folder 3.

52. "Harvard Law School Dean Backs Right to Take Fifth Amendment," Allen's Press Clipping Bureau, August 26, 1955, Griswold Papers, box 88, folder 5. Since there is no transcript of the meeting, we must rely on accounts of the debate in articles and correspondence.

53. "Attorneys' Use of '5th' Debated: Dean of Harvard and Coast Lawyer Disagree on Issue of Automatic Disbarment," *New York Times*, August 25, 1955, 12, Griswold Papers, box 77, folder 18.

54. See "Attorneys' Use of '5th' Debated," 12.

55. See Erwin N. Griswold, "The Individual and the Fifth Amendment," *New Leader*, October 29, 1956, 20, 23, Griswold Papers, box 77, folder 18.

56. Erwin N. Griswold, "The Fifth Amendment Today," *Marquette Law Review* 39 (1955–56): 191, 202.

57. David Cole, *Enemy Aliens: Double Standards and Constitutional Freedoms in the War on Terrorism* (New York: New Press, 2003), 148.

THE RISE OF THE NATIONAL SECURITY STATE AS A TECHNOLOGY ENTERPRISE

LINDA WEISS

There is one thing we do know: we cannot settle for anything short of technological leadership in R&D [research and development] related to national security.

—MELVIN LAIRD, 1970 Senate Hearings on Appropriations FY 1971

Although I use the concept in a quite specific and distinctive way in this essay, the genesis of the national security state (NSS) has been richly detailed in several historical studies. I highlight the rise and evolution of the NSS *as an innovation enterprise* that concentrates national responsibility for science and technology. How that role emerged and took shape and how it embraced a variety of actors in the private sector is a fascinating story in itself. Nothing like it had ever been created before. I emphasize four important points. First, the national security state emerged not fully formed but in fits and starts in the aftermath of World War II, in response to a persistent and intensely felt geopolitical threat. Second, its creation had a major impact on American political development in that it led to significant expansion (and concentration) of the state's transformative capacity within the executive branch of government. Third, the national security state has been Janus-like in its responsiveness to threats arising from both the international security environment and weaknesses in its domestic sources of supply, wherever these were perceived to challenge America's technological leadership. And fourth, rather than relying on heavy-handed top-down controls or simply counting on the private sector to foster innovation from the bottom up, the NSS has fostered relations of "governed interdependence" throughout the American economy. These public–private relationships would often take the form of contractual synergistic partnerships between the NSS, industry, and academic institutions. However, they also generated more lasting institutional fusions that created distinctive hybrid arrangements for the pursuit of public purpose. Through these partnerings and hybrid arrangements, the NSS came to revolutionize the nation's technological capabilities and stimulate commercial innovation for the purpose of national defense.

Several excellent accounts of the early postwar period have described the emergence of institutions that have come to be identified with national security functions, and I draw amply on many of them. However, the purpose of this essay is both narrower and broader than the extant literature. Its key objective is to clarify the nature, scope, and sources of the NSS (qua technology leadership/innovation enterprise). My account is accordingly narrower in focus, being concerned chiefly with those components of the NSS that play a significant role in technology development.

I frame my discussion of the rise and evolution of the NSS in terms of four broad "phases." These correspond roughly rather than neatly to the designated periods of emergence (1945–1957), growth (1958–1968), crisis (1969–1979), and reform and reorientation in two phases (1980–1998). In each phase, I seek to highlight those aspects of the international security environment, the domestic political context, and the technology leadership challenges that have influenced the formation and evolution of the NSS innovation enterprise. However, I also consider these phases as two distinctive but interconnected eras: the "procurement era" (up to and including the 1970s) and the "commercialization era" (1980s and beyond). The implication is not that procurement was abandoned after the 1970s but rather that there was a heightened emphasis on bringing innovations to market in a way that met both mission-centered and commercial goals.[1]

EMERGENCE (1945–1957)

It is no secret that World War II was a watershed event for both American political development and US technology leadership. Prior to that national emergency, America could be characterized as neither a national security state nor a technology leader.² In the early postwar decades, however, the United States could lay claim to being both, though neither development was inevitable. The surprise attack on American territory in 1941 helped to strengthen the postwar case for permanent military preparedness, which gave birth to a vast national security infrastructure, but it was by no means a fait accompli at war's end. As public policy historian David Hart explains, "The establishment of the military as a patron worth having and national security as a label worth fighting for did not occur automatically or immediately after the victory in World War II." Rather, the immediate postwar years were marked by "frustration and bitterly won incremental gains for proponents of the national security state."³ Intense struggles ensued between different parts of the bureaucracy, between the executive and Congress, and between powerful political actors over different organizational designs that conflicted with established power prerogatives and offended that cluster of American values aptly captured by Aaron L. Friedberg under the label of "antistatism."⁴ It would take the Korean War to most effectively "break this bottleneck."⁵ And it would take the shock of Sputnik to propel the NSS into a sustained race for technological supremacy, and in a way that transcended partisan rivalries.

The emergence of the NSS was kick-started and carried forward by a series of geopolitical events that spanned the marked deterioration of US–Soviet relations after 1945 and the outbreak of the Korean War in 1950. But the eventual shape of the new structure was a product of domestic conflict and compromise, as the Truman administration sought to reconcile American antistatist values with the new ideology of national security and the expansion of executive power that this implied.⁶

The birth of the NSS is conventionally traced to the 1947 National Security Act. The 1947 act provided a foundation for the expansion and centralization of the federal government's defense and intelligence operations under the direct authority of the president as commander in chief.⁷ The Truman administration unified the army, navy, and recently established air force within the National Military Establishment—a body replaced in 1949 by the newly created Department of Defense (DoD)—placing all under the authority of a civilian secretary of defense. It also created the Central Intelligence Agency

(CIA) and the National Security Council (NSC) and provided a statutory identity to the Joint Chiefs of Staff. Finally, President Truman established several science and technology boards, which proved ineffective and were later recast in a more centralized form under Dwight D. Eisenhower. In the final weeks of his presidency, Truman united all signals intelligence within the National Security Agency, an agency within the DoD. In so doing, he created the four institutions—the NSA, along with the NSC, DoD, and CIA—that evolved into the main hard power pillars of US national security.

Washington's national security networks converged in the Oval Office. This was the node through which the incumbent president could use his authority to coordinate the activities of the many and varied agencies that came to constitute the NSS. Through special advisory councils, strategic programs, and the Bureau of the Budget, the president was positioned to coordinate technology policy, as shaped by its separate NSS components.[8] It would take a little over a decade for the key agencies of the national security state to acquire their longer-lasting institutional identities. Battles over missions, budgets, and influence would subsequently transform many of the new entities; nevertheless, the foundations were now in place.

Having established a set of powerful institutions for concentrating the management of science and technology, President Truman set about containing their budgets.[9] Geopolitical developments, however, soon trumped balanced budgets. Following several successive events—the Soviet blockade of Berlin in June 1948, the "loss" of 500 million inhabitants of China to the Communist camp in 1949, and the Soviets' successful detonation of a nuclear weapon that same year—Truman and many of his closest advisers cast communism as a direct military threat, not just a dangerous subversive force. The Soviets' explosion of the atom bomb had such a profound impact that it generated vast new programs for a continental air and missile defense system as well as a strategic nuclear deterrent capable of retaliating.

In response to the newly perceived direct external threat of destruction to the American homeland, a landmark document, *National Security Council Paper 68* (NSC-68), outlined justifications for a rapid and massive US military buildup. It cited Soviet consolidation of power in Eastern Europe as evidence of its expansionist intentions and called for the West to contain the Soviet

Union as justification for the United States to pursue a major buildup of its conventional military and nuclear resources. Reticent about its cost projections, Truman held off approving the plan until after the outbreak of the Korean War, until finally removing the cap that he had imposed on defense spending.

Technological Leadership beyond Defense: National Institutes of Health, Atomic Energy Commission/Department of Energy

Looking beyond the DoD to the other arms of the NSS, we soon see how the process of establishing a national security state geared to securing technological supremacy could not stop with the DoD and the intelligence agencies. At various stages, it also drew into its orbit the Atomic Energy Commission, which in 1973 became the Department of Energy (DoE), as well as the National Institutes of Health (NIH), the National Science Foundation (NSF), and a little later, the National Aeronautics and Space Administration (NASA).

The NIH inherited the responsibilities and contracts of the wartime Office of Scientific Research and Development Committee on Medical Research and continued to work closely with the NSS. Indeed, the NIH budget was not permitted to grow until it inherited wartime projects.[10]

Wartime biomedical research was intended to ensure the health of US service personnel and to defend against biological and chemical warfare, an effort that NIH activity continues to support. The Public Health Service, in partnership with the army and the Department of Agriculture, then began research in the field of biological warfare in 1941 under the auspices of the Chemical Warfare Service.[11] Shortly thereafter, a Biological Warfare Committee composed of civilian scientists was established to advise the armed services, and the military began funding research relevant to biological warfare in dozens of universities and industrial plants. The principal effect of the committee was to draw attention to the potential dangers of biological weapons to human beings, crops, and livestock. It called for an extensive program of biodefense, emphasizing the development of vaccines and protection of the national water supply.

Commenting on this early history, Barton Bernstein notes that the US secretary of war, Henry L. Stimson, hoped to legitimize the research at the Chemical Warfare Service by naming civilians as monitors, and that senior army officials preferred the establishment of a civilian agency with ties to the armed services. Stimson's reasoning is instructive: "civilianizing" it, or "entrusting the matter to a civilian agency . . . would help in preventing the public from being exercised over any ideas that the War Department might be contemplating the use of this weapon offensively."[12]

The second point to note in establishing the national security relevance of the NIH is the fact that biomedical research did not lose its military significance simply because the nation had entered an era of "armed peace." The Chemical-Biological Coordination Center that succeeded the Biological Warfare Committee continued to provide a forum to promote close cooperation between the army, the navy, the NIH, and the American Cancer Society, each of which provided the center with financial support. This mechanism allowed the armed services to exploit innovations and research driven by the NIH.

Third, the NIH remains an integral part of the NSS because the body of knowledge required to cure naturally occurring human disease is in many cases the same as the knowledge required to counteract the threat of biological and chemical warfare, or to understand the cellular effects of exposure to other environmental hazards, such as radiation.[13] Cancer research has thus become another mechanism through which the NIH also serves national security. Not coincidentally, the National Cancer Institute shares the same address as the US Army Health Services Command at Fort Detrick, exploiting facilities originally used for research and development related to biological warfare. This cohabitation was the result of the Nixon administration's 1969 decision to convert the nation's biological warfare program to a commercial biotechnology industry. It signifies the close and continuing relationship between the DoD and the NIH, whose synergies have made lasting contributions to the postwar development of the US biotechnology industry.

Another core component of the NSS, the Department of Energy, traces its origins to the former Atomic Energy Commission, the roots of which lay in the nuclear Manhattan Project. In taking over the Manhattan laboratory system in 1947, the commission acquired virtually unlimited control over all nuclear energy research and development (R&D). One of its early tasks was to assess the nascent atomic weapons program of the Soviet Union. "Since then," according to the Office of the Director of National Intelligence, "its security and intelligence functions have come to reside within DoE."[14]

As the agency responsible for nuclear weapons development and testing during the Cold War, and subsequently for stockpile stewardship, a major part of the DoE's budget has been dedicated to national defense objectives. Later, a smaller share of its budget would also support the development of new energy-saving and renewable energy technologies, with more direct relevance to the civilian economy. Today, the DoE's primary missions include stewardship of the nuclear stockpile. Like the armed services, it has relied on a system of contracting out R&D as an adjunct to the important work conducted in its extensive network of national laboratories.

The national laboratories, otherwise known as Federally Funded Research and Development Centers, form another key component of the NSS innovation enterprise. With thirty-nine labs overall, the DoE has the largest network, including the famous nuclear labs at Los Alamos, Lawrence Livermore, and Sandia, originally constituted for the purpose of creating nuclear weapons. Initially established under the Atomic Energy Commission to perform R&D for the mission agencies, their activities range from basic research all the way to patenting and licensing inventions. As the Manhattan program wound down, the labs were given new missions, some of which included R&D applied to the use of fissionable and radioactive materials for biomedical, health, and military purposes. As a result, these in-house laboratories developed strong connections with private contractors, paving the way for entirely new industries, ranging from radioisotopes in nuclear medicine to biotech and bioengineering.

Constructed as organizational hybrids for conducting research and developing technologies, in addition to sponsoring entrepreneurship and commercializing innovations (since the 1980s), these government-owned, privately operated labs have come to play a much broader role in the NSS innovation story than is conventionally conveyed by the term "R&D." Similar public–private fusions were engineered by the DoD in its bid to outflank the Soviet Union. Thus, in 1951, the US Office of Naval Research, together with the air force and army, jointly requested the creation of MIT's Lincoln Laboratory. Its brief, a direct response to the Russians' atom bomb explosion, was to develop an air defense system known as the semi-automatic ground environment, or SAGE. Following a pattern similar to the energy agency's research labs, the MIT lab was a hybridized arrangement that melded public and private resources to serve a national mission.

From Contracting Revolution to Radical Innovation

Mobilization for World War II revolutionized technology procurement through new contracting arrangements that shifted the risk of innovation to the public sector. This was a turning point in the nation's science and technology development because it paved the way for a more radical and sustained form of innovation. In the process, the role of firms and universities was transformed as well.

Prior to World War II, the armed services relied on technological change driven mainly by private demand and the public sector initiatives of European powers, especially Great Britain and Germany. This situation changed dramatically under the National Defense Appropriation Act (1940) driven by Franklin Roosevelt before America entered the war. Together with the War Powers Act (1941), this made a sweeping break with procurement tradition. Henceforth, the armed services could undertake developmental projects in partnership with the private sector through contractual arrangements that transferred the cost and risk from private actors to the federal government. The act gave the armed services authority to negotiate contracts using either a fixed-fee or cost-plus-fixed-fee payment. Contracting reforms were most important because they allowed the armed services to steer developmental projects throughout the private sector while protecting private sector partners from risk. In effect, by no longer relying on private–commercial demand to set the pace of innovation, the services came to occupy a leading position on the technological frontier.

The war transformed not only the federal government's role within high-technology sectors of the national economy but also the role of American firms within the global economy. American firms tended to excel at using and (sometimes) improving technologies created elsewhere, but the US economy rarely spawned radically new technological fields or industrial sectors. Prior to World War II, American firms "had few equals" in their ability to use and (sometimes) improve technologies created abroad, but until World War II, the US position in science and technology was not one of leadership.[15] The notable exception was the agricultural sector, historically a stronghold of federal government support.

The American university was another institution remade by the Cold War and the rise of the NSS, in turn generating an industrial ecosystem. Both MIT and Stanford figured prominently in Pentagon patronage, which established permanent labs designed to achieve strategic goals. At MIT, the air force's Lincoln Laboratory, in partnership with IBM, created the massive air defense system known as SAGE. At a cost of $8 billion over ten years, it was the largest science and technology enterprise mounted since the Manhattan Project.[16] On the West Coast, Stanford University became a key institution in the growth of a radio and microelectronics industry that evolved into Silicon Valley. From modest beginnings, Stanford grew rapidly, and by 1950 it was drawing almost one-quarter of its electronics research budget from the DoD, little of it "undirected."[17]

These changes, together with the growing weight of large military contractors, were not viewed in a wholly positive light. President Eisenhower, in his 1961 farewell address, first raised the alarm, referring to the danger of a "military-industrial complex." Yet it was not until the Vietnam War that the term came into its own in public discourse, whence it has emerged as both "lobby and trope."[18]

The fledgling national security state thus emerged incrementally and somewhat messily, the product of geopolitical imperatives filtered through domestic politics and antistatist impulses. By the early 1950s, the principal components of today's national security state were largely in place, actively harnessing the nation's scientific and technical resources for the purpose of military preparedness. Ironically, domestic political conflict over the nature of that enterprise helped translate geopolitical challenges into a technology policy that was heavily oriented toward the military and defense-related agencies.[19] Nevertheless, the NSS role in national technology policy had yet to be fully established, through a process that crystallized in response to Sputnik.

GROWTH (1958–1968): THE SPUTNIK EFFECT

It's really an impressive story of how we turned a negative into a positive. We won the space race. We built miniaturized objects that became cell phones and GPS systems. We built the Internet. And at the end of the day, there is no Soviet Union.

—DAVID HOFFMAN, in CBS News, "How Sputnik Changed America"

In October 1957, at the height of the Cold War, the USSR launched Sputnik, a small earth-orbiting satellite hardly bigger than a beach ball. In America, this world first achievement met with a mix of fear and awe. Its impact was momentous—broad, deep, and lasting. As Eisenhower's chief science adviser, James Killian, recalled, "As it beeped into the sky, Sputnik 1 created a crisis of confidence that swept the country like a windblown forest fire. Overnight there developed a widespread fear that the country lay at the mercy of the Russian military machine and that our own government and its military arm had abruptly lost the power to defend the mainland itself.... Confidence in American science, technology, and education suddenly evaporated."[20]

The Sputnik effect planted new shoots in the NSS and instituted a system of perpetual innovation for military preparedness. NSC-68 had emphasized the relationship between technological superiority and national defense; suddenly, however, it seemed that it was the USSR that had been actively building such a relationship, while the United States had been caught sleeping. The nation was still reeling from Sputnik 1 when, one month later, the Russians sent their second satellite into space. The contrast with America's own failed December effort (fast-tracked by the navy) had a devastating impact on morale and led to a period of "genuine consternation, followed by a veritable orgy of national self-examination and self-criticism."[21]

In response, Sputnik triggered the so-called space age and a new era of institution (and nation) building. School curricula were strengthened, science education was prioritized, R&D funding was increased. In addition, to boost the innovation effort, the federal government founded two new research-and-technology-oriented agencies, the Defense Advanced Research Projects Agency (DARPA) and NASA; created another hybrid institution, the Small Business Investment Corporation, to seed a modern venture capital industry; expanded the NIH; and centralized DoD science and technology policy by creating the position of deputy director of research and engineering. As Walter McDougall writes, "Sputnik triggered an abrupt discontinuity," transforming governments into "self-conscious promoters, not just of technological change but of perpetual technological revolution"[22]

As for institutional development relevant to formation of the NSS technology enterprise, the Sputnik moment had four important effects. First, it made it politically easier to appropriate funds for defense-and national security–led research and development.[23] In the name of defense, Congress provided NSS agencies with large infusions of funds to assist in the national innovation effort.

Adjusted for inflation, the NSF budget increased from just under $173 million in 1957 to more than $1.2 billion in 1967, while NIH funding climbed from $950 million to $3.8 billion. Overall federal obligations for the five NSS agencies conducting R&D during this period more than tripled, climbing from just over $20 billion to more than $72 billion.[24] Whereas before Sputnik, the nation spent roughly 1.5 percent of gross domestic product on R&D, with government and the private sector contributing equal shares, a decade on, that investment exceeded 3 percent of GDP, some 70 percent of which was provided by the federal government.

Second, Sputnik paved the way for centralizing the organization of technology development, giving President Eisenhower the opportunity to drive through the Defense Reorganization Act of 1958. This act enhanced the authority of the secretary of defense and the Joint Chiefs of Staff by giving them the power to impose a unified program on all the armed services. Most importantly, as mentioned, it established the position of director of defense research and engineering, who assumed the role of chief technologist for the DoD, responsible for research and engineering. As Friedberg has observed, whenever the secretary of defense was prepared to use it, "he now had available to him, for the first time, an instrument with which to exert substantial control over the pace and direction of the nation's entire military research effort."[25]

Third, Sputnik provided an imperative for preparedness against future "technological surprise," leading to the creation of two new agencies, the Advanced Research Projects Agency (ARPA; the word "Defense" was added later and the agency became DARPA) and NASA. DARPA was founded in 1958 as a defense research agency, independent of the three services, with a mandate to create and prevent technological surprise. The agency's broad charter gives it authority to develop both military and dual-use (general-purpose) technologies in collaboration with commercial industry. As the central arm of the DoD's research program, DARPA became responsible for long-range, high-risk R&D of interest to the military as a whole, including the building of prototypes for new military systems. It is often credited with helping to put the DoD at the forefront of high technology. Although small by DoD standards (receiving less than 4 percent of the military's research, development, test, and evaluation budget), the agency's broad remit and agile form would spark numerous breakthroughs, stimulating military and commercial innovation ranging from stealth aircraft to the Internet.

Whereas DARPA was intended to lead investigation and development of revolutionary technologies from within the Defense Department, NASA was established as an independent agency tasked with increasing national opportunities for scientific and technological advancement in space-related fields. Although it was designated as a civilian agency, NASA formed a key component of the "defense establishment," as former science adviser to three administrations, Harvey Brooks, remarked to a congressional committee in 1970.[26] NASA's technological prowess was a vital component of the national prestige on which America's soft power depended. In particular, the new agency spawned the Apollo program, which mobilized American science and technology in ways reminiscent of the World War II Manhattan Project. In a direct, "hard power" manner, too, NASA served specific military purposes, working closely with the armed services, the CIA, and the DoD.[27] As a result of its broad congressional mandate, NASA, like DARPA, engaged in dual-use technology development, and in 1962 it created the Technology Utilization Program, which promoted commercial spin-offs through dedicated field offices and industrial applications centers.

Mirroring the armed services, DARPA and NASA relied predominantly on the judicious use of contracts to conduct their work, further expanding the federal government's technology procurement networks and strengthening the role of the American research university in the national security system. Federal funding for university research rose by 200 percent during the half decade from 1959 to 1964, compared with a 91 percent increase in the preceding five years.[28]

Notwithstanding incremental adjustments, the institutional complex in place at the end of the Eisenhower administration lives on. Whereas most of the arrangements implemented by the Truman administration were temporary, Eisenhower established a permanent and preeminent role for the national security state in the nation's science and technology policy, organizing it and equipping it for war on the technological frontier. The response of his administration to the Sputnik crisis completed the lineaments of the NSS as we know it, and its infrastructural reach grew in scale and scope right through the 1960s. It was the debacle of Vietnam that halted this trajectory.

CRISIS (1969-1979): LEGITIMATION AND INNOVATION DEFICITS

When Richard Nixon took over the presidency in 1969, he inherited a legacy of crises at home and overseas. Domestically, the nation's universities—drawn into the orbit of the NSS during and immediately after World War II—became battlegrounds as radical students demanded the expulsion of the military and a small but vocal group of academic researchers called for sources of funding other than the DoD.[29] Internationally, the strategic logic of the Vietnam War was being called into question, and there was a growing awareness that the United States had to try to defuse a Cold War that was spinning out of control and that—as some in the administration feared—the nation was set to lose.

The new decade also brought fresh concerns about an innovation deficit, heightened to an increasing extent by the seemingly relentless rise of Japan as a rival technological power. The implications for US technological leadership and defense strategy would pave the way toward a new emphasis on military and commercial integration. The decade starting in the late 1960s began with a legitimation crisis and closed with an emerging innovation crisis. Each challenge generated a distinctive response that tilted the NSS toward a more direct role in fostering commercial innovation, beginning with biotechnology.

The Legitimation Crisis and Its Impacts

The impact of the anti-Vietnam legitimation deficit was felt in three main ways: first, it sparked a biological weapons conversion effort, which catalyzed the formation of a commercial biotechnology industry; second, it redefined the DoD–DARPA relationship with the university sector; and finally, it ramped up the NSS relevance of the National Science Foundation and National Institutes of Health, rerouting DoD's "nondefense" funding through these agencies.

Nixon's November 1969 decision to ban development of offensive biological weapons was responsive to the intense antiwar sentiment that gripped the country. It was also motivated by the realization that in an offensive bioweapons race, a secretive authoritarian system like the USSR would always have a large advantage. That calculation was reflected in the concurrent decision to ratify the Biological and Toxin Weapons Convention, finalized in 1972. Determined to lead the emerging revolution in microbiology, the federal government deployed the conversion process to kick-start a commercial "dual-use" biotechnology industry, transferring to the private sector a good deal of the technology that had been locked up in government labs. Keeping control of US technology once conversion to peacetime use had been achieved was also important. It was the desire to protect US inventions, once they were transferred to the private sector, that set federal authorities on a path to major intellectual property reform, starting with a strengthening of the patent act in 1971 and culminating in the Bayh–Dole Act and the Stevenson–Wydler Technology Innovation Act, both in 1980.[30]

In the conversion process, a major beneficiary was the Department of Health, Education, and Welfare. In 1972, its National Institutes of Health acquired a new biological research arm, the Frederick National Laboratory for Cancer Research, as part of the National Cancer Institute (NCI). The NCI was the organization designated to fight a new battle, the so-called war on cancer, launched by Nixon during his reelection campaign. The NCI would become highly relevant to the NSS, given that cancer research involves a knowledge base similar to that required for biodefense. In 1970, the journal *Nature* reported that the new NIH-run facility would "use Fort Detrick for the containment and large-scale production of suspected viral tumor agents," while another NIH-run facility, the National Institute for Allergy and Infectious Diseases, would undertake "research on hazardous viruses," among other viral diseases.[31] Both NIAID and NCI are the mostly highly funded institutes of the NIH, working in areas that also feed into the biomedical work of their next-door neighbor, the US Army Medical Research Institute of Infectious Diseases.

Symbolic of its entwinement with the NSS, the National Cancer Institute took possession of the army's former biological warfare facilities. An official history of Fort Detrick remarks how "unusual" it was that a civilian agency establishing itself on a military reservation would be given "full title to the land," including seventy buildings.[32] But the NIH–NCI relationship with the NSS went beyond the occupation of military premises to also embrace its human resources. Following demilitarization of the biological labs, several hundred displaced Fort Detrick scientists and technicians were moved into the positions that were opened up by the new cancer institute. The move allowed the retention of critical scientific expertise that could deliver knowledge relevant to this quintessentially dual-use field of biotechnology.

Indeed, the complementarity of Defense and NIH interests in this arena played no small part in building a biotechnology industry, funding projects of fledgling companies aimed at both mission-oriented and commercial applications.[33] Today, in two-hatted mode, the US Army Medical Research and Development Command runs an extramural research program that targets various forms of cancer. Thus, the conversion process provided the United States with the makings of a biotechnology industry that played to the dual needs of defense and commerce. The critical point, however, is that in doing so, conversion forged another link connecting the NIH to the NSS.

The legitimation crisis also helped to redefine the relationship of the military to the university sector, producing two outcomes relevant to the NSS technology enterprise. The first was an expanded role for the NSF and NIH, which stepped into the breach created by the military's partial retreat from the funding of university research. As the Vietnam War escalated, unrest at university campuses inflamed debates over the propriety of DoD–DARPA sponsorship of university research, a good deal of which had included nondefense activities. As antiwar sentiment increased across American campuses, Congress responded with the Mansfield amendment to the Defense Procurement Authorization Act of 1970, which required mission agencies to divest themselves of broader, "non-mission-oriented" research. Ironically, to comply, the military services were forced to cancel numerous university research projects that did not have a "direct and apparent relationship" to the defense mission, while continuing to fund defense-specific projects.[34] Though the requirement was softened a year later and was eventually removed from legislation, for almost a decade DoD–DARPA funding of university research emphasized military relevance.

In the meantime, however, the extramural programs of the NSF and NIH expanded to fill the vacuum created by the departure of the DoD from nonmilitary funding. Thus, in 1971, the NSF assumed responsibility for Defense's materials research laboratories to pursue industrial applications. The university-based program had been set up in response to post-Sputnik concerns but faced extinction when Congress banned the use of Pentagon-sourced money to fund non-mission-related research. At one stroke, responsibility for the DARPA program was transferred to the NSF.

The second outcome can best be described as a "hybridizing" response. Because of fierce reaction to the perceived militarization of research universities, several institutions were induced to hive off research units that owed their existence to military sponsorship. Innovation-focused ventures such as the famed Stanford Research Institute (renamed SRI International in 1977) and Draper Laboratory (divested from MIT in 1973), among several others, were formally separated from their university base and reconstituted as independent nonprofits that effectively—in the spirit of public purpose institutions—continued to draw the bulk of their income and research agendas from the NSS.

Innovation Deficit and the "Offset" Strategy

As détente ended in 1977, the new Carter administration confronted a darkening geopolitical and economic landscape. Strategically, the military establishment saw itself struggling to stay ahead of the USSR in defense technology. Economically, there appeared to be no escape from the malaise that had gripped the US economy since the mid-1970s, attributed by many not to the Vietnam War or the oil crisis but to the rise of Japan and a loss of innovation capacity. In due course, as Japan began to outflank the United States in many of its own high-technology markets, the economic challenge would increasingly take on geopolitical significance. The Japan factor thus came to add a distinctive geopolitical threat of its own to these strategic and economic concerns.

Overlaying and intersecting with these concerns was the perception of a mounting "innovation deficit"—a diminished ability of the NSS to access the advanced capabilities of the private sector as innovative firms turned their backs on the government market. It is worth pausing to consider both the geostrategic challenge and innovation deficit as they emerged in the late 1970s, because it was their intersection that provided the impetus in the subsequent decade to expand and consolidate the commercial reorientation of NSS technology policy. As discussed earlier, this reorientation had haltingly begun in the biotech-biodefense arena, with Nixon's conversion decision to ensure US leadership in the microbiology revolution.

The Cold War was not simply an arms race but a science and technology race, as both the United States and the Soviet Union concentrated their resources to gain a technological edge and impose technological surprise on their foes. By the late 1970s, technology development initiatives begun under

Eisenhower had achieved outstanding progress, an upshot of which was that US intelligence agencies now had a relatively clear picture of Soviet military capabilities and technological accomplishments. By 1977, US intelligence suggested that the Soviet Union had achieved parity with the United States in terms of nuclear weapons and their delivery systems. Since the USSR also had quantitatively superior conventional forces, it now possessed a potentially large strategic advantage. As a result, senior officials feared that deterrence was being threatened and looked for a strategy "to restore the conventional military balance."[35]

This fear coincided with a collapse in détente, accelerated by the Soviet invasion of Afghanistan in 1979. Secretary of Defense Harold Brown thus determined that the United States needed to once again target its resources toward the development of technologically superior weapons systems able to offset the USSR's quantitative edge. He named this the Offset Strategy and gave Director of Defense Research and Engineering William Perry the responsibility and resources to develop the relevant technology as quickly as possible. Looking back, Perry recalled what this meant for technology development: "I decided . . . to base the Offset Strategy on information technology, a field in which the United States, even in those days, had a commanding lead. Very early in my tenure, I went to an organization called DARPA . . . for detailed briefings on the advanced sensors and smart weapons that were to be the basis of the Offset Strategy."[36]

The Offset Strategy has a particular analytical relevance because it coincided with what was described as an innovation deficit. This concern became the subject of testimony before the House Armed Services Committee and led to formation of a special Defense Industrial Base Panel. In its report, *The Ailing Industrial Base*, the panel's key finding was that there had been "a serious decline in the nation's defense industrial capability. . . . An alarming erosion of crucial industrial elements, coupled with a mushrooming dependence on foreign sources for critical materials," the panel concluded, "is endangering our defense posture at its very foundation."[37]

Even allowing for some hyperbole, there was genuine cause for concern. The case of semiconductors generated the most disquiet. These devices, known as integrated circuits, typically had been sourced from smaller specialized firms such as Fairchild Semiconductor and Texas Instruments. Although government contracts had been critical to their crucial start-up stage, these younger but fast-growing firms began to turn their backs on defense-space work in favor of higher returns in expanding commercial markets where integrated circuits were being incorporated into all manner of electronic goods.

As commercial demand for mass-produced chips soared, dwarfing the government market, the defense-space agencies found it ever more difficult to interest semiconductor firms in designing and manufacturing integrated circuits for their use.[38] As the Congressional Budget Office commented in a 1987 report, stringent technical and other requirements, had made defense-related semiconductors too expensive for the commercial market, "discouraging semiconductor firms from producing the integrated circuits needed by military planners."[39] As a result, the armed services began to experience shortages of customized chips. Addressing this problem was made more urgent by the renewed tensions with the Soviet Union and the decision to rely more heavily on an information technology–intensive strategy on the battlefield. Making the problem even more pressing was Japan's challenge to US technology leadership, most vitally in microelectronics, the very basis of the Pentagon's Offset Strategy.

The significance of this point should not be lost. This Offset Strategy meant having fewer, but technologically more advanced, weapons than the Soviet Union. However, many of the advanced design and manufacturing capabilities for achieving that goal were in the commercial arena, not among the large defense contractors, conventionally identified with the military-industrial complex. This meant that the DoD had to explore new ways of procuring advanced technology that could also meet commercial interests if it was to access the so-called nontraditional suppliers.

As America entered the new decade, its political and national security leaders thus confronted the two-pronged challenge of a rising power in high technology and an "ailing industrial base," one they saw as compromising the nation's technology leadership and endangering its military primacy. How they responded to this challenge marked the deepening and broadening of NSS engagement with commercial undertakings. However, it left unresolved the erosion of high-tech manufacturing, whose flight abroad would intensify from the mid-1980s onwards.

The distinctiveness of the American experience must also be recognized. Although most modern industrialized countries have instituted "permanent preparedness" by building armed forces and arsenals for defense, no country engaged in that process, with the singular exception of the United States, has created an institutional complex resembling a national security state. This is the difference that sets the United States apart, for here, permanent preparedness is not just about "the military" or "defense," or even "intelligence." It is about the strategic goal of technology leadership that drives the quest for perpetual innovation. In the US setting, the goal of military preparedness was immediately added to the ambition of scientific and technological superiority. This powerful American cocktail created an encompassing political-economic system in which the national security state became intricately bound to the development of the private sector and its capacity for innovation.

NOTES

This essay is a condensed and abridged version of "Rise of the National Security State as Technological Enterprise," in Linda Weiss, *America Inc.? Innovation and Enterprise in the National Security State* (Ithaca, NY: Cornell University Press, 2014), 21–50, copyright © 2014 Cornell University and is used with permission of Cornell University Press.

1. This essay concentrates on the emergence, consolidation, and expansion of the national security state as it responded to the Soviet threat. For detailed discussion of its evolution beyond the Cold War, see Weiss, *America Inc?*. For discussion of high-tech procurement during the "commercialization" period, see chapter 2 of that volume.

2. David C. Mowery and Nathan Rosenberg, *Paths of Innovation: Technological Change in 20th-Century America* (Cambridge: Cambridge University Press, 1998), 6.

3. David M. Hart, *Forged Consensus: Science, Technology, and Economic Policy in the United States, 1921–1953* (Princeton, NJ: Princeton University Press, 1998), 174.

4. Aaron L. Friedberg, "American Antistatism and the Founding of the Cold War State," in *Shaped by War and Trade: International Influences on American Political Development*, ed. Ira Katznelson and Martin Shefter (Princeton, NJ: Princeton University Press, 2018), 239–265.

5. Hart, *Forged Consensus*, 174.

6. For an extended discussion of the forms and influence of antistatism in the development of the national security state, see Aaron L. Friedberg, *In the Shadow of the Garrison State: America's Anti-Statism and Its Cold War Grand Strategy* (Princeton, NJ: Princeton University Press, 2000), chapter 1.

7. Michael J. Hogan, *A Cross of Iron: Harry S. Truman and the Origins of the National Security State, 1945–1954* (New York: Cambridge University Press, 1998), 24.

8. Anna Kasten Nelson, "The Evolution of the National Security State: Ubiquitous and Endless," in *The Long War: A New History of US National Security Policy since World War II*, ed. Andrew J. Bacevich (New York: Columbia University Press, 2007), 265–301, at 266.

9. Hogan, *Cross of Iron*, 69.

10. Donald Swain, "The Rise of a Research Empire: NIH, 1930–1950," *Science* 138 (3546), 1233–1235.

11. This paragraph draws on Harlyn O. Halvorson, "Civilian Control of Biological Defense Research," *Annals of the New York Academy of Sciences* 666 (1992): 191–201.

12. Barton J. Bernstein, "The Birth of the US Biological-Warfare Program," *Scientific American* 256, no. 6 (1987): 116–121, at 117.

13. Robert P. Kadlec and Alan P. Zelicoff, "Implication of the Biotechnology Revolution for Weapons Development and Arms Control," in *Biological Warfare: Modern Offense and Defense*, ed. Raymond A. Zilinskas (Boulder, CO: Lynne Reinner), 11–54, at 14.

14. *An Overview of the United States Intelligence Community for the 111th Congress*, 2019, 14, at Federation of American Scientists, Intelligence Research Program, https://irp.fas.org/eprint/overview.pdf.

15. Mowery and Rosenberg, *Paths of Innovation*, 6.

16. Stuart W. Leslie, *The Cold War and American Science: The Military-Industrial-Academic Complex at MIT and Stanford* (New York: Columbia University Press, 1993).

17. Roger Geiger, "Science, Universities and National Defense, 1945–1970," *OSIRIS* 7, 26–48, 33–34.

18. Alex Roland, "The Military-Industrial Complex: Lobby and Trope," in *The Long War: A New History of US National Security Policy since World War II*, ed. Andrew J. Bacevich (New York: Columbia University Press, 2007), 335–369.

19. Hart, *Forged Consensus*, 176.

20. James R. Killian Jr., *Sputnik, Scientists, and Eisenhower* (Cambridge, MA: MIT Press, 1982), 7.

21. Robert Watson, official historian of the Office of the Secretary of Defense, quoted in Douglas T. Stuart, *Creating the National Security State: A History of the Law that Transformed America* (Princeton, NJ: Princeton University Press, 2008), 139.

22. Walter A. McDougall, "Technocracy and Statecraft in the Space Age—Toward the History of a Saltation," *American Historical Review* 87, 1010–1040, at 1011.

23. *A History of Science Policy in the United States, 1940–1985* (Washington, DC: US Government Printing Office, 1986), https://doi.org/10.5962/bhl.title.4170.

24. The national security state data here are from National Science Foundation, Federal Funds for Research and Development, Detailed Historical Tables (1951–2009). National Institutes of Health data for 1952 to 1957 are not standardized with later years and hence are slightly inflated. NIH data for 1958 to 1966 supplied by Michael Yamaner (National Science Foundation) from printed publications of Department of Health, Education, and Welfare.

25. Friedberg, *In the Shadow of the Garrison State*, 319.

26. Geiger, "Science," 26.

27. Marvin Berkowitz, *The Conversion of Military-Oriented Research and Development to Civilian Uses* (New York: Praeger, 1970), 9.

28. Roger Geiger, "What Happened after Sputnik? Shaping University Research in the United States," *Minerva* 35, 349–367.

29. Bruce L. R. Smith, *American Science Policy since World War II* (Washington, DC: Brookings Institution Press, 1990), 73–74.

30. Shelley Hurt, "Military's Hidden Hand: Examining the Dual-Use Origins of Biotechnology, 1969–1972," in *State of Innovation: The US Government's Role in Technology Development*, ed. Fred Block and Matthew R. Keller (Boulder, CO: Paradigm, 2011).

31. "Biological Warfare: Relief of Fort Detrick," *Nature* 228 (November 28, 1970): 803.

32. Norman M. Covert, *Cutting Edge: A History of Ft. Detrick, Maryland, 1943–1993* (Fort Dietrick, MD: Public Affairs Office, 1993), 110.

33. Maryann P. Feldman, "Role of the Department of Defense in Building Biotech Expertise," in *The Small Business Innovation Research Program (SBIR): An Assessment of the Department of Defense Fast Track Initiative*, ed. Charles W. Wessner (Washington, DC: National Academy Press, 2000).

34. *History of Science Policy*, 51–52.

35. William J. Perry, "Technology and National Security: Risks and Responsibilities," Conference on Risk and Responsibility in Contemporary Engineering and Science: French and US Perspectives, 2, https://stanford.edu/dept/france-stanford/Conferences/Risk/Perry.pdf.

36. Perry, "Technology," 3.

37. *The Ailing Defense Industrial Base: Unready for Crisis*, 96th United States Congress, House Committee on Armed Services, Defense Industrial Base Panel (Washington, DC: US Government Printing Office, 1980), https://www.hsdl.org/?view&did=712063.

38. John A. Alic, Lewis M. Branscomb, Harvey Brooks, Ashton B. Carter, and Gerald L. Epstein, *Beyond Spinoff: Military and Commercial Technologies in a Changing World* (Boston, MA: Harvard Business School Press, 1992), 260.

39. Philip C. Webre, *The Benefits and Risks of Federal Funding for Sematech* (Washington, DC: Congressional Budget Office, 1987), 61.

THE COLD WAR AND US IMMIGRATION POLICY

The Legacy of Migrant Screening on Diaspora Communities in America

PETER J. VEROVŠEK

The Cold War had profound and long-lasting effects on almost all aspects of American life and policy formation. Fears of terrorists entering the United States by posing as migrants or refugees have become common once again after the attacks of September 11, 2001. However, this discourse builds on similar anxieties expressed in the aftermath of World War II, when government officials worried about the infiltration of the United States by Communist agents at the start of the Cold War.

Before 1945, American immigration policy was primarily governed by racial quotas but involved little vetting of the backgrounds of the individuals entering the country. This changed after the end of World War II in response to fears that infiltrators and spies from the Soviet Union and the newly Communist states of Central and Eastern Europe might seek to infiltrate the county as migrants or refugees. As part of a broader American response to the outbreak of the Cold War, policymakers in Washington created a screening system designed to check the backgrounds of potential migrants and refugees to ensure that Communist agents did not enter the country via this channel. In addition to changing the immigration system, this new screening process also had a profound effect on the existing diaspora communities from these countries.

The geopolitical concerns expressed in these changes to America's postwar immigration policy resulted in the systematic selection of hard-line nationalists and anticommunists from East-Central Europe for admission to the United States. In addition to granting these individuals entry, the same geopolitical factors provided political opportunities for exiles from the Eastern Bloc to mobilize politically and to form powerful and influential ethnic lobbies.[1] Although there is little evidence that the vetting system prevented the entry of communist subversives, one unintended consequence was the creation of a cohort of vigorously anticommunist activists. After settling in the United States, these individuals mobilized to create powerful ethnic lobbies that sought to push America to adopt hard-line policies vis-à-vis the Soviet Union and the new Communist regimes in their homelands. In this sense, reflecting on the long-term policy effects of the new migrant screening procedures installed at the start of the Cold War reveals what I refer to as the "unexpected dangers" of extreme vetting.[2]

The German Jewish political theorist Hannah Arendt, who came to the United States from Germany as an immigrant during the war, was among the first to recognize that migrants could be catalysts for conflict diffusion across state borders. By 1951 she had already developed an argument demonstrating the role that stateless people, refugees, and minorities played in the rise of totalitarianism in Europe and in the onset of World War II.[3] Many other scholars have confirmed and built on her claims. For example, Douglas Woodwell argues, "International militarized disputes arise when ethnic nationalist pressure groups successfully influence state foreign policy in such a way that state interests are seen to coincide with ethno-national group interest."[4] Exiles thus play an important part in spreading domestic conflicts beyond the borders of their homelands by shaping public opinion in their new host states, promoting international intervention, and raising money to support continuing warfare.[5]

The power of these ethnic lobbies has grown with the historical expansion of the American president's ability to make unilateral policy changes over the course of the twentieth century. Migrant communities have taken advantage of "this relatively new center of policy development in American politics to supplement long-established ties with Congress and bureaucrats."[6] Due to their access to the global media and the sensitivity of Congress to lobbying, Nathan Glazer and Daniel Patrick Moynihan claim that migrants and diaspora communities have become "the single most important determinant of policy" in America.[7]

This immigration policy helps to explain the rise of highly unified, politically mobilized ethnic lobbies in America during the postwar period. At the start of the Cold War, the United States was faced with an unprecedented refugee crisis in Europe. In response to the geopolitical situation, the government created an immigration system that allowed extremely anticommunist—in some cases even fascist—migrants from East-Central Europe to enter the country. The newly arrived exiles from the Eastern Bloc mobilized quickly, forming uncompromising lobbies that opposed any form of cooperation or détente with the USSR. While promoting national ideals, they called for their homelands to be granted political freedom and independence.

The rapid mobilization of these anticommunist ethnic lobbies took place in two steps. First, the fear of Soviet infiltration led to the creation of an immigration apparatus that systematically granted visas to extremist individuals. The evidence contained in government documents and congressional hearings shows how the United States created a screening process that gave preference to individuals who espoused hard-line anticommunist views. The legislatively mandated vetting procedures designed to keep Communist agents out of the United States systematically skewed the political views of the individuals granted entry into the country. This model demonstrates the role immigration policy plays in distorting the composition of migrant communities by favoring individuals with certain characteristics.

Second, the effects of this migration procedure were amplified by government policies that sought to make use of exiles in the nascent Cold War. The same geopolitical concerns that led to the creation of the vetting procedures also created the "dimensions of opportunity" that enabled their politicization.[8] Throughout the 1950s, a number of American policies sought to take advantage of immigration from East-Central Europe to open what George Kennan's Policy Planning Staff called "a wide breach in the Iron Curtain."[9] For example, the government sought to utilize exiles by forming them into a Volunteer Freedom Corps (VFC) that would fight to liberate their homelands. The VFC and similar initiatives unintentionally gave a political ear to migrants who had already been radicalized by their postwar experience of communism in their homelands.[10] When the government later abandoned these plans, it was surprised by the strength of exile opposition and even had to warn its agencies to resist the pressure of this highly mobilized ethnic lobby.

The proposals for the VFC and other, similar initiatives are crucial for understanding the postwar era because they "emerged as the United States was still developing most of the security and foreign policy instruments on which it relied throughout the Cold War."[11] Given the changes involved in reorganizing the American immigration system in the aftermath of World War II,[12] as well as the stickiness of policy legacies, many of these measures continue to affect US policy—and debates about vetting and immigration—to this day.[13] Examining how these policies were developed in the context of the early Cold War can therefore shed light on the present.

MIGRATION POLICY AND THE COLD WAR

Focusing on the effects of migration from East-Central Europe on American life during the early Cold War may seem somewhat esoteric given the more active scholarly interest in other migrant communities, such as the Cuban diaspora and the so-called Israel lobby.[14] However, migration from the newly Communist states of the Eastern Bloc dominated a "dynamic era in US foreign and defense policy" in the aftermath of World War II.[15] This example has garnered renewed attention after the release of a Justice Department report in 2006 detailing how American intelligence created a "safe haven" for Nazis and their collaborators after 1945.[16] The fact that the archival records relating to this wave of migration have been declassified also allows insight into the thinking and motivations of policymakers that is not available in other, more recent cases. In addition, this temporal distance makes it possible to track the full effects of the vetting process designed to prevent communist infiltration.

The anticommunist migrants from East-Central Europe mobilized quickly and began to effectively lobby the US government on behalf of what they perceived to be their homeland interests. For example, Tony Smith observes, "During the Cold War, American liberals typically lamented the visceral anticommunism of East European ethnic groups as an impediment to better relations with Moscow." He argues that Henry Kissinger lost considerable influence in the Republican Party after Ronald Reagan's election in 1981, due to the backlash from this lobby, which saw détente as a betrayal of US promises.[17]

Arguing along similar lines, Yossi Shain contends that US–Soviet differences could have been resolved earlier had it not been for the steady pressure of American descendants from East-Central Europe, who rejected anything that fell short of unconditional freedom for their homelands.[18] Through much of the postwar period America's aversion to communism reinforced the views of the hard-line anticommunist views of many migrants. This encouraged the activities of East-Central European lobbies in the United States, which raised funds to promote regime change.[19] However, as the United States later sought to improve relations with the East, ethnonationalist agitation was discouraged. In some cases, the CIA even acquiesced to the activity of foreign agents who intended to silence dissident voices in the United States.[20]

Despite this evidence, the overall impact of this anticommunist lobby on US policy is hard to determine. In part, this is because "the impact of US diasporic communities on the demise of communism in Eastern Europe has been accumulative rather than direct."[21] In trying to draw attention to the connection between geopolitics, immigration policy, and immigrant mobilization, the focus here is on the causes and long-term consequences of migrant mobilization, not its effectiveness.

Mobilization is usually defined in terms of a community's ability to coordinate its members, select spokespeople, and engage in collective action.[22] Drawing on this basic definition, government documents reveal how organizations created by migrants from East-Central Europe lobbied the US government. These records show that these dissidents took an active role in politics soon after their arrival in the United States and that they quickly obtained access to the upper channels of government.

There are many explanations for the differing levels of political mobilization among ethnic communities.[23] First, the nature of a migrant's exit is an important variable. While some migrants choose to leave voluntarily, refugees often are "pushed" out of their homelands because of fear for their lives or livelihoods.[24] Those who are forced to leave are more likely to mobilize politically than those who leave to pursue economic opportunities abroad. Second, given the costs of mobilization, the resources available to migrants (often tied to their economic success) are also important in determining the political activity of diasporas.[25] Third, the ability to mobilize may depend on receptivity, that is, how the norms of the community "fit" with those of the host state.[26]

While helpful, these explanations are not satisfactory. For example, resource-based arguments do not predict the political direction (for simplicity, from left to right) of mobilization. While the nature of exit may predict mobilization, it does not explain how and why large numbers of migrants end up in the same host state. Additionally, receptivity is generally analyzed in terms of "societal security" as measured by cultural distance, not on the political opportunities presented by geopolitical situation.[27]

The basic problem is that these existing explanations take the composition of immigrant communities as given. By contrast, my approach pushes the explanation of mobilization back a step, treating selection as a variable instead of a constant. The vetting conducted by the United States played a crucial role in selecting hard-line anticommunist individuals for admission into the country. The admission of a "victim diaspora" with preexisting, extremist political views, whose members are shaped by their flight from the regime in their homelands, is potentially dangerous for host states.[28] These experiences help to explain the activity of exiles in homeland politics, since they increase "their inclination or motivation to maintain their solidarity and exert group influence."[29] Additionally, the trauma of exile creates a psychological void that can make political migrants easy prey for extremism.[30]

The second stage of this study bears some resemblance to the existing explanations stressing receptivity. However, the focus here is on the "political opportunity structures" presented to migrants upon their arrival in the United States, not on cultural distance. Following Sidney Tarrow, the "dimensions of the political environment . . . provide incentives (or disincentives) for people to undertake collective action by affecting their expectations for success or failure."[31] After 1945, concerns about the Soviet Union facilitated the collective action of anticommunist migrants from East-Central Europe. Exiles from Communist Europe were able to take advantage of the openness and vulnerability of US institutions (particularly Congress) to lobbying, and of the presence of influential allies within the government and the national security establishment who shared their views about communism and the Soviet Union.[32]

Unlike many other studies of exiles and refugees, the present study offers a transnational perspective. In line with the policy of the US government at the time, postwar anticommunist émigrés are classified as a distinct group. This perspective reflects the key role that these migrants played in the propaganda war between the United States and the USSR at the start of the Cold War. It also emphasizes the shared anticommunism of these groups and their cooperation in seeking to influence US foreign policy toward East-Central Europe.

POSTWAR MIGRATION TO THE UNITED STATES FROM EAST-CENTRAL EUROPE

In 1945, there were more than 7 million Eastern and Central European refugees in Western Europe. These displaced and stateless people posed a problem for the Allies, who were bound by the Treaty of Yalta to repatriate "Soviet citizens" back to the USSR after the war. The Western alliance adopted a broad interpretation of the agreement. US general (and later president) Dwight D. Eisenhower wrote in 1944, "These displaced persons are a constant source of misunderstanding and controversial discussion with representatives of the Soviet Military Mission. . . . The only complete solution to this problem from all points of view is the early repatriation of these [individuals]."[33]

In the end, the military forces of the Allies and the United Nations Relief and Rehabilitation Administration repatriated about 5.5 million of the 7 million East-Central European refugees living in Western Europe. The International Refugee Organization took charge of the remainder, leaving under Allied control only about 100,000 refugees who had fled the Nazis during the war.[34] However, refugee flows to Western Europe did not stop with the end of the war, as individuals "liberated" by the Red Army sought to avoid persecution by the Soviets.[35] By 1952, more than 18,000 people had escaped from Communist Europe. Unlike the first wave of migrants who had fled fascism, this population was broadly anticommunist. Many had played an active role within the Nazi wartime client regimes as administrators, police officers, officials, or even soldiers. Once in power, the Communists imprisoned and executed many Nazi sympathizers on charges of collaboration.

To relieve the pressure on its allies in Western Europe and take advantage of the skills and increasing psychological value of Eastern Bloc defectors, the "legal statutes and instruments [of the United States] were hastily reconfigured to facilitate these prized individuals' entrance to America. This entailed parallel adjustments to domestic and international law."[36] These legislative changes were part of a broader policy of "calculated kindness" on the part of the

Truman and Eisenhower administrations.[37] Although America began accepting individuals from East-Central Europe immediately after the war, migration started in earnest with the admission of this second, anticommunist wave of refugees. This corresponded with the passage of the Displaced Persons Act of 1948, which "authorize[d] for a limited period of time the admission into the United States of certain European displaced persons for permanent residence, and for other purposes."[38]

The admission of so many émigrés from East-Central Europe into the United States did not go unnoticed domestically. Episodes like Oksana Kasenkina's highly publicized "leap for freedom" from the third-floor window of the Soviet consulate in New York City in August 1948 made escapees hard to ignore.[39] The Policy Planning Staff observed that the stories of escapees had done more "to arouse the Western World to the realities of the nature of communist tyranny than anything else since the end of the war."[40]

The Communist coup in Hungary in the spring of 1947, followed by the Czechoslovak revolution in February 1948 and the Berlin Blockade, starting in June 1948, convinced American policymakers that the United States had to take a harder line against the Soviet Union. Following the creation of the Central Intelligence Agency in 1947, President Truman announced a propaganda offensive that sought to win the "struggle for the minds of men." Exiles with firsthand knowledge of the situation behind the Iron Curtain would help by "getting the real story across to people in other countries."[41]

With the election of Eisenhower in 1952, a more "aggressive rollback" of communism appeared to be in the offing. This was signaled by John Foster Dulles's promise of an "an explosive and dynamic" policy of liberation. Although Eisenhower was initially skeptical of this more uncompromising approach, many of his aides, including chief national security adviser C. D. Jackson, supported it wholeheartedly.[42] Eventually the Eisenhower administration even drafted plans to create an army of exiles who would engage in battle to liberate their homelands.

Regardless of how Truman and Eisenhower sought to take advantage of escapees, the problem of East-to-West migration in Europe still needed to be addressed. By 1952, the Mutual Security Agency estimated that the rate of flight from behind the Iron Curtain had increased to one thousand people per month.[43]

In response to this, the deputy director of the agency urged Congress to consider "the threat this [European surplus population] poses to political stability."[44]

As a result, the Displaced Persons Act was extended repeatedly before expiring in 1954, and while this posed domestic political problems, it was also an opportunity. According to Senate testimony, "The caliber of the expellee is such as to make them rather desirable immigrants into the United States. In other words, they are not left-overs. The expellees we can choose from, and we can choose those whom we need in this country."[45] Intellectuals and businessmen had been targeted by the Communist regime due to their bourgeois background. Others were experienced craftspeople and farmhands deemed necessary to maintain the growth of the postwar American economy.

The Displaced Persons Act was only the first in a series of actions taken by Congress to bring refugees from World War II to the United States. The government found so many of the émigrés to be "desirable" that it kept expanding immigration quotas for East-Central Europe.[46] These exiles were important not only because of their skills but also as pawns in the growing conflict with the USSR. According to a report from the Department of State, granting these individuals entry was part of a broader US plan to pressure on the Soviet Union in three ways: by emphasizing to Soviet rulers and peoples the reckless nature of Soviet policy and its consequences; by establishing a reservoir of goodwill between the peoples of the USSR and those of the free world; and by widening the schism which exists between the Soviet peoples and their rulers.[47]

As an administrator at the Mutual Security Agency explained, "One of the best ways to keep alive faith in freedom and democracy behind the iron curtain is to let the people enslaved by communism know that those who make the dangerous flight to safety will find refuge in the west and will be given an opportunity to start a new life."[48] Individuals who had escaped from East-Central Europe after the war were frequently hired by Radio Free Europe or had their stories told on programs broadcast back into their homelands.[49] This propaganda battle was so important that the United States was unwilling to deport anyone for fear of the negative publicity this would generate in the Communist Bloc.[50]

Due to the economic advantages of some and the strategic position of others, refugees from Communist Europe comprised nearly half of all immigrants admitted to the United States from 1945 to 1955.[51] Most of those who had fled during the war were classified as refugees, stateless, or displaced persons. Those expelled by or fleeing communism after the end of the war required a new category. Though they were sometimes referred to as "expellees" or "political asylees," the government soon coined the term "escapees." When used within government documents and acts of Congress, "'Escapee' means any person who ... after World War II has left the Union of Soviet Socialist Republics or other Communist, Communist-dominated, or Communist-occupied area of Europe, including those parts of Germany under military occupation by the Union of Soviet Socialist Republics and who because of persecution or fear of persecution on account of race, religion, or political opinion refuses to return thereto and who has not been permanently resettled."[52]

Today, it is a truism that "refugees can become pawns in global power struggles, and refugee assistance can be used to discredit an opponent."[53] However, at this time, migration was just one front in the geopolitical battle between the United States and the USSR. Regardless of the program under which immigrants from East-Central Europe entered the United States, they were all subject to a thorough screening process that Acting Secretary of State General Walter Bendell Smith called "even more rigorous than that which applies under normal immigration requirements."[54]

SCREENING COMMUNISTS OUT (AND ANTICOMMUNISTS IN)

Although the US government saw clear economic and political advantages to admitting desirable immigrants, there was also great concern about the possibility of communist "subversives" infiltrating the United States. A former military intelligence officer (G-2) stationed in Berlin after the war noted that by the fall of 1945, he and his colleagues had become "convinced with adequate evidence that deliberate attempts were being made by the Soviet Government ... [to send agents] to the United States, to South America and to Canada under the guise of being displaced persons or being political refugees."[55]

To combat infiltration by Communist agents, Congress authorized the executive branch to set up a system to screen all individuals eligible for immigration to America. The vetting process was instituted in response to article 13 of the Displaced Persons Act of 1948, which required immigration officials to ensure that no visas were granted to any individual "who is or has been a member of, or participated in, any movement which is or has been hostile to the United States or the form of government of the United States." Based on this and on the legislative mandate included in other displaced persons laws, the agencies responsible for overseeing the postwar immigration to the United States gradually developed a screening system to ensure both the eligibility and the desirability of migrants seeking entrance.

Several agencies participated in carrying out the required investigation. First, the International Refugee Organization carried out a background check of individuals before they were even considered for eligibility. Next, the information sheet was turned over to the Federal Bureau of Investigation, which made a check against their records. In his testimony before Congress, the chairman of the Displaced Persons Commission noted that "it is surprising how much [FBI agents] know about people that have never even seen these shores."[56]

This was followed by a monthlong investigation by the Counter Intelligence Corps of the US Army, which was assisted by the Immigration and Naturalization Service. The background check included an interview with three neighbors; obtaining a good-conduct certificate from local police, a camp officer, or another authority to establish that the individual had not been convicted of any crimes; cross-checking to see whether the individual was ever associated with any party/organization hostile to the United States; a fingerprint check of local records for subversive activity; and multiple rounds of individual interrogation. The State Department also conducted a full inquiry before handing the case off to a case analyst at the Displaced Persons Commission. By the end of the process, the case analysts had an extensive file on every potential migrant.[57]

As a result of this thorough background check, the displaced persons camps in Western Europe became "manufactories of evidence."[58] The burden of proof was always on the potential immigrants to establish their eligibility and prove their "political desirability."[59] The applicants had to establish that that neither they nor anyone in their family had ever been a member of any party or organization hostile to the United States. They were required to account for each month of their life, corroborated by character statements. Consular officers were instructed to act with caution, barring anyone from entry "if [the interviewer] has a reasonable doubt that they are politically inadmissible."[60]

The officers conducting the required interrogations took their jobs very seriously. A relief agency official who witnessed the interrogations described the consular interviewers as "case-hardened" with "no more tears, no more pity for their fellow man." He noted that the escapees are "treated in such a manner as to make them wonder whether the free world is their friend."[61] Although about two-thirds of the individuals rejected by the screening process appealed to the Displaced Persons Commission or tried to get back into the system at a different camp under a different name, only 1 or 2 percent succeeded in having their status changed. In total, the screening process took four to six weeks. In many cases, the camps filled less than two-thirds of their allotted visas, as migrants were not being screened quickly enough.[62]

During oversight hearings, members of Congress frequently expressed concerns about the effectiveness of the vetting procedures. Some outsiders, such as the chairman of the National Americanism Commission of the American Legion, expressed their skepticism, arguing, "It is completely and utterly impossible to screen [escapees]."[63] Although Nazi Germany kept meticulous records on the political activities of individuals under its occupation, the growing conflict with the Soviet Union meant that many of the records were not accessible or were incomplete. There is considerable evidence that the screening apparatus was inadequate for catching Communist infiltrators, since agents from the Eastern Bloc expected to be screened and were prepared for it. In fact, in their search for "those that measured up to the highest physical, mental, moral, and *ideological* American standards" (emphasis added), the US interrogators likely turned away more eligible individuals, who did not express their anticommunism ardently enough for the interrogators, than actual Communist agents.[64]

Despite these problems, immigration officials were able to convince Congress that "the security check is as adequate as it can be under the circumstances."[65] The system undoubtedly affected the general composition of the migrant community granted immigration visas to the United States after World War II. In many cases, it was easier for erstwhile fascists to enter the country than those with more moderate political views. Members of the Nazi Party were officially ineligible for admission to the United States, since the party was classified as "an organization hostile to the US." However, the changed geopolitical situation meant that Nazi affiliations were often overlooked if the individual had other redeeming characteristics. For example, the United States recruited many Nazi scientists and intelligence agents at the start of the Cold War.[66] In other cases, serious war criminals were given immigration visas because of their language skills, local knowledge, or anticommunism.

Although immigration officials were instructed to ignore the requests of prominent Nazi war criminals, they helped many others bypass the vetting process.[67] By the mid-1950s, this kind of "bleaching" was no longer necessary, as investigations carried out by the CIA only had to ensure that "no derogatory information" existed. Since the Nazi party was anticommunist, information that an individual had been a Nazi or a member of another fascist organization was not considered an impediment.

Although it is unclear how many "Nazi persecutors" were admitted because of these programs and an immigration system that focused on ferreting out Communist agents, the government estimate of ten thousand is broadly reported.[68] As a result, the United States ended up selecting hard-line, anticommunist individuals for admission. This included many individuals who had been active Nazi persecutors. This selection bias, along with the self-conscious attempts by the government to mobilize these individuals, upon their arrival in the country, directly against the Communist regimes in East-Central Europe, helps to explain their high degree of political mobilization.

MOBILIZING ESCAPEES IN THE UNITED STATES

The Truman administration had seen the escapees as part of a propaganda battle with the USSR. However, the Eisenhower administration began to change the role of the escapee in 1953 as part of its "aggressive rollback of communism." The supporters of this policy hoped to take advantage of the politically mobilized migrants from East-Central Europe to form an émigré army. In a secret memorandum from 1953, President Eisenhower wrote, "In the interest of our national security, the burden now resting upon the youth of America in the world struggle against Communism should be relieved by providing additional combat manpower." To do this, he argued, "We should find a way to mobilize the will to oppose Communism which exists in countries under the Communist yoke. One way to meet these objectives is . . . [the] proposal for a 'Volunteer Freedom Corps.'"[69]

Loosely based on the Free French Forces organized in opposition to the

Vichy regime in occupied France during World War II, the Volunteer Freedom Corps was conceptualized as a military organization for exiles from East-Central Europe to join the fight to liberate their homelands. It was a response to earlier offers such as that of Polish general Władysław Anders, who promised more than 6 million men to fight with the United States for the anti-Soviet cause in 1951.[70] Although this was not the first attempt to create an émigré army to fight communism, it was the only one that received explicit support from the president. In the view of the administration, giving escapees an opportunity to fight for their homelands would help the United States in its battle against communism and encourage continued emigration from East-Central Europe. In the words of C. D. Jackson, the opportunity to help the West in the Cold War would give escapees "something to hang on to."[71]

In 1951, Representative Charles J. Kersten of Wisconsin introduced an amendment to the Mutual Security Act, proposing the creation of national legions of escapees associated with the North Atlantic Treaty Organization. He argued, "Just imagine that the United States had been taken over by the Communists, and there were 100,000 young Americans available for military service outside the country. What a magnetic force that would be for the eventual liberation of this country. The same situation exists in Poland, in Hungary, in Rumania, and in Bulgaria."[72]

The so-called Kersten amendment led to proposals for the Volunteer Freedom Corps. While President Eisenhower initially hoped to recruit an army of 250,000 escapees, other groups within the administration questioned his optimism. CIA director Allen W. Dulles noted that the United States should avoid "overenthusiasm at the start," aiming instead for the more realistic figure of about thirty thousand. Detailed plans were made for the organization of national units affiliated with NATO. A full range of issues was discussed, including the use of national insignia, flags, and command structure. There was even some debate about expanding the Volunteer Freedom Corps to fight in Korea.[73] The US ambassador to the United Nations remarked, "Escapees can give the United States the initiative in psychological warfare, and can be the biggest, single, constitutive, creative element in our foreign policy."[74]

Despite the promise seen in the VFC by President Eisenhower and many senior security officials, the escapee army was never implemented. There are several reasons for this. In the first place, the USSR reacted strongly to the Kersten amendment in the United Nations, condemning the "appropriation of 100 million dollars to pay for the recruitment of persons and the organization of armed groups in the Soviet Union, Poland, Czechoslovakia, Hungary, Romania, Bulgaria, [and] Albania."[75]

Second, the administration was unable to overcome lingering reservations in the State Department and objections from its allies in Western Europe. Most notably, for the leadership of the newly created Federal Republic of Germany and other US allies along the Iron Curtain, "the prospect of housing units of recruits itching for World War III was more alarming than reassuring." Carruthers points out that "without the support of those states in which [the VFC's] units would be based, nothing . . . could be done."[76]

Finally, the gradual thaw that followed Stalin's death in 1953 convinced the government that the VFC was not valuable enough to risk endangering America's improving relations with the USSR. The suppression of the East German uprising by Soviet troops later that year also "shattered the notion of an aggressive rollback." By this point, John Foster Dulles and others within the Eisenhower administration had begun to question this strategy as too costly and too risky. By 1955, Dulles told the Senate Foreign Relations Committee that "the US is getting closer to a relationship [where] we can deal [with the Soviet Union] on a basis comparable to that where we deal with differences between friendly nations."[77] This was the death knell of the VFC. Although some escapees had been recruited into the US Army and were already in training, the administration officially rescinded the proposals for a VFC in 1960, incorporating the existing escapees into regular army units.[78]

The escapees and refugee organizations representing exiles from Eastern and Central Europe were disappointed when government programs to fight communism were abandoned. They had lobbied Congress hard in support of the VFC and other anticommunist measures.[79] These émigrés saw themselves as the perfect soldiers to lead the fight against communism. They had written many letters to the president and to their representatives in Congress, promising to do anything to defeat the Communists. In many cases, exiles succeeded in penetrating and forming relationships with the American political elite.[80]

By the time the plans for the VFC were abandoned, the political support given to forming an army of émigrés had already encouraged the escapees from East-Central Europe to form "refugee-warrior communities."[81] For example, a group of veterans of the Slovak army formed the Union of Slovak Combatants in 1953. Similar organizations sprang up in every Eastern and Central European diaspora, including the Free Armenia Committee, the Union of Estonian Fighters for Freedom, the Latvian Association for the Struggle Against Communism, and the Croatian National Liberation Movement, to name just a few.

During the Cold War, many of these organizations banded together under the banner of the Anti-Bolshevik Bloc of Nations. Inspired by the anticolonial movements in Africa, the ABN was a coordinating center for anticommunist organizations dedicated to destroying the Warsaw Pact. Founded by the Bandera faction of the Organization for Ukrainian Nationalists, the ABN had US chapters in New York, Chicago, Detroit, and Cleveland. Though its rhetoric was on the fringe of the diaspora community, it was very prominent and highly mobilized.[82]

The government was surprised by the intensity of the support for these programs and even sought to diminish their impact. A top secret report warned, "All agencies concerned with the VFC must be prepared to minimize the impact of pressures from the various émigré groups. Such pressure can be anticipated in direct approaches to members of Congress, to the participating agencies and to the press."[83] In its attempt to improve relations with the USSR, the administration was deeply concerned about the possible impact of lobbying by extremist ethnic groups. This demonstrates the influence that geopolitically motivated selection mechanisms and political opportunities had in helping migrants mobilize into powerful lobbies. It also shows how the policy legacies of decisions dictated by world politics can backfire when the geopolitical situation changes.

CONCLUSION

The concerns that drove the implementation of the migrant screening processes during the early Cold War continue to exercise a considerable effect on American life, despite important geopolitical and economic differences between the early Cold War and the start of the twenty-first century. In particular, the events of September 11, 2001, and subsequent attacks by individuals residing in the country, such as the Boston Marathon bombings of April 2013, have highlighted the importance of migration for national security.[84] The ongoing debate over the power of the Israel lobby has also raised concerns about the influence of mobilized diasporas, especially when the policies advocated by these communities antagonize a region of the world crucial to US security interests.

Even though scholars of international relations have highlighted the importance of migration in contributing events as disparate as the rise and fall of the Roman Empire and the development the United States and Russia in the nineteenth century, migration has not played a particularly prominent role in contemporary studies.[85] There are many reasons for this oversight. Rey Koslowski suggests that the issue of human movement has been bypassed "because it does not easily fit into the state-centric conceptualizations of world politics as an international system of territorially delineated states."[86] This perspective is seconded by James Carafano, who blames the failure of the VFC on the "US predilection for state-focused solutions that largely ignored the role of civil society in building peace and stability."[87]

By focusing on a case drawn from the early Cold War, this chapter aims to "bring the state back in" by highlighting state influence on diaspora mobilization through responses to the structure of the international system.[88] The geopolitical concerns at the start of the Cold War led the United States to adopt immigration selection criteria that favored the admission of hard-line anticommunist migrants to America. Had the United States not screened applicants from East-Central Europe, it probably still would have received a broadly anticommunist population, given the memories of expulsion carried by these individuals.[89] However, this population would have displayed more diversity in the vehemence of its views and its willingness to act upon them. Overall, while lobbies would still have formed, they probably would have had fewer actively ideological "core members."[90]

Although the problems of global terrorism that have brought migration into the spotlight of national security today differ from the case of postwar migration from East-Central Europe in many ways, this case still can help us reflect on contemporary issues and theoretical concerns. Since the nineteenth century,

Congress has restricted immigration using three main mechanisms: excluding individuals, favoring certain nationalities, and giving priority to certain individuals.[91] While the criteria have changed, immigration officials continue to conduct interviews and vet potential immigrants.

The Refugee Act of 1980 incorporates into US law the first definition of refugees that is not ideologically or geographically based. However, it still searches for signs of persecution, which opens the possibility for the admittance of many individuals who share the deep-rooted political opinions of "core" ethnic lobbyists.[92] In particular, the political influence of such migrant communities on the policies of their host states deserves further attention, especially within geopolitical powers like the United States, because immigration procedures create structural conditions in which motivated, politically active migrant communities can exert a significant impact by lobbying the government, as well as by providing expertise and local knowledge of regions that few other Americans can dispute.

In addition to lobbying, ethnic groups can also affect US policy through their influence in the intelligence services and academia. It is difficult to judge the extent to which the use of former Nazi intelligence networks from the *Abwehr* and the so-called Gehlen group affected US policy, but the possibility is certainly disturbing.[93] Within academia, the presence of foreign intellectuals with stridently anti-Soviet views at many American institutes and universities was also important. In some cases—one need only think of individuals such as Zbigniew Brzezinski and Richard Pipes—these individuals also crossed over from academia to take on important positions within the policy apparatus of the United States. Overall, the ideological commitments of intellectuals and policymakers from the diaspora, who could claim direct knowledge of the Communist system and the USSR, resulted in highly propagandized views of the Soviet Union that worked their way into US policy.[94]

With the end of the Cold War and rise of terrorism, the emphasis of research into migration policy has shifted from military technology to locating extremists within transnational networks. In this new security environment, the issues surrounding immigration vetting procedures and migrant radicalization are becoming more important. With this shift in international concerns, the topics theorized by scholars must shift as well. However, the lessons of the past, particularly with regard to the policy legacies and unexpected dangers of extreme vetting, must also be considered.

NOTES

An earlier, longer version of this essay was published as Peter J. Verovšek, "Screening Migrants in the Early Cold War: The Geopolitics of US Immigration Policy," *Journal of Cold War Studies* 20, no. 4 (2018): 154–179.

1. The absence of migrants with opposing opinions enhanced their power, as governments overvalued the expertise of émigrés that had settled within their borders. Stephen M. Walt, *Revolution and War* (Ithaca, NY: Cornell University Press, 1996), 31–32.

2. Peter J. Verovšek, "The Unexpected Dangers of 'Extreme Vetting,'" *Eurozine* 10 (February 2017), https://www.eurozine.com/the-unexpected-dangers-of-extreme-vetting.

3. Hannah Arendt, *The Origins of Totalitarianism* (New York: Brace Harcourt, 1951), chapter 9.

4. Douglas Woodwell, "Unwelcome Neighbors: Shared Ethnicity and International Conflict During the Cold War," *International Studies Quarterly* 48, no. 1 (Spring 2004): 197. See also William Safran, "Diasporas in Modern Societies: Myths of Homeland and Return," *Diaspora* 1, no. 1 (Winter 1991): 83–99; Sarah Wayland, "Ethnonationalist Networks and Transnational Opportunities: The Sri Lankan Tamil Diaspora," *Review of International Studies* 30, no. 2 (Summer 2004): 405–426; Nevzat Soguk, "Transversal Communication, Diaspora, and the Euro-Kurds," *Review of International Studies* 34, no. 1 (Winter 2008); Jennifer M. Brinkerhoff, "Digital Diasporas and Conflict Prevention: The Case of Somalinet.com," *Review of International Studies* 32, no. 1 (Winter 2006): 25–47; John Armstrong, "Mobilized and Proletarian Diasporas," *American Political Science Review* 70, no. 2 (Spring 1976): 393–408; John F. Stack, ed., *Ethnic Identities in a Transnational World* (Westport, CT: Greenwood Press, 1981); Michael S. Tietelbaum, "Immigration, Refugees, and Foreign Policy," *International Organization* 38, no. 3 (Summer 1984): 429–450.

5. Idean Salehyan and Kristian Skrede Gleditsch, "Refugees and the Spread of Civil War," *International Organization* 60, no. 2 (Spring/Summer 2006): 335–366; Idean Salehyan, "Transnational Rebels: Neighboring States as Sanctuary for Rebel Groups," *World Politics* 59, no. 2 (Winter 2007): 217–242; Sarah Kenyon Lischer, *Dangerous Sanctuaries: Refugee Camps, Civil War, and the Dilemmas of Humanitarian Aid* (Ithaca, NY: Cornell University Press, 2005); Gabriel Sheffer, "Ethnic Diasporas: A Threat to Their Hosts?," in *International Migration and Security*, ed. Myron Weiner (Boulder, CO: Westview Press, 1993), 268–285. Diasporas are a key factor increasing the likelihood of renewed conflict. Five years after the end of active warfare, diasporas increase the chances of renewed conflict by a factor of six. See Paul Collier and Anke Hoeffler, "Greed and Grievance in Civil War," *Oxford Economic Papers* 56, no. 4 (Fall 2004): 563–595; Daniel Byman, *Trends in Outside Support for Insurgent Movements* (Santa Monica, CA: Rand, 2001); Mary B. Anderson, *Do No Harm: How Aid Can Support Peace—Or War* (Boulder, CO: Lynne Rienner, 1999).

6. Joseph A. Pika, "Interest Groups and the White House Under Roosevelt and Truman," *Political Science Quarterly* 102, no. 4 (Winter 1987–1988): 649; also 655 for more on minority interest groups.

7. Nathan Glazer and Daniel P. Moynihan, eds., "Introduction," in *Ethnicity: Theory and Experience* (Cambridge, MA: Harvard University Press, 1975), 23–24.

8. Graham Smith and Andrew Wilson, "Rethinking Russia's Post-Soviet Diaspora: The Potential for Political Mobilisation in Eastern Ukraine and North-East Estonia," *Europe-Asia Studies* 49, no. 5 (Summer 1997), 848.

9. US Department of State, Policy Planning Staff, "Policy Relating to Defection and Defectors from Soviet Power," June 28, 1949, records of the PPS, RG 59, microfiche 1171, 62, quoted in Susan L. Carruthers, "Between Camps: Eastern Bloc 'Escapees' and Cold War Borderlands," *American Quarterly* 57, no. 3 (Fall 2005), 917.

10. Peter Hägel and Pauline Peretz, "States and Transnational Actors: Who's Influencing Whom? A Case Study in Jewish Diaspora Politics During the Cold War," *European Journal of International Relations* 11, no. 4 (Fall 2005); Fiona B. Adamson and Madeleine Demetriou, "Remapping the Boundaries of 'State' and 'National Identity': Incorporating Diasporas into IR Theorizing," *European Journal of International Relations* 13, no. 4 (Fall 2007): 491.

11. James Jay Carafano, "Mobilizing Europe's Stateless: America's Plan for a Cold War Army," *Journal of Cold War Studies* 1, no. 2 (Spring 1999): 61.

12. Fiona B. Adamson, "Crossing Borders: International Migration and National Security," *International Security* 31, no. 1 (Summer 2006): 165; Roxanne Lynn Doty, "Immigration and the Politics of Security," *Security Studies* 8, no. 2 (Spring 1998): 71–93.

13. Christopher Rudolph, "Security and the Political Economy of International Migration," *American Political Science Review* 97, no. 4 (Fall 2003): 612.

14. John Mearsheimer and Stephen Walt claim that the "Israel lobby" has diverted US foreign policy "far from what the national interest would otherwise suggest." Mearsheimer and Walt, "The Israel Lobby," *London Review of Books* 28, no. 6 (March 23, 2006).

15. Carafano, "Mobilizing Europe's Stateless," 61.

16. Judy Feigin, *The Office of Special Investigations: Striving for Accountability After the Holocaust* (Washington, DC: Department of Justice, 2006).

17. Tony Smith, *Foreign Attachments: The Power of Ethnic Groups in the Making of American Foreign Policy* (Cambridge, MA: Harvard University Press, 2000), 57.

18. See Yossi Shain, *Marketing the American Creed Abroad: Diasporas in the US and Their Homelands* (Cambridge: Cambridge University Press, 1999).

19. Yossi Shain, "Ethnic Diasporas and US Foreign Policy," *Political Science Quarterly* 109, no. 5 (Winter 1994–1995): 834; Shain, "The Mexican-American Diaspora's Impact on Mexico," *Political Science Quarterly* 114, no. 4 (Winter 1999–2000): 667.

20. Jack I. Garvey, "Repression of the Political Émigré—the Underground to International Law: A Proposal for Remedy," *Yale Law Journal* 90, no. 1 (Fall 1980): 78–120.

21. Shain, "Ethnic Diasporas and US Foreign Policy," 833.

22. See Smith and Wilson, "*Rethinking Russia's Post-Soviet Diaspora*," 845–848; Charles King

and Neil J. Melvin, "Diaspora Politics: Ethnic Linkages, Foreign Policy and Security in Eurasia," *International Security* 24, no. 3 (Winter 1999/2000): 116–117; Doug McAdam, John D. McCarthy, and Mayer N. Zald, *Comparative Perspectives on Social Movements: Political Opportunities, Mobilizing Structures, and Cultural Framings* (New York: Cambridge University Press, 1996); Doug McAdam, Sidney G. Tarrow, and Charles Tilly, *Dynamics of Contention* (New York: Cambridge University Press, 2001).

23. Rogers Brubaker, "The 'Diaspora' Diaspora," *Ethnic & Racial Studies* 28, no. 1 (Winter 2005): 13; Nedim Ögelman, "Documenting and Explaining the Persistence of Homeland Politics Among Germany's Turks," *International Migration Review* 37, no. 1 (Spring 2003): 164.

24. Peter Doerschler, "Push-Pull Factors and Immigrant Political Integration in Germany," *Social Science Quarterly* 87, no. 5 (December 2006): 71–93; Nicholas Van Hear, *New Diasporas: The Mass Exodus, Dispersal and Regrouping of Migrant Communities* (London: UCL Press, 1998); John D. McCarthy and Mayer N. Zald, "Resource Mobilization and Social Movements: A Partial Theory," *American Journal of Sociology* 82, no. 6 (May 1977): 1212–1241. The importance of push and pull factors was also observed by US officials at the time. Carruthers, "Between Camps," 922.

25. Fiona B. Adamson, "Globalisation, Transnational Political Mobilisation, and Networks of Violence," *Cambridge Review of International Affairs* 18, no. 1 (Spring 2005): 35–36.

26. Luis Eduardo Guarnizo, Alejandro Portes, and William Haller, "Assimilation and Transnationalism: Determinants of Transnational Political Action Among Contemporary Migrants," *American Journal of Sociology* 108, no. 6 (May 2003): 1217; Kenneth D. Wald, "Homeland Interests, Hostland Politics: Politicized Ethnic Identity Among Middle Eastern Heritage Groups in the United States," *International Migration Review* 42, no. 2 (Summer 2008): 273–301.

27. Ole Wæver, Barry Buzan, Morten Kelstrup, and Pierre Lemaitre, *Identity, Migration and the New Security Agenda in Europe* (London: Pinter, 1993).

28. Robin Cohen, "Diasporas and the Nation-State: From Victims to Challengers," *International Affairs* 72, no. 3 (July 1996): 507–520.

29. Milton J. Esman, "Diasporas and International Relations," in *Modern Diasporas in International Politics*, ed. Gabriel Sheffer (London: Croom Helm, 1986), 336.

30. Fathali M. Moghaddam and Anthony J. Marsella, *Understanding Terrorism: Psychosocial Roots, Consequences, and Interventions* (Washington, DC: American Psychological Association, 2004).

31. Sidney G. Tarrow, *Power in Movement: Social Movements, Collective Action, and Contentious Politics* (New York: Cambridge University Press, 1994), 85.

32. See McAdam, McCarthy and Zald, *Comparative Perspectives on Social Movements*; Doug McAdam, *Political Process and the Development of Black Insurgency, 1930–1970* (Chicago: University of Chicago Press, 1982); Herbert P. Kitschelt, "Political Opportunity Structures and Political Protest: Anti-Nuclear Movements in Four Democracies," *British Journal of Political Science* 16, no. 1 (Winter 1986): 57–85; Hanspeter Kriesi, Ruud Koopmans, Jan Willem Duyvendak, and Marco G. Giugni, "New Social Movements and Political Opportunities in Western Europe," *European Journal of Political Research* 22, no. 2 (Spring 1992): 219–244; Wayland, "Ethnonationalist Networks," 415–418; Fiona B. Adamson, "Mobilizing for the Transformation of Home: Politicized Identities

and Transnational Practices," in *New Approaches to Migration? Transnational Communities and the Transformation of Home*, ed. Nadje Al Ali and Khalid Koser (London: Routledge, 2002); Michael Hanagan, "Irish Transnational Social Movements, Migrants, and the State System," *Mobilization* 3, no. 1 (Spring 1998): 107–126; Patrick R. Ireland, *The Policy Challenge of Ethnic Diversity: Immigrant Politics in France and Switzerland* (Cambridge, MA: Harvard University Press, 1994); Ruud Koopmans and Paul Statham, *Challenging Immigration and Ethnic Relations Politics: Comparative European Perspectives* (Oxford: Oxford University Press, 2000).

33. Quoted in Malcolm Jarvis Proudfoot, *European Refugees: 1939–52—A Study in Forced Population Movement* (Evanston, IL: Northwestern University Press, 1956), 177–178.

34. United States Congress, *Mutual Security Act Extension. Staff Memorandum on Manpower Provisions of Mutual Security Act of 1951*, CMP-1952-FOA-0051, 82nd US Congress, session 2 (1952), 11. For more on the United Nations Relief and Rehabilitation Administration and the International Refugee Organization, see Michael Robert Marrus, *The Unwanted: European Refugees in the Twentieth Century* (New York: Oxford University Press, 1985), 317–319, 340–345.

35. For more on this wave of migrants, their motivations, and their connection to the Nazi Party during the war, see Feigin, *Office of Special Investigations*, 1.

36. Carruthers, "Between Camps," 912.

37. See Gil Loescher and John A. Scanlan, *Calculated Kindness: Refugees and America's Half-Open Door, 1945 to the Present* (New York: Free Press, 1986).

38. Displaced Persons Act of 1948, 80th US Congress, session 2 (June 25, 1948), section 1. See also Robert Barde, Susan B. Carter, and Richard Sutch, "Immigrants, by Country of Last Residence—Europe: 1820–1997," table Ad106–120, in *Historical Statistics of the United States, Earliest Times to the Present: Millennial Edition*, ed. Susan B. Carter et al. (New York: Cambridge University Press, 2006). http://dx.doi.org/10.1017/ISBN-9780511132971.Ad90-221.

39. See Susan L. Carruthers, *Cold War Captives: Imprisonment, Escape, and Brainwashing* (Berkeley: University of California Press, 2009), 23–32.

40. US Department of State, "Policy Relating to Defection and Defectors from Soviet Power."

41. Walter L. Hixson, *Parting the Curtain: Propaganda, Culture, and the Cold War, 1945–1961* (New York: St. Martin's Press, 1997), 12–13.

42. László Borhi, "Rollback, Liberation, Containment, or Inaction? US Policy and Eastern Europe in the 1950s," *Journal of Cold War Studies* 1, no. 3 (Fall 1999): 88–89.

43. *Admission of 300,000 Immigrants*, HRG-1952-HJH-0009, House Committee on Judiciary, Subcommittee no. 1, 82nd US Congress, session 2 (1952), 15–16.

44. C. Tyler Wood, quoted in, *Admission of 300,000 Immigrants*, 105–106.

45. "Statements of Otto R. Hauser, National President, and Bernard H. Hofmann, Secretary, American Relief for Germany, Inc.," in *Displaced Persons*: Hearings Before the Subcommittee on Amendments to the Displaced Persons Act of the Committee on the Judiciary, United States Senate, Eighty-First Congress, First and Second Sessions (Washington, DC: US Government Printing Office, 1950), 186.

46. J. Kolaja, "A Sociological Note on the Czechoslovak Anti-Communist Refugee," *American Journal of Sociology* 58, no. 3 (Fall 1952): 289–291.

47. This list is copied directly from "Psychological Offensive Vis-à-Vis the USSR: Objectives, Tasks, Theme, Confidential," in United States Department of State, *Foreign Relations of the United States, 1951: Eastern Europe* (Washington, DC: US Government Printing Office, March 3, 1951), 1234.

48. Quoted in "Statement of Mr. Harrison on the Cellar Bill Before House Judiciary Subcommittee" in *Admission of 300,000 Immigrants*, 16.

49. Edward W. Barrett, "Memorandum by the Assistant Secretary of State for Public Affairs (Barrett) to the Deputy Under Secretary of State (Matthews), Secret," in United States Department of State, *Foreign Relations of the United States, 1951: Eastern Europe* (Washington, DC: US Government Printing Office, January 25, 1951), 1207. See also Operations Coordinating Board for the National Security Council, "Progress Report on US Policy Toward Soviet-Bloc Escapees," in United States Department of State, *Foreign Relations of the United States, 1955–1957: Eastern Europe* (Washington, DC: US Government Printing Office, April 18, 1956), 149–152.

50. See Dean Acheson, "The Secretary of State to the Embassy in Sweden, Confidential," in United States Department of State, *Foreign Relations of the United States, 1951: Eastern Europe* (Washington, DC: US Government Printing Office, October 13, 1951),1290–1292.

51. Robert Barde, Susan B. Carter, and Richard Sutch, "Refugees and Asylees Admitted and Granted Permanent Resident Status, By Continent of Birth: 1948–1997," table Ad1005–1013, in *Historical Statistics of the United States*.

52. *Emergency Immigration Program*, HRG-1953-HJH-0006, House Committee on Judiciary, Subcommittee no. 1, 83rd US Congress, session 1 (1953), 1.

53. Claudena M. Skran, *Refugees in Inter-War Europe: The Emergence of a Regime* (Oxford: Clarendon Press, 1995), 2.

54. "Statement of Gen. Walter Bendell Smith, Acting Secretary of State, Accompanied by Mr. George L. Warren, Advisor on Refugees, Daniel L. Horowitz, Labor Advisor, Bureau of European Affairs, George O. Gray, Congressional Liaison, and Edward Maney, Visa Division," in *Emergency Immigration Program*, 5.

55. "Statement of a Former Officer, Military Intelligence, United States Army," in *Displaced Persons*, 1156.

56. "Statement of Ugo Carusi, Chairman, Displaced Persons Commission, Washington, DC—Resumed," in *Displaced Persons*, 33.

57. "Statement of Hon. Emanuel Celler, A Representative in Congress from the State of New York—Resumed," in *Displaced Persons*, 315.

58. Carruthers, "Between Camps," 929.

59. *Displaced Persons*, HRG-1949-SJS-0016, House Committee on Judiciary, Subcommittee on Amendments to Displaced Persons Act, 81st US Congress, session 1 (1949), section 10.

60. "Statement of Robert James, Vice Consul, Ludwigsburg," in *Displaced Persons*, 1208–1210.

61. "Statement of Walter Gallan, Executive Director of United Ukrainian American Relief Committee, Inc.," in *Admission of 300,000 Immigrants*, 121.

62. "Statement of Robert James," 1208–1211.

63. "Statements of Crete Anderson, Chairman, Subcommittee on Immigration and Nat-

uralization of the National Americanism Commission, the American Legion, and Clarence H. Olson, Assistant Director, National Legislative Commission, the American Legion," in *Emergency Immigration Program*, 149. For more on the difficulties presented by the need to screen these migrants, see also Feigin, *Office of Special Investigations*, 36–37.

64. "Statement of George A. Polos, Chairman, Ahepa Displaced Persons Committee" in *Admission of 300,000 Immigrants*, 205.

65. "Statement of Walter C. Young, Displaced Persons Commission," in *Displaced Persons*, 1222.

66. Tom Bower, *The Paperclip Conspiracy: The Battle for the Spoils and Secrets of Nazi Germany* (London: M. Joseph, 1987); Christopher Simpson, *Blowback: America's Recruitment of Nazis and its Effects on the Cold War* (New York: Weidenfeld & Nicolson, 1988). For more on the importance of foreign scientists in maintaining the US lead in military science and technology, see Robert L. Paarlberg, "Knowledge as Power: Science, Military Dominance, and US Security," *International Security* 29, no. 1 (Summer 2004): 125.

67. Nazi War Criminal Records Interagency Working Group, *Implementation of the Nazi War Crimes Disclosure Act: An Interim Report to Congress* (Washington, DC: US National Archives and Records Administration, 1999); Mark Fritz, "The Secret History of World War II," *Boston Globe*, March 11, 2001; John Loftus and Mark Aarons, *Secret War Against the Jews* (New York: St. Martin's Press, 1994), 214; John Kolasky, *Prophets and Proletarians: Documents on the History of the Rise and Decline of Ukrainian Communism in Canada* (Edmonton: Canadian Institute of Ukrainian Studies Press, 1990), 367; Mark Aarons and John Loftus, *Unholy Trinity: How the Vatican's Nazi Networks Betrayed Western Intelligence to the Soviets* (New York: St. Martin's Press, 1991), 223.

68. This estimate is from the director of the Office of Special Investigation, in Allan A. Ryan, *Quiet Neighbors: Prosecuting Nazi War Criminals in America* (San Diego: Harcourt Brace Jovanovich, 1984), 26–27. Since then, this figure has been challenged as too high. Feigin, *Office of Special Investigations*, v.

69. Dwight D. Eisenhower, "Memorandum by the President to the Executive Secretary of the National Security Council (Lay)," in United States Department of State, *Foreign Relations of the United States, 1952–1954: Eastern Europe; Soviet Union; Eastern Mediterranean* (Washington, DC: US Government Printing Office, February 14, 1953), 180–181.

70. In Borhi, "Rollback, Liberation, Containment, or Inaction?," 87.

71. "Record of Meeting of the Ad Hoc Committee on NSC 143," in United States Department of State, *Foreign Relations of the United States, 1952–1954: Eastern Europe; Soviet Union; Eastern Mediterranean*, vol. 8 (Washington, DC: US Government Printing Office, March 30, 1953), 208.

72. Quoted in United States Congress, *Mutual Security Act Extension*, 2.

73. Eisenhower, "Memorandum by the President to the Executive Secretary of the National Security Council (Lay)," 182; "Record of Meeting of the Ad Hoc Committee on NSC 143," 196, 209.

74. Quoted in Bennett Kovrig, *Of Walls and Bridges: The United States and Eastern Europe* (New York: New York University Press, 1991), 64.

75. In Warren Austin, "The United States Representative to the United Nations (Austin) to the Secretary of State," in United States Department of State, *Foreign Relations of the United*

States, 1951: The United Nations; the Western Hemisphere, vol. 2 (Washington, DC: US Government Printing Office, November 23, 1951), 478.

76. Carruthers, *Cold War Captives,* 74.

77. Borhi, "Rollback, Liberation, Containment, or Inaction?," 89–90.

78. Kovrig, *Of Walls and Bridges,* 64–65. President Eisenhower complained of the slow progress made in the implementation of this legislation, "the objective of which was to produce from stateless, anti-Communist young men elite officer material." Eisenhower, "Memorandum by the President to the Executive Secretary of the National Security Council (Lay)," 182.

79. See *Investigation of Communist Aggression* [part 8], *Tenth Interim Report, Poland, Rumania, and Slovakia,* H1475-1-E, and *Investigation of Communist Takeover and Occupation of Poland, Lithuania, and Slovakia* [part 4], *Sixth Interim Report,* H1475-1-A, House Select Committee to Investigate Communist Aggression and the Forced Incorporation of the Baltic States into the Soviet Union, 83rd US Congress, session 2 (1954); *Emergency Migration of Escapees, Expellees, and Refugees,* 83 S1057-6, Senate Committee on Judiciary, 83rd US Congress, session 1 (1953).

80. See photos of ex-Nazis with prominent American politicians in Brooklyn Byelorussian-American Association, *Byelorussia's Independence Day, March 25, 1918: Documents, Facts, Proclamations, Statements, and Comments* (New York: Byelorussian-American Association, 1958).

81. Aristide R. Zolberg, Astri Suhrke, and Sergio Aguayo, *Escape from Violence: Conflict and the Refugee Crisis in the Developing World* (New York: Oxford University Press, 1989), 275–278.

82. Vic Satzewich, *The Ukrainian Diaspora* (London: Routledge, 2002), 158; Albert Hunt, "Bitter in Yorkshire," *New Society,* November 16, 1986, 14–16.

83. Operations Coordinating Board, "Report to the National Security Council on the Activation of a Volunteer Freedom Corp, Top Secret," in United States Department of State, *Foreign Relations of the United States, 1955–1957: Eastern Europe* (Washington, DC: US Government Printing Office, June 14, 1955), 63.

84. Robert S. Leiken, *Bearers of Global Jihad? Immigration and National Security After 9/11* (Washington, DC: Nixon Center, 2004); Audrey Kurth Cronin, "Behind the Curve: Globalization and International Terrorism," *International Security* 27, no. 3 (Winter 2002/2003): 30–58; Marc Sageman, *Understanding Terror Networks* (Philadelphia: University of Pennsylvania Press, 2004); John Arquilla and David F. Ronfeldt, *Networks and Netwars* (Santa Monica, CA: Rand, 2001).

85. See Niccolò Machiavelli, *Discourses on Livy,* translated by Harvey Claflin Mansfield and Nathan Tarcov (Chicago: University of Chicago Press, 1996); Edward Gibbon, *The Decline and Fall of the Roman Empire* (New York: Modern Library, 1932); Alexis de Tocqueville, *Democracy in America,* translated by George Lawrence (Garden City, NY: Doubleday, 1963), 413; Hans J. Morgenthau, *Politics among Nations: The Struggle for Power and Peace,* 5th ed. (New York: Knopf, 1978), 131.

86. Rey Koslowski, "Human Migration and the Conceptualization of Pre-Modern World Politics," *International Studies Quarterly* 46 (2002): 376.

87. Carafano, "Mobilizing Europe's Stateless," 62.

88. Hägel and Peretz, "States and Transnational Actors," 468.

89. Jane Perry Clark Carey, "Political Organization of the Refugees and Expellees in West Germany," *Political Science Quarterly* 66, no. 2 (Summer 1951): 200.

90. Alicja Iwańska, *Exiled Governments: Spanish and Polish—An Essay in Political Sociology* (Cambridge, MA: Schenkman, 1981), 43–44.

91. Andrew M. Isserman, "United States Immigration Policy and the Industrial Heartland: Laws, Origins, Settlement Patterns and Economic Consequences," *Urban Studies* 30, no. 2 (Spring 1993): 239; John Hawkes Noble, "The Present State of the Immigration Question," *Political Science Quarterly* 7, no. 2 (Summer 1892): 235–240. These issues are especially important given the convergence of immigration control policies around the world. See Eytan Meyers, "The Causes of Convergence in Western Immigration Control," *Review of International Studies* 28, no. 1 (Winter 2002): 123–141.

92. John A. Scanlan and G. D. Loescher, "Mass Asylum and Human Rights in American Foreign Policy," *Political Science Quarterly* 97, no. 1 (Spring 1982): 40.

93. Mary Ellen Reese, *General Reinhard Gehlen: The CIA Connection* (Fairfax, VA: George Mason University Press, 1990); Burton Hersh, *The Old Boys: The American Elite and the Origins of the CIA* (New York: Scribner's, 1992).

94. For instance, the Policy Planning Staff noted that escapees from behind the Iron Curtain provided a "goldmine of vital information [to] be systematically exploited to the fullest possible extent." US Department of State, Policy Planning Staff, "Utilization of Refugees from the Soviet Union in US National Interest," March 4, 1948, records of the PPS, RG 59, microfiche 1171, 24, quoted in Carruthers, "Between Camps," 917. See also John Gimbel, "US Policy and German Scientists: The Early Cold War," *Political Science Quarterly* 101, no. 3 (Summer 1986): 433–451; Clarence G. Lasby, *Project Paperclip: German Scientists and the Cold War* (New York: Atheneum, 1971); Linda Hunt, *Secret Agenda: The United States Government, Nazi Scientists, and Project Paperclip, 1944–1990* (New York: St. Martin's Press, 1991).

CREATING A COLD WAR IDENTITY

By the end of the 1940s and into the 1950s, the Cold War began to impact the lives of everyday Americans in often dramatic ways, and it transformed how they saw themselves and their country. Two years after Winston Churchill's warning about the descent of an Iron Curtain across Europe, the United States was embroiled in the trial of accused Soviet spy Alger Hiss—and Richard Nixon, Hiss's chief accuser in Congress, successfully used the trial to springboard his political career. Even more importantly, the USSR successfully tested its first atomic bomb in 1949, ending the short US monopoly on this devastating weapon. The test was followed by the 1950 arrest of Julius and Ethel Rosenberg for passing US nuclear weapons secrets to the Soviets, plans which had helped to accelerate the Soviet nuclear program. In 1951, the couple was convicted, and they were executed two years later. It is no wonder, then, that anticommunism reached a fever pitch in the United States by the early 1950s.

The Red Scare, McCarthyism, loyalty oaths, and the House Un-American Activities Committee were overt examples of the way in which Americans sought ideological loyalty and even conformity. But the inculcation of a red-blooded Cold War identity emerged in both overt and subtle ways—in the embrace of a consumer society, in family and gender roles, in views on sexuality, in leisure activities, and in religion. There was, of course, not one monolithic "American" during the Cold War, and—this cannot be overstated—postwar identities varied widely based on such factors as race and socioeconomic status. Similarly, many of these identities were scrutinized and evolved over time as early Cold War conformity became increasingly challenged during the counterculture movements of the 1960s. But for much of the conflict, manufacturers, advertisers, activists, and policymakers created a set of ideals and built environments that sought to define a vision of Americanism that contrasted with the collectivist ideals of communism. As with the structural transformations discussed in part 1, many of these ideals endured long after the collapse of the Soviet Union.

Enjoying the bounteous consumer goods of the capitalist system became a fundamental part of Americans' identity, in large part, due to the Cold War. As Lizabeth Cohen demonstrates in *A Consumers' Republic: The Politics of Mass Consumption in Postwar America,* mass consumption became a way of both rejuvenating the postwar economy and demonstrating the superiority of the US economic system. Purchasing became a patriotic duty to ensure the vitality of the capitalist system. In a model home created for a 1959 American cultural exhibit in Moscow, US vice president Richard Nixon proudly boasted to Soviet premier Nikita Khrushchev of such innovations as color television and domestic labor-saving devices. Throughout the resulting Kitchen Debate, the two bickered for several minutes in front of the assembled press about the relative strengths of their systems. Nixon highlighted the consumer choices available as the key to America's strength, contending that "diversity, the right to choose, the fact that we have one thousand builders building one thousand different houses is the most important thing. We don't have one decision made at the top by one government official. This is the difference."

The advertising and consumption of alcohol and cigarettes became synonymous with the freedoms Americans enjoyed. Budweiser advertisements from the 1950s and 1960s frequently featured young couples on some version of dates, or with Bud as an accompaniment to activities like billiards or a beach party. Tobacco industry advertisers promoted the widespread choices Americans could make in their cigarettes, in contrast to the limited choices available in the Soviet Bloc. Advertising often depicted smoking as a cultural choice, the reward of a capitalist culture. Nearly one-quarter of American women and more than half of American men smoked by the mid-1950s. Given the preferred treatment tobacco received in terms of domestic subsidies and as part of the Marshall Plan to rebuild Europe, cigarettes were, indeed, a reward for Americans and allies alike.

Similar themes emerged decades later, in a mid-1980s ad for Highland Superstores, which depicted a Soviet submariner defecting when he is confronted with the overwhelming consumer choices available—VHS recorders, electric dryers, stereos—after his crew sets foot in the United States. An ad campaign for Wendy's hamburgers from the same era contrasted the wide variety of burger toppings Americans could choose with a drab Soviet fashion show depicting the same gray, misshapen dress as the only choice women had for day, night, and swimwear. The tagline, "Having no choice is no fun," was far more a statement on the two opposing economic systems than it was on Americans' condiment options.

In addition to promoting an idea of American society, some advertisers also sought to project notions of the ideal citizen embodying American values. The Marlboro Man—an ad campaign begun in 1955—is an enduring image of Cold War smokers and tobacco advertising. By the 1960s, the Marlboro Man was a cowboy, portraying the fabled individuality of the American West. The campaign embodied the nostalgic, masculine portrayal of the American (white) male—bold, silent, strong. The depiction of the American male was also important to the American motor industry. Muscle cars such as Ford's Mustang, Pontiac's GTO, and Chevy's Camaro were famously, purposefully, and unapologetically an "integral part of the American culture, representing freedom, power and speed."

Similarly, the motorcycle became a symbol of the American identity. Brands such as Harley-Davidson could reflect both the unshackled nature of the liberal 1960s and the conservative counteraction. When young Americans began to protest the Vietnam War, the notorious Hells Angels biker group fought back, though according to Hunter S. Thompson in his book *Hell's Angels* (1967), "The difference between the student radicals and the Hell's Angels is that the students are rebelling against the past, while the Angels are fighting the future. Their only common ground is their disdain for the present, or the status quo." By 1969, at the end of a decade of famed counterculture, civil rights, and the height of the Vietnam War protests, the movie *Easy Rider*—a tale of motorcycling hippies and drug users taking a trip across the American South—captured the rebellious antiauthoritarian spirit of the late 1960s. Despite the infamous 1969 stabbing by a Hells Angels security guard at the Rolling Stones' Altamont

Speedway free concert in Northern California, motorcycle culture and the lure of the open road still captured the imagination.

While calls arose for the American male to restore and retain the hardy masculinity of the days of yore, other notions of gender and sexuality changed, too. The classic role of the stay-at-home mother and wife had been challenged by the need for industrial workers on the home front during World War II. The Victorian ideal was rejuvenated early in the Cold War era, in part due to anticommunist fears of liberated women undermining men's job opportunities and virility as the family breadwinners. There arose a concomitant—and predominantly white and middle-class—view that the "traditional" family unit was an essential bulwark to communist subversion and collectivist identity—a literal nuclear family. Marriage and family were the expected norm, and even women who attended college were often encouraged to limit their aspirations to getting their "Mrs. Degrees."

At the Kitchen Debate, Nixon boasted that domestic appliances were conceived "to make life easier for women." When Khrushchev challenged this restrictive "capitalistic attitude toward women," Nixon countered, "I think that this attitude toward women is universal. What we want to do is make life more easy for our housewives." As with all aspects of Cold War society, these cultural trends and expectations were neither permanent nor monolithic.

The publication of Betty Friedan's *The Feminine Mystique* in 1963 helped spur a sexual revolution and a women's rights movement to challenge this family ideal. Significant breakthroughs occurred that expanded women's horizons. Women increasingly joined the workforce in the 1960s and 1970s, the average age of marriage increased, the number of children born dropped, and women's incomes rose. Many women could not even open a bank account separate from their husbands until the 1960s, and not until the 1974 Equal Credit Opportunity Act was discrimination based on gender prohibited in extending credit. But the early Cold War family ideal retained a strong influence on American life.

During the 1950s, activist Phyllis Schlafly came to prominence in St. Louis for her warnings about encroaching communism. She charged Democrats with being too soft on communism and predicted that the nation would be communist by 1970 if Americans did not acknowledge the threat. She gained national prominence in 1964 by writing *A Choice Not an Echo*, which castigated the

Republican Party for its elitism and neglect of grassroots conservatives. In the early 1970s, she began to see feminism as an equal threat to American society. Arguing that the Equal Rights Amendment would deny women the special privileges that their status as wives and mothers provided, she launched a remarkably successful campaign to halt its ratification.

Given the early Cold War focus on heteronormativity and conformity, it is no surprise that homosexuality came under increased scrutiny. In 1952, North Carolina senator Clyde R. Hoey released an influential report which claimed that national security was at risk from what he deemed "sexual deviants" who were more susceptible to blackmail and more likely to cavort with communists. The following year, Dwight Eisenhower signed Executive Order 10450—a wide-ranging statement on individuals likely to be security risks—which not only forbade the hiring of gay men and lesbians but also began to actively purge them from government positions. The resulting "Lavender Scare" had a devastating impact on the lives of tens of thousands and contributed to the stigmatization of homosexuality as a sexual perversion. As with the women's rights movement, the discriminatory environment of the 1950s led to increased gay rights activism, which was catalyzed following the 1969 Stonewall riots in New York. It was not until 1995 that a Bill Clinton executive order prevented sexuality from being a determinant in federal security clearances. However, many of the prejudicial attitudes of the Cold War era, and some of the discriminatory laws, persisted.

These examples reveal just some of the fundamental ways in which the Cold War changed the ways that Americans lived and viewed themselves. But, as the essays in this section reveal, the ways were myriad. In "Race Relations and the Cold War," Ann V. Collins illustrates that for post–World War II Black leaders, racial equality was an extension of the decolonization of empires. Additionally, the issues facing the Black community became part of the Cold War language, as both civil rights leaders and Soviet leaders asked the question: If the United States cannot, or will not, offer equal political and economic rights to its own citizens, how can it export democracy to the world?

Angela F. Keaton's essay "Guns, Manhood, and the Cold War" shows that Cold War hunting and gun cultures were intertwined efforts to retain a traditional view of manhood and masculinity during turbulent years. Hunting and guns served as a fortification against the threat of communism; were the war to turn hot, hunting skills would translate onto the battlefield. Hunting and competing with the elements kept men rugged, hardy, and ready.

As Kurt Kemper makes clear in "No Substitute for Football: Cold War Culture and College Football," the Cold War shaped the way in which college football was discussed, played, coached, and governed. Athletic conferences, college administrations, and coaches treated football as a successful "antidote to domestic subversion" and a preventive measure against juvenile delinquency. Football built men and represented a contest of will as much as skill. Physical and moral fitness went hand in hand, and only these traits could prevent the crumbling of American culture.

Few areas of national identity differentiated Americans from their communist foes as much as religion. In "Televangelism and the Transformation of American Christianity," Randi Barnes-Cox and Charity Rakestraw explore how evangelicals used the threat of communism to support their crusades and apocalyptic visions. Televangelists then allied these Cold War fears with new media to usher in an era of profitable "Christian capitalism," which transformed the ways Americans consumed religion.

Finally, adding nuance to the discussion of consumer choice and Cold War advertising, Francesco Buscemi starkly reveals, in "A War of Colors: Cold War Food Advertising in US Newspapers and Magazines, 1946–1960," that the use of color in advertising differentiated Americans from Soviets. In the United States, color clearly communicated the rich tapestry of choice available to Americans, in literal contrast to the gray, drab lack of options in a Soviet economy.

RACE RELATIONS AND THE COLD WAR

ANN V. COLLINS

"Your problems will never be fully solved," Malcolm X wrote to Organization of African Unity conference participants in Cairo, Egypt, in July 1964, "until and unless ours are solved. . . . You will never be recognized as free human beings until and unless we are also recognized and treated as human beings. Our problem is your problem. It is not a Negro problem, nor an American problem. This is a world problem; a problem for humanity."[1] The members of the OAU had invited Malcolm X to attend their second annual gathering. He used the opportunity to draw a correlation between the plight of African Americans and the people in Africa gaining economic and political freedom. His observations that summer on US race relations and their connectedness to the rest of the world lay at the very center of US policy concerns during part of the Cold War era.

Malcolm X's speech exposed what US leaders had come to realize profoundly affected their actions in the aftermath of World War II. The country's systemic racism posed at least three serious foreign policy struggles during the Cold War: convincing people across the globe that US democracy was superior to communism while African Americans had second-class status at home; contending with communist exploitation of the United States' race problem and the hypocrisy of US leaders in their effort to win over the developing world; and reacting to the battles that African Americans were waging on segregation within the United States as debates occurred over what actions—if any—to take on apartheid and colonization in other parts of the world.[2] As with many other aspects of US politics and society, racism and the contentious race relations in the United States proved to be central to Cold War deliberations—indeed, "a problem for humanity."

Not until recently did scholars begin a deeper investigation into the association between the Cold War and US race relations.[3] Cold War scholarship had tended to focus more on outward foreign policy concerns than on the link between domestic turmoil and debates over options abroad. Meanwhile, examinations of US race relations proved more inward looking, with little mention of the international geopolitical ramifications. Academics looked at issues such as systemic racism, segregation, and the civil rights movement in national isolation rather than through the lens of the Cold War.[4] Rare exceptions included W. E. B. Du Bois, Gunnar Myrdal, and Richard Wright, who recognized that race played a crucial role in international concerns.[5] Ultimately, however, more research has explored the connections between the Cold War and US race relations and how the two realms interacted with and affected each other: policy debates over the Cold War shaped US race relations, and US race relations affected the trajectory of the Cold War. Scholars began to recognize and analyze that relationship.[6] Indeed, the Cold War and US race relations go hand in hand—it is difficult to understand the full scope of one without comprehending its link to the other.

After World War II, US policymakers quickly discovered just how race relations at home would affect the country's role in shaping the new world order. At the United Nations Conference on International Organization in San Francisco in April 1945, Black leaders led the charge in highlighting the parallels between the situation of African Americans in the United States and of subjugated people—especially those of color—elsewhere. National Association for the Advancement of Colored People (NAACP) executive secretary Walter White asserted that the war had fostered within African Americans "a sense of kinship with other colored—and also oppressed—peoples of the world." He continued, "The struggle of the Negro in the United States is part and parcel of the struggle against imperialism and exploitation in India, China, Burma, Africa, the Philippines, Malaysia, the West Indies, and South America." He predicted, "A wind is rising—a wind of determination by the have-nots of the world to share the benefits of freedom and prosperity which the haves of the earth have tried to keep exclusively for themselves."[7] To White and others, the time for racial equality in the United States and the end of colonization for people of color abroad were long overdue.

For African Americans, the end of World War II signaled an opportunity to push for equality both at home and abroad as the war's aftermath began to take shape. The *Chicago Defender,* a prominent Black periodical, ran several pieces in 1945 addressing the question "When Peace Comes . . . What?." "To white America," one editorial read, "the peace will mean joyous tidings. To Black Americans and the colored peoples of the earth, it may mean the outbreak of another war, a bloody racial conflict." As the issue of US race relations became more embroiled in the larger global debate over race, some Black leaders suggested that the Conference on International Organization negotiations would prove crucial. "Today the status and standing of Negro America," the editors of the *Defender* wrote, "is part and parcel of the color problem of the world, known as the colonial question. The Negro is the colonial of America, exploited and robbed of the fruits of his labor just as men of color in the Congo or India or the South Seas. . . . San Francisco will set the temper of the times to come."[8] If a new world charter came from the discussions, African Americans wanted to ensure that US policymakers included them in its design.

Decolonization and a world bill of rights espousing equality among all races became the conference's end goal for Black leaders. "The proposed Charter," stressed scholar and activist W. E. B. Du Bois, "should, therefore, make clear and unequivocal the straightforward stand of the civilized world for race equality, and the universal application of the democratic way of life. . . . What was true of the United States in the past is true of world civilization today—we cannot exist half slave and half free."[9] At the end of the deliberations, however, Du Bois and other proponents of a robust human rights provision had to settle for a much more tempered charter. Fueled by two predominant fears—about the spread of communism and the embarrassment of the history of systemic racism in the United States—(white) US delegates to the conference played it safe. Although they had some apprehension about European colonization of Africa and Asia, US government leaders held more trepidation about the potential vacuum left by immediate independence and therefore the opportunity for communist access. Moreover, forceful human rights language would expose the hypocrisy of the United States and its own record of racial violence and oppression.[10] In his closing remarks to the conference delegates, President Harry Truman admitted that the charter was "only a first step."[11] Nonetheless, this tentative action taken toward human rights and equality shaped Cold War deliberations and set the tone for decades to come.

Many African American leaders continued to express frustration with the direction of US and Western policy. Even Winston Churchill's "Iron Curtain" speech drew a strong reaction from Black newspapers. The *Pittsburgh Courier* labeled the former prime minister's plan a "suicide pact," "crazy KuKlux philosophy," and "white hope for the dying cause of imperialism." The *Chicago Defender* asserted that "Churchill's cry that Russia is threatening world peace through an expansion of Communism is only a smoke screen" obscuring "white supremacy" and "rule by oppression." "We shudder to contemplate the fate of colonials already oppressed by the British," the *Baltimore Afro-American* concurred, "should such an imperialist partnership become a reality."[12]

For US government officials, however, the primary motivation changed from conquering the Nazis and fascism to crushing communism (with the Soviet Union as its primary purveyor)—not decolonization. Truman declared to a joint session of Congress in March 1947:

> At the present moment in world history, nearly every nation must choose between alternative ways of life. The choice is too often not a free one. . . . The seeds of totalitarian regimes are nurtured by misery and want. They spread and grow in the evil soil of poverty and strife. They reach their full growth when the hope of a people for a better life has died. We must keep that hope alive. The free peoples of the world look to us for support in maintaining their freedoms. If we falter in our leadership, we may endanger the peace of the world.[13]

In what came to be called the Truman Doctrine, he promised that the United States would provide aid "to support free peoples who are resisting attempted subjugation by armed minorities or by outside pressures." At that moment, he asserted, Greece and Turkey needed US aid to counter communism.

To African American leaders and many in the Black press, though, the funds allocated for the fight against communism in Greece and Turkey—$400 million—could be put to better use to combat poverty and discrimination in the

United States. The *Pittsburgh Courier*'s Marjorie McKenzie Lawson suggested that the money would be more effective advancing democracy in the South rather than propping up a Greek monarch. Morehouse College president Benjamin Mays was skeptical as well. "I wish I could believe that we were really concerned about establishing freedom in these countries," he declared. "I am troubled at this point because there are so many areas in the United States where democracy doesn't work."[14]

The fight against communism abroad was completely intertwined with the race situation at home. Segregationists considered communism to be the force behind the march for integration, blaming it for the attempts to upend the white power structure. At the same time, leaders of the NAACP suggested that their efforts to reform US society paralleled the cause of battling communism. NAACP executive director Roy Wilkins asserted:

> The survival of the American democratic system in the present global conflict of ideologies depends upon the strength it can muster from the minds, hearts, and spiritual convictions of all its people. . . . The Negro wants change in order that he may be brought in line with the *American* standard . . . [, which] must be done not only to preserve and strengthen that standard here at home, but to guarantee its potency in the world struggle against dictatorship.[15]

Ultimately, however, the United Nations failed to act on the NAACP's position.

President Truman did take some measures to counter discrimination in the United States, including creating the President's Committee on Civil Rights. Its December 1947 report concluded that issues abroad should be incorporated into the reasons to address civil rights violations at home. "Our foreign policy is designed to make the United States an enormous, positive influence for peace and progress throughout the world. We have tried to let nothing, not even extreme political differences between ourselves and foreign nations, stand in the way of this goal. But our domestic civil rights shortcomings are a serious obstacle. . . . We cannot escape the fact that our civil rights record has been an issue in world politics."[16]

Truman followed up the report with a special address to Congress on civil rights, on February 2, 1948. He recommended ten specific actions for Congress to take in addressing civil rights violations in the United States, including legislation on a permanent civil rights commission, federal protection against lynching, securing the right to vote, and augmenting current civil rights laws. A few months later—on July 26, 1948—Truman issued Executive Order 9980 and Executive Order 9981, which ordered "fair employment practices" in the federal government and "equality of treatment and opportunity" in the US military, respectively.[17] Of course, Truman's actions on desegregation within the federal government and the military did not put a stop to US racism—and some political leaders laid out the call for Congress to act.

As the world plunged deeper into the Cold War, other events and government actions dealing with race became framed through its lens. US Supreme Court cases such as *Shelley v. Kraemer* in 1948 and *Brown v. Board of Education* in 1954, for example, invoked human rights and nondiscrimination espoused by the United Nations. One amicus curiae brief in the *Shelley* case quoted the legal adviser to the US Department of State as saying, "The United States has been embarrassed in the conduct of foreign relations by acts of discrimination taking place in this country."[18] Justice Department officials, in their amicus curiae brief for the plaintiffs in the *Brown* case, stated, "It is in the context of the present world struggle between freedom and tyranny that the problem of racial discrimination must be viewed." The brief then explored this theme at length: "The United States is trying to prove to the people of the world, of every nationality, race, and color, that a free democracy is the most civilized and most secure form of government yet devised by man." But "racial discrimination furnishes grist for the Communist propaganda mills, and it raises doubts even among friendly nations as to the intensity of our devotion to the democratic faith." US race relations clearly played a vital role in the broader concerns over the future course of world governance.

The brief continued by also quoting Acting Secretary of State Dean Acheson regarding the impact of US race discrimination on foreign affairs: "The undeniable existence of racial discrimination gives unfriendly governments the most effective kind of ammunition for their propaganda warfare. . . . In such countries the view is expressed more and more vocally that the United States is hypocritical in claiming to be the champion of democracy while permitting practices of racial discrimination here in this country."[19] He drew a direct link between the systemic racism in the United States and the problems it posed during the Cold War.

Some US newspapers praised the *Brown* decision, not only for how it would promote racial equality at home but also for how it would affect the rest of the world. "This clarion announcement will . . . stun and silence America's Communist traducers behind the Iron Curtain," the *Pittsburgh Courier* proclaimed. "It will effectively impress upon millions of colored people in Asia and Africa the fact that idealism and social morality can and do prevail in the United States, regardless of race, creed or color."[20]

The decision made international news as well. The *Sydney Morning Herald* declared, "The most powerful item of propaganda available to Communists has been the alleged second-class citizenship of more than 15 million of those Americans." *Brown*, the newspaper suggested, "should go a long way toward dissipating the validity of the Communist contention that Western concepts of democracy are hypocritical." NAACP officials tuned in to other countries' responses and emphasized that African Americans would not be the only ones to gain from the Supreme Court's action. "Steady progress toward integration undermined the charge of hypocrisy so often and so effectively leveled against our country whenever our national leaders espouse human freedom," they submitted in the organization's annual report.[21]

World public opinion would be tested again just a few years later by events in Little Rock, Arkansas. In September 1957, nine African Americans attempted to attend Central High School as the *Brown* decision had ordered. However, Governor Orval Faubus deployed the National Guard to prevent their entry. President Dwight Eisenhower felt compelled to act. "When I became President," he pledged to Faubus, "I took an oath to support and defend the Constitution of the United States. The only assurance I can give you is that the Federal Constitution will be upheld by me by every legal means at my command." Both Secretary of State John Foster Dulles and, later, President Eisenhower in his memoirs suggested that Little Rock was a defining moment during the Cold War. "Overseas," the president recalled, "the mouthpieces of Soviet propaganda in Russia and Europe were blaring out that 'anti-Negro violence' in Little Rock was being 'committed with the clear connivance of the United States government.'" Dulles also acknowledged that "Radio Moscow has been chirping happily about the troubles of integration," especially in Little Rock. The US ambassador to the United Nations, Henry Cabot Lodge, also expressed his frustration when he wrote to Eisenhower, "Here at the United Nations I can see clearly the harm that the riots in Little Rock are doing to our foreign relations. More than two-thirds of the world is nonwhite and the reactions of the representatives of these people is easy to see." Dulles himself also suggested that "this situation was ruining our foreign policy."[22]

Finally, on September 24, 1957, in an address from the White House, Eisenhower explained that he had to act in Little Rock by sending in troops:

> At a time when we face grave situations abroad because of the hatred that Communism bears toward a system of government based on human rights, it would be difficult to exaggerate the harm that is being done to the prestige and influence, and indeed to the safety, of our nation and the world. Our enemies are gloating over this incident and using it everywhere to misrepresent our whole nation. We are portrayed as a violator of those standards of conduct which the peoples of the world united to proclaim in the Charter of the United Nations.[23]

Calling on the country's patriotism, Eisenhower hoped Americans would see the events in Little Rock as a national security concern, not a sectional crisis. Unfortunately, the following year, officials in Arkansas closed the schools in Little Rock rather than integrate.[24] US government officials had to carry on in their debate over foreign policy strategies and their connection to race relations at home.

During the early 1960s, President John Kennedy acknowledged that racial discrimination, tension, and violence had plagued US society—and continued to persist. And he knew the corrosive effects that this had on the country's image abroad.[25] Even during the lead-up to the 1960 presidential election, both Kennedy and his Republican opponent, Richard Nixon, linked the centrality of race relations at home to the status of the United States in the world. "In the world-wide struggle in which we are engaged," Nixon highlighted in a campaign booklet, "racial and religious prejudice is a gun we point at ourselves." He stressed, "I know of nothing that does more harm to United States foreign policy abroad."[26] Likewise, Kennedy's secretary of state, Dean Rusk, expressed in 1961, "The biggest single burden that we carry on our backs in our foreign relations in the 1960s is the problem of racial discrimination here at home."[27]

In June 1961, Malick Sow, Chad's first ambassador to the United States, was himself a victim of this treatment. Driving from New York to Washington, DC, he stopped at a Maryland diner for coffee but was promptly rebuffed. The DC chapter of the Congress of Racial Equality (CORE) led protests against the segregated restaurants along Route 40, and one leader, Julius Hobson, pushed for Freedom Rides throughout all of Maryland. "The international implications of such a project would be tremendous," he urged, "and would serve to rally many individuals and organizations to CORE's support."[28]

Indeed, by 1961, groups such as CORE and the Student Nonviolent Coordinating Committee used these Freedom Rides and lunch counter sit-ins to shed light on the continued injustices of racial discrimination. Even after the Supreme Court, and eventually Congress, contributed the weight of the federal government in the fight for desegregation, inequities continued throughout the country, and civil rights activists fought on. When some of the riders met a mob in Alabama in May 1961 and suffered violence, an exasperated Kennedy pleaded with civil rights adviser Harris Wofford to call off the Freedom Rides, in part, because communists could use the bloodshed as propaganda. Kennedy was also planning to embark on his first trip abroad as president—a meeting with Soviet premier Nikita Khrushchev in Vienna—and wanted to be perceived as a leader in command of his country, particularly in the wake of the Bay of Pigs debacle. The United States Information Agency (USIA), charged with boosting the country's reputation abroad, later revealed, however, that "the Alabama racial incident was highly detrimental" to the country's status in the world and "had dealt a severe blow to US prestige, which might adversely affect its position of leadership in the free world as well as weaken the overall effectiveness of the Western alliance."[29]

Over the next two years, challenges in the South continued. In the fall of 1962, for example, Kennedy sent federal marshals and then National Guard units to Oxford, Mississippi, when white mobs descended on the campus in response to James Meredith's integration of the University of Mississippi. Two people died during the ensuing clash, including a foreign correspondent, and countless more suffered injuries. Some overseas sources lauded what they saw as decisive steps by Kennedy. Upon hearing that the former governor general of India had praised Kennedy's action during the incident, US ambassador Chester Bowles stated that it was "a turning point not only in our struggle against segregation in this country, but in our efforts to make the people of Asia, Africa and Latin America understand what we are trying to do." Moreover, he pointed out, "Three weeks after Oxford, [Guinean leader] Sékou Touré and [Algerian president] Ben Bella were prepared to deny refueling facilities to Soviet planes bound for Cuba during the missile crisis."[30]

Government officials remained vigilant. "Racial prejudice," an October 1962 USIA report declared, "is the chief blemish on the image of the American people abroad, even among citizens of non-Communist nations who hold the United States in high esteem."[31] As senator, Kennedy had condemned Eisenhower's response to the Little Rock incident, and according to journalist Richard Reeves, as president himself, Kennedy wanted "no photo opportunities on his watch that would embarrass the United States all over the world."

But further damning images circulated across the country and the world in 1963, when Birmingham police used dogs and high-pressure fire hoses to attack demonstrators, many of them teenagers and children, marching to desegregate public facilities. Black leaders purposely chose the city to push for integration because of its notoriety for the most severe segregation in the country. Although he asserted that the sight of children being attacked disgusted him, Kennedy chose a subtle response. Rather than deploying the National Guard, he dispatched Burke Marshall, assistant attorney general for the Civil Rights Division of the Department of Justice, to Birmingham to facilitate deliberations for a peaceful resolution. Though he was at first optimistic about a deal forming between the activists and city leaders to desegregate Birmingham's restrooms and other public spaces, Kennedy's hopes were quickly dashed on May 11, when the home of Martin Luther King's brother and a motel that served as King's office suffered damage from firebombs. In response, the city's Black neighborhoods exploded. Kennedy now stood ready to send in the National Guard, but King called for calm, and an uneasy peace emerged.[32]

The world again weighed in. On May 14, the USIA communicated that reporting in many countries proved "moderate and factual" but that the Soviet Union had "stepped up its propaganda on Birmingham over the weekend to campaign proportions, devoting about one fifth of its radio output to the subject." Furthermore, countries in Africa responded negatively to the news coming out of Birmingham. One Nigerian reporter suggested that the United States was on its way to being "the most barbarian state in the world."³³ In Kenya, a newspaper headline read, "Riots Flare in US South—Infants Sent to Jail," and US embassy officials conveyed that the United States had suffered a "heavy beating in Ghana over Birmingham" and "definitely lost ground."³⁴

Other African countries reacted as well. At the end of May, participants at the Conference of Independent African Heads of State and Government assembled in Ethiopia to form the Organization of African Unity (the entity that Malcolm X addressed the following July in Cairo). They took this opportunity to criticize the United States for its continued legacy of discrimination and racial violence, and most recently for what they saw in Birmingham. Ugandan prime minister Milton Obote, for instance, issued a public letter to Kennedy regarding the recent events. "Nothing is more paradoxical than that these events should take place in the United States and at a time when that country is anxious to project its image before the world screen as the archetype of democracy and the champion of freedom."³⁵

Secretary of State Rusk wasted no time in reiterating the detrimental effect race relations continued to have on foreign affairs. In a message sent to posts around the world, he stressed that the administration remained "keenly aware of [the] impact of [the] domestic race problem on [the] US image overseas and on achievement [of] US foreign policy objectives." He continued, "We have a certain amount of time before our racial problem will impinge even more seriously upon our policies and objectives." Importantly, civil rights activists also knew this, and they used that fact to force the Kennedy administration to act more decisively on civil rights policy. "What is demanded now, and at once," author and activist James Baldwin asserted, "is not that Negroes continue to adjust themselves to the cruel racial pressures of life in the United States but that the United States readjust itself to the facts of life in the present world."³⁶ King also made a point of telling activists that "the United States is concerned about its image. When things started happening down here, Mr. Kennedy got disturbed. For Mr. Kennedy . . . is battling for the minds and the hearts of men in Asia and Africa."³⁷

In June, Kennedy called on Congress to pass meaningful civil rights legislation. He also appealed to people's moral compass to put an end to discrimination: "We preach freedom around the world, and we mean it, and we cherish our freedom here at home, but are we to say to the world, and much more importantly, to each other that this is the land of the free except for the Negroes; that we have no second-class citizens except Negroes; that we have no class or caste system, no ghettoes, no master race except with respect to Negroes?"[38] The next week, Kennedy spoke to a joint session of Congress to lay out his vision of legislative reform. In this speech, he focused on the urgent need to desegregate public facilities, schools, and employment and suggested that it would take the federal government, specifically Congress, to lead the way. Moreover, he stressed, not acting would mean "weakening the respect with which the rest of the world regards us."[39]

In July, Kennedy asked Secretary Rusk to appear before the Senate Commerce Committee to articulate the administration's concerns over racial discrimination, its effect on the country's image abroad, and the pressing need for civil rights legislation. "Racial discrimination here at home has important effects on our foreign relations," Rusk testified. "The United States is widely regarded as the home of democracy and the leader of the struggle for freedom, for human rights, for human dignity. We are expected to be the model.... So, our failure to live up to our proclaimed ideals are noted—and magnified and distorted.... Communists clearly regard racial discrimination in the United States as one of their most valuable assets." According to a public opinion poll a few weeks after Rusk's testimony, a solid majority of Americans concurred that race issues at home affected foreign affairs. Some 78 percent of white Americans believed that discrimination damaged the country's image overseas.[40]

Meanwhile, civil rights activists planned a massive rally in DC to keep the momentum for civil rights reform going. The March on Washington stirred both hope and disquiet for the president—hinging on whether the event proved peaceful or violent, and whether it was supportive or critical of the administration. King shared his dream of a better tomorrow with the quarter of a million people stretched out in front of the Lincoln Memorial on August 28, 1963. The day played well to a world audience. But events in Birmingham less than a month later, on September 15, again shone a light on the ugly nature of

US race relations, when a bomb blast at the Sixteenth Street Baptist Church killed four girls. Kennedy strongly denounced the violence, and the world was horrified. Racial violence did not seem to be abating. It appeared that Kennedy would have to act decisively and bring the full power of the federal government to the realm of civil rights if he wanted to burnish the country's image abroad.

The president's chance to make a difference, however, was cut short on November 22, 1963, and his assassination sparked outrage throughout the world, as well as concern about the future of African American civil rights. But Lyndon Johnson appeared ready to carry on Kennedy's legacy. Shortly after the funeral, President Johnson stood before Congress and the world and declared:

> No memorial oration or eulogy could more eloquently honor President Kennedy's memory than the earliest possible passage of the civil rights bill for which he fought so long. We have talked long enough in this country about equal rights. We have talked for one hundred years or more. It is time now to write the next chapter, and to write it in the books of law.
>
> There could be no greater source of strength to this Nation both at home and abroad.[41]

Even so, the war in Vietnam continued to sustain the incongruity between what the United States purported to be to the rest of the world and the harsh realities of how some citizens existed in US society. African Americans—who still strove for rights at home—bore much of the burden of fighting a war abroad. The Black Panther Party asserted that African Americans should not be forced to "kill other people of color in the world who, like Black people, are being victimized by the white racist government of America."[42]

As was the case throughout the post–World War II era, activists reiterated that US race relations should continue to be a "world problem" and "a problem for humanity," just as Malcolm X had asserted in 1964. But, for the most part, by the end of Johnson's administration, race relations and Cold War foreign policy were not inextricably intertwined. And with Richard Nixon in office, the Cold War started to become less acute in general as détente took hold. As both desegregation at home and decolonialization abroad gained traction, US race relations changed in scope and tenor when it came to Cold War considerations.[43]

NOTES

1. George Breitman, ed., *Malcolm X Speaks: Selected Speeches and Statements* (New York: Grove Press, 1994), 75.

2. Michael L. Krenn, ed., *Race and US Foreign Policy during the Cold War* (New York: Garland, 1998), ix.

3. See John David Skrentny, "The Effect of the Cold War on African-American Civil Rights: America and the World Audience, 1945–1968," *Theory and Society* 27, no. 2 (1998): 237–285.

4. Krenn, *Race and US Foreign Policy*, vii.

5. Tilden J. LeMelle, "Race, International Relations, US Foreign Policy, and the African Liberation Struggle," in Krenn, *Race and US Foreign Policy*, 161.

6. See James H. Meriwether, "Worth a Lot of Negro Votes," *Teaching the JAH* 95, no. 3 (December 2008), http://archive.oah.org/special-issues/teaching/2008_12/article.html.

7. Robert L. Harris Jr., "Racial Equity and the United Nations Charter," in Krenn, *Race and US Foreign Policy*, 2.

8. Harris, "Racial Equity and the United Nations Charter," 12–13.

9. Paul Gordon Lauren, "First Principles of Racial Equality: History and the Politics and Diplomacy of Human Rights Provisions in the United Nations Charter," in Krenn, *Race and US Foreign Policy*, 44–45.

10. Krenn, *Race and US Foreign Policy*, ix.

11. Lauren, "First Principles of Racial Equality," 45.

12. James L. Roark, "American Black Leaders: The Response to Colonialism and the Cold War, 1943–1953," in *The African American Voice in US Foreign Policy since World War II*, ed. Michael L. Krenn (New York: Garland, 1998), 44.

13. Harry S. Truman, "Special Message to the Congress on Greece and Turkey: The Truman Doctrine," March 12, 1947, American Presidency Project, https://www.presidency.ucsb.edu/node/232818; Mary L. Dudziak, "Desegregation as a Cold War Imperative," in Krenn, *Race and US Foreign Policy*, 189–190.

14. Mark Solomon, "Black Critics of Colonialism and the Cold War," in Krenn, *African American Voice in US Foreign Policy*, 67–68.

15. Dudziak, "Desegregation as Cold War Imperative," 191–192.

16. Mary L. Dudziak, *Cold War Civil Rights: Race and the Image of American Democracy* (Princeton, NJ: Princeton University Press, 2000), 80.

17. Harry S. Truman, "Special Message to Congress on Civil Rights," February 2, 1948, American Presidency Project, https://www.presidency.ucsb.edu/node/232898; Truman, "Executive Order 9980—Regulations Governing Fair Employment Practices Within the Federal Establishment," July 26, 1948, American Presidency Project, https://www.presidency.ucsb.edu/node/278504; Truman, "Executive Order 9981—Establishing the President's Committee on Equality of Treatment and Opportunity in the Armed Services," July 26, 1948, American Presidency Project, https://www.presidency.ucsb.edu/node/231614.

18. Lauren, "First Principles of Racial Equality," 49.

19. Brief for the United States as amicus curiae, *Brown v. Board of Education*, 347 US 483 (1954), filed December 1952, 6–7.

20. Dudziak, "Desegregation as Cold War Imperative," 231.

21. Mary L. Dudziak, "*Brown* as a Cold War Case," *Journal of American History* 91, no. 1 (2004): 36. See also Richard Lentz and Karla K. Gower, *The Opinions of Mankind: Racial Issues, Press, and Propaganda in the Cold War* (Columbia: University of Missouri Press, 2010), 79–83.

22. Dudziak, *Cold War Civil Rights*, 117–119, 131; Lentz and Gower, *Opinions of Mankind*, 98–102.

23. Dwight D. Eisenhower, "Radio and Television Address to the American People on the Situation in Little Rock," September 24, 1957, American Presidency Project, https://www.presidency.ucsb.edu/node/233623.

24. Melba Pattillo Beals, *Warriors Don't Cry*, abridged ed. (New York: Simon Pulse, 1995), 218–219.

25. Ofra Friesel, "Changing the American Race Narrative, 1962–1965: Transparency as a Guiding Rule in American Cold War Diplomacy," *Journal of Social History* 49, no. 1 (2015): 168–169.

26. Skrentny, "Effect of the Cold War on African-American Civil Rights," 261.

27. Renee Romano, "Moving Beyond 'The Movement That Changed the World': Bringing the History of the Cold War into Civil Rights Museums," *Public Historian* 31, no. 2 (2009): 35–36.

28. Dudziak, *Cold War Civil Rights*, 153; Romano, "Moving Beyond 'The Movement That Changed the World.'"

29. Dudziak, *Cold War Civil Rights*, 158–159; Jonathan Rosenberg and Zachary Karabell, *Kennedy, Johnson, and the Quest for Justice: The Civil Rights Tapes* (New York: W. W. Norton, 2003), 250.

30. Dudziak, *Cold War Civil Rights*, 165; Lentz and Gower, *Opinions of Mankind*, 143–147.

31. Dudziak, *Cold War Civil Rights*, 166.

32. Julian E. Zelizer, *The Fierce Urgency of Now: Lyndon Johnson, Congress, and the Battle for the Great Society* (New York: Penguin, 2015), 43–46.

33. Dudziak, *Cold War Civil Rights*, 169-170; Thomas Borstelmann, *The Cold War and the Color Line: American Race Relations in the Global Arena* (Cambridge, MA: Harvard University Press, 2003), 160.

34. Dudziak, *Cold War Civil Rights*, 169–170.

35. Dudziak, *Cold War Civil Rights*, 169–172; Lentz and Gower, *Opinions of Mankind*, 162, 167–168.

36. Dudziak, *Cold War Civil Rights*, 177–178; James Baldwin, *The Price of the Ticket: Collected Nonfiction, 1948–1985* (Boston: Beacon Press, 1985), 274.

37. Borstelmann, *Cold War and the Color Line*, 160.

38. John F. Kennedy, "Radio and Television Report to the American People on Civil Rights," June 11, 1963, American Presidency Project, https://www.presidency.ucsb.edu/node/236675.

39. John F. Kennedy, "Special Message to the Congress on Civil Rights and Job Opportunities," June 19, 1963, American Presidency Project, https://www.presidency.ucsb.edu/node/236711.

40. Dudziak, *Cold War Civil Rights*, 184–185, 187.

41. Lyndon B. Johnson, "Address Before a Joint Session of Congress," November 27, 1963, American Presidency Project, https://www.presidency.ucsb.edu/node/238734.

42. Peter B. Levy, "Blacks and the Vietnam War," in Krenn, *African American Voice in US Foreign Policy*, 284.

43. Borstelmann, *Cold War and the Color Line*, 222.

GUNS, MANHOOD, AND THE COLD WAR

ANGELA F. KEATON

In his 1946 work *Hunting North American Deer,* noted conservationist, hunter, and writer Arthur Hawthorne Carhart lauded the many benefits of outdoor recreation, emphasizing, "There is hardly a situation that cannot be met if one is fortified with a fire and his gun." Hunting offered a special allure and captured men's imagination and loyalty. "It's something American that calls you back," he insisted. "The free America, where it is a birthright to bear arms, where you have the privilege of the sovereign to hunt without let or hindrance, except for the rules of the game and the laws of the land that you and your brothers have set up to guide human conduct." When reflecting on the hunt, "You forget how cold it was up on the ridge, how the new boots you wore pinched a little at the heel, how you wondered at the time why in Sheol you came all the way out here every year just to get half frozen, spavined, full of aches, blessed with blisters. You wonder at the moment; but around the table, over the cups of coffee, you know."[1]

Carhart did not need to articulate the many meanings of the hunt for his readers. Confident in this shared knowledge, he knew that readers agreed that a hunter's masculinity would be tested by the ability to endure harsh conditions in order to kill an animal with a gun. In addition, though very few hunters after 1945 were "pot hunters" who killed game to provide meat for their families' survival, Carhart and his readers nonetheless relished the hunt for the opportunity it afforded to escape the pressures of modern life, particularly domesticity and other effeminizing influences. Carhart and his compatriots also believed that they carried on traditions of hunting and gun use that reinforced American heritage, a worthy quest during the early Cold War era. Ultimately, Carhart's description of the hunting experience serves as a window into attitudes about one of America's most popular pastimes of the early post–World War II era.

Before the post–World War II explosion of hunters, sport hunting struggled to overcome a tarnished reputation and declining popularity as a legitimate outdoor pursuit.[2] The advent of World War II, however, proved a godsend to those struggling to rehabilitate the image and enlarge the population of hunters. Magazine articles and advertising campaigns harnessed the war effort to convince Americans that hunters made better soldiers.[3] During the war, Colonel Charles A. Ranlett authored multiple articles for *Sports Afield*, explaining the usefulness of applying shooting skills to the battlefield. "On the big game hunt or the field of battle," he insisted, "the best gunner is the man who can shoot his rifle skillfully at targets which do not stand still."[4] David Newell, editor of *Field & Stream*, agreed. In an article about the benefits of hunting for young boys, he declared, "If he can hit a running deer, he can hit a running Jap."[5] Similar articles peppered the pages of outdoor magazines during the war, helping to restore the image of hunting and hunters.

The post–World War II era also heralded a period in which interest in and use of firearms significantly increased. Millions of World War II servicemen had become familiar with firearms during their service training or combat experience. Returning to the states, they sought firearms for recreational purposes. Nine million demobilized veterans brought their interest in firearms home, and "tens of thousands of ex-GIs joined the NRA."[6] The interest in the sporting use of guns grew so large that the National Rifle Association witnessed a doubling of its membership.[7] At the same time, manufacturers seeking to maintain wartime production levels increased their efforts to market their wares. A reported one-quarter of the NRA's revenue came from gun advertisers in the postwar era.[8] As a result, a type of symbiosis resulted between consumers and producers that fanned the flames of steadily growing firearms ownership. Many of the consumers of those guns were hunters, fueling what can be termed "a postwar renaissance in hunting."[9] *Life* magazine put the number of hunters in fall 1954 at 15 million, "twice the number that hunted before World War II."[10]

Yet the increased popularity of hunting and firearms cannot be attributed entirely to wartime rhetoric. The Cold War itself presented circumstances that attracted men to the sport in droves. Added to concerns about creeping communism and the economic impact of returning GIs were fears about new geopolitical realities that led people to construct bomb shelters, store canned goods, and strike a balance between the destructive yet promising powers of the atom. The specter of the Cold War suffused the magazines Americans read (*Parenting, Life, Field & Stream*), the television shows they watched (*The Man from U.N.C.L.E.*), the games their children played (Uranium Rush), and the food they consumed (survival biscuits, anyone?). "Duck and cover" became a routine part of life, not just a vehicle to fame for a quirky turtle named Bert.

Beyond pop culture's harnessing of atomic imagery to financially capitalize on the moment, the fact of living in a nuclear world dominated news headlines. The Cold War became more than a term to describe new geopolitical realities. It was fast becoming a way of life. As such, the Cold War's tentacles reached into every cultural crevice, weaponizing recreation, gender roles, and American history in the fight against communism.

In this context, among white, middle-and working-class men, hunting became a favorite weapon in the war against the Red menace in the postwar era, especially between 1945 and 1963.[11] The assumption that hunting and guns formed an integral part of the nation's heritage became a cornerstone of hunting, and by extension, of gun culture. Dismayed by pronouncements about the decline of the American male and communists' desire to exploit that vulnerability, many men also embraced hunting to showcase and cultivate a particular strain of masculinity. Fearful of threats from social change at home and new geopolitical realities abroad, men hunted to reassert their control over a rapidly changing world through experiences like those described by Carhart. In waging these battles, hunting with firearms became a panacea for the ills of the age, offering a means to cultivate masculinity, practice martial skills, and connect with frontier heritage. As a result, American gun culture dramatically intensified, becoming more deeply intertwined with notions about gender and American heritage.

Publications about outdoor recreation and shooting proliferated after World War II, providing men with constant reminders about the importance to American history of hunting and guns, and their restorative powers for the woes beleaguering men of the atomic age. Titles such as *Sports Afield, Field & Stream*, and *Outdoor Life* each enjoyed more than 1 million monthly readers.[12] By the early 1960s, interest in hunting had quadrupled the prewar circulation of outdoor magazine staples *Field & Stream* and *Outdoor Life*.[13] Not limited to merely magazines, stories and advice about hunting appeared in numerous popular books. For instance, shooting editor Warren Page of *Field & Stream* witnessed his collected edition of writings, *One Man's Wilderness*, published seventeen times between 1952 and 1970.

Outdoor writers like Page wielded considerable talent and influence, producing literature so popular that their names—Jack O'Connor, Archibald Rutledge, Havilah Babcock—became synonymous with superb writing and award-winning hunting skill. These and other outdoor writers helped hunters articulate the meanings of their hunting and shooting experiences while also molding the contours of American gun culture. One of the most notable features to emerge in this culture was the role of the gun and hunting in American history.

Many postwar American men viewed hunting as a means to connect with American heritage and to forge a patriotic identity at a time when communism threatened the very way of American life they sought to celebrate. Looking backwards, hunters and gun enthusiasts found solace in a past full of legendary, revered gunslingers, frontiersmen, soldiers, hunters, and even presidents. Postwar popular culture showcased guns and the men who wielded them as the architects of America, as well as the evangelists and protectors of its values. Outdoor writers, especially, rarely divorced the importance of hunting and its role in the American past from the gun. "As you trace each step toward the rifle of today," Carhart explained, "you will gather appreciation of the tradition back of the gun you own. For there is a fine American heritage back of every rifle you take into the field—the heritage of the American rifleman."[14] Rutledge, whose prolific writing garnered him a national reputation as one of the twentieth century's most popular outdoor writers, enjoyed a devout following from readers of his hunting books and features in *Field & Stream*.[15] Referred to as "Flintlock" or "Dixie Deer-Slayer," he reminded readers, "In a deep sense, this great land of ours was won for us by hunters."[16]

The most important tool of those hunting heroes, the gun, did not escape attention. The executive director of the NRA, Louis F. Lucas, articulated what many Americans believed when he wrote in 1959, "One of the prize possessions of manhood since our forefathers first settled America always has been the gun." In this American past, "It was necessary and accepted that young and old alike be intimately acquainted with firearms and use them as tools of everyday life."[17] Gun expert C. E. Hagie asserted, "Of no other country in the world can it be said that its very existence rests on the rifle as a foundation—that its independence sprang from proficiency with the rifle, and that the rifle was basically responsible for its expansion and development; and in no other country than the United States is practically every male citizen familiar with the rifle as a part of his civilian activities."[18] Leveraging history, writers cemented a facet of American gun culture.[19]

The association between guns and the formation, and implicitly the survival, of America held particular resonance. At a time when civil defense preparations were not mere abstractions, reminders of past victories reassured uneasy Americans and gave them confidence that with enough fortitude and guns, they would again triumph over threats posed to national security. The constant references to hunting and gun use as a democratic tradition helped gun culture grow dramatically, because many men defined hunting as a quintessentially "American" activity and therefore an antidote to creeping communism. Rhetoric about pioneer reliance on the gun grew as a defining and enduring feature of American gun culture.

Though it was a potent force in Cold War America, however, the glorification of a mythic, American heritage did not act as the only factor intensifying men's attachment to firearms and hunting. A preoccupation with maintaining strict gender roles also fed the hunting craze. Americans saw their fears about the instability of gender roles captured in allusions to "trousered mothers and dishwashing dads."[20] Men's changing roles especially caused concern, as evidenced in magazine articles with titles such as "Our Fighting Men Have Gone Soft," "The Abdicating Male," and "The New Burdens of Masculinity," while books like *The Decline of the American Male* appeared on bookshelves across the nation.[21]

A new form of masculinity based on leisure, conformity, and corporate work threatened to eclipse the dominant, or hegemonic, masculine ideal of the self-made man that emphasized competition, individualism, ruggedness, and entrepreneurship. Fear that the hegemonic masculine ideal might be upended produced shock waves.[22] Arthur Schlesinger, a noted historian, political consultant, and Pulitzer Prize–winning author, lamented, "What has happened to the American male? For a long time, he seemed utterly confident in his manhood, sure of his masculine role in society, easy and definite in his sense of sexual identity." Schlesinger noted a change during the mid-twentieth century, however, when "the male role had plainly lost its rugged clarity of outline. Today men are more and more conscious of maleness not as a fact but as a problem. The ways by which American men affirm their masculinity are uncertain and obscure."[23] Another essayist complained, "Today's breadwinner must be a part-time nursemaid, kitchen helper, handyman and mechanic." He warned, "The danger, of course, is that we will become too soft, too complacent and too home-oriented to meet the challenge of other dynamic nations like China and the Soviet Union."[24]

Domesticity posed a fundamental threat to male virility. J. Robert Moskin, an editor of *Look* and a World War II veteran, lamented, "Our younger generation [of men] already shows signs of being fagged out and of having lost . . . the 'hunting instinct.'"[25] Gallup statistics also provoked considerable hand-wringing when 1949 polling revealed that "four out of ten husbands were helping to cook" and "nearly a third of all American husbands were doing the dishes." Polls in 1952 indicated that men had slid deeper into the domestic abyss when respondents agreed that if a dominant party in a marriage could be identified, "a majority of both sexes said it was the wife." Wives' power even extended to dominating husbands' clothing choices, resulting in such unforgivable atrocities as men's slacks "being made in peach and lemon" and men "wriggling into girdles" at unprecedented rates.[26] Locked in an epic "struggle against the taffeta tide," American men worried about "a general male emasculation" at the hands of wives who rid the house of their hunting prints. Seeking to escape castration by decoration, millions of men grabbed their guns and escaped to the great outdoors.[27]

Hunting provided a fitting antidote to the detrimental influence of women. If one wished to find "the hard core of resistance to woman's insane determination to supercivilize the male animal," a *Field & Stream* article urged readers to look no further than "the outdoorsman." Among the "stout men of the fish and the fowl" could be found the only men "who will refuse to knuckle under" the control of women.[28] Likewise, in 1960 the *Saturday Evening Post* posited:

> Deer hunting is mostly an excuse. It's an excuse to get away from jutting-jawed bosses, mean-dispositioned customers, international crises; from shaving, neckties, the 8:10, desks, memos, boredom. And—even though you love them dearly—the women and the family. You get away into a world of pipe-smoking, poker playing, wood smoke, wet wool and sweaty males. . . . For a few days you're not a little person any longer. You're a he-man among men. In the woods with that rifle in hand you're three sizes bigger than Paul Bunyan.[29]

Hunting offered a remedy for all types of anxiety generated by the Cold War. Hoping to reassert their manliness "with that rifle in hand," hunters deepened attachment to firearms by investing them with the power to augment their masculinity as they vicariously became a rugged pioneer hunter. Hunting became a preferred leisure activity because in contrast to "little lisping men," hunters could show they cared little if "a lavender tie will match mauve socks." Instead, they spent their energies developing "discipline and iron nerve" through the pursuit of game.[30]

In this climate, hunting became a concrete activity that reaffirmed the abstract concepts of masculinity and patriotism while also propelling gun sales to new heights. As early as 1947, the Winchester gun company reported that only a "dent" had been made in the "unprecedentedly large demand for guns." Gun sales amounted to $41 million the first six months of 1947, which surpassed the total of more than $28 million for the entire year of 1946.[31] While sales of hunting guns grew, so too did a gun culture rooted in a mythic American past, heterosexual virility, and resistance to domesticity. In the postwar era, an American gun culture crystallized around these various notions associated with the sporting use of guns.

Hunters often commented about the important relationship between firearms and masculinity. Robert Ruark, a well-known hunter, respected outdoor writer, and one of the associate editors of *Field & Stream*, described how a quail hunt became the proving ground for masculinity because of how a man did, or did not, handle his gun. He described a hunter whose "heart is pounding a rumba-beat. He is carrying a shotgun, generally with a 26-to 28-inch barrel. The gauge of the gun is an index to the ability of the man to prove his manhood at that moment. If it is a 12-gauge, he is so-so at his business. If it is a 16, he is pretty good. If it's a 20-gauge he is excellent, and if it's a .410 he is bragging."[32] The larger the gauge, the better shot, and the more skilled he will prove himself.

Ruark added, "At the very moment he feels like a bull-fighter awaiting a *toro bravo*, a big-game hunter preparing to meet an African buffalo's charge, a soldier verging on a desperate destruction of a machine-gun emplacement. . . . His reputation is at stake." Even hunting small birds became a test of masculinity equal to that of bullfighting or warfare. Waiting for the dogs to retrieve the birds, the hunter "lights a cigarette, and for a moment he is Belmonte, the bull-fighter. He is Dwight Eisenhower. He is Clark Gable. . . . He is David, standing over the prostrate form of Goliath. He is one hell of a big guy—to himself, if he is alone—to the others, if he is accompanied."[33] If the hunter wields his firearm successfully, he not only joins a brotherhood of masculine icons but also has given a fine performance, demonstrating his own masculinity. Firearms, then, became required tools for the performance of masculinity on the hunting stage.[34]

Hunting and shooting provided men a means to exert some control over their lives in the face of a looming communist threat. The hunter could feel quite safe anywhere if he had his gun. Jack O'Connor, who received mountains of fan mail during his thirty-one-year tenure as shooting editor of *Outdoor Life*, explained, "The hunter who stalks the grizzly above timberline in some great open basin, who has an adequately powerful rifle, who can shoot, and who keeps his cool, is in about as much danger as he is in his living room sitting before the fireplace reading a book." He elaborated, "The combination of a powerful rifle and a well-placed shot made the grizzly about as dangerous as a chipmunk."[35] Armed and properly trained, a hunter could triumph over any threat, from menacing communists to domesticating wives.

Sportsmen also frequently invoked sexual metaphors and gendered language to describe their connection to guns. Numerous sources characterized relationships with guns as marriages, stories and advertisements routinely employed sexualized language to discuss firearms, and outdoor writers often penned stories romanticizing their bond with specific guns. Some accounts even encouraged gun owners to find pleasure in having a tactile experience with their firearms. Chapman J. Milling explained that a man's collection of guns "is not only pleasing to own and to fondle with pride; it is also very highly practical."[36] Likewise, in the 1951 *Field & Stream* Christmas gift guide, shoppers looking for a gift for Dad are urged to find out which "shotgun Pop has been fondling down at the store."[37]

It may seem surprising that men would mention or even encourage other men to fondle an object so closely associated with males in a period of intense gender scrutiny. The frequent use of sexualized language when discussing guns indicates that such rhetoric was the norm, however. Coupling guns and sexual language raised no cries of alarm about deviant behavior because it was accepted that guns elicited pleasure.

Despite all of the talk about rugged masculinity, hunters could become quite sentimental about their firearms. The gun remained an integral part of an experience that granted men much pleasure. At times, various writers characterized the relationship between a man and his gun as a marriage, because some men considered their guns loyal companions. For instance, Archibald Rutledge explained, "It just is not natural for a man to shoot well with a strange gun. And one reason is that under these circumstances most men may have a nervous feeling that they are stepping out on the Little Woman who has been faithful to them so long." It would not be unusual for men to engage in a monogamous relationship with their preferred gun, and Rutledge enthusiastically encouraged readers to mate with their gun for life.[38]

The connection between man and gun could have been described as a friendship. Or Rutledge could have chosen to discuss caliber, design, or any other feature. Instead, he chose to use the metaphor of matrimony. "Before he can come really to count on his gun, a man has to be married to it," he insisted. "And usually, as in marriage itself, after a few unhappy experiences and disillusions, the two may settle down to many long years of success and happiness."[39] That a relationship existed at all between man and gun, and that Rutledge chose such a metaphor, suggests that hunters would readily recognize his meaning.

Writers and hunters often discussed firearms using the language of romance, at times expressing their ardor for guns and giving them female traits. Jack O'Connor once admitted, "I like a handgun. I hold a shotgun in high regard; but rifles—well, I love the darned things. To me they stand for wilderness, mystery, romance." One would of course expect the twentieth-century's foremost gun writer to be enthusiastic about guns, but his choice of language uncovers the nature of that enthusiasm. In another piece, O'Connor explained, "There are almost as many different varieties of taste in firearms as there are in women. My own taste in both is on the conservative side. I like graceful shape along classic lines in either a rifle or shotgun stock."[40]

In this description, the gun is cast as an attractive woman, reflecting the routine feminization of guns. Even those who were not gun authorities, like business journalist John Carlyle, similarly feminized guns, stating that riflemen's weapons were "as delicately made as watches and are beautiful as girls at a fountain."[41] In these descriptions, read by countless numbers of men, the gun became a feminized object of beauty that evoked an emotional attachment, rather than just another piece of hunting gear.

The sexualization of guns and males' emotional attachment to them added another dimension to gun culture. For instance, O'Conner, who was noted for both his gun expertise and his clear, accessible writing, decided that an anecdote about women would be the most effective means to illustrate to readers his main point about gun stock design. In a description of gun stocks, O'Connor explained, "Sometimes very slight changes in curves and angles make the difference between a beautiful and graceful stock and a homely and ordinary one." He then illustrated his point:

> I am thinking now of two sisters I once knew. Both were blond, witty and charming. But one, though she was a fine cook and had a heart of gold, was a rather ordinary lass who got by on her good disposition and winning ways. The other was a stunning beauty, a creature so lovely that one look sent young men's blood pressure skyward and set them to uttering wild hoarse cries and tearing telephone directories apart with their bare hands. Yet these two girls looked much alike, and it was easy to see they were sisters. What made the difference was an angle here, a line there, small dimensional differences in features.[42]

Writing that compared a gun's features to women's appearance helped O'Connor appeal to his readers and, in the words of Robert Anderson, accounted for

"Jack's ability to write of such esoteric subjects as the aesthetics of gun stock design in a way that the average man could relate to."[43] O'Connor knew the best means to appeal to and educate his readers—to sexualize guns. Even if it was intended as an entertaining rhetorical trope, however, such descriptions nonetheless popularized the feminization of firearms and made sexualizing them a standard practice.

One of the best examples of framing discussion about guns in the context of women and romance is a story by Havilah Babcock. Known in hunting circles as the "the nation's leading expert on quail shooting," and a popular writer, Babcock authored a piece about his own relationship with his favorite firearm, a Parker double. Reminiscing about his longing for the gun, he began the story by recalling, "I once called her Fallen Lady. Not inappropriately, either, for it should have been apparent to any kindly and discerning eye that the aged fowling piece had been quite a lady in her day." Settling into a rocking chair, he recounted how he "smiled sadly, fingering the well-remembered gash in her once comely stock."

He recounted how he came to meet Fallen Lady. Fearing embarrassment because he had lapsed into a shooting slump, Babcock reluctantly agreed to tag along as a spectator on a quail hunting trip, and then spotted a large covey of quail. Just as he chastised himself for not bringing a gun, he spotted at the edge of the field a rabbit hunter, "Unc Spiller," who had one. Despite a warning that the gun was unsuitable for quail, Babcock insisted on borrowing it. Describing what happened next, he declared, "I had no recollection of putting the gun up or of pulling the trigger. It seemed to have shot itself. That feeling, I have since decided, is the touchstone of perfect gun fit." It seemed to be love at first shot.

Babcock later yearned for the gun to such a degree that his desperation drove him to rent it over a period of time, because the owner consistently refused to sell it. Babcock's infatuation was so intense that he admitted to driving sixty miles round trip to use it, and he confessed, "Three times during the week following, I sneaked by Unc Spiller's and rented his gun. And this kept up week after week . . . the countless side trips to Unc Spiller's was running me ragged." Unc Spiller, enjoying the rental profits, teased Babcock, "Yessir, I sho' got myself a fat possum!" Babcock, rendered irrational by his obsession, had already paid Spiller exorbitant rental fees and agreed that "he did indeed have himself a fat possum."

At last, Unc Spiller relented and agreed to sell Babcock the gun. "Back at home," Babcock gleefully proclaimed, "still shaken, I hurried to my room and locked the door against interruption. . . . I would gloat over my beauty alone. I'd doll her up in just a bit." In a cruel twist of fate, however, the makeover revealed that the barrels were Damascus, lethal to the shooter if used with modern, smokeless powder. Babcock was devastated to learn that the object of his affection was a femme fatale. Years later he wistfully recalled, "Since that time I have often thought of Fallen Lady and of our brief but fruitful romance. I came out of that experience with a conviction I have since verified again and again: the feeling a gunner has toward his gun is part of the gun."[44]

In the gendered drama of hunting, the gun became a key prop in assisting men to perform this strain of masculinity.[45] Babcock, a popular writer with a large fan base, anthropomorphized his gun because he knew it would resonate with his audience.[46] Feminizing firearms also reinforced the heterosexual masculinity of hunting culture and fit well into the expectations for the performances of masculinity demanded by the era.[47]

Sport hunting grew in popularity as a leisure activity from the end of World War II through much of the 1960s as a result of various facets of Cold War society and culture. In that tumultuous decade, however, hunting faced challenges from several quarters, most notably the gun control movement that began to formalize after the assassination of President John F. Kennedy. Prior to that tragedy, hunting with guns had spoken to the anxieties of the age, including assumptions about declining masculinity, Cold War geopolitical uncertainties, and the need to demonstrate Americanness.

In the early postwar era, then, hunting and firearms enjoyed popular support even as they gained meaning as important symbols. Outdoor writers and their hunting audiences considered firearms significant because of what they afforded—a connection to a heroic heritage and a remedy for waning masculinity. Prowess, whether sexual or that represented by the killing of game via mastery of one's favorite "lady," offered men an antidote to some of the ills of the era. Millions of men escaped the domesticating influence of suburbs, work, and wives by pursuing wild animals with their guns, just as they imagined their pioneer predecessors had done.

The use of firearms and hunting to combat atomic age anxieties became one of the most significant, if unintended, features of the Cold War. Due to the popularity of hunting, gun culture deepened its roots and acquired new significance, raising the stakes for the unfettered ability to own and access guns. After all, what would it bode if hunting and gun use, key means to display martial manliness and patriotism, were circumscribed or eliminated?

The conviction that opposition to hunting and guns was antidemocratic, antimale, and pro-domesticity helps to explain the lack of any successful widespread efforts to regulate firearms during this period. In fact, in the early Cold War era, public officials, psychiatrists, school administrators, parenting experts, a host of social scientists, and pop culture icons routinely encouraged and celebrated the use of firearms by adults and children as a healthy, patriotic recreation that had benefits for instilling proper gender roles and strengthening the nation's defenses. A formal gun control movement in America did not, and perhaps could not, operate in such a high tide of support for the recreational use of guns. Hunting had come to embody so many ideals and to satisfy so many needs that a complex gun culture became entrenched among the throngs of postwar hunters—a group that would dig in its heels and join forces with other gun rights advocates in the coming decades to form the backbone of opposition to almost any effort to control guns. This is perhaps one of the most notable, if overlooked, impacts of the Cold War on American life.

NOTES

1. Arthur Hawthorne Carhart, *Hunting North American Deer* (New York: Macmillan, 1946), 150, 227.

2. For more on hunting and conservation at this time, see Andrea L. Smalley, "'Our Lady Sportsmen': Gender, Class, and Conservation in Sport Hunting Magazines, 1873–1920," *Journal of the Gilded Age and Progressive Era* 4 (October 2005): 355–380. Also see Louis S. Warren, *The Hunter's Game: Poachers and Conservationists in Twentieth-Century America* (New Haven, CT: Yale University Press, 1999); John F. Reiger, *American Sportsmen and the Origins of Conservation*, 3rd ed., revised (Corvallis: Oregon State University Press, 2000); and Tara Kathleen Kelly, *The Hunter Elite: Manly Sport, Hunting Narratives, and American Conservation, 1880–1925* (Lawrence: University Press of Kansas, 2018).

3. Thomas L. Altherr, "Mallards and Messerschmitts: American Hunting Magazines and the Image of American Hunting During World War II," *Journal of Sport History* 14, no. 2 (Summer 1987): 151–163.

4. Charles A. Ranlett, "The Rifle and Moving Targets," *Sports Afield*, June 1942, 14.

5. David M. Newell, "Food for Thought," *Field & Stream* 47 (October 1942), 15.

6. Gregg Lee Carter, *The Gun Control Movement* (New York: Twayne, 1997), 69.

7. Richard Feldman, *Ricochet: Confessions of a Gun Lobbyist* (Hoboken, NJ: John Wiley and Sons, 2008), 38.

8. Stanley Meisler, "Get Your Gun from the Army," *The Nation*, June 8, 1964, 569.

9. Feldman, *Ricochet*, 38.

10. "Bumper Year for Guns and Game," *Life* 37, no. 21 (November 22, 1954), 33.

11. Women and African Americans also hunted. Unfortunately, little scholarship has been produced on either group as recreational hunters, particularly during this era. This study focuses on white males because they dominate popular literature of the era.

12. David Abrahamson, *Magazine-Made America: The Cultural Transformation of the Postwar Periodical* (Cresskill, NJ: Hampton Press, 1996), 53.

13. Andrea L. Smalley, "'I Just Like to Kill Things': Women, Men, and the Gender of Sport Hunting in the United States, 1940–1973," *Gender and History* 17, no. 1: 183–209.

14. Carhart, *Hunting North American Deer*, 126.

15. Archibald Rutledge's writing covered numerous hunting topics and appeared in a variety of publications, ranging from boys' magazines to scientific journals. James Casada, ed., *America's Greatest Game Bird: Archibald Rutledge's Turkey Hunting Tales* (Columbia: University of South Carolina Press, 1994), 209. Rutledge, South Carolina's first poet laureate (1934), earned three Pulitzer Prize nominations, a John Burroughs Medal for nature writing (1930), and seventeen honorary degrees. Rob Wegner, "Flintlock: A Dixie Deer-Slayer," *Deer & Deer Hunting*, June 1990, 23–44. See also Jim Casada, *Remembering the Greats: Profiles of Turkey Hunting's Old Masters* (Rock Hill, SC: High Country Press, 2012).

16. Casada, *America's Greatest Game Bird*, 209. See also Archibald Rutledge, "An American Hunter," in James A. Casada, ed., *Hunting and Home in the Southern Heartland: The Best of Archibald Rutledge* (Columbia: University of South Carolina Press, 1992), 30.

17. Louis F. Lucas, "A Man and His Gun," *American Rifleman* (1959), reprinted in *Gun Digest*, ed. John T. Amber (Chicago: Gun Digest Company, 1961), inside front cover.

18. C. E. Hagie, *The American Rifle for Hunting and Target Shooting* (New York: Macmillan, 1944), v. See also Daniel Justin Herman, *Hunting and the American Imagination* (Washington, DC: Smithsonian Institution Press, 2001), xii.

19. Louis S. Warren also notes Americans' reverence for hunters. See Warren, *The Hunter's Game: Poachers and Conservationists in Twentieth-Century America* (New Haven, CT: Yale University Press, 1997), 7; Charles Bergman, *Orion's Legacy: A Cultural History of Man as Hunter* (New York: Dutton, 1996).

20. Dorothy Barclay, "Trousered Mothers and Dishwashing Dads," *New York Times*, April 28, 1957, 25.

21. Hanson Baldwin, "Our Fighting Men Have Gone Soft," *Saturday Evening Post*, August 8, 1959, 13–15, 82–84; Philip Wylie, "The Abdicating Male," *Playboy*, September 1958, 51–52, 77–79; Helen Mayer Hacker, "The New Burdens of Masculinity," *Marriage and Family Living*, August 1957, 227–233; editors of *Look* magazine, *The Decline of the American Male* (New York: Random House, 1958).

22. For more on the transition from one masculine ideal to another, see Michael Kimmel,

Manhood in America: A Cultural History (Oxford: Oxford University Press, 2006). For more on nineteenth-century masculinity, see E. Anthony Rotundo, *American Manhood: Transformations in Masculinity from the Revolution to the Modern Era* (New York: Basic Books, 1993).

23. Arthur Schlesinger, "The Crisis of American Masculinity," in *The Politics of Hope* (Boston: Houghton-Mifflin, 1963), 237. See also James Gilbert, *Men in the Middle: Searching for Masculinity in the 1950s* (Chicago: University of Chicago Press, 2005), 63.

24. William Attwood, "Why Does He Work So Hard?," in *Look* magazine, *Decline of the American Male*, 58, 64.

25. J. Robert Moskin, "Why Do Women Dominate Him?," in *Look* magazine, *Decline of the American Male*, 3, 11.

26. Richard Gehman, "Toupees, Girdles and Sun Lamps: The American Male," *Cosmopolitan*, May 1957, 39–41.

27. Philip Wylie, "The Womanization of America," *Playboy*, September 1958, 52, 77–78.

28. Gordon MacQuarrie, "All Girls Turn into Women," *Field & Stream* 59 (October 1954), 127.

29. Murray Hoyt, "Beware the Untamed Deer Hunter," *Saturday Evening Post*, December 3, 1960, 27.

30. Archibald Rutledge, "Why I Taught My Boys to Be Hunters," in Casada, *Hunting and Home*, 33–34.

31. "Guns Are Plentiful—But Are Ducks?," *Business Week*, October 25, 1947, 42–44.

32. Robert C. Ruark, "The Brave Quail," in *Field & Stream Treasury*, ed. Hugh Grey and Ross McCluskey (New York: Holt, 1955), 330. The original story appeared in *Field & Stream*, December 1951, 18–21, 110–111.

33. Ruark, "Brave Quail," 330.

34. This association explains why hunters fought vehemently against gun regulation in the late 1960s, perceiving it as an attack on masculinity. Feeling emasculated by government, progun males sought to reassert their masculinity by curbing state power, especially with regard to firearms regulation, thereby transferring that paternalism back to men. Gun-oriented masculinity, according to Jennifer Carlson and Kristin A. Goss, depended on men, not the state, fulfilling the role of protector. See Carlson and Goss, "Gendering the Second Amendment," *Law and Contemporary Problems* 80, no. 2 (2017): 103–128. See also Chip Berlet and Matthew N. Lyons, *Right-Wing Populism in America: Too Close for Comfort* (New York: Guilford Press, 2000); Jennifer Carlson, "Mourning Mayberry: Guns, Masculinity, and Socioeconomic Decline," *Gender and Society* 29 (2015); and Angela Stroud, "Good Guys with Guns: Hegemonic Masculinity and Concealed Handguns," *Gender and Society* 26 (2012): 216–238.

35. Jack O'Connor, *The Big-Game Rifle* (New York: Knopf, 1952), 9–10.

36. Chapman J. Milling, *Buckshot and Hounds* (New York: A. S. Barnes, 1967), 65.

37. "Christmas Gift Guide," *Field & Stream*, December 1951, 83.

38. Archibald H. Rutledge, *Those Were the Days* (Richmond, VA: Dietz Press, 1955), 401–402.

39. Rutledge, *Those Were the Days*, 399.

40. Robert Anderson, *Jack O'Connor: The Legendary Life of America's Greatest Gunwriter* (Huntington Beach, CA: Safari Press, 2001), 174–175.

41. John Carlyle, "The Rifle Is America's Heritage," *Nation's Business*, October 1947, 48.

42. Anderson, *Jack O'Connor*, 176.

43. Ibid.

44. Havilah Babcock, *Jaybirds Go to Hell on Friday and Other Stories* (New York: Holt, Rinehart, and Winston, 1964), 30–31, 34, 37–39. This work was reprinted eight times between 1958 and 1965.

45. Brian Luke argues, "Hunting men are not frustrated and sexually impotent, they typically enjoy sexual relations with other people, *and* they enjoy the erotics of stalking and shooting wild animals." Luke, "Violent Love: Hunting, Heterosexuality, and the Erotics of Men's Predation," *Feminist Studies* 24, no. 3 (Autumn 1998): 633.

46. "Havilah Babcock: Virginia Carolinian," *Georgia Review* 21, no. 3 (Fall 1967): 297.

47. *Playboy* also exemplifies connections between hunting and sexuality via the bunny symbol, "a sexualized image that identifies women with a domesticated animal that is also hunted for sport, meat, and as a varmint." Luke, "Violent Love," 646.

NO SUBSTITUTE FOR FOOTBALL

Cold War Culture and College Football

KURT EDWARD KEMPER

In October 1950, the *Saturday Evening Post* published a splashy cover story on nefarious concepts such as free speech and open inquiry endangering American higher education. Provocatively entitled "UCLA's Red Cell: A Case Study of Campus Communism," the article, as was often the case with such sensationalized fear mongering during the Cold War, offered little substantive proof of communism run amok on UCLA's campus, let alone that it served as a case study of communist infiltration. It embarrassed the nascent university, however, which was only two years removed from earning its status as a junior campus of the University of California, and the administration fervently sought to dispel such a popular sentiment.

So when the *Los Angeles Examiner* began nosing around in 1953, intending to run a multipart series on communist infiltration at UCLA, the university went on the offensive to derail the series. Andrew Hamilton, the university's public information officer, developed a host of talking points for his meeting with the *Examiner* reporter. Hamilton's list mostly denied that UCLA had ever had any undue communist influence on campus, but it also contained a trump card, in his mind. Hamilton's tactic was to admit UCLA's Leftist student activity but to claim that it never reached the level of infiltration by the Communist Party and that any such activity had predated World War II and was long gone by the 1950s. Then, as if to suggest that the soul of the university remained unsullied, Hamilton authoritatively declared, "No Communist has ever been a member of the football squad."[1]

Far from being seen as an outrageous or irrelevant claim, Hamilton's assertion demonstrated that he, and countless others, during the Cold War understood football as representative of the antithesis of communism. If a school like UCLA played college football, the campus, and by extension the very fabric of the republic, remained impervious to the communist challenge. Thus, UCLA administrators not only saw football as a necessary antidote to domestic subversion but also implicitly saw the Cold War as a crucible in which college football would be tempered for its distinctive postwar mission.

The process by which Americans came to explain college football in the language of the crises of the postwar period, and vice versa, came from the intense anxiety of the period and concerns over national fitness, character development, and moral rectitude. The willingness of so many Americans to find these attributes as natural outgrowths of football and thus to see the game as a bulwark against communism nurtured the cultural institution of football during the postwar years.

By the early 1950s, Americans understood that the doctrine of containment required a tremendous investment in money and resources for an indefinite period. Under these circumstances, containment bred frustration among many Americans because it was contrary to unconditional surrender, requiring instead a patient, passive response that ran counter to the wishes of many Americans. As a result, containment, and the absence of a shooting war that would bring unqualified victory, created an irresolvable malaise. Additionally, nuclear proliferation magnified the potential consequences of such a shooting war, meaning that containment created the need for Americans to see progress and victory in other, less satisfying and dangerous, areas.

Thus, sports evolved as a natural outlet for Cold War tensions, and American "athletic excellence" illustrated *a priori* evidence of the superiority of "our free system of government and vast educational network."[2] Though sport enjoyed a prominent place in American society by the middle of the twentieth century, Americans could not take athletic superiority over the Soviets for granted. In fact, several indicators in the early 1950s suggested that the United States was falling behind the Soviets in both mental and physical fitness.

Throughout the 1950s, popular assumptions about an America grown soft took root amid the material affluence of the postwar period. Such concerns were not unique to the period; national apprehension over softness has recurred in waves since the onset of industrialization. However, Americans put their postwar anxieties over softness explicitly within the interrelated contexts of the Cold War and the pitfalls of prosperity. During the Korean War, many were stunned to learn that perhaps 70 percent of American prisoners of war collapsed under Communist interrogation and deprivation, which brought about a "wholesale breakdown in morale" both at home and at the front.[3]

In addition, concerns about the mental fitness of adults occurred alongside popular paranoias about juvenile delinquency. In the face of daunting FBI statistics, Congress established a standing Subcommittee on Juvenile Delinquency in 1954. The following year, the issue achieved pop culture status with the release of *Blackboard Jungle*, a film featuring out-of-control high school students, set to the soundtrack of Bill Haley's "Rock Around the Clock."[4]

Americans also found much about physical fitness to concern them. The well-publicized 1956 Kraus–Weber tests revealed that the fitness and dexterity of American youths lagged behind that of their European counterparts. The authors explicitly identified American abundance and material comfort in the form of automobiles, elevators, and televisions as the culprit. The military made plain the consequences of physical and mental softness when it estimated that by the end of the decade such issues would disqualify 5 of every 7 candidates for military service. Indeed, the military now saw the Kraus–Weber study as an explanation for the otherwise baffling results of military induction physicals.[5]

Such evidence made for easy links to the Cold War and the concern that physical and emotional softness threatened national security. Senator Hubert Humphrey ominously warned that such conditions endangered the United States. "One thing is certain—each day, each week, each year—the Soviet Union and its captive nations are increasing their efforts for the physical fitness of their populations."[6] Humphrey's rhetoric both reflected and helped create the growing American paranoia of communist bogeymen everywhere. Just as the American public had heard of a Soviet economy outdistancing their own in terms of gross national product, and a Soviet military producing a growing missile gap, they now saw themselves on the losing end of a "muscle gap" as well.

Responding to such fears, American elites consciously began crafting what historian Donald Mrozek has labeled "the cult and ritual of toughness." According to Mrozek, leaders believed that mere physical fitness, though still necessary, was no longer enough to combat the growing Soviet menace. In addition to fit bodies, Americans needed to cultivate mental toughness by inuring themselves to pain and deprivation, and by accepting such conditions as necessary for the assurance of victory, either on the playing field or on the battlefield. This required confronting the consequences of the material abundance that marked the postwar American experience.[7]

Dartmouth president Ernest Hopkins noted his concerns about the feminizing influence of material abundance in American society. "I believe quite definitely that in a generation like ours where nothing in the way of physical hazard, to say nothing of physical effort, is demanded under ordinary circumstances, [physically demanding] games have a definite merit and that up to the limit of personal injury it is advantageous to a man to have some knowledge of the fact even of what physical pain is."[8]

The new cult of toughness extended even to the spiritual realm. The evangelist Billy Graham criticized depictions of Christ that would show him as "effeminate." Instead, Graham described Christ as a prototypical linebacker—strong, virile, manly. "He would have been a star athlete on any team." For Graham, the depiction of Christ as a tough, manly athlete also served as an antidote to the growing concern over juvenile delinquency. At a revival in North Carolina, Graham recited FBI juvenile delinquency statistics but claimed that tough, manly sports countered the causes of juvenile delinquency: "insecurity, bad environment, [and] too much leisure."[9]

Such concerns for developing toughness in American youth emerged alongside conversations on parenting and the role of mothers. In 1942, Philip Wylie published *Generation of Vipers*, his scathing indictment of American society. His criticism of American mothers overly concerned with material consumption and overly protective of their children gained new credence during the Cold War. Wylie's allegation of "momism" found a receptive audience, such that the book went into a second printing in 1955.[10]

But Wylie was not the only writer to hold mothers accountable for the development of Cold War toughness. *Ladies Home Journal* asked, "How Fit Are Our Children?," while *Cosmopolitan* was even more explicit, "Are We and Our Children Getting Too Soft?" No less an authority than the American Medical

Association endorsed the exposure of American youth to painful and dangerous play in a 1959 pamphlet on the importance of youth fitness, while implicitly echoing Wylie's "momism" allegation. "A fractured ankle may leave less of a scar than a personality frustrated by reason of parental timidity over participation in contact sports."[11] For these commentators and observers, embracing the cult of toughness was necessary to arrest the American slide into dissipation.

The cult of toughness hinted at the hard road ahead for American claims of global supremacy. Only a resolute toughness could develop "the vigor and determination necessary to satisfy the awakening aspirations for progress and the elimination of poverty and want," both at home and abroad. Thus, the elevation of toughness as a cultural value established its primacy not only in defeating the Soviets but also in enabling America to overcome the barriers to progress everywhere and assume the mantle of world leadership. In his inaugural address, John Kennedy linked these themes by declaring that the United States was summoned by the "trumpet" of a historical moment, "a call to bear the burden of a long twilight struggle . . . against the common enemies of man: tyranny, poverty, disease, and war itself." Americans must "be willing to work for the physical toughness on which the courage and intelligence and skill of man so largely depend."[12] The stakes of the Cold War demanded that Americans search for material progress while simultaneously developing a national character of toughness and self-denial. Americans needed the greatness to create material comfort and the fortitude to keep it from corrupting them.

No team sport better represented the route to the new cult of toughness than football, a sport that evoked manliness, deprivation, and violence. Coaches often denied water to players during practices to teach such lessons, and they revered players who denied injury to continue playing. Thus, just as Kennedy challenged Americans to "pay any price, bear any burden" in their quest for world leadership, Paul "Bear" Bryant told his players that winning football was only achieved by those willing to "pay the price."[13] In these constructs, football during the Cold War emerged not so much as a game decided by skill and talent as a contest of want, will, and self-denial.

At a time when Americans sought to differentiate themselves from the Soviets, football emerged in the eyes of many as representative of a distinct American exceptionalism. Few individuals more prominently advocated football as a game of Cold War toughness than Presidents Dwight Eisenhower and

John Kennedy. Both presidents made the elevation of toughness and fitness a component of their national agendas and seldom missed an opportunity to connect those efforts with football. Eisenhower, himself a former player, frequently harkened back to his playing days at West Point. In reviewing his wartime service, he once remarked that he was constantly on the lookout for the "natural leaders" created by football and acknowledged that the outstanding men on his entire staff were ex-football players. Eisenhower believed that "football, almost more than any other sport, tends to instill in men the feeling that victory comes through hard—almost slavish—work." Although Eisenhower's own career was cut short by injury, he felt that such occurrences, and by extension the possibility of injury to all players, were acceptable costs of a game that taught its players the necessary character and values the republic needed in its time of crisis.[14]

Eisenhower firmly believed that football embodied uniquely American values while simultaneously demanding the toughness necessary to counter Soviet advances. In his 1958 acceptance speech as the first recipient of the National Football Foundation and College Hall of Fame's Gold Medal, the president noted that "wherever human liberty is respected, competition is the animator of progress. In football, in business, in politics, the normal urge to excel provides one of the most hopeful assurances that our kind of society will continue to advance and prosper." Eisenhower declared that "morale—the will to win, the fighting heart—are the honored hallmarks" of the game, and that such competitive values were crucially applicable in the defense of the republic "For there is another kind of competition which America must meet—ponderous, persistent, deadly. It is clever and powerful, and it is out to win by whatever means and at whatever cost." The benefit of football, in Eisenhower's view, was that it so successfully married the physical with the mental. The struggle with the Soviets "requires fitness—fitness in its deepest and broadest sense. We know that fitness is far more than a healthy body. It is more than an alert, disciplined, mind. Fitness is the sum of all values which enable a man to act effectively in his nation's behalf in this great contest. In this environment, fitness is man's maximum development to make all of us a stronger nation."[15]

Eisenhower's embrace of football and those associated with it elevated the game's cultural prominence, but his efforts paled in comparison to the support football received from John Kennedy. Commenting forty years after Kennedy's death on the importance of football in the president's mind-set, Charles Pierce wrote, "Football was what they played on the New Frontier. . . . There was a tyranny of the new at work, stretching from outer space to Southeast Asia. Football was a part of all that."[16] Kennedy seldom passed up a chance to connect with voters over the issue of college football, particularly in the South as confrontations over civil rights created southern white hostility toward his administration. When the University of Alabama won the 1961 national championship, Kennedy met with the team at the New York awards ceremony. And he called Tuscaloosa to offer encouragement to the team during a pep rally before the team's 1962 Sugar Bowl game against Arkansas.

Kennedy frequently referred to football as a cultural touchstone common to all Americans. During the 1962 crisis at the University of Mississippi surrounding the enrollment of James Meredith, the university's first Black student, the president urged Mississippians to avoid violence. Hoping to appeal to a common source of pride, he reminded them, "You have a great tradition to uphold, a tradition of honor and courage, won on the field of battle and on the gridiron."[17]

Few moments better symbolized Kennedy's belief in the values and meanings of football than his speech announcing the US entry into the space race. Declaring in 1962, in his finest New Frontier rhetoric, that America would put a man on the moon by the end of the decade, Kennedy staked the prestige of the nation to success in space. The president gave his address in Houston, Texas, the future home of the space program, on the campus of Rice University, a school distinguished in academics but with limited football success, particularly against the nationally prominent University of Texas. Kennedy acknowledged that space travel would be difficult and the struggle would be marked by those who would say success was unobtainable. Kennedy asserted that Americans, however, did things "not because they are easy, but because they are hard." Such efforts marked the best of the American spirit, and success under those circumstances illustrated the leadership, progress, and "peaceful cooperation" America had to offer the world in its hour of peril. "Why choose the moon?" the president asked rhetorically. "Why climb the highest mountain? Why, thirty-five years ago, fly the Atlantic?" And then, to thunderous applause, "Why does Rice play Texas?"[18] In Kennedy's equation, America would go to the moon, demonstrating its greatness in the face of overwhelming obstacles in the same way that tiny Rice University struggled against the mighty Texas Longhorns on the gridiron. The magnitude of the obstacle glorified the nobility of the effort and amplified the satisfaction of success.

Robert Kennedy, himself a former Harvard player, similarly elevated the game's social and cultural significance. The attorney general, like his brother, linked physical fitness with mental toughness. Addressing the American Football Coaches Association, Robert Kennedy claimed that such qualities delivered American victory in World War II but that the nation had abandoned both fitness and toughness in the years since. The individuals best suited to reverse such a decline, according to Kennedy, sat before him in that very room. Football coaches could "exert a tremendous influence for good in this country . . . You who participate in football, who have played well and trained others to play well, symbolize the needs of the nation." Kennedy, like his brother and Eisenhower before them and American elites dating back to the nineteenth century, continued to see football as the peacetime crucible in which national character was forged. "Except for war, there is nothing in American life which trains a boy better for life than football. There can be no substitute for football."[19]

Eisenhower and Kennedy were only the most prominent supporters of football who placed the game at the center of the emerging postwar culture of toughness. Republican senator from Kentucky John Sherman Cooper noted on the floor of the Senate that the game's "emphasis on discipline, competitive spirit, physical fitness, teamwork and courage contributes to the vigor and moral and physical fiber of our country."[20] Popular assumptions that football represented values crucial to American Cold War success allowed many to link the game to an explicit American exceptionalism. Michigan State's head coach, Clarence Munn, declared, "I would rather my son be a football player than a Phi Beta Kappa [because] . . . you learn democracy and Americanism in the game of football."[21] Similarly, an Ivy League coach was so blunt as to assert that "football is our best defense against communism," a sentiment echoed almost exactly by Army head coach Red Blaik, who described "football as a disciplinary force, and as the antithesis of communism."[22] Even Pasadena's storied Rose Bowl posited itself as a bastion against the encroaching communist foe. "In these times of international tensions, with the spectre of war and attempted domination casting shadows on a free United States . . . the Tournament of Roses lightens the dark corners of fear. . . . So long as there is a Tournament of Roses, so long as there is a Rose Bowl Game . . . there will there be a free United States."[23]

Perhaps the most insistent advocate of football as a key component to national security was the National Football Foundation and College Hall of Fame. Established in 1947 by former coaches, players, and benefactors of the game to build a college football hall of fame, the foundation emerged during the Cold War as the game's most ardent defender, cloaking football in the rhetoric of national defense and the cult of toughness, declaring that "there shall be no softening of our fiber as we face the task of world leadership." The fear of Americans gone soft played a prominent role in the foundation's message, which was that the game "will serve as an inspiration so that our youth, unlike the ancient Greeks and Romans, will not grow soft." The group viewed with alarm the potential by-products of America's postwar affluence but saw football as the antidote. "In an age where there has been considerable tendency to softness and the relaxing of our standards of fortitude and physical preparedness, the foundation believes that football will continue to be a significant and vital factor in helping to strengthen and prepare the physical and moral fiber of the Nation for our defense in the years to come."

The foundation frequently placed the game in explicit Cold War contexts. Football was "a vital force in the life of the nation, developing the rugged virtues and tough leadership qualities indispensable for the survival of a free world menaced by a ruthless and conspiratorial tyranny." Similarly, the foundation viewed the game "as an incubator of 'competitive fiber,'" claiming it turned out men capable of directing an "economy toward defeating Russia in its avowed aim to destroy us." The benefits of football, according to the foundation, would accrue not just to its players but to the nation they represented, and it touted the game's "important role in the advancement of our way of life." Striking a tone of Kennedy-esque global citizenship, the foundation argued that football promised "a better life for all mankind."[24]

In equating football with the defense of the republic, the foundation looked with hostility upon individuals who challenged or criticized the game. The group included as a formal program initiative its mission "to combat the unwarranted attacks made on football in the public press by those who are uninformed or prejudiced." Chester LaRoche, the foundation's president in the late 1950s and early 1960s, took every opportunity to attack the game's critics, but he focused his most acidic rhetoric on those who had dropped football altogether, particularly the University of Chicago. "We should dig into the facts concerning Chicago. It is probable that the character of their student body has dropped off badly, and they are now overloaded with beatniks, leftists, and undesirables. It could be proved that dropping football was a disaster." On another occasion, LaRoche asserted that Chicago had "suffered" so extensively from dropping football that the university might now be receptive to its return.[25]

LaRoche was not the only one who saw attempts at deemphasizing the game as a threat to national security and character. Broadcaster Bill Stern asserted on the air in October 1958 that schools that dropped or minimized football, such as Chicago, Harvard, City College of New York, and New York University, were "hotbeds of communism." In the absence of big-time football, according to Stern, the wholesome energies of college youth that could have gone to constructive character-building exercises found no outlet. "In many cases, too many of them have turned to Communism."[26]

Individuals who publicly voiced opposition to football faced the harshest reprisals. In 1959, Wade Thompson, a Brown University English professor, proposed the abolition of intercollegiate football at Brown. The responses to Thompson's proposal brought allegations of treason, homosexuality, and communism, among others.[27] Similarly, Gary Althern, undergraduate student editor of the University of Colorado's *Colorado Daily*, editorialized in September 1962 his desire to abandon big-time football in Boulder. When Althern followed his football editorial with one harshly critical of strident anticommunist Senator Barry Goldwater, many observers linked the two pieces as intertwined evidence of Althern's subversiveness. Responding to such critics, the university president subsequently removed Althern as editor.[28] Thus, by directing the code words for subversion and deviance at football's critics, defenders of the game helped craft a culture that elevated football to national importance while simultaneously placing those critics beyond the respectable pale of that culture.

Defenders of college football so easily linked attacks on opponents of football with communism because the game represented one of the most time-honored campus institutions, and any challenge to such tradition appeared un-American. Joseph McCarthy saw criticisms of football as evidence of communist subversion and a repudiation of such institutions as marriage, social conformity, and the American Legion. In his infamous hearings into alleged communist subversion in American government, McCarthy called the State Department's Reed Harris to testify in February 1953. McCarthy spent much of Harris's three days on the witness stand questioning him about the book *King Football*, which Harris wrote in 1932 as an undergraduate at Columbia. By Harris's own admission, the book was a sophomoric attempt to criticize a host of institutions representing paternalism and authority, one of which was college football. McCarthy focused on Harris's attack of intercollegiate athletics, especially football, with the Wisconsin senator reading into the record a passage that noted, "Russia has barred football from her new athletic program" because the sport appealed "to the least desirable emotions."[29] Thus, McCarthy saw football as representative of a generic American way of life and readily marginalized its critics by linking them with communism.

Americans viewed football during the Cold War as evocative of a distinct national exceptionalism that embodied values of universal acclaim. To reject the game, then, was to reject these values and this sense of American distinctiveness. Thus, critics found themselves linked with communism, homosexuality, and a host of alleged character flaws that existed outside the bounds of the American way of life. The suggestion that anything less than a lusty embrace of football during the period could be linked to all manner of deficiencies emerged most often in popular discussion of the newly created Ivy League. Formally created in 1956, the Ivy League sought to distance itself from "the contaminants of big-time football," in the words of John Watterson, by restricting or abolishing many of the game's accepted practices.[30]

The move away from big-time football earned the game's founders a barrage of criticism. George Preston Marshall, owner of the professional Washington Redskins, declared, "The Ivy League is destroying the game it created." One Big Ten alum simply stated that "Ivy League football stinks," while a UCLA partisan dismissed the Eastern brand of the game relative to big-time football: "We play football, not potsy." Descriptions of Ivy League football as "potsy" suggested that its critics saw it as unmanly, effeminate. One critic of Ivy League football restrictions feared that it marked a surrender to "over-stimulated introverts and pinkish weaklings."[31]

The notion of effeteness soon dominated descriptions of Ivy League football. An electronic keyword search of the *New York Times* historical database reveals that the description of football at Ivy League schools as "effete" did not appear in the pages of that paper prior to the creation of the formal Ivy League. After the consummation of the Ivy Group Agreement in 1954, however, the phrase appeared with regularity. Notions of Ivy League effeteness so successfully colored national perceptions of football reform that the Ivy League haunted proponents of big-time football like a specter to be avoided at all costs. When considering Ohio State's decision not to accept the 1962 Rose Bowl invitation, one Buckeye partisan lamented, "I hope our university does not . . . imitate some of the effete Eastern Colleges with the consequent loss of vigor, both in mind and body."[32]

Linking Ivy League football with "effeteness" and "pinkish weaklings" illustrated the ease with which Americans perceived a hostility to football as a proxy for a host of un-American traits. The charge of effeteness in post–World War II America bore distinct implications, suggesting not just a masculine shortcoming but an ideological one as well. To be effete, to be unmanly, was to be soft, weak, both physically and mentally, and thus to be corruptible. Commentators during the Cold War universally agreed that the defense of the republic required a fit populace, capable of stoic sacrifice and self-discipline, in both the personal and an ideological sense. It is not coincidental that one of President Kennedy's favorite terms was "vigor."

Critics claimed that communism promised easy solutions, offered easy protections, by placing all responsibilities on the state rather than the individual. Success in American society required constant perseverance and striving, a lifetime of struggle unnavigable by individuals too weak to resist the promise of a socialized society. To be effete in postwar America was to be un-American, possibly a threat to national security.

This perverse logic informed the intense homophobia of the period, which manifested itself in ways both profane and profound, from popular assumptions to governmental action. Senator Joseph McCarthy once crudely declared that anyone who opposed him was "either a Communist or a cocksucker." With little more subtlety, Congress passed the McCarran Act, which barred homosexuals from becoming US citizens and forbade those already in the country from traveling abroad, while President Eisenhower issued an executive order barring homosexuals from federal employment. Allegations of Ivy League football as effete were thus challenges to the schools' loyalty and commitment to waging the Cold War.[33]

The decision by the Ivy League to distance itself from big-time football at the exact moment that many Americans identified the game as so thoroughly evocative of American life not only led to criticisms of Ivy League football as effete but also coincided with increasing criticisms of Ivy League schools for their alleged ambivalence toward moral development in general and communist sympathies specifically. Noted conservative intellectual William F. Buckley Jr. indicted his alma mater, Yale, for its abandonment of Christian and capitalist values that had served as the school's foundation for three centuries, and his criticisms were not the only ones. A letter to the *New York Times* noted that recent scandals in college athletics marked a wholesale "collapse of conscience in these United States." The culprit, according to the author, resided in the elite halls of American academia, where "a slavish devotion to an entirely false concept of academic freedom is turning our colleges into booby traps for young and impressionable minds." Describing the intellectual discourse that occurred in American higher education in the 1950s as "evil and alien influences," the letter placed the blame on professors. "Too often today the American way of life—from a belief in free enterprise to faith in democracy—is belittled by our enlightened professors. These men decry the past, scorn the present and offer various forms of socialism and collectivism as the only hope for the future." The salvation of American higher education could be found by "turn[ing] again towards the ideals and simple faith that made us great," including institutions of church, education, and sports as a means of instructing patriotism, "rectitude, and high moral principles." In this fashion, the United States would avoid not only the scandals of college athletics but also the erosion of the American character. Thus, the distancing of the Ivy League from big-time athletics was an assault, and not even a thinly veiled one, on the future of the republic.[34]

An editorial in the Mobile, Alabama, *Press-Register* made an even more explicit link between Ivy League sports policies and its supposed unwillingness to challenge the communist menace. The author noted that while the Ivy Group Agreement required all athletes to sign a pledge stating they would abide by the agreement's provisions, particularly that they would disclose financial assistance, half of the Ivy League schools at the same time opposed loyalty oaths that "Congress thinks would assist our government in stamping out Communism and subversive activities. For it is well-known [sic] that the Communist technique is to try to influence members of the faculty as well as the students."[35] According to such logic, the limitations of Ivy League football and sympathy to communism were born from the same bankrupt values.

At the height of the Cold War, football's supporters understood the game as a vital cog in the emerging cult of toughness. These individuals interpreted football as a purveyor of desired American values representative of the Cold War mind-set. Some observers at the time also linked the game to the waging of the Cold War itself. Joseph Kaplan, a renowned physics professor at UCLA and chair of the US Committee on the International Geophysical Year, offered a series of articles for popular consumption in the 1950s espousing football's Cold War role. Kaplan firmly accepted existing assumptions linking the physical with the mental, refusing to "distinguish between the need and fittingness of scientific activity on one hand and athletic activity on the other. Our nation seriously needs both." Kaplan also embraced the increasing specialization and rationalization of the game, which for so many Americans was disorienting and ambiguous. Kaplan argued that football should not reject the two-platoon system but should embrace it as integral not only to the rationalization of college football but also to the rationalization of the Cold War economy that would lead to American supremacy over the Soviets. "If we are to gain any superiority over [the Soviets] in any given essential category, in peace or war, we must do it by concentrating on the development of specialists." In that way, according to Kaplan, the game—and by extension society—intensified competition and bred excellence. He explicitly linked the increase of specialization within college football to the similar occurrences in the larger economy that created better talent. "Since competition fosters growth, it is logical for highly competitive football to grow big—and sometimes rapidly." He pointed to his own academic discipline as a good example, citing the intense competition for scientists among the nation's elite university research labs, a phenomenon known as "Big Science." The most specialized labs, directed by the most talented researchers, would be rewarded with federal grant dollars, allowing the rich to get richer and larger, thereby allowing them to attract more talent and make greater scientific discoveries.[36]

Kaplan argued that specialization created excellence from the crucible of competition, and no better crucible existed than football. Not surprisingly, the National Football Foundation echoed Kaplan's assumptions on the relationship between the game and competition, claiming that football offered "a unique training ground for leadership in our competitive economy."[37] Like so many others during the time, Kaplan understood football to be indicative of a kind of American exceptionalism. "Football is the most competitive of sports. Its teamwork, its ruggedness, its Spartan spirit, a throwback to our pioneering ancestry, all have tremendous appeal to our basic American characteristics."[38]

A uniquely American game, football thus appealed to a uniquely American experience, creating, in Kaplan's mind, a culture of uniquely American values. Having linked football to an American past of frontier individualism, however, he also viewed the game as analogous to a bureaucratized American experience that was necessary to conquer the final frontier, space. Noting the prominence of space as a Cold War battleground, Kaplan argued that the acceptance of specialization was a necessary evolution of American culture to achieve Cold War victory. "The Space Age is geared to specialization, and there's no room for amateurism. Amateurs cannot make the 20,000 moving parts of a Vanguard rocket function. It is also a fact that amateurs cannot participate smoothly in a complicated football play."[39]

Kaplan was not the only academic who embraced sports for its competitive values. James B. Conant, former president of Harvard, argued, "The spirit of competition . . . is a healthy aspect of our American emphasis on sports. There is no reason why the same type of motivation could not be utilized in the study of mathematics, and foreign languages, provided, as in athletics, selection of the naturally talented is accepted as a matter of course."[40] Thus, the culture of football during the Cold War era represented not merely toughness and fitness but also Americans' desire for competition and national exceptionalism, all of which Americans easily fit into existing assumptions about their way of life.

If football helped illuminate America's Cold War path to the moon, Kaplan also envisioned the Cold War as a means to reform college football. The intertwined national priorities of space and the Cold War, according to Kaplan, created ever greater demands on intellectual talent. Such demands would rapidly intensify the academic performance of capable individuals while leaving behind those left unprepared for such competition. "The athlete in the Space Age will face an even stiffer fight to justify a classroom seat."

Kaplan argued that the values of football helped players to maintain that seat. As a result, football would produce competitors fit and tough enough to compete with the Soviets, and the intellectual demands of the space age would banish the academic abuses identified with college football. Because "academic curves trend upward," Kaplan argued, and "improvement will be intensified in the Space Age," only those who mastered football specialization in addition to academic excellence would prosper. He predicted that "in the next ten years, the player who barely gets by" would become obsolete.[41]

Kaplan presumed that the postwar abuses of college football, particularly the search for football talent based on the going rate rather than academic potential, would resolve itself, allowing for a natural return to some fictional day when legitimate amateurism prevailed and "real" students played college football. As a result, Kaplan saw football providing Cold War victory while Cold War necessities would ensure college football reform, allowing the game to return to its allegedly pristine bygone era. Thus would the future deliver the past.

Moreover, Kaplan's argument that Cold War necessity would deliver both academic and athletic achievement fit within the prevailing post–World War II ethos of abundance and assumptions of a society without limits. Lyndon Johnson promised Americans that they could have a Great Society at home and Cold War victory abroad, proclaiming, "We can do it all." Proponents of the game said much the same thing in declaring that big-time football and scholastic excellence were not mutually exclusive but in fact were both means to the same end—the defeat of the Soviets. Concurrent with the idea of the liberal consensus that dominated American politics in the decades following World War II, which promised domestic abundance at home and global security abroad, the vision of Kaplan, LaRoche, Kennedy, and others proposed that the culture of football in the postwar years did not require Americans to choose athletics over academics; they could have both.[42]

Kaplan's insistence on seeing academic reform and intellectual development emerge from the ultracompetitive world of big-time college football illustrated not merely the optimism of the period but also the insistence that the culture of abundance would deliver both "more" and "better." If the specialization of two-platoon football created a more rational game merely for the aggrandizement of spectators and coaches but came with long-term negative consequences, then it was little more than opulent luxury, serving no purpose but to appease insatiable consumerist desires. Americans raised the specter of luxury throughout the period by frequently warning that American abundance could lead to the valueless decadence of ancient Rome. Here, again, was the dilemma of the postwar culture of abundance: to create wealth and leisure while keeping its corrupting influences at bay. Kaplan's claim that the postwar version of the game would better both football and America deftly linked football with the larger American cultural imperative of the Cold War, to use progress for the benefit of all.

By the mid-1950s, the United States was mired in an undefined, indefinite confrontation with the Soviet Union. Inundated with evidence of Soviet economic growth and military strength, many Americans grew increasingly uncertain about their own superiority. Worse, symbols of domestic weakness in the form of declining physical fitness and mental toughness, along with moral dissipation, caused many to make critical self-comparisons to a decadent Rome. As a result, many Americans feared a powerful Soviet enemy abroad and an anxious and insecure American character at home. This Cold War anxiety caused them to seek out distinctive aspects of American society and culture that flattered their sense of American exceptionalism and reassured them about American strength. In this regard, they elevated football as a unique American experience that helped breed and inculcate distinct American values necessary for Cold War victory.

While many of the claims made by football's supporters strained credulity, their relevance comes not from their accuracy or even their rationality but from their willingness to encode football with specific Cold War meaning. Cold War football was not football changed by the Cold War but rather a demonstration of how Americans viewed football through the prism of a changed American life and identity wrought by the Cold War.

NOTES

This essay is excerpted from Kurt Edward Kemper, *College Football and American Culture in the Cold War Era* (Urbana: University of Illinois Press, 2009). Copyright © 2009 by the Board of Trustees of the University of Illinois. Used with permission of the University of Illinois Press.

1. William L. Worden, "UCLA's Red Cell: A Case Study of Campus Communism," *Saturday Evening Post*, October 23, 1950, 42–44; letter from Andrew Hamilton to Raymond Allen, Sep-

tember 16, 1953, in Records of the Chancellor's Office, UCLA University Archives, box 266, file 228, "Loyalty Oath and Subversive Activities." The culture of postwar anticommunism at UCLA is discussed in Kurt Edward Kemper, "Reformers in the Marketplace of Ideas: Student Activism in Cold War Los Angeles" (PhD diss., Louisiana State University, 2000), chapter 2.

2. Thomas Michael Domer, "Sport in Cold War America, 1953–1963: The Diplomatic and Political Use of Sport in the Eisenhower and Kennedy Administrations" (PhD diss., University of Wisconsin-Milwaukee, 1976), 20.

3. Adam J. Zweiback, "The 21 Turncoat GIs: Nonrepatriates and the Political Culture of the Cold War," *Historian* 60, no. 2: 345–362; Tom Englehardt, *The End of Victory Culture: Cold War America and the Disillusioning of a Generation* (New York: Basic Books, 1995), 65.

4. James Gilbert, *A Cycle of Outrage: America's Reaction to the Juvenile Delinquent in the 1950s* (New York: Oxford University Press, 1986), particularly chapter 4; James B. Gilbert, *Men in the Middle: Searching for Masculinity in the 1950s* (Chicago: University of Chicago Press, 2005), chapter 4. On Bill Haley and *Blackboard Jungle*, see James Miller, *Flowers in the Dustbin: The Rise of Rock and Roll, 1947–1977* (New York: Simon and Schuster, 1999), 87–94.

5. Shelly McKenzie, *Getting Physical: The Rise of Fitness Culture in America* (Lawrence: University Press of Kansas), 2013, 14–19.

6. Domer, "Sport in Cold War America," 108–109; Robert L. Griswold, "The 'Flabby American,' the Body, and the Cold War," in *A Shared Experience: Men, Women, and the History of Gender*, ed. Laura McCall and Donald Yacavone (New York: New York University Press, 1998), 322–348; Hubert H. Humphrey, "A Five-Point Fitness Program," *Journal of Health, Physical Education, Recreation* 33 (October 1962): 21–22, 72–74.

7. Donald J. Mrozek, "The Cult and Ritual of Toughness in Cold War America," in *Rituals and Ceremonies in Pop Culture*, ed. Ray B. Browne (Bowling Green, OH: Popular Press, 1980), 178–191.

8. Mark F. Bernstein, *Football: The Ivy League Origins of an American Obsession* (Philadelphia: University of Pennsylvania Press, 2001), 178.

9. "View and Preview," *Daily Tar Heel*, October 8, 1958, 2; "Graham Heard by 200,000 in Charlotte Drive," *Atlanta Journal-Constitution*, October 8, 1958, 6.

10. Philip Wylie, *Generation of Vipers* (New York: Rinehart Books, 1942); "*Generation of Vipers* Loses Its Bite," *Washington Post*, July 30, 2005, C1.

11. Elizabeth Pope, "How Fit Are Our Children?," *Ladies Home Journal*, March 1954, 69, 90–93; Harry Henderson, "Are We and Our Children Getting Too Soft?," *Cosmopolitan*, August 1954, 16–22; Griswold, "Flabby American."

12. John F. Kennedy, "The Soft American," *Sports Illustrated* (December 26, 1960), 15–17; Kennedy, "Inaugural Address, 20 January 1961," Historic Speeches, John F. Kennedy Presidential Library and Museum, https://www.jfklibrary.org/learn/about-jfk/historic-speeches/inaugural-address.

13. Keith Dunnavant, *Coach: The Life of Paul "Bear" Bryant* (New York: Simon & Schuster, 1996), 100; Jim Dent, *Junction Boys: How Ten Days in Hell with Bear Bryant Forged a Championship Team* (New York: St. Martin's Press, 2000); Tom Stoddard, *Turnaround: The Untold Story of Bear Bryant's First Year at Alabama* (Birmingham, AL: Black Belt Press, 1996); Jim Dent, *The Undefeated: The Oklahoma Sooners and the Greatest Winning Streak in College Football History* (New York: St. Martin's Press, 2001).

14. Gene Schoor, *100 Years of Army-Navy Football* (New York: Henry Holt, 1989), 48; Wanda Ellen Wakefield, *Playing to Win: Sports and the American Military 1898–1945* (New York: State University of New York Press, 1997), 61.

15. "Eisenhower Receives Award from Football Hall of Fame," *New York Times*, October 29, 1958, 40.

16. Charles P. Pierce, "Black Sunday," *Sports Illustrated*, November 24, 2003, 56–62.

17. E. Culpepper Clark, *The Schoolhouse Door: Segregation's Last Stand at the University of Alabama* (New York: Oxford University Press, 1993), 146; William Doyle, *An American Insurrection: James Meredith and the Battle of Oxford, Mississippi, 1962* (New York: Anchor Books, 2003), 154.

18. John F. Kennedy, "Address at Rice University on the Nation's Space Effort," September 12, 1962, Historic Speeches, https://www.jfklibrary.org/learn/about-jfk/historic-speeches/address-at-rice-university-on-the-nations-space-effort.

19. "Robert Kennedy Calls Coaches Key to Fitness," *New York Times*, January 12, 1961, 34; Griswold, "Flabby American," 333.

20. Extension of Remarks of the Honorable John Sherman Cooper of Kentucky, given July 2, 1960, *Congressional Record*, appendix, July 5, 1960, A5832–5833.

21. John R. Thelin, *Games Colleges Play: Scandal and Reform in Intercollegiate Athletics*, (Baltimore: Johns Hopkins University Press, 1996), 109.

22. Meeting minutes of the National Football Foundation, April 19, 1961, Archives of the University of Notre Dame, Records of the National Football Foundation and College Hall of Fame (hereinafter NFF), box 79, folder 15.

23. "Tournament of Roses-Rose Bowl Game: Our First 70 Years," 1961 folder, Tournament of Roses Collection, Pasadena Museum of History, California.

24. "Men with Missions," *New York Times*, February 28, 1958, 24; advertisement for the National Football Foundation, in 1958 official football program, 38, and in Oklahoma-Notre Dame football program, September 30, 1961, reprinted in Football Programs, 1958–1960, Archives of the University of Notre Dame; Extension of Remarks of the Honorable John Sherman Cooper of Kentucky; "The Foundation and the Hall of Fame," NFF, box 79, folder 15.

25. Meeting minutes of the National Football Foundation, April 19, 1961, and January 26, 1961, both in NFF, box 79, folder 15.

26. "Lack of Football Cited as Reason for Communism," *Daily Bruin*, November 7, 1958, 1. Paul Tillett, in his 1965 study "The Social Costs of the Loyalty Programs," also noted the Stern comment; see Victor Navasky, *Naming Names: The Social Costs of McCarthyism* (New York: Viking, 1980), 335. Not everyone took Stern's comments seriously, however. *The Nation* editorialized that such utterances allowed Stern to make "a sufficiently grotesque public ass of himself." "Stern's Law," *The Nation*, November 15, 1958, 350–351.

27. Wade Thompson, "My Crusade Against Football," *The Nation*, April 11, 1959, 313–316.

28. Lawrence G. Weiss, "Goldwater and Colorado U," *The Nation*, December 8, 1962, 402–404.

29. Testimony of Reed Harris, March 4, 1953, Hearings Before the Permanent Subcommittee on Investigations of the Committee on Government Operations (Washington, DC: US Govern-

ment Printing Office, 1953), 365, 446; David Oshinsky, *A Conspiracy So Immense: The World of Joe McCarthy* (New York: Free Press, 1983), 274–276.

30. John Sayle Watterson, *College Football: History, Spectacle, Controversy* (Baltimore: Johns Hopkins University Press, 2002), 245–255, at 253. See also John R. Thelin, *The Cultivation of Ivy: A Saga of the College in America* (Cambridge, MA: Schenkman, 1976).

31. "Still Ivied Autumn?," *Newsweek*, October 15, 1956, 75–78.

32. "Festooned with Ivy," *New York Times*, October 23, 1959, 37; "The Foot in Football," *New York Times*, October 16, 1959, 37; "Peering Through Ivy," *New York Times*, May 3, 1961, 47; "A Novel Idea," *New York Times*, May 24, 1962, 43; letter from J. W. Blackwell to Jack Fullen, December 4, 1961, "Rose Bowl, 1962," 3/i/28, Papers of Novice G. Fawcett, Ohio State University Archives.

33. David Halberstam, *The Fifties* (New York: Fawcett Columbine, 1993), 54; John D'Emilio, *Sexual Politics, Sexual Communities: The Making of a Homosexual Community in the United States, 1940–1970* (Chicago: University of Chicago Press, 1983); David K. Johnson, *The Lavender Scare: The Cold War Persecution of Gays and Lesbians in the Federal Government* (Chicago: University of Chicago Press, 2004); Robert Dean, *Imperial Brotherhood: Gender and the Making of Cold War Foreign Policy* (Boston: University of Massachusetts Press, 2001).

34. William F. Buckley Jr., *God and Man at Yale: The Superstitions of Academic Freedom* (Chicago: Regnery, 1951); "To Fight Corruption," *New York Times*, January 5, 1952, 10.

35. "But It Goes Beyond Four Sport Seasons," *Press-Register*, December 14, 1959, 4A.

36. Joseph Kaplan, "The Case for Big-Time Football," *Look*, December 11, 1956.

37. "Foundation and the Hall of Fame."

38. Kaplan, "Case for Big-Time Football."

39. Joseph Kaplan, "Clean House or Else," *Look*, December 9, 1958, 33–38.

40. Kaplan, "Case for Big-Time Football."

41. Kaplan, "Clean House or Else."

42. The definitive source on the liberal consensus remains Godfrey Hodgson, *America in Our Time: From World War II to Nixon—What Happened and Why* (New York: Knopf, 1978), 65–98. The term itself was coined in John Higham, "The Cult of 'American Consensus': Homogenizing Our History," *Commentary* 27 (January 1959): 93–100. See also Robert M. Collins, "Growth Liberalism in the Sixties: Great Societies at Home and Grand Designs Abroad," in *The Sixties: From Memory to History*, ed. David Farber (Chapel Hill: University of North Carolina Press, 1994), 11–44.

TELEVANGELISM AND THE TRANSFORMATION OF AMERICAN CHRISTIANITY

RANDI BARNES-COX AND CHARITY RAKESTRAW

When Pat Robertson announced his candidacy for the Republican presidential nomination in September 1987, the television star boasted that 3.3 million people had petitioned him to run for the nation's highest office. Unlike the outgoing president, Robertson was not a Hollywood celebrity with acting chops and a camera-ready smile. The conservative leader, whom many deemed a "fringe" candidate, claimed his fame from a relatively new and lucrative development in entertainment media: televangelism.[1] An early pioneer of Christian television, Robertson founded Christian Broadcasting Network (CBN) in 1959 and built an evangelical empire out of his original, humble studio in Virginia.[2] Robertson was a passionate preacher and controversial voice for the Christian Right, and he did not shy from promoting his beliefs in the already charged Cold War political climate. He claimed to control the direction of hurricanes with prayer, to possess the gift of the "word of knowledge," and to heal believers through their television screens.[3] And he could be the next man anointed to be commander in chief of a nation involved in a lengthy and tense conflict with a communist power that he deemed evil and an agent of Satan.[4]

Despite his claims of an anointed campaign and mass popular support, Robertson did not win the nomination and returned to his *700 Club* studio in Los Angeles. From their electric pulpits, however, Robertson and his televangelist colleagues and competitors shaped popular religious rhetoric and evangelical worldviews in the Cold War era. Millions of Americans tuned in to hear them connect Christianity with American civil religion in stark, apocalyptic terms as they claimed to have prayerful answers to the perceived communist threat. Televangelists like Robertson turned Cold War anxieties into profitable mass media businesses, proving the potential of Christian capitalism while simultaneously claiming it was under siege.

ORIGINS OF THE (ANTICOMMUNIST) ELECTRONIC CHURCH

Although his network capitalized on the Bible-thumping potential of the new medium, CBN was not the first foray into television sermonizing for a Cold War audience. A Catholic auxiliary bishop of New York, Fulton Sheen, helped set the stage for Christian anticommunist television preaching during the "fifties revival."[5] Sheen, a staunch Catholic conservative, made direct connections between communism and evil spiritual forces, arguing that Satan had created communism in a war against Christianity. Beginning his mass media career in the 1930s as a radio host of *The Catholic Hour*, he joined the ranks of Father Charles Coughlin, the famous "radio priest," to blast anticommunist messages over the airwaves and into God-fearing Americans' homes.[6]

Sheen's fervent belief in the iniquities of communism, combined with a strong academic background and a plain and clear delivery, made him one of the most well-known religious figures in the United States at the time. Sheen claimed to convert former communists to Christianity, and he argued that the Christian faith was the only bulwark against secularization, the fall of society, and the loss of American souls to the communist threat. Some of his sermons on *The Catholic Hour* garnered more than 4 million listeners, which in conjunction with successful publishing efforts, propelled him into a prominent television career in 1952, on *Life Is Worth Living*.[7] After moving his message from radios to increasingly affordable television sets, Sheen expanded his audience to 30 million Catholic, Protestant, and Jewish viewers and helped to spawn a new spiritual marketplace of television preachers and religious celebrities.[8]

At the center of this burgeoning popular religious marketplace stood one of America's most recognizable figures—Billy Graham, preacher to the presidents. Beginning his ministerial career just as the world was splitting into Cold War factions, Graham found a national stage and popular recognition in the late

1940s through huge revival meetings called Crusades, which combined evangelical preaching with anticommunist jeremiads. Both US and Soviet newspapers considered the revivalist to be "Communism's Public Enemy Number One." He gained this reputation by attaching his proselytizing firmly to his patriotism and contrasting Christian America with what he deemed a godless Soviet threat. "Communism is a fantastical religion," he declared, "that has declared war upon the Christian God." Graham continued to employ this vitriolic rhetoric through the 1960s, but he did shift in the 1970s and 1980s as he expanded his international reach and missionizing and witnessed the atrocities of the Korean and Vietnam Wars.[9] The prominent Holy Roller—who filled stadiums, was piped into living room radios, and witnessed to millions through television sets—represents the contours of Protestant thought in this complex era, and the relationship between religion and Cold War culture.

Sheen's *Life Is Worth Living*, Graham's hawkish anticommunism, and Robertson's presidential campaign serve as a through line for the rise of religious television broadcasting during the Cold War and reveal the power and persuasiveness of the medium. The confluence of advancements in broadcasting, a reawakening of Christian fervor, and the perceived perils of a godless communist threat led to a mushrooming televangelism industry. Television preachers harnessed revivalist spirit to expand their audiences and save American souls, while often turning a major profit in the process. This electronic church (or electric church) emerged as a formidable force in the 1960s and 1970s. Using the tropes of old revivalist religion, religious broadcasters modernized the message to directly connect Christ to the defeat of communism. This linking of Christian faith with Cold War fears created a formula for success that elevated electric preachers to the status of national celebrity and granted them significant influence in American culture and politics.

AMERICAN EVANGELISM FOR A POPULAR AUDIENCE

These successful Christian broadcasters did not build their following out of entirely new methodology. They instead drew tens of millions of viewers by tying contemporary anticommunist themes to familiar revivalist themes of the American past. Nineteenth- and early twentieth-century preachers like Charles

Grandison Finney, Dwight Moody, Billy Sunday, and Aimee Semple McPherson served as models of mass appeal for these modern television preachers. The "most important legacy" of these preachers, scholar Razelle Frankl contends, "was their revivalist ethos, or use of 'appropriate means' to stir religious enthusiasm."[10] "Appropriate means" took many forms, depending on the preacher, audience, and era, but the core elements of American revivalism remained rooted in mass appeal obtained through anecdotal sermonizing, colloquial language, and a simplified, entertaining delivery of the Gospel.

In the tradition of these earlier American revivalists, television evangelists often used any means possible to reach their audience, but they tailored their approach to a nuclear generation. Perhaps one of the most effective themes to galvanize believers after World War II was the notion of an impending apocalypse, a concept that seemed all the more tangible in a postbomb society. This apocalyptic rhetoric, too, referenced the work of previous radical evangelicals, such as John Nelson Darby, who in the 1860s and 1870s promoted a controversial theology called premillennial dispensationalism. This belief held that humanity was entering a final phase before the Second Coming of Christ—a phase (or "dispensation") that can be seen in current events as analyzed through scriptural interpretation and application. Adherents looked for enemies who would aid the Antichrist in establishing global domination during these end times. "Radical evangelicals' preoccupation with anticipating who those enemies would be," historian Matthew Avery Sutton explains, "drove them to become serious students of geopolitical developments."[11]

This nineteenth-century framework of premillennialism informed the messages of later generations of evangelicals and took on enhanced meanings and creative theological interpretations in an increasingly globalized society mired in ideological conflict. By the mid-twentieth century these apocalyptic themes morphed into a globalized nuclear narrative, with televangelists engaging in end times prophesies based on Cold War developments and foreign activities.[12]

THE CONTEXT OF COLD WAR CULTURE

Thus, electronic evangelicals were part of a larger, shifting Cold War culture that both affected their message and was influenced by it. When historians use the phrase "Cold War culture," they are not merely referring to social trends of the years 1947 to 1991. Rather than denoting just the periodization, the term makes an implicit argument that there was something about the Cold War itself that shaped American culture and society. The impossibly high stakes of the conflict with the Soviet Union encouraged both elites and ordinary Americans to define themselves and their nation in terms that emphasized the contrast with their communist adversary. If the Cold War was a global debate over what made for a meaningful life, Americans made the case that their values and institutions were at once both exceptional and universally appealing. While decrying communism as a form of enslavement to the state, Cold War culture in the United States linked American patriotism with respect for traditional institutions, support for free market capitalism, and faith in America's civilizing mission. As is often the case in cultural transitions, new ideas such as anticommunism were bolstered by appeals to (and refashioning of) old ideas and traditions, ranging from gender norms to religious faith.

Early scholarship on the cultural history of the Cold War emphasized the importance of religion in shaping both cultural values and government policy, especially in the United States.[13] Although there are minor disagreements over emphasis, historians have developed a common narrative about the intersection of the Cold War and American religion during the first half of the period. Research and analysis on the later Cold War period of the 1970s to 1980s has only just begun to emerge. The existing scholarship can be broken into three overlapping categories: religion and American foreign policy, religion and secular culture, and the impact of the Cold War on religious ideas and institutions.

These religious beliefs played a vital role in shaping elites' understanding of America's proper role in the world, and political leaders often employed religious rhetoric in explaining their policies.[14] Although there was nothing new about religious rhetoric in political speeches, such language reinforced the urgent tone that politicians used to define the Cold War as an existential struggle between good and evil. Harry Truman, the first US president of the Cold War era, frequently spoke of faith and religious freedom as twin pillars of democracy. Citizens who enjoyed the freedom to worship as they chose would be quick to insist on other types of natural rights, including property rights. During the Eisenhower administration, Secretary of State John Foster Dulles's strident anticommunism reflected his devout faith as the son of a Presbyterian minister. It was Dulles who persuaded Eisenhower to include a prayer in his inaugural address, to demonstrate American commitment to Christianity.[15]

The impact of religion on Cold War elites was not limited to rhetoric and ritual, however. It also directly affected foreign policy in several ways. Truman, for example, sought to improve relations with the Vatican as part of an effort to use interfaith religious cooperation to build a global alliance against communism. Diplomatic historian Seth Jacobs has convincingly argued that Ngo Dinh Diem's Catholicism was a key factor in the Eisenhower administration's support for Diem as leader of South Vietnam.[16]

CONNECTING CHRISTIANITY AND PATRIOTISM

In addition to the diplomatic significance of Christianity abroad, the early Cold War was also a period of increased religiosity at home, particularly in secular political culture. New public rituals linked American patriotism with Christian faith, while new cultural narratives suggested (with some exaggeration) that the two had been inextricably intertwined since the American Revolution.[17] Several scholars have pointed out that the dramatic growth of American civil religion, as sociologist Robert Bellah termed it in 1967, cannot be separated from the Cold War; a renewed sense of religious righteousness as an essential and enduring component of American exceptionalism promised to reinforce claims that the government of the United States had the moral authority to lead the global struggle against Soviet communism.[18]

President Eisenhower, like Truman, saw the Cold War in religious terms, and under his administration the federal government introduced a number of new practices that emphasized the religious nature of American patriotism. The most famous of these was the introduction of the phrase "under God" into the Pledge of Allegiance in 1954, but that is far from the only example.[19] The Post Office issued a postage stamp that same year with the phrase "In God we trust" inscribed above the Statue of Liberty, and in 1955 Congress ordered that the phrase be added to paper currency; it already appeared on coins. The following year it was adopted as the national motto, replacing *E pluribus unum*.

Congressional debates over adding "In God we trust" to paper currency reveal the lines legislators drew between Christian faith, American patriotism, and anticommunism. The bill's sponsor, Representative Charles Bennett (D-

Florida), argued for its passing by invoking both anticommunism and American heritage. "In these days when imperialistic and materialistic communism seeks to attack and destroy freedom," he proclaimed, "we should continuously look for ways to strengthen the foundations of our freedom. At the base of our freedom is our faith in God and the desire of Americans to live by His will and by His guidance. As long as this country trusts in God, it will prevail."[20] Eisenhower himself called for annual days of prayer, which evolved into the annual National Prayer Breakfast, and in 1956 the Congressional Prayer Room was opened in the Capitol building.

Historian Jonathan Herzog has argued that these new practices led to the "sacralization" of secular government institutions. Furthermore, he demonstrates that political elites cooperated with economic leaders and media figures to promote a religious revival that they believed was a necessary condition for success in the fight against communism. If earlier periods of revival had been organic movements in which ordinary believers challenged the complacency of established churches, much of the religious revival of the 1950s was the result of intentional planning by elites in what Herzog evocatively terms the "spiritual-industrial complex."

"Worried that the spread of Communist ideas would undermine the home front," he explains, "[American] leaders concluded that religious faith was one of the most potent arrows in the quiver of domestic security. They did not hesitate to call the Cold War a holy crusade."[21] To counter this perceived vulnerability to communist subversion, corporate leaders sponsored a wide variety of efforts to counter secularization and to promote Christian faith as central to American identity, ranging from traveling displays of historical documents to campaigns for state laws requiring prayer in schools to calls to celebrate the Fourth of July as a religious holiday.[22]

This cultural relationship between the Cold War and American religion was not a one-way street. While religious perspectives shaped American understandings of the Cold War, theologians and religious communities were changed by their encounter with Cold War politics. Communism was an explicitly atheist philosophy that maintained that religion was mere superstition that the wealthy used to control the poor, an accusation that required a theological response. Furthermore, the lack of religious freedom and the persecution of believers in communist countries required religious institutions to seek a political response. Communism did not only present an existential threat to capitalist democracies; it also directly threatened faith communities, which encouraged religious leaders—especially from evangelical denominations—to engage with politics much more than they had in previous generations.

NUCLEAR WEAPONS, EVANGELICALS, AND PREMILLENNIAL DISPENSATIONALISM

Looming over this landscape of political religiosity was the ultimate apocalyptic fear: nuclear war. The arms race was one of the most terrifying aspects of the Cold War, and as weapons technology improved with each passing year, the possibility of nuclear war became increasingly disturbing. In the 1950s, the Eisenhower administration pursued a strategy of "massive retaliation," threatening to hit the USSR with a devastating nuclear attack should the Soviets invade Western Europe. Civil defense officials urged Americans to build family bomb shelters and to lay in supplies in the event of a Soviet nuclear attack. In the early 1950s, they suggested preparing three days' worth of food and water, but by the late 1950s, with the development of more powerful bombs and intercontinental ballistic missiles, the recommendation had increased to seven days' worth.

The Kennedy administration, recognizing the contradiction of "winning" a nuclear war, shifted to a policy of deterrence that became known as "mutually assured destruction," or MAD. Given the unimaginable consequences of an all-out nuclear conflict, neither the United States nor the USSR could dare to launch an attack. Instead, both sides would have to tolerate an uneasy awareness of the other's destructive ability. At the same time, federal civil defense officials increased their recommendation to fourteen days' worth of food and water.[23]

Many scholars have noted that popular anxiety about nuclear war—a literal apocalyptic event—created a space for Christian revival as Americans tried to make sense out of the possible end of the world. Secular society had no way to explain nuclear war, other than as a maddening, senseless tragedy. It was incomprehensible. On the other hand, American Christianity, with its emphasis on divine providence, offered both an explanation and reassurance. No matter what happens, God has a plan. As televangelist Jerry Falwell put it in 1983, "While considering all these things, let us not forget that there is a God who is in control."[24]

American evangelical sects had a significant advantage over other Christian denominations: interpreting biblical prophecies about the apocalypse had been central to their theology since the nineteenth century. Before the Cold War, evangelicals' embrace of premillennial dispensationalism kept them on the fringes of American Christianity, but the development of nuclear weapons brought them closer to mainstream culture. Suddenly everyone was talking about the end of the world, whether they were religious or not. As historian Angela Lahr has pointed out, nuclear anxieties created an opening for evangelicals both to join the national political discourse and to appeal to Americans trying to find meaning in the face of an incomprehensible threat.[25] Participation in a faith community could calm fears, reinforce a sense of national belonging, and even serve as a preemptive rebuttal to any accusations of subversion.[26]

Dispensationalism emphasizes literal interpretation of scripture, which leads evangelicals to a unique understanding of time. The Bible is not only a guide for the faithful but also reveals God's plans for history. Prophecy identifies certain events as inevitable and unalterable. The task for the believer is to "read history backwards" by examining current events in terms of how they will lead to known future events.[27] Interpretations of prophecy often change over time, as believers seek to define their own contemporary context through the application of Bible passages. As folklorist Daniel Wojcik observes, earlier generations interpreted prophecies of catastrophic destruction as predictions of natural disasters, whereas Cold War believers interpreted those same passages as predictions of nuclear war.[28]

For example, in *The Late Great Planet Earth*, author Hal Lindsey devotes nearly two hundred pages to detailed explications of scripture to support his claim that the biblical prophets were describing events that would take place in the late twentieth century, including an invasion of Israel by the Soviet Union that would lead to nuclear war. Lindsey, a graduate of Dallas Theological Seminary, stated that the ancient prophets could not have understood God's revelations in their own time, but as these events grew closer, Christians could recognize their prophecies as descriptions of modern military technology: "[In

Revelation, John] also predicts that entire islands and mountains would be blown off the map. It seems to indicate an all-out attack of ballistic missiles upon the great metropolitan areas of the world. . . . All of these verses seem to indicate the unleashing of incredible weapons the world over."[29]

With *The Late Great Planet Earth,* published in 1970 and made into a movie in 1978, Lindsey popularized Cold War interpretations of prophecies in the books of Ezekiel, Daniel, and Revelation that had first appeared in evangelical circles in the late 1940s and 1950s.[30] Written in a breezy style that combined informal language with claims of unavoidable truth, the book sold 28 million copies by 1990 and 35 million by 1999.[31] For millions of American believers, Lindsey's book established a basic plotline for the End of Days that would reappear, with minor variations, in the teachings of 1970s–1980s televangelists, including Jerry Falwell, Oral Roberts, Jimmy Swaggart, and Pat Robertson.[32]

The countdown begins in 1948, with the creation of the modern nation of Israel, which dispensationalists saw as partial fulfillment of God's promise to restore the homeland of the Israelites. The importance of Israel in prophecy led Falwell and Robertson to call for an aggressive American foreign policy to help Israel take full control of Jerusalem, destroy key Muslim sites, and build a new Jewish temple on the Temple Mount as fulfillment of the rest of the promise.[33]

After an indeterminate period of social, spiritual, and economic decline, during which the United States will lose its status as an international leader due to "internal political chaos caused by student rebellions and communist subversion,"[34] the Soviet Union will launch an unsuccessful invasion of Israel in fulfillment of the prophecy in Ezekiel 38–39, which describes an attack on Israel by Gog, a prince of Magog, a nation to the north, which is allied with Persia (Iran), Gomer (East Germany), and Ethiopia and Libya, which Falwell interpreted as the Black nations of sub-Saharan Africa and the Arabic nations of North Africa.[35] As punishment for attacking Israel, the USSR will be destroyed, most likely in a nuclear war that God allows. The resulting chaos will allow the Antichrist to gain power during seven years of tribulation. Finally, Christ will return and defeat the Antichrist at the battle of Armageddon, ushering in a thousand years of earthly reign.

As frightening as this timeline might appear, premillennialism offered believers an escape from inevitable nuclear war: the Rapture. Originally developed in the nineteenth century by John Nelson Darby, this term refers to a miraculous end times event in which the faithful are swept up bodily into heaven just before the tribulation, allowing them to escape both the Antichrist and death itself.[36] Although Cold War premillennialists were vague about the exact timing and order of events, they assured believers that the Rapture would take place before nuclear war. Only the enemies of God would suffer in that horrific war. All one had to do to avoid such a terrible fate was accept God. The saved had absolutely nothing to worry about.[37]

In fact, rather than fear, believers should feel joy. They lived in a special time, when God would finally fulfill promises that he had made more than two thousand years before. They would see the end of history. Indeed, an unsettling sense of excitement and anticipation is often evident in premillennialists' lurid descriptions of imminent nuclear destruction, which read like a thrilling movie script. As part of God's unalterable plan, nuclear war is morally justified and meaningful, because it will lead to the final redemption of humanity.

Historically, apocalyptic narratives have developed on the fringes and usually are not supported by mainstream institutional churches. During the Cold War, as during other periods of crisis, these narratives became more mainstream, bringing evangelical preachers and their end times theology into greater view. However, as they became more visible and more popular, many of them moderated the more frightening aspects of their theology. For example, from the late 1940s to the 1950s, Billy Graham's sermons often included warnings that if Americans did not turn to God, He might allow the Soviets to launch a nuclear attack on the United States. By the 1980s, after more than three decades as "America's pastor," Graham's message was closer to that of the old mainline Protestant churches.[38] In *Approaching Hoofbeats: The Four Horsemen of the Apocalypse,* published in 1983, he still sees nuclear war as a possibility, but rather than it being God's inevitable plan or divine retribution, he describes it as a sinful human action and calls on Christians to oppose nuclear proliferation: "To limit the growing threat of nuclear warfare seems perfectly in line with Christ's call to be peacemakers on the earth."[39] Biblical prophecies served as a warning of what *could* happen, but these events could also be avoided or postponed by human action.

Susan Friend Harding has noted an even more extreme shift in Jerry Falwell's theology. In the early 1970s, Falwell rejected political activism as pointless. Because Americans were living in the prophesied period of decline that preceded the return of Christ, no human action could improve society or prevent nuclear catastrophe. However, by the early 1980s, as the leader of the Moral Majority, he had rewritten the timeline to reassure his followers that they need not worry about nuclear war. In a 1983 "prophecy packet" comprising a short book and two cassette tapes, he argued that nuclear weapons were so destructive that they could not be part of a Soviet invasion of Israel, or even of the battle of Armageddon that would follow. It was possible that God might use them to destroy the world, but that would not take place until after the millennium of Christ's earthly rule. "Therefore, the earliest that a worldwide nuclear confrontation could happen is at least 1,007 years away if Jesus would come for his saints [in the Rapture] today!"[40]

It is worth noting that despite their interest in other religious implications of the Cold War, most American policymakers did not discuss nuclear weapons in these terms—with the exception of Ronald Reagan. Several observers have noted that while he was governor of California, Reagan studied end times theology with his friend Pat Boone, a well-known singer and evangelical Christian. In 1971, Reagan read *The Late Great Planet Earth* and was convinced by Lindsey's application of biblical prophecy, especially Ezekiel 38–39, to contemporary geopolitical events. As a presidential candidate in 1980, he commented in an interview with televangelist Jim Bakker, "We may be the generation that sees Armageddon." Reagan even went so far as to invite both Hal Lindsey and Jerry Falwell to the White House to brief Pentagon officials and the National Security Council on the link between prophecy and nuclear war.[41] Reagan's comments in the early 1980s terrified Soviet officials, who worried that his apocalyptic religious beliefs could lead him to launch nuclear war in order to fulfill prophecy.[42]

AMERICAN ABUNDANCE IN APOCALYPTIC TIMES

In this atmosphere of Cold War anxiety and apocalyptic talk, religious ideas became intimately entwined with capitalist agendas. For example, American postwar economic prosperity was often described as evidence of the superiority of the capitalist system over communism; the heart of Vice President Richard

Nixon's comments to Nikita Khrushchev in the famous Kitchen Debate in 1959 was that capitalism provided American working-class families with stable lives and a comfortable standard of living.[43] It was a short step from arguing that American abundance was proof of capitalism's superiority to arguing that American abundance was a sign of God's favor, a view with roots planted by John Winthrop and the early Puritan settlers.[44] Television preachers and Christian networks stepped right into this nexus of politics, culture, and faith to bolster the spiritual-industrial complex, to serve as partners of anticommunist American politicians, and to connect capitalist prosperity with Christian godliness.

When viewed as evidence of God's favor, prosperity served multiple purposes for televangelists. Adopting the prosperity gospel (or "health and wealth") connected them with capitalist ideals, allowed them to build massive business empires, and provided a foundational and appealing theology for many of their ministries. Building on past models of corporate Christian media ventures like Billy Sunday's large, electrified revivals and Aimee Semple McPherson's radio and screen presence in Hollywood, televangelists delivered entertaining programming, engaged in funding drives, and offered retail items to expand their brands and their network of believers. The sales and funding drives, themselves, also fit neatly into Cold War ideology, as popular preachers exhibited the capitalist identity of affluence and growth.

And grow they did. Evangelicals took over Americans' tubes, with prosperity preachers having what historian Kate Bowler deems "a market share that came close to a theological monopoly." Within ten years, from 1971 to 1981, independent preachers gobbled up so much airtime that they went from composing 42 percent of the top syndicated religious programming to a dominating 83 percent. By 1980, the industry was bringing in about $1 billion a year, and their audiences could see the fruits of this evangelical enterprise in the multimillion-dollar churches and gilded sets that propped up their favorite celebrity pastors.[45]

In this climate of Cold War capitalism and increasingly profitable Christian ministries, monetary success became a sign of God's blessing, and many television preachers taught that one simply must ask, believe, and one shall receive. As with capitalist conspicuous consumption, television pastors showed off these blessings by building churches with opulent architecture and appointing their sanctuaries (or sets) with lavish furniture and expensive features like waterfalls. Famous televangelist Rex Humbard built the Cathedral of Tomorrow in Cuyahoga Falls, Ohio, spending millions on a campus that included a revolving tower restaurant and a thirty-two-ton cross hanging behind the pulpit, illuminated by thousands of color-changing lights.[46]

Robert Schuller delivered the nationally syndicated *Hour of Power* broadcasts from one of the most recognizable modern megachurches, the Crystal Cathedral in Garden Grove, California. Completed in 1980, the imposing mirrored structure cost his ministry $18 million to construct, including the "Cape Canaveral" doors designed with the assistance of NASA engineers. The mechanized glass doors stood at eighty feet, directly behind Schuller's pulpit, where the camera crew could easily capture the grandeur of the design, and they ultimately symbolized the interaction of Cold War culture and televangelist empires.[47] The Crystal Cathedral was meant to reflect American technological advances and the might of capitalism and Christianity working in tandem.

Schuller's commitment to American Cold War ideologies and capitalism infused much of his spiritual teachings, which reached a million television viewers by the mid-1980s, including the audience of the Armed Forces Network. He proselytized "Possibility Thinking," the notion that individuals have the power to change their circumstances by believing in that change. Schuller in effect "assured financial success of those who followed his 'biblically based' principles" by combining free will with free market capitalism. This message, combined with Christian libertarianism and a steadfast desire to expand his brand and business, led Schuller to engage in aggressive fundraising and growth models, all while consistently using his platform to condemn communism. According to an *Eternity* magazine feature at the time, "The Soviet Union apparently considers Schuller's ministry to be such a totem of God'n'Country American civil religion that they have featured a display of the Garden Grove Church, complete with photographs of its pastor, in the Soviet Museum of Atheism in Leningrad." If true, this characterization was well earned. In his sermon "I Am the American Flag," the showy silver-haired evangelist exhorted that American capitalist democracy was the Christian way. "Freedom to borrow and build," he opined, "to buy and sell, to make an honest profit in return for real service sincerely offered" is the society that believers should defend.[48]

While televangelists all participated in this free (and largely unregulated) burgeoning spiritual marketplace, they did not all adhere to the call for honest profits. Infamously, Jim and Tammy Faye Bakker exploited the frenzied moment to create one of the most popular religious television shows of the 1980s—until excess and scandal took down the entire operation and landed Jim in prison. Starting their television ministry with Pat Robertson at CBN in the 1960s and continuing to develop a prosperity-driven ministry with Paul Crouch at Trinity Broadcasting Network in the 1970s, the Bakkers established their own empire with *Praise the Lord* (*PTL*) and combined evangelicalism with American pop culture to reach a wide audience. They innovated the format of television evangelism, airing a *Phil Donahue*–like talk show rather than a traditional sermonizing format, and the method of distribution, launching a satellite network that rivaled HBO and the Turner Broadcasting System.[49]

By 1986, *PTL* was projected into homes in forty nations and was making $129 million a year. The couple's ambitions led them to open a popular Christian-themed amusement park with an adjacent resort, attached to the television studio. Heritage USA in Charlotte, North Carolina, sat on 2,300 acres and boasted a water park and shopping mall for followers to get their fill of biblically (and *PTL*-) inspired merchandise. Sinking $175 million into building costs, Jim and Tammy Faye ultimately created a Disneyland for Christ.[50]

With such provocative ventures, the Bakkers represented both the rise of corporate Christianity and the perils of capitalist greed. While their colleagues and competitors were touting the morality of capitalism, Jim was engaging in illegal fundraising and exploiting vulnerable *PTL* viewers, exhibiting the darker side of free market economics. Heritage USA and *PTL* espoused jingoistic rhetoric with a "city on a hill" vision of an exceptional nation where all of Christ's faithful could enjoy the blessings of prosperity—all while selling a false bill of goods to those faithful followers.[51]

Several scandals swirled around the Bakkers, including stories of affairs, alleged rape, cover-ups, and drug dependencies. But the scandal that landed Jim in prison for almost five years involved the overselling of partnerships to Heritage USA in his telethons. In 1988, the disgraced evangelical entrepreneur was convicted of wire fraud, mail fraud, and conspiracy charges.[52]

THE NEXT CRUSADES

Despite his fall from grace, Bakker is back, with prophetic warnings for viewers who either forgot or forgave his past sins. After his parole in 1994, he publicly repented and published *I Was Wrong*, in which he denounces the prosperity gospel.[53] This public relations campaign set Jim up for another foray into religious programming with *The Jim Bakker Show*, which first aired in 2003, traffics in prophetic warnings, and promotes survivalist fare like buckets of bunker food. Cleverly forsaking his prosperity preaching, which would seem gauche, considering his financial crimes, his recent evangelizing doubles down on apocalyptic end times theology that borrows from and builds on Cold War constructs. "The Prosperity Gospel, with all its glitz and money, fit the culture of the 1980s and Jim found that was a very successful component of his message," historian John Wigger assesses. "In this post-9/11 era, he's found that the Apocalypse and survivalism make for a very compelling message that will also gain him an audience."[54] A theology of fear and promises of a Second Coming pervade his messaging as renewed global tensions emerge, and in 2022, with Russia once again a central player.

The failed presidential candidate and successful television personality Pat Robertson has not lost his zeal for political commentary, nor his audience for millennialism and prosperity teachings. After hosting *The 700 Club* on CBN for fifty-five years, the host retired briefly, only to return to the airwaves in March of 2022 to deliver a prophecy based on Russia's invasion of Ukraine. Drawing on the very same passages from Ezekiel 38 to bolster his claims, the ninety-one-year-old Robertson deemed the invasion an "act of God."

"I think you can say, well, Putin's out of his mind. Yes, maybe so," Robertson admitted. "But at the same time, he's being compelled by God. He went into the Ukraine, but that wasn't his goal. His goal was to move against Israel, ultimately."[55] And this action, according to the televangelist, is all part of God's larger design to bring about the battle of Armageddon. Despite the failure of his earlier predictions, made at the height of the Cold War, to manifest—or perhaps because they have not manifested yet—Robertson and his fellow televangelist crusaders continue to find an audience and plenty of revenue as they carry their apocalyptic and prosperity-fueled preaching into the new millennium.

NOTES

1. Wayne King, "Robertson, Displaying Mail, Says He Will Join '88 Race," *New York Times*, September 16, 1987, D30.

2. J. Gordon Melton, Phillip Charles Lucas, and Jon R. Stone, "Christian Broadcasting Network," in *Prime-Time Religion: An Encyclopedia of Religious Broadcasting* (Phoenix, AZ: Oryx Press, 1997), 57–58.

3. David Edwin Harrell Jr., *Pat Robertson: A Personal, Religious, and Political Portrait* (San Francisco: Harper & Row, 1987), 118–120.

4. For more recent anticommunist statements from Robertson, see Lee Marsden, *For God's Sake: The Christian Right and US Foreign Policy* (London: Zed Books, 2008), 63.

5. Irvin D. S. Winsboro and Michael Epple, "Religion, Culture, and the Cold War: Bishop Fulton J. Sheen and America's Anti-Communist Crusade of the 1950s," *Historian* 71, no. 2 (2009): 212.

6. Winsboro and Epple, "Religion, Culture, and the Cold War," 213. For more on early religious radio, see Quintin J. Schultze, "Evangelical Radio and the Rise of the Electronic Church, 1921–1948," *Journal of Broadcasting and Electronic Media* 32, no. 3 (1988): 289–306.

7. Jonathan P. Herzog, *The Spiritual-Industrial Complex: America's Religious Battle Against Communism in the Early Cold War* (New York: Oxford University Press, 2011), 60, 77, 85.

8. Winsboro and Epple,"Religion, Culture, and the Cold War," 218. Although televangelism is usually associated with evangelical denominations, Bishop Sheen's television ministry was notable for the religious diversity of its viewers.

9. Grant Wacker, *America's Pastor: Billy Graham and the Shaping of a Nation* (Cambridge, MA: Belknap Press of Harvard University Press, 2014), 232, 234–237.

10. Razelle Frankl, *Televangelism: The Marketing of Popular Religion* (Carbondale: Southern Illinois University Press, 1987), 4.

11. Matthew Avery Sutton, *American Apocalypse: A History of Modern Evangelicalism* (Cambridge, MA: Belknap Press of Harvard University Press, 2014), 16–20.

12. Angela M. Lahr, *Millennial Dreams and Apocalyptic Nightmares: The Cold War Origins of Political Evangelicalism* (New York: Oxford University Press, 2007).

13. See, especially, Stephen J. Whitfield, *The Culture of the Cold War*, 2nd ed. (Baltimore: Johns Hopkins University Press, 1996), 77–100.

14. This topic has proved fruitful for Cold War historians. In addition to Herzog, see T. Jeremy Gunn, *Spiritual Weapons: The Cold War and the Forging of an American National Religion* (Westport, CT: Praeger, 2009); and William Inboden, *Religion and American Foreign Policy, 1945–1960: The Soul of Containment* (Cambridge: Cambridge University Press, 2008).

15. Herzog, *Spiritual-Industrial Complex*, 92–94.

16. Jonathan P. Herzog, "From Sermon to Strategy: Religious Influence on the Formation and Implementation of US Foreign Policy in the Early Cold War," in *Religion and the Cold War: A Global Perspective*, ed. Philip E. Muehlenbeck (Nashville: Vanderbilt University Press, 2012), 54; Seth Jacobs, "'Our System Demands the Supreme Being': The US Religious Revival and the 'Diem Experiment,' 1954–55," *Diplomatic History* 25, no. 4 (Fall 2001): 589–624.

17. Many of the practices that underlie the contemporary popular belief that America was founded as a Christian nation originated in the 1950s, not the 1780s.

18. Robert N. Bellah, "Civil Religion in America," *Daedalus* 96 (Winter 1967): 1–21. For more recent scholarship, see Herzog, *Spiritual-Industrial Complex*; Gunn, *Spiritual Weapons*; and Raymond Haberski Jr., *God and War: American Civil Religion since 1945* (New Brunswick, NJ: Rutgers University Press, 2012).

19. Lee Canipe, "Under God and Anti-Communist: How the Pledge of Allegiance Got Religion in Cold War America," *Journal of Church and State* 45, no. 2 (Spring 2003): 305–323.

20. "HR 619: United States Currency Inscription," in *Miscellaneous Hearings: Hearings Before the Committee on Banking and Currency,* House of Representatives, 84th US Congress, session 1 (Washington, DC: US Government Printing Office, 1956), 47–57, at 49. Ironically, despite Congress's explicitly religious goals, the Supreme Court has dismissed legal challenges to the Pledge of Allegiance and other elements of civil religion on the grounds that such language was merely "ceremonial deism . . . [which has] lost through rote repetition any significant religious content."

21. Herzog, *Spiritual-Industrial Complex,* 16.

22. Ibid., 135–163. New York's Regent's Prayer, which was at the center of *Engel v. Vitale* in 1962, had been introduced only a few years before, in 1955. School officials explicitly listed anticommunism as one of the goals of the prayer.

23. Laura McEnaney, *Civil Defense Begins at Home: Militarization Meets Everyday Life in the Fifties* (Princeton, NJ: Princeton University Press, 2000).

24. Jerry Falwell, *Nuclear War and the Second Coming of Jesus Christ* (Lynchburg, VA: Old Time Gospel Hour, 1983), 2.

25. Lahr, *Millennial Dreams,* 25, 31.

26. Whitfield, *Culture of the Cold War,* 83.

27. Susan Friend Harding, *The Book of Jerry Falwell: Fundamentalist Language and Politics* (Princeton, NJ: Princeton University Press, 2000), 230.

28. Daniel Wojcik, "Embracing Doomsday: Faith, Fatalism, and Apocalyptic Beliefs in the Nuclear Age," *Western Folklore* 55, no. 4 (Autumn 1996): 301–302. See also Paul Boyer, *When Time Shall Be No More: Prophecy Belief in Modern American Culture* (Cambridge, MA: Belknap Press of Harvard University Press, 1992).

29. Hal Lindsey, *The Late Great Planet Earth* (Grand Rapids, MI: Zondervan, 1970), 166–167.

30. Paul Boyer observed that Lindsey's former classmates at Dallas Theological Seminary "complained that Lindsey had simply repackaged his lecture notes!" Boyer, *When Time Shall Be No More,* 126.

31. Erin A. Smith, *What Would Jesus Read? Popular Religious Books and Everyday Life in Twentieth-Century America* (Chapel Hill: University of North Carolina Press, 2015), 223.

32. See Larry Jones, "Apocalyptic Eschatology in the Nuclear Arms Race," *Transformations* 5, no. 1 (1988): 25–27; Michael Barkun, "The Language of Apocalypse: Premillennialists and Nuclear War," in *The God Pumpers: Religion in the Electronic Age,* ed. Marshall Fishwick and Ray B. Browne (Bowling Green, OH: Bowling Green State University Popular Press, 1987), 160–161.

33. Mark G. Toulouse, "Pat Robertson: Apocalyptic Theology and American Foreign Policy,"

Journal of Church and State 31, no. 1 (Winter 1989): 88–90. See also Grace Halsell, *Prophecy and Politics: Militant Evangelists on the Road to Nuclear War* (Westport, CT: Lawrence Hill, 1986); Tim LaHaye, *The Beginning of the End* (Wheaton, IL: Tyndale House, 1972), 43–60; Jack Van Impe, *Israel's Final Holocaust* (Nashville: Thomas Nelson, 1979), 87–109; Lahr, *Millennial Dreams*, 133–168.

34. Lindsey, *Late Great Planet Earth*, 184.

35. Falwell, *Nuclear War*, 18.

36. On Darby and the concept of the Rapture in evangelical theology, see Sutton, *American Apocalypse*.

37. LaHaye, *Beginning of the End*, 21–30; Lindsey, *Late Great Planet Earth*, 186–188; Van Impe, *Israel's Final Holocaust*, 115–118.

38. Throughout the Cold War, mainline Protestant churches had encouraged ecumenism and called for nuclear disarmament. See, for example, Andrew Preston, "Peripheral Visions: American Mainline Protestants and the Global Cold War," *Cold War History* 13, no. 1 (2013): 109–130.

39. Billy Graham, *Approaching Hoofbeats: The Four Horsemen of the Apocalypse* (New York: Avon Books, 1983), 140. See also Boyer, *When Time Shall Be No More*, 139; and Harding, *Book of Jerry Falwell*, 243.

40. Harding, *Book of Jerry Falwell*, 243–244; Falwell, *Nuclear War*, 8. See also Barkun, "Language of Apocalypse," 160–161.

41. Halsell, *Prophecy and Politics*, 42–50, at 47. See also Lawrence Jones, "Reagan's Religion," *Journal of American Culture*, December 1985, 59–70.

42. Multiple stories in *Pravda* drew attention to Reagan's eschatological beliefs, including "'Fatalist' iz Belogo doma" ['Fatalist' in the White House], *Pravda*, December 22, 1982, 5.

43. On the diplomatic background of the American National Exhibition in Moscow, see Walter L. Hixon, *Parting the Curtain: Propaganda, Culture, and the Cold War* (New York: St. Martin's Press, 1997), 151–183. For Nixon's comments, see *Bulletin of the Department of State* 41, no. 1051 (August 17, 1959): 227–236.

44. Although Nixon did not make this point explicitly, others did. During the congressional debates over adding "In God we trust" to currency, Representative Lawrence Fountain (D-North Carolina) noted that the phrase would indicate that Americans recognized that "because of the goodness of God, we have become a prosperous and powerful nation." The chairman of the House Banking and Currency Committee, Representative Brent Spence (D-Kentucky), supported the bill, stating, "I think if ever there was a nation that has, by its course, demonstrated that God had a hand in its making and its progress, it is this nation." "HR 619: United States Currency Inscription," 51, 56.

45. Kate Bowler, *Blessed: A History of the American Prosperity Gospel* (New York: Oxford University Press, 2013), 74–75.

46. Humbard also struggled with monetary problems that invited criticism of his theology and approach to evangelism, underscored by a 1973 Securities and Exchange Commission suit against his organization. See Douglas E. Kneeland, "Rex Humbard: From Sawdust Trail Impresario to Head of the Cathedral of Tomorrow," *New York Times*, February 22, 1973.

47. Mark T. Mulder and Gerardo Martí, *The Glass Church: Robert H. Schuller, the Crystal

Cathedral, and the Strain of Megachurch Ministry (New Brunswick, NJ: Rutgers University Press, 2020), 175.

48. Mulder and Martí, *Glass Church,* 18, 98, 125.

49. John Wigger, *PTL: The Rise and Fall of Jim and Tammy Faye Bakker's Evangelical Empire* (New York: Oxford University Press, 2017), 4–5.

50. Darren E. Grem, The Blessings of Business: How Corporations Shaped Conservative Christianity (New York: Oxford University Press, 2016), 162, 170.

51. The "city on a hill" imagery harkens back to colonial governor John Winthrop, who delivered the famous sermon to fellow settlers on their journey to Massachusetts Bay. Grem, *Blessings of Business,* 172.

52. Wigger, *PTL,* 301–328.

53. Jim Bakker, *I Was Wrong: The Untold Story of the Shocking Journey from PTL Power to Prison and Beyond* (Nashville: Thomas Nelson, 1996).

54. Tim Funk, "Fallen PTL Preacher Jim Bakker Is Back with a New Message About the Apocalypse," *Charlotte Observer,* February 19, 2008.

55. Timothy Bella, "Pat Robertson Says Putin Was 'Compelled by God' to Invade Ukraine to Fulfill Armageddon Prophecy," *Washington Post,* March 1, 2022.

A WAR OF COLORS

Cold War Food Advertising in US Newspapers
and Magazines, 1946–1960

FRANCESCO BUSCEMI

During the Cold War, communication strategies honed by both the West and the East extolled the perception of "us" and demonized the view of "them" in official political communication and popular culture. This was particularly true of one of the most prevalent aspects of popular culture, advertising. Beginning in the 1930s, advertising attracted consumers who were particularly thirsty for new products. In the postwar consumer society of the 1950s, however, economic growth increased the presence of advertisements as both commerce and ideology.[1] Scholars of propaganda have long debated the boundaries of the term "propaganda," whether it pertains only to dictatorships or also to democracies. This essay addresses advertising in the capitalist West—specifically, an analysis of the ideological use of color in food advertising published in US newspapers and magazines between 1946 and 1960—and uses the term to mean any form of communication that is strategically conceived to support one ideology to the detriment of another.[2]

EXISTING STUDIES ON COMMUNICATION IN THE COLD WAR

Many media studies on the Cold War focus on how the military and state apparatuses communicated ideologically. Brian McNair points out that political communication in the Cold War demonstrates how wars can be fought without arms and shows us how, beginning in the late 1950s, this strange weapons-free conflict became an excuse to limit progressive movements.[3] Martin Medhurst analyzes the coherent and consistent construction of the enemy through rhetorical techniques.[4] Matthew Aid and Cees Wiebes's edited collection centers on the codes of intelligence communication during those years.[5] Thomas McPhail tells the stories of the scientists and technicians who were hired in the United States to hone the secrecy of military communication and ended up creating the Internet.[6]

In 2004, a Defense Science Board report, confirming the centrality of communication in times of threat and duress, specified that some communication strategies adopted during the Cold War were reactivated after the terror attacks of September 11, 2001.[7] Greg Barnhisel suggests that visual communication, specifically the artistic movement of modernism, was used in the service of American cultural diplomacy, as anti-Soviet propaganda.[8]

In popular culture, James Schwoch highlights how American television became global during the Cold War and featured widespread anticommunist ideology.[9] Nancy Bernhard adds that in the United States, the government partnered with TV networks to instill the fear of the enemy in the American public.[10] Frances Stonor Saunders examines the Congress for Cultural Freedom, which from 1950 to 1967 spread anticommunist propaganda in thirty-five countries by producing art exhibitions, conferences, public performances, and magazines.[11]

Barnhisel analyzes magazines in the United Kingdom and the United States—London's *Encounter* and New York's *Perspectives USA*—which linked "artistic modernism, intellectual freedom, and anticommunism among members of the Anglo-American literary and cultural establishment."[12] *Encounter* also repeatedly accused Jean Paul Sartre of communist sympathy and service.[13] Advertisements in the West frequently related to the concept of abundance, with images brimming with colorful products and goods, though as Jonathan Nashel argues, "advertisements always promised and never completely supplied."[14] Batchelor argues that this focus on quantity developed as an American propagandist obsession to draw a contrast with the Soviet Union's poverty.[15]

Children and women were often targeted by advertising and merchandizing. For example, "from September 1948 through May 1949, America's 'Candy Bomber' Gail Halvorsen and 25 aircraft crews dropped 23 tons of chocolate, chewing gum, and candy over Berlin."[16] New models of beauty and femininity, such as the Avon ladies, marked the difference between Western beauty and communist ugliness.[17] For Dawn Spring, the Advertising Council demonstrates the alliance between politicians and advertisers such as J. Walter Thompson, which allowed advertising to become a fundamental weapon during the Cold War.[18]

Nathan Abrams explores the way terms such as "Jewishness" and "Americanness" were rediscussed during the Cold War, particularly after the case of Julius and Ethel Rosenberg.[19] In this rediscussion, Jewish food had a relevant role and acquired political meanings. Nickie Charles and Marion Kerr discuss meat as an ideological food in their discussion of gender roles in the kitchen.[20] Karen Syse mentions the ideological role of celebrity chefs on TV during the Cold War.[21] Notably, all of this literature lacks a coherent analysis of colors in communication during the Cold War, which is the issue under discussion here.

THEORY: COLOR, JEAN BAUDRILLARD, AND FOOD PROPAGANDA

This research draws on theories analyzing the relationships between color and communication. William Ryan and Theodore Conover point out that color "floods our sense. Color may be explosive, subtle, arresting, calming, symbolic, numbing, or seductive. It is pervasive, and it is everywhere."[22] Martti Huttunen considers that color may constitute a theoretical framework.[23] Even more specifically, Dennis Puhalla argues that color is a form of language through which people view, understand, interpret, and make an experience.[24] Color impacts emotions and thus affects the deepest parts of the user's comprehension.[25]

As with any system of representation, colors are organized according to signs, codes, and symbols, and this makes them suitable for semiotic investigation. Colors also have syntax to express thoughts and semantics that convey meaning.[26] Symbols related to colors change according to culture. For example, death is frequently expressed by the color black in Western societies but by white in many Asian countries.[27] Thus, every culture has its own color symbolism, precise codes of signification that relate to its various forms of representation.[28] Theories of color have also permeated popular culture. For Susan Murray, color TV was an ideological technology adopted by the United States during the Cold War to display a colorful world, in contrast with the gray imagery of the Soviet Union.[29] This chapter also draws on Jean Baudrillard's hyperreality and his reading of Jorge Louis Borges's short story *Of Exactitude in Science*.[30] In the story, a group of cartographers try to draw the most detailed map of their empire, ultimately creating a map that is identical to the empire and covers it in total. This creates confusion among the inhabitants, who take the real territory for the map and thus the representation for reality. Baudrillard points out that this is an example of hyperreality, in which signifieds and signifiers do not play their roles any longer and intertwine. He warns that this is exactly what is happening in postmodern societies, in which people only gain knowledge from media representations (the map). The reality, conversely, remains inaccessible, and thus people consider what the media represent to be true. However, the reality that is created is not identical to the original, as the media have somehow manipulated it.[31] In the end, Baudrillard sees hyperreality as a process of mutual detachment of reality and representation. The final part of this theoretical framework looks at food and its relationships with propaganda. As with colors, food is intrinsically bound to emotions. It may mean subsistence, life, or nurturing, but it also is frequently linked to the relationships to the Other, love, beliefs, nostalgia, and death. Food's ability to touch the most profound and hidden chords of human beings is why it has been used many times as a means of propaganda. Food and the nation, for example, share a strong bond, and in many cases we can witness the phenomena of overt food nationalism, in which food becomes a symbol of the nation, used to underline the superiority of "us" contrasted to "them."[32]

In recent studies, I have analyzed how food has been adopted to persuade people politically and even to support totalitarian regimes.[33] Moreover, I have underlined color as a powerful means through which to communicate food and ideology.[34] Ken Albala finds that food ideologies follow the same mechanism as political ideologies and that they have extraordinary abilities to promise social transformations.[35]

The three parts of this theoretical framework explain the point of view from which this research has been carried out. This chapter explores how the use of color in US food advertising created meaning with regard to the Cold War and the differences between the United States and the Soviet Union, from 1946 to 1960. To answer this question, I adopt the methodology developed in the next section.

METHODOLOGY

This essay applies multimodal analysis as theorized by the social semiotician Theo Van Leeuwen and other scholars of social semiotics. The object of this investigation is a sample of advertisements published in the United States from 1946 to 1960. Social semiotic and multimodal analysis examines how colors, positions, shapes, and other visual elements create meaning in relation to social contexts. Jewitt has found three different applications of multimodal analysis.[36] The first gives great attention to the connections between the analyzed items and what happens in the respective societies.[37] The second is a functional grammar approach,[38] and the third is an interactional application principally analyzing spoken languages.[39] This study follows the first strand and centers on advertisements in relation to the Cold War and its social effects.

Multimodal analysis is based on the analysis of various modes. The modes are single elements of an item. In a multimedia text, for example, there are visual modes such as color, shape, position, and the like; audio modes such as music, noise, voice, and others; and written modes like words, messages, and so on. Multimodal analysis breaks up a message into various modes, analyzes them separately, and obtains final results by combining all the analyses to discover how all the modes orchestrate meaning in a text.[40] While color is certainly the principal mode here, other written and visual elements also will be analyzed. Multimodal analysis is particularly fruitful when it considers social, cultural, and political differences and historical change.[41]

More specifically, I adopt Theo van Leeuwen's four multimodal categories of discourses, genre, style, and modality. *Discourses* are categories largely recognized, such as the Cold War, the United States, the Western world, and the like. *Genre*, instead, concerns "templates for doing communicative things," such as advice columns in magazines, Western films, or in this case, various types of advertising, from the educational to the purely commercial. *Style* relates to the ways a text is written, how objects are positioned in a picture, or how colors are used. Finally, *modality* is the way in which representations talk to the audience to underline their realness or fictitious nature, such as the realistic or unrealistic ways colors are used in an advertisement.[42] This essay analyzes advertisements through these four levels of social semiotic analysis.

For the selection of the items to be analyzed, I employed purposive sampling, "a nonrandom sampling technique in which the researcher selects elements supporting a particular theory or presenting specific characteristics."[43] This kind of sampling is used in qualitative research and involves participants or items that "have a particular type of experience, characteristic, or understanding to share." As with any qualitative insight, this method focuses on a small number of participants or items, and this offers advantages and disadvantages. On the one hand, it allows the researcher to go in-depth and catch essential traits of behavior or signification that a quantitative analysis would not consider; on the other hand, it presents "the possibility of prematurely focusing the data collection on one experience or understanding, and missing the broader range of data."[44] I selected three advertisements, published by newspapers and magazines in the United States during the analyzed period, which present a relevant use of color and other modes relating to the Cold War. Ultimately, qualitative research always implies that the researcher interprets the data they have found. To some this is a downside, while to others it is its strength. A third group of scholars argue that interpretation is necessary for qualitative research but that it must never become biased or prejudiced.[45] This is the balance I strive for here.

THIS IS LIFE

Leo Burnett's famous "This Is Life" advertising campaign relied on color as a fundamental element of signification. Commissioned before World War II by the American Meat Institute, which was aiming to push meat consumption in the United States, the campaign was first published in 1945. Because of its widespread success, it was republished in subsequent years.[46] The campaign was based on a simple and revolutionary idea: representing red meat on a red background. It in fact consists of a red image, half of which is occupied by a cut of raw red meat that is as red as the background. Conversely, the fat part of the cut is white. The other elements of the image are the white text reading "This is Life," which is the only element positioned above the cut; more white text just below the cut that says "Standing Rib Roast of Prime Beef"; a dark carving knife and fork about two-thirds of the way down the image; and another, longer block of white text below that.

This ad's copy underlines the idea that meat is life, that it feeds the body like nothing else, that its substances are complete and essential to life. "The protein of all meat (regardless of cut or kind) is complete," it says. Meat contributes to the physical development of both young and old people. Thus, eating meat is important as it gives enjoyment and, more relevantly, is nutritionally useful. A more educational portion of the text recommends eating meat "to maintain tissues, regenerate blood, resist infections, rebuild the body after injury or illness." A seal and some fine print guarantee that what is said in the ad has been checked by the American Medical Association. The rest of the text has to do with gendered roles in the kitchen. Meat is in fact defined as "a symbol of man's desire, his will to survive. For as old as man's instinct to live is his liking for meat." Women, conversely, are more simply "proud of their meals." Finally, the ad assures the consumer that if meat is not at the shop, it will arrive soon.

In terms of discourse, the general topic around which all the elements of the image gather, "life" seems to me the most recurrent. The red color plays a fundamental role here. We know that red is has been assigned many meanings and much symbolism, including its association with communism—that is, the enemy. Another recurring association with red is blood, however, and blood gives life like no other substance.[47] The claim of the ad, "This is life," immediately communicates the concept that meat is necessary to human life. As a result, we can say that in this case all the modes go in the same direction.

In terms of genre, this advertisement may be easily associated with the educational genre, or institutional campaigns that do not promote a private company but support a habit or a social activity, in this case eating meat. Institutional campaigns have the state or its institutions behind them, and in this case, the presence of the state, and its approval, is also reinforced by the seal and the writing stating that the content of the message is guaranteed by the American Medical Association. What is said in it is thus also approved by the United States, as if it were endorsed by the nation. "Life" therefore becomes something different in this light, as it is also the life of American citizens and the good health they have achieved. The dominant red color of the image, in the end, also symbolizes the (life) blood of the nation.

The first element regarding style is the fact that meat is portrayed raw and not cooked, as was almost always the case before this campaign. Leo Burnett said that representing uncooked red meat was a real novelty at the time. The campaign intended to communicate the idea of a virile item of food—bleeding, flavorful, and strong. To further add dramatic feeling, Burnett also decided to present red meat on a red background, and he added that he was surprised that the meat did not disappear. In the end, the entire bloodred page communicated a sense of drama without weak points or interruptions. Burnett said he found the image entirely natural, with the red background increasing the natural character of the image of meat.[48]

Finally, Burnett added a dark fork and knife strongly emerging from the red background, the only elements in the image, apart from the white fat and the text, that are not red. The two utensils are two spots that break the continuity of the red. If we consider, with Burnett, that the color red recalls nature, we may also suggest that the dark knife and fork symbolize culture. These are tools built by humans and with which humans deal with nature. As a result, meat is represented as a natural element that has been mediated by culture, underlines masculinity, is essential to human life, is supported by medical doctors, and relates to male desire, the will to survive, home, and enjoyment.

Mode, or the relationship with truth that the image suggests, is relevant here, due to the saturated color flooding the entire image. The red of the meat is enhanced and the background artificially has the same tonality as the cut. Baudrillard would have defined this image as an example of hyperrealism, in which the representation goes beyond reality. When reality becomes more complex, its traditional realistic representation is not sufficient to fully explain it. Rather, it is necessary to manipulate the traditional codes of representation and to represent reality in a nonrealistic way. Finally, because red is also the color of communism, America reappropriates it, refusing to leave to the enemy the exclusive use of it.[49]

The advertisement refers to meat as a material and immaterial good at the same time. Certainly, Burnett's ad relates to the medical, physical, and positive effects of meat on the human body; however, color, as we have seen in the theoretical framework, hits at the emotional level. In the end, the combination of the visual and the written modes links to the immaterial abilities of meat to improve human life, to give enjoyment, to create good health, and thus to better Americans (and "Americanism"), with state approval in the form of the

American Medical Association. Meat is no longer exclusively something to eat; it is also something immaterially giving consumers joy, a better life, and pride in being Americans. Interpreting this advertisement through Van Leeuwen's four categories highlights color as key to understanding many elements of the image. Blood, life, good health, enjoyment, and the relationship between nature and culture are the principal elements that color reinforces and promotes. Certainly, this advertisement was not thought of in relation to the Cold War, even though it repurposes the color of the enemy. In the end, this is the image that the United States created to represent one of its national foods, meat, and through it, to represent itself. The extraordinary combination of different languages, made up of words, colors, and objects, gives back a colorful image of America, in contrast to the gray representation of the Soviet Union described by Murray.[50]

YOU BET YOUR LIFE THEY'RE GR-R-REAT!

The second item analyzed here is Burnett's 1955 advertisement for Kellogg's Sugar Frosted Flakes.[51] It consists of a black-and-white photo of Groucho Marx, with a cigar between his lips, looking skeptically to his right, where a color drawing representing an anthropomorphized tiger has been added. The tiger has taken the NBC microphone from Groucho and is offering him a bowl full of Kellogg's flakes. Under the photo is written, "Tony the Tiger says: 'You bet your life they're Gr-r-reat'"! In smaller font, the text continues, "No wonder Groucho's speechless. What if a tiger stole *your* microphone and *your* favorite line. But that's Tony for you. And he's *all* for you when he tells you to try these big, crackly flakes of corn. Because they are the ones with the secret Kellogg's sugar coating all over. Gr-r-reat? You bet your life." At the bottom of the page, finally, is written, "Kellogg's Sugar Frosted Flakes."

As in the case of "This Is Life," analyzing this image through Van Leeuwen's categories may better explain what this image signifies and connotes, especially through color. In terms of discourse, what first emerges is the encounter (or clash) between two different worlds, the black-and-white and the color. The image, in fact, is entirely black-and-white, but the colored stain of the anthropomorphized tiger is the most evident element, as it breaks the regularity of the black-and-white. Incidentally, the microphone that the tiger has stolen and is taking in his hands (legs?) is also in black-and-white, a gray island in the colored part of the picture.

Here it is clear that the black-and-white represents the old world, while color is the novelty, and that in this image color brings something new to the old world of Groucho. It is thus the product that represents the novelty, arriving to change the old world. As a result, the flakes are promoted not only because they are good but also because they can change things and bring color to a black-and-white world.

In terms of genre, this is a fully commercial advertisement with a testimonial. A company is overtly stating its aims to sell, is showing its product, and is providing a testimonial by a famous actor supporting this message. It seems a traditional genre, and it certainly is. However, a second, unusual testimonial is more hidden: NBC, the television network that aired *You Bet Your Life*, the popular show hosted by Groucho Marx and to which the advertisement copy refers. The "NBC" on the microphone relates to the show but also adds another testimonial supporting the product, lending the credibility of a TV network. Thanks to this strategy, the product is much more strongly supported. With regard to style, what comes up immediately is the anthropomorphism and "cutification" of the tiger, which is also given a name, Tony. Representing a tiger with hands, a smile, offering a bowl, and even being called Tony renders it almost human. This cancels all the negative elements of the animal (in this case, ferocity) and transforms it into a sympathetic living being, close to humans and tender like a pet.[52] Moreover, many scholars have underlined that animal anthropomorphism confirms our dominion over nonhuman beings.[53] By expropriating their ways of feeling emotions, of speaking, and other characteristics, we deny their nature and conform them to ourselves. With regard to the mode and the idea of reality and truth that this image confers, it is evident that again the traditional and fair representation of reality is surpassed. As in the previous analysis, this analysis suggests a hyperrealistic approach that inserts an anthropomorphized tiger, distorts the figure of the animal, and relies on an actor and a TV network to sustain the commercial message and the promotion of the product. And as in the previous analysis, in this case, a tiger named Tony serving flakes to a comedian detaches the viewer from the traditional representation of reality to reinterpret it.

"SO LIGHT THEY ALMOST FLY"

The third advertisement for analysis is the 1956 promotion of Puffin biscuits. About 70 percent of the ad is occupied by a drawing of flying biscuits and a smiling young boy wearing a space helmet, set against a blue background. A young girl behind him looks at the scene in amazement. The tagline is "So light they almost fly," and the body of the text says, "So quick, so easy too! Puffins are completely mixed, shaped, and ready to bake. Remarkably white, light, and fluffy. A secret blend of premium flours makes them that way. Puffins are double-foil wrapped to guarantee freshness! Sweet milk or Buttermilk . . . begin enjoying Puffins today! In your grocer's dairy case." Under one of the two images of the product there is the "Guaranteed by Good Housekeeping" seal. Under the other is written, "Pick the package with the string." The bottom of the advertisement repeats the slogan, "Puffin Biscuits: So light they almost fly."

The discourse that is overtly manifested here is signaled by the blue sky where biscuits fly and the boy wears the space helmet: the space race. The competition between the United States and the Soviet Union to conquer space began in 1956, the year of the publication of the advertisement. On July 30 of that year, the United States announced that it would launch an artificial satellite into space. Two days later the Soviet Union stated the same intention (and Sputnik would be launched in 1957).

The space race was a competition between the two international powers, each seeking to reach space, and later the moon, to lend credibility and the perception of being stronger than the other.[54] The ad thus seems to actively support the United States through the representation of the biscuits flying in space and the boy among them. In this sense, whereas the other advertisements analyzed here did not mention the Cold War but only offered a colorful and promising image of the country and its inhabitants, this example overtly refers to the competition with the Soviet Union.

In terms of genre, this ad may be assimilated into the wide group of American advertisements displaying smiling young boys and girls. The image belongs to the category of advertising portraying the so-called American dream, a series of promotional messages relying on a happy America with its smiling boys and girls, used to promote foods and other products.[55] This representation certainly helped the process of quantitatively extolling consumerism, thanks to abundance, and turned children into consumers.[56] However, the passive role of the girl in comparison to the boy certainly demonstrates that although women were targeted by the media, they still played a secondary role.[57]

As regards style, it is important to note that the ad adopts two different modes, the written and the drawn. On the one hand, the written mode never hints at what is drawn, that is, the blue sky, the children, and the flying biscuits. Moreover, it has no educational content. Rather, it describes the product and invites the reader to buy it. On the other hand, the drawn mode does not describe the product but only makes people dream of a space race also involving the promoted product. In the end, we have a descriptive written mode and a dreamy visual mode. The first involves the public rationally, while the second does it emotionally. Colors are fundamental here, with the blue of the sky occupying the majority of the page and projecting the biscuits onto infinite space. Even in this case, the environment is represented as an example of domesticated nature, with the space somehow dominated by the (American) humans. As in the mode of the previous examples, there is an imaginary representation of reality. Space is evoked but not fairly represented. It is, rather, a funny and comfortable environment where children may go around along with their favorite biscuits. As Albala notes, food is paramount when someone promises social transformations, and these are the same transformations that were denied due to the emergence of the Cold War.[58] This and the other representations of reality led to a hyperrealism that, as in Baudrillard, manipulates the common rules of the representation of reality to detach from it, and at least in these cases, it supports the American ideology of the Cold War.

CONCLUSION: COLORED IDEOLOGIES

What emerges in a broader sense from this investigation is that food has been ideologically represented to support the United States in the Cold War and that color was decisive in this regard. Color has been relevantly adopted to create a different truth, another reality, in which the United States could show its cultural and material power, made up of joy, vitality, domesticated nature, optimism, and in the end, colorful life. Color can change reality, as in Groucho Marx's advertisement.

The great absence in this approach is the Soviet Union. The first ad is based on the color of the enemy and the third hints at the space race and thus at the Cold War. However, failure to overtly mention the enemy does not matter. It is sufficient to show a colorful and optimistic America made up of vital blood, anthropomorphized animals, and smiling children and then to say that these are the strengths of the nation. It was enough to underline the colorfulness of "us," leaving to others the representation of the gray "them."[59]

Certainly, Cold War propaganda relied on ostentation of abundance, as some studies have noted. However, the present study has found that there also was ostentation of color. Propaganda here was not based on the quantity of goods and products but on the quality of color and its ideological messages. By coloring ideology, these ads communicated the Cold War to an enormous mass of people and contributed to the creation of what has been termed "consumer-oriented anticommunism."[60] In doing so, color has been revealed to be a language.[61] Though color is the focus of this study, the other modes follow the same trend, both visually and textually. Together, they have constructed the United States as a nation domesticating nature. Meat has been saturated and portrayed along with a fork and knife, Tony the Tiger has been humanized and has lost his overt animalism, and space has been conquered by a boy and a dozen flying biscuits. America is not winning by chance. Representing a nation that has won the war against nature, meaningfully, will persuade people that it also will win the next conflict, the Cold War.

Color has therefore been assisted by other modes in this optimistic representation celebrating the wealth and the abundance of American consumerism. The center of this ideological discourse is the construction of a hyperrealistic world in which, as in Baudrillard, things are distorted to become more than real. While the traditional way of representing reality forced the cartographers to create a map identical to the territory, these advertisements manipulated reality, saturated its colors, inserted in it speaking tigers and flying biscuits to communicate the power of the United States against the enemy. The media and the old representation of reality do not do justice to the new, complex world. The NBC brand on the microphone is real, but because it appears next to a speaking tiger, it participates in the new, confusing world of hyperrealism, bearing its past but signifying other meanings, as theorized by Baudrillard.

Relevantly, even the food in these ads is never real. The analysis shows that colors present in two of the three analyzed ads were well beyond a realistic representation of what people eat. The cut of meat of the first case is too red, and the flakes of the second cannot be recognized clearly and are an undistinguishable yellow mass in a bowl. However, it is a new relationship with the consumer that these items of food are describing. They ask to be consumed not because of their closeness to what the consumer will find at the supermarket. Rather, they ask to be bought because they belong to a nation that is at war.

In relation to this, when a nation is at war, it addresses its soldiers—at those times, men. Underlining the virile role of meat, therefore, or giving way to the boy and not to the girl, makes soldiers feel proud of their masculine mission. The sense of drama described by Burnett completes the construction of tension crawling below the surface of the page.

As noted in discussing the theoretical framework, food itself is a powerful weapon for spreading nationalism.[62] It usefully hits the emotional side of the consumer. Color and food together have a special ability to touch the emotional chords. Showing a country full of variety and wealth perfectly served the ideological purpose of celebrating consumerism and demonizing communism. This idea of abundance and the joy of consuming further detached the United States from the gray idea of poverty and scarcity in the Soviet Union. In doing so, ideology was colored and served its purpose.

NOTES

    1. Bob Batchelor, "Introduction: Creating Advertising Culture, Beginnings to 1930s," in *We Are What We Sell: How Advertising Shapes American Life . . . and Always Has*, ed. D. Sarver Coombs and Bob Batchelor (Santa Barbara, CA: Praeger, 2014), xi–xxi.

    2. Tran Van Dinh, *Communication and Diplomacy in a Changing World* (New York: Ablex, 1987), 42.

    3. Brian McNair, *An Introduction to Political Communication* (Abingdon: Routledge, 1995).

    4. Martin J. Medhurst, *Cold War Rhetoric: Strategy, Metaphor, and Ideology* (East Lansing: Michigan State University Press, 1997).

    5. Matthew M. Aid and Cees Wiebes, *Secrets of Signals Intelligence during the Cold War and Beyond* (London: Frank Cass, 2001).

    6. Thomas L. McPhail, *Global Communication: Theories, Stakeholders, and Trends* (Malden, MA: Wiley Blackwell, 2010).

7. Defense Science Board, *Report of the Defense Science Board Task Force on Strategic Communication* (Washington, DC: Office of the Under Secretary of Defense for Acquisition, Technology, and Logistics, 2004).

8. Greg Barnhisel, *Cold War Modernists: Art, Literature, & American Cultural Diplomacy* (New York: Columbia University Press, 2015), 2.

9. James Schwoch, *Global TV: New Media and the Cold War, 1946–1969* (Urbana: University of Illinois Press, 2009).

10. Nancy E. Bernhard, *US Television News and Cold War Propaganda, 1947–1960* (Cambridge: Cambridge University Press, 1999), 2.

11. Frances Stonor Saunders, *The Cultural Cold War: The CIA and the World of Arts and Letters* (New York: New Press, 1999).

12. Barnhisel, *Cold War Modernists*, 138.

13. Saunders, *Cultural Cold War*, 182.

14. Jonathan Nashel, *Edward Lansdale's Cold War* (Amherst: University of Massachusetts Press, 2005), 52.

15. Batchelor, "Introduction: Creating Advertising Culture," xi–xxi.

16. Victoria M. Grieve, *Little Cold Warriors: American Childhood in the 1950s* (Oxford: Oxford University Press, 2018), 124.

17. Lindsey Feitz, "Ding Dong! Avon Calling! Selling Beauty and Femininity in the Cold War," in Coombs and Batchelor, *We Are What We Sell*, 101–112.

18. Dawn Spring, *Advertising in the Age of Persuasion: Building Brand America, 1941–1961* (New York: Palgrave Macmillan, 2011)

19. Nathan Abrams, "More than One Million Mothers Know It's the Real Thing," in *Edible Ideologies: Representing Food and Meaning*, ed. Kathleen LeBesco and Peter Naccarato (New York: State University of New York Press, 2008), 79–103.

20. Nickie Charles and Marion Kerr, *Women, Food and Families* (Manchester: Manchester University Press, 1988).

21. Karen L. Syse, "Celebrity Chefs, Ethical Food Consumption and the Good Life," in *Sustainable Consumption and the Good Life: Interdisciplinary Perspectives*, ed. Karen L. Syse and Martin L. Mueller (London: Routledge, 2015), 165–182.

22. William Ryan and Theodore Conover, *Graphics Communications Today*, 4th ed. (New York: Delmar Learning, 2004), 178.

23. Martti Huttunen, *Beneath the Surface of Colours* (Helsinki: Books on Demand, 2018).

24. Dennis Puhalla, "Color Language Hierarchy," in *Visual Communication*, ed. David Machin (Berlin: De Gruyter, 2018), 195–214.

25. Donis A. Dondis, *A Primer of Visual Literacy* (Cambridge, MA: MIT Press, 1973), 55.

26. Puhalla, "Color Language Hierarchy," 196.

27. Ryan and Conover, *Graphics Communications Today*, 178.

28. John Gage, *Color and Meaning: Art, Science, and Symbolism* (Berkeley: University of California Press, 1999).

29. Susan Murray, "Color TV Transformed the Way Americans Saw the World, and the World Saw America," *Smithsonian Magazine*, January 25, 2019.

30. Jean Baudrillard, *Simulacra and Simulation* (Ann Arbor: University of Michigan Press, 1994); Jorge Louis Borges, "On Exactitude in Science," in *Collected Fictions*, ed. Andrew Hurley (New York: Viking, 1998), 325.

31. Jean Baudrillard, *Selected Writings*, 2nd ed., ed. Mark Poster (Stanford, CA: Stanford University Press, 2001), 149.

32. Atsuko Ichijo, Venetia Johannes, and Ronald Ranta, *The Emergence of National Food: The Dynamics of Food and Nationalism* (London: Bloomsbury Academics, 2019).

33. Francesco Buscemi, *From Body Fuel to Universal Poison: Cultural History of Meat, 1900–The Present* (Doredecht: Springer, 2018), 49–62; Buscemi, "The Sin of Eating Meat: Fascism, Nazism and the Construction of Sacred Vegetarianism," in *Proteins, Pathologies and Politics: Dietary Innovation and Disease from the Nineteenth Century*, ed. David Gentilcore and Matthew Smith (London: Bloomsbury Academic, 2019), 137–147.

34. Buscemi, *From Body Fuel*, 64–65.

35. Ken Albala, *Three World Cuisines: Italian, Mexican, Chinese* (London: Altamira Press, 2012).

36. Carey Jewitt, "Different Approaches to Multimodality," in *The Routledge Handbook of Multimodal Analysis*, ed. Carey Jewitt (London: Routledge, 2014), 31–43.

37. Robert Hodge and Gunther Kress, *Social Semiotics* (Cambridge: Polity Press, 1988); Gunther Kress and Theo van Leeuwen, *Multimodal Discourse: The Modes and Media of Contemporary Communication* (Oxford: Oxford University Press, 2001).

38. Kay O'Halloran, *Multimodal Discourse Analysis: Systemic Functional Perspectives* (London: Continuum, 2004); Michael O'Toole, *The Language of Displayed Art* (Leicester: Leicester University Press, 1994).

39. Sigrid Norris, *Analyzing Multimodal Interaction: A Methodological Framework* (London: Routledge, 2004).

40. Roberta Taylor, "Multimodal Analysis of the Textual Function in Children's Face-to-Face Classroom Interaction," in *Multimodal Epistemologies: Towards an Integrated Framework*, ed. Arianna Maiorani and Christine Christie (New York: Routledge, 2014), 228–244.

41. Jeff Bezemer, "What Is Multimodality?," *University College London*, Institute of Education, February 16, 2012, https://mode.ioe.ac.uk/2012/02/16/what-is-multimodality; Arianna Maiorani and Christine Christie, "Introduction," in *Multimodal Epistemologies*, 1–12.

42. Theo van Leeuwen, *Introducing Social Semiotics* (London: Routledge, 2005), 91, 94, 128.

43. Francesco Buscemi, "How 'Il Caffé Sospeso' Became 'Suspended Coffee': The Neo-liberal re-'Invention of Tradition' from Bourdieu to Bourdieu," *European Journal of American Culture* 34 (2015): 2, https://doi.org/10.1386/ejac.34.2.123_1.

44. Carol L. Macnee and Susan McCabe, *Understanding Nursing Research: Using Research in Evidence-Based Practice*, 2nd ed. (Philadelphia: Lippincott Williams & Wilkins, 2008), 122.

45. Stacey Menzel Baker and James W. Gentry, "Framing the Research and Avoiding Harm: Representing the Vulnerability of Consumers," in *Handbook of Qualitative Research Methods in Marketing*, ed. Russell W. Belk (Cheltenham: Edward Elgar, 2006), 322–332.

46. Grad Conn, "100 Days of Leo Burnett, the Midwestern Master of Mascots: Day 14," *Copernican Shift*, March 14, 2017, http://www.copernicanshift.com/100-days-of-leo-burnett-the-midwestern-master-of-mascots-day-14.

47. Gage, *Color and Meaning*, 110–112.

48. Denis Higgins, *The Art of Writing Advertising: Conversations with Masters of the Craft* (Chicago: NTC Business Books, 1965).

49. Jesse Owens Hearns-Branaman, *Journalism and the Philosophy of Truth: Beyond Objectivity and Balance* (New York: Routledge, 2016).

50. Murray, "Color TV Transformed the Way Americans Saw the World."

51. Brian Braiker, "Before Frosted Flakes Had Netflix, It Had Groucho Marx," *AdAge*, January 23, 2019. https://adage.com/article/creativity/frosted-flakes-netflix-groucho-marx/316318.

52. Buscemi, *From Body Fuel*, 67–68; Frans de Waal, *Good Natured: The Origins of Right and Wrong in Humans and Other Animals* (Cambridge, MA: Harvard University Press, 1996).

53. Siobhan O'Sullivan, Barbara Creed, and Jenny Gray, "Low Down Dirty Rat: Popular and Moral Responses to Possum and Rats in Melbourne," *Relations beyond Anthropocentrism*, no. 2 (2014): 2, https://doi.org/10.7358/rela-2014-002-osul.

54. Sally Spray, *Awesome Engineering Spacecraft* (North Mankato, MN: Capstone Press, 2018), 6.

55. Barry Richards, Ian MacRury, and Jackie Botterill, *The Dynamics of Advertising* (Amsterdam: Harwood Academic, 2000), 59.

56. Batchelor, "Introduction: Creating Advertising Culture," xi–xxi.

57. Feitz, "Ding Dong! Avon Calling!," 101–112.

58. Albala, *Three World Cuisines*; McNair, *Introduction to Political Communication*.

59. Murray, "Color TV Transformed the Way Americans Saw the World."

60. Bernhard, *US Television News*, 2.

61. Puhalla, "Color Language Hierarchy," 196.

62. Ichijo, Johannes, and Ranta, *Emergence of National Food*.

CULTURE AND POPULAR ENTERTAINMENT

The ideological nature of the Cold War necessitated an unprecedented mobilization of nearly every aspect of American society responsible for molding the nation's values and identity. By the mid-twentieth century, the broad scope and impact of mass media, art, entertainment, and leisure pastimes brought cultural activities to the forefront of this battle. Allied to the structural militancy and concomitant vigilance required of Cold War preparedness, many aspects of American culture became weaponized in the struggle to assert the nation's supremacy. Over time, the contribution of American culture to the consensus building of the grand American narrative gave way to a critique of the nihilism of mutually assured destruction and of the stifling restrictions imposed by Cold War conformity.

Overseas, the government prosecuted a "soft power" war of influence on several fronts. Dwight Eisenhower once noted the need to "promot[e] the American story throughout the world to friend and enemy alike," adding that it is "hopeless to do this by lecturing and pontification. It must be done in many ways." The vanguard of this effort was the CIA, which covertly funded initiatives such as the Congress for Cultural Freedom, a global enterprise that, beginning in 1950, produced magazines, journals, and artistic events dedicated to promoting Western liberal-democratic principles. The CIA also helped to fund international exhibitions of modern art, dance recitals, and classical music concerts to extol the vitality and individual expressiveness of a free society. The agency also produced and distributed works that could sow discord in Communist societies. The most notable example was their dissemination of Boris

Pasternak's novel *Dr. Zhivago* behind the Iron Curtain. A CIA memo noted that with this book, "we have the opportunity to make Soviet citizens wonder what is wrong with their government." More overtly, beginning in 1947 and extending through the end of the Cold War and beyond, the federally funded Voice of America provided a positive image of American society on radio sets across the globe. The Cold War similarly influenced the form and content of American cultural activities at home, though the effort was less centrally coordinated.

Few forms of media in the twentieth century had as much ability to capture hearts and minds as movies, and American filmmakers fully embraced the nation's Cold War concerns. Alongside anticommunist government documentaries, some early Cold War commercial movies barely rose above the level of propaganda, including *The Red Menace* (1949), *I Married a Communist* (1950), and *Invasion USA* (1952). The John Wayne movie *The Green Berets* continued this trend in 1968 and received significant material support and input from the Pentagon in its depiction of the Vietnam War. The nihilistic absurdity of the mutually assured destruction nuclear strategy found expression in movies such as *On the Beach* (1959), *Dr. Strangelove* (1964), and *WarGames* (1983). The covert side of the Cold War proved fertile ground in the spy genre, spawning such films as *The Spy Who Came In from the Cold* (1965) and the James Bond series.

The continued popularity of Westerns reminded Americans of the rugged individualism and steely vigilance of frontier life, in direct contrast to the collectivist mentality of the Soviet state. Biblical epics extolled the pious nature of American life compared to the godlessness of communism. Science fiction and horror movies provided an allegorical canvas on which to paint the nation's hopes and fears. In *The Day the Earth Stood Still* (1951), for instance, an alien figure threatens to destroy the world if humanity continues its belligerent ways. The story of a farm boy doing battle against an evil empire in the original *Star Wars* trilogy (1977–1983) echoed filmmaker George Lucas's concerns over the geopolitical struggle between democracy and authoritarianism.

During the 1980s, many filmmakers embraced the militarism and anticommunist rhetoric of Ronald Reagan's presidency in movies such as *Red Dawn* (1984), *Rambo: First Blood Part II* (1985), and *Top Gun* (1986). Musclebound actors such as Sylvester Stallone and Arnold Schwarzenegger became part of the image of American virility, promoting what one critic described as the "Pecs

Americana." Movies also had the ability to critique Cold War society, and films such as *Easy Rider* (1969) assailed the nation's conformity while *Hearts and Minds* (1974) eviscerated the militarism of the Vietnam era.

Similar themes played out on the small screen. The postwar expansion of television brought the cultural war into Americans' living rooms on a nightly basis. Shows such as *Father Knows Best* (1954–1960) established the family as the central organizing unit of society. *Gunsmoke* (1955–1975) and *Bonanza* (1959–1973) continued the theme of settling the frontier as a defining process in America's national identity. The realm of television science fiction spoke to the nation's hopes through the utopian visions presented in series such as the original *Star Trek* series (1966–1969), while several episodes of *The Twilight Zone* (1959–1964) aired genuine anxieties about nuclear annihilation or the corrosive social impact of anticommunist hysteria. The ABC-produced movie *The Day After* became a television event of profound significance when it aired in 1983. Depicting with grim realism a nuclear attack on Kansas, it attracted more than 100 million viewers. Ronald Reagan wrote in his diary that the movie left him both depressed and determined to do what was necessary to avoid nuclear war.

Many of the most notable popular movies of the Cold War era were based on best-selling novels, including Nevil Shute's *On the Beach* (1957), Richard Condon's *The Manchurian Candidate* (1959), Eugene Burdick and Harvey Wheeler's *Fail-Safe* (1962), and Tom Clancy's series of novels involving the character of Jack Ryan, which began with *The Hunt for Red October* (1984). As with their big-and small-screen counterparts, science fiction writers created alternate worlds in which to examine Cold War themes. George Orwell's novel *1984* (1949) continues to serve as a cultural touchstone warning against the dangers of a centralized totalitarian state. Robert Heinlein's *Starship Troopers* (1959) depicted a society in which military service and vigilance against foreign foes was foundational to citizenship. Some authors used science fiction to both explore and warn about a postapocalyptic world, as in Walter M. Miller Jr.'s *A Canticle for Leibowitz* (1959), in which an order of monks strives to preserve mankind's scientific knowledge in the wake of a nuclear holocaust. As with some counterculture filmmakers, writers often took up the mantle of assailing the conformity of American society. Most notably, authors of the Beat generation and New Left movement launched scathing critiques of the nation's racial, economic, and sexual mores.

Literature more oriented toward younger readers was similarly influenced by Cold War anxieties. Dr. Suess's *The Butter Battle Book* (1984) is an unsubtle allegory for the (nuclear) arms race, played out here between the Yooks and the Zooks who live on opposite sides of a dividing wall. A seemingly trivial cultural difference between the two leads to the creation of new weapons on either side, culminating in the mighty Bitsy Big-Boy Boomeroo. The book concludes with a standoff at the wall and an ominous wait for who will strike first.

Comic book readers gained some respite from the dread of annihilation thanks to superheroes promising salvation from existential threats. The 1960 iteration of *Green Lantern* featuring test pilot Hal Jordan, and *Fantastic Four* launched in 1961, offered the hope that American ingenuity and derring-do could transcend the fear of technological inertia caused by the Soviet launch of Sputnik in 1957. Many comic book characters were literal creations of the Cold War, such as the Hulk, who was born from a failed experiment with a gamma bomb. In 1963, long before becoming a twenty-first-century big-screen phenomenon, the original comic book version of *Iron Man* fought communists, and Tony Stark created his first metallic suit to escape a ruthless Vietnamese foe. In the graphic novel *Watchmen* from the mid-1980s, the central antagonist, Ozymandias, seeks to prevent the United States and the Soviet Union from fighting each other by creating a fictional extraterrestrial enemy against whom they can align.

Away from the page, international sport offered little respite from Cold War tensions, and events such as the Olympic Games provided a natural stage on which to play out the struggle for ideological supremacy. The martial values and physical prowess of sporting conflict gave an opportunity to portray the strength and vitality of a society through the athletes it produced. Consequently, both the United States and the Soviet Union devoted significant resources toward ensuring the primacy of their athletes on the global stage. Any victory of one side over the other had the potential to carry huge psychological significance. When the Soviet Union competed in its first Olympics, in Helsinki in 1952, a *New York Times* columnist rallied Americans to support their athletes, arguing that the "communist propaganda machine must be silenced so that

Part III: Culture and Popular Entertainment 223

there can't be even one distorted bleat out of it." The rivalry continued, reaching its height for the American public with the 1980 "Miracle on Ice" when, at the Lake Placid Winter Olympics in New York, a group of predominantly amateur ice hockey players defeated a heavily favored professional Soviet team.

Songwriters from Bob Dylan ("Masters of War") to Billy Joel ("Leningrad," "We Didn't Start the Fire"), and Diamond Head ("Dead Reckoning") released songs with overt Cold War themes, while the antiwar songs of the Vietnam era by artists including Credence Clearwater Revival ("Fortunate Son") and Neil Young ("Ohio") gave us some of the more memorable rock tunes of the twentieth century. On the stage, Arthur Miller's *The Crucible* (1953) turned a dramatization of the Salem witch trials into a critique of the paranoia of the McCarthy era. The fashion industry became an arena in which to promote Western abundance. In the waning years of the Cold War, the nascent video game industry produced titles such as *Missile Command* (1980) and *Raid over Moscow* (1984). Teenagers could also face off against an advanced fictional Soviet fighter jet in *Firefox* (1984), based on the 1977 novel and 1982 Clint Eastwood movie of the same name.

The essays in this section highlight the ways in which the Cold War influenced the production and consumption of culture and entertainment. In the first essay, "Hollywood's Cold War: The Battle for Hearts and Minds on Film," Tony Shaw divides American Cold War movies into five phases in which filmmakers both reflected and amplified the undulating cultural shifts of either consensus building or critique across the decades of Cold War society. In "To Condense a Mockingbird: Harper Lee, *Reader's Digest,* and the Cold War," Kristen Popham and Simon Stow demonstrate how Harper Lee's seminal 1960 work, *To Kill a Mockingbird,* was filtered through a Cold War lens for consumers of the popular *Reader's Digest* condensed book series. Published in 1961, the truncated version of the book sanitized much of the nuance and racial tension in the original novel and presented a more palatable vision of race relations— and of American society—for its readers, both at home and overseas. Matt Sprengeler's "Playing by New Rules: Board Games and Cold War American Culture, 1945–1965," examines how popular board games such as Scrabble, Chess, Clue, and Risk offered a palliative for Cold War anxieties by allowing players to exert a degree of control over complex scenarios. In "The Cops versus the

Commies: Cold War Cuba and Chile in US Folk Music," Eunice Rojas explores how US folksingers highlighted interventions in Latin America, particularly in Cuba and Chile. Collectively, their songs reflected and amplified the concerns over the morality of US Cold War policy in Latin America. The final essay, "Us and Them: The Eagle versus the Hammer and Sickle in the Cold War Sporting Arena," by Kurt Jefferson, focuses on the centrality of sports as a spectacle of the Cold War from 1945 to 1991. In contrast to Kurt Kemper's essay on college football in part 2, Jefferson explores how sport became a shared national experience for Americans as they rallied behind their surrogate warriors on metaphorical fields of battle.

HOLLYWOOD'S COLD WAR

The Battle for Hearts and Minds on Film

TONY SHAW

For more than a century, America's film executives have habitually prided themselves on creating harmless, feel-good, apolitical entertainment. We give the people what they want, they say: the chance to laugh, to cry, to be thrilled, and above all, to escape. The truth is that American film—just like the nation's theater, radio, newspapers, and television—has always been political in one way or another. In particular, the big screen has traditionally been hostile to what it loosely defines as extremism.

This helps to account for the dozen or so explicitly anticommunist films that appeared in the immediate aftermath of the 1917 Bolshevik Revolution. Bristling with titles like *Dangerous Hours* (Fred Niblo, 1920) and *Starvation* (George Zimmer, 1920), these films depicted Bolsheviks as the bringers of murder, rape, chaos, and destruction.[1] Communists continued to be portrayed negatively on the American screen intermittently throughout the 1920s and 1930s— though in a more gentle and thus arguably more effective fashion politically—in movies such as *Trouble in Paradise* (Ernst Lubitsch, 1932), *Little Man, What Now?* (Frank Borsage, 1934), and *Ninotchka* (1939).[2]

The American government played no direct part in the making of these early "Cool War" movies. It had no need to, for Hollywood shared Washington's ideological worldview. Hollywood—both the place and the way of doing business—came into being in the 1920s, when the geographically scattered array of small and medium-sized producers, distributors, and exhibitors that had characterized the American filmmaking industry since the early 1900s was supplanted by an increasingly oligarchic, vertically integrated studio system with production centered in Los Angeles and business offices in New York. By the end of the 1920s, eight major studios controlled more than 90 percent of the films made and distributed in the United States.

The executives who ran Columbia, MGM, Paramount, RKO, Twentieth Century-Fox, United Artists, Universal, and Warner Bros. were hostile to communism owing to political conviction and economic self-interest, not because they felt beholden to officialdom. Men like Louis B. Mayer at MGM and Joseph Schenck at Twentieth Century-Fox instinctively equated patriotism with capitalism. Throughout this period and beyond, the major studios' films consistently reinforced the reigning cultural ethos and political-economic order in the United States, abounding with what many in the industry saw as the quintessentially American ideals of democracy, social mobility, capitalist consumption, justice, and cross-class harmony.[3]

By the time of the World War II, cinema had become the prime entertainment medium in the United States and across large parts of the world. Talkies had taken over from silent movies, and cinema admission figures in the United States had reached almost 100 percent of the population. During the war, American filmmakers, like their Soviet counterparts, played an enthusiastic, imaginative, and vital role in the struggle against fascism. In accordance with guidance from one of the government's propaganda arms, the Office of War Information, a small number of movies sought to transform the Soviet Union from an erstwhile enemy into a valuable wartime partner. These films—*Mission to Moscow* (Michael Curtiz, 1943), *Tender Comrade* (Edward Dmytryk, 1943), *The North Star* (Lewis Milestone, 1943), and *Song of Russia* (Gregory Ratoff, 1944)—would come back to haunt the studios when the Cold War proper started in the late 1940s, providing spurious evidence that Hollywood was infested with communists. Meanwhile, the links established between the film community and the Office of War Information during World War II would help facilitate cooperation between Hollywood and the government once the renewed but now more pressing propaganda battle with Soviet communism got under way.[4]

This overview of Hollywood's Cold War output divides the years 1947 to 1990 into five periods: 1947–1953 (dominated by hard-line negative propaganda); 1953–1962 (soft-core, positive propaganda mixed with the beginnings of negotiated dissent); 1962–1980 (pro-détente propaganda); 1980–1986 (New Right propaganda); and 1986–1990 (a call for peace). None of these dates are definitive and there is scope for considerable overlap between some of the sections. More space is allotted to the 1940s and 1950s due to film's role in the development of America's early Cold War consensus and because this period also marked the high point of the state's involvement in Cold War filmmaking.

DECLARING WAR, 1947–1953

Having challenged and ridiculed communists (usually as pathetic individuals) for the best part of three decades, Hollywood went several steps further in the late 1940s by declaring full-scale war on international communism. As would be the case for the next forty years or so, Hollywood followed rather than led political and public opinion during this era. Its first full-fledged Cold War movie, for instance, *The Iron Curtain,* a fact-based exposé of Soviet espionage in postwar Canada directed by William Wellman for Twentieth Century-Fox, appeared in May 1948, fourteen months after the announcement of the Truman Doctrine.[5] Nevertheless, once it got into its Cold War stride, the American film industry pretty much hit Soviet communism with all it had. Many historians have tended to belittle this campaign by suggesting it amounted to little more than a cycle of crudely made box office flops.[6] Evidence indicates otherwise.

Hollywood came under tremendous pressure to establish its anticommunist credentials once US–Soviet diplomatic relations froze soon after the defeat of fascism in 1945. The chief turning point came in October 1947, when the House Un-American Activities Committee (HUAC) arrived in Hollywood to root out those who had turned the American film industry into, as the committee's chairman J. Parnell Thomas put it, a "Red propaganda center." HUAC failed, both in 1947 and again in the early 1950s, to uncover any hard proof of communist infiltration or Marxism on celluloid. Nevertheless, the blacklisting of real or suspected communists was introduced, spreading like a tapeworm throughout the industry into the 1960s.

The wounds left by HUAC's inquisition would be felt across Hollywood for decades, not least by those such as the Hollywood Ten, who were jailed for actively opposing the committee, and the relatives of actor Philip Loeb, after persecution helped drive Loeb to suicide.[7] HUAC's investigations were part of an uncoordinated yet ferocious campaign fought by conservative forces inside and outside the government in the late 1940s and 1950s, which was designed to draft the media into the Cold War.

Five organizations played a key role in ensuring Hollywood acted in the national interest during this period. First, the Catholic Legion of Decency, a militant right-wing group established in the 1930s, acted as guardian of the big screen's moral and political rectitude. It was quick to categorize any politically or sexually dubious film material as potentially "subversive." The Legion of Decency enjoyed an especially close relationship with Hollywood's own Production Code Administration, another highly conservative censorship body, which had been set up in 1934 and until the mid-1950s was run by the Catholic intellectual Joseph Breen. The PCA selected stories, examined scripts, and approved the final cuts of movies. During the early phases of the Cold War, it managed to control the content of nearly all films shown in the United States, domestic and foreign.[8]

Third, the Motion Picture Alliance for the Preservation of American Ideals issued regular advice to filmmakers on how they should best express their patriotism in the Cold War's battle for hearts and minds. Established in Hollywood in 1944 to vanquish "the growing impression that this industry is made up of, and dominated by, Communists, radicals, and crackpots," the alliance was headed by, among others, Eric Johnston, who was president of the Motion Picture Association of America, Hollywood's main trade body, and Roy Brewer, leader of the most powerful film labor union, the International Alliance of Theatrical Stage Employees. In 1948, the alliance published a highly influential booklet by novelist and conservative ideologue Ayn Rand, *A Screen Guide for Americans*, which warned studios against, among other things, smearing the free enterprise system or deifying "the common man."[9]

Fourth, the American Legion, a veterans' organization founded in 1919, campaigned against those identified as suspect by the alliance, the Legion of Decency, or HUAC, organizing boycotts of films it deemed subversive or that featured actors labeled as communist sympathizers. With more than seventeen thousand posts and nearly 3 million members nationwide in the 1950s, the legion, like the numerous other established social organizations of the Right, such as the Daughters of the American Revolution, carried considerable economic and political weight in the film industry. During the 1970s, Legionnaires were more than willing to put a stop to movies criticizing America's presence in Vietnam by tearing up theater seats.[10]

Finally, and perhaps most importantly, the Federal Bureau of Investigation, which from 1924 to 1972 was run by one of the nation's most ardent anticommunists, J. Edgar Hoover, operated its own triangular-shaped film strategy. First, the bureau ran a comprehensive surveillance operation in Hollywood, pinpointing supposed communists with the aid of secret informers and identifying those movies that were being used as "weapon[s] of Communist propaganda." Second, the FBI secretly laundered its intelligence through HUAC, pressuring the industry into establishing and then strengthening a blacklist. Third, the bureau helped to produce movies that fostered its image as the protector of the American people. It provided script material, editing expertise, production consultation, and even special agents as actors for at least eight feature films between 1945 and 1959.[11]

Given this measure of policing, it is hardly surprising that the content of American movies in the late 1940s and early 1950s lurched decisively to the political right. We should also consider the numerous film artists who voluntarily contributed to the anticommunist onslaught on screen—some because they were conservative Catholics, others because they were liberal anticommunists, others still due to their strong links with the government or military. These included the world's preeminent animator, Walt Disney; Columbia Pictures president Harry Cohn; the head of censorship at Paramount, Luigi Luraschi; big-name directors such as Leo McCarey and John Ford; the legendary producer-director Cecil B. DeMille; and A-list actors such as John Wayne and James Stewart.[12]

Hollywood turned out approximately seventy explicitly anticommunist movies between 1948 and 1953, roughly 5 percent of the total film output for those years. This, the high point of the American film industry's full-frontal assault on the Soviet Union, took place when cinema attendance in the United States numbered roughly 6 million patrons per week (down from an all-time peak of 80 million patrons per week in 1945).[13] None of these films reached anywhere near the top of the annual box office charts; indeed, many failed to recoup their costs. But some did not do too badly financially. Alfred E. Green's *Invasion USA*, for instance, which was distributed by Columbia in 1952 and foretold a Soviet atomic attack on America through Alaska, only cost $120,000 but grossed a respectable $1.2 million.[14] MGM's *Never Let Me Go* (Delmer Daves, 1953), a Clark Gable vehicle telling the story of an American journalist stationed in Moscow just after World War II who falls for a Russian ballet dancer, made $1.5 million.[15]

Critics justifiably panned most of these movies for being poorly constructed and transparently propagandistic. Historians have since used the term "agitprop" to describe this material, denoting its resemblance to the Soviet Union's highly politicized, often clumsy style of mass persuasion.[16] There were some exceptions, however. Alfred L. Werker's *Walk East on Beacon*, for example, a Boston-set spy docudrama made by Columbia in association with the FBI in 1952, eschewed sensationalism in favor of a factual, no-frills portrait of communist fifth columnism in the United States. The Central Intelligence Agency leased copies of this movie for showings overseas well into the 1970s.[17] George Seaton's *The Big Lift* (1950), a romantic drama that extolled the bravery of the US Air Force during the 1948–1949 Berlin Airlift, was nominated for a Golden Globe. Made on location in collaboration with the Defense Department's public relations directorate, *The Big Lift* was an early example of the Pentagon–Hollywood axis during the Cold War.[18]

Other anticommunist movies of this era garnered Academy Award nominations. These include the Warner Bros. drama *I Was a Communist for the FBI* (Gordon Douglas, 1951) and Sam Fuller's crime thriller *Pickup on South Street* (1953).[19] Dore Schary's *The Hoaxters* won the Oscar for best documentary in 1953 and was endorsed by the FBI, the State Department, and the Psychological Strategy Board, the coordinator of the US government's Cold War propaganda activities from 1951 to 1953. Narrated by a host of MGM actors, this thirty-six-minute film likened the lure of communism to "that of the old-time medicine man whose phony brew promised to cure everything, being swallowed cheerfully by the gullible until rigor mortis set in."[20]

The overriding theme to emerge from Hollywood's Cold War material in this early phase of the conflict is the fear of communist subversion. The theatrical trial of Julius and Ethel Rosenberg in 1951 on atomic espionage charges—they were executed in 1953—provided many people with compelling evidence that the Reds really were under Americans' beds. What is striking, however, is Hollywood's versatility in depicting subversion, and the film industry's ability to incorporate this and other Cold War themes across the full range of genres.

Communists were shown to be infiltrating the United States from all directions—east, west, north, and south. They were sabotaging military installations, controlling labor unions, twisting the minds of university students, and masquerading (though not very successfully) as Christians on church pews. Film fans could watch them doing all this in dramas, comedies, documentaries, espionage thrillers, science fiction shockers, crime capers, and even Westerns. To an extent, many of these movies simply amounted to a retooling of World War II plot lines, in which communists played the new Nazi infiltrators with identical personality flaws, false idealism, and brutal methods. In some cases, the Red–fascist totalitarian link was made explicit. RKO's *The Whip Hand* (William Cameron Menzies, 1951), for example, focused on a former Nazi scientist, since converted to communism, who was carrying out germ warfare experiments in sleepy Wisconsin.[21]

Other films showed communism to be spreading across the world, thereby emphasizing the global, total dimensions of the Cold War and calling upon the American people to support Washington in its duty to defend the cause of freedom. Sometimes Americans were depicted as fighting the scourge of communism as private individuals (as in Fred T. Sears's 1953 drama *Target Hong Kong*), on other occasions as professional spies (as in Robert Parrish's 1952 *Assignment—Paris*). Established Hollywood stars added to the general picture of American Cold War heroism. Thus, the Indian-born actor Sabu and former Tarzan star Johnny Weissmuller (now the hunter Jungle Jim) fought communist insurgencies on tropical islands in *Savage Drums* (William Berke, 1951) and *Savage Mutiny* (Spencer Gordon Bennet, 1953), respectively.[22]

Wherever Americans were countering the threat from the new enemy, communists were usually portrayed according to a set of easily identifiable conventions. While their American (read democratic and capitalist) adversaries were innocent, courageous, clever, and law-abiding freethinkers, communists were evil-doing, cowardly, mentally unstable, heartless automatons who worked for the Party. Sporting cheap suits and murdering opponents in cold blood, they looked and acted like gangsters. The Communist Party did not stand *for* anything in these films, only *against* sacred American principles: God, motherhood, and love for one's family and country. Communism's political and economic principles might receive token expression in crudely distilled comments and speeches, but Hollywood's overall attitude toward ideological matters during these years can be summed up in a line from R. G. Springsteen's *The Red Menace* (1949): "I don't know what communism is," says a Party member's mother to a recent convert, "but it must be bad if it makes you do the things you do."[23]

Perhaps those movies that spelled out the bankruptcy of communism more starkly than any others during the late 1940s and the 1950s are those that purported to depict the reality of life behind the recently installed Iron Curtain. One notable B feature was Felix Feist's *Guilty of Treason* (1949), which, like Columbia's more prestigious *The Prisoner* (Peter Glenville, 1955), accused the Communist government in Hungary of torturing and brainwashing the nation's Catholic primate, Cardinal József Mindszenty, after his highly publicized real-life arrest in 1948.[24] As information about the degradations faced by many living under communism began to leak into the West, especially after Khrushchev's famous "Secret Speech" of 1956, Hollywood went more on the attack by alleging widespread human rights abuses behind the curtain. One film, Elia Kazan's *Man on a Tightrope* (1953), set in Czechoslovakia and released just after Stalin's death in 1953, anticipated this enduring portrait of communist dictatorship.

ACCENTUATING THE POSITIVE, 1953–1962

Hard-line, negative cinematic propaganda continued to appear even after the era dominated by HUAC and Senator Joseph McCarthy. In the mid-1950s, however, a small number of American filmmakers started to question cinema's role in this Cold War propaganda campaign. As the perceived threat from the communist enemy within receded and McCarthy's own witch-hunt tactics were famously exposed on television in 1954, space opened for liberals within Hollywood to challenge aspects of the Cold War consensus. The result was what can be termed the beginnings of negotiated dissent on the screen in the

United States, of images that offered an alternative perspective on the Cold War but that, at this stage of the conflict at least, were still largely contained by long-standing industrial constraints and contingent political pressures. Any filmmaker who went too far in subverting the Cold War consensus in the 1950s still had to reckon with the blacklist and the American Legion. Projects also had to get past the Production Code Administration.

Two movies led the field in questioning American Cold War orthodoxy in the mid-to late 1950s. In Daniel Taradash's 1956 melodrama *Storm Center*, Bette Davis played an elderly small-town librarian who is hounded out of her job for refusing to remove from her shelves a tome, *The Communist Dream*, which local officials deem to be subversive "garbage."[25] *Storm Center* made only a small impression at the box office but it represented Hollywood's most direct assault on McCarthyism until the mid-1970s. Stanley Kramer's star-studded drama *On the Beach*, released three years later, in 1959, was the first American movie to challenge seriously the feasibility of nuclear war survival. Set in Melbourne, its plot followed the fates of the crew of a US atomic submarine and their Australian hosts, who are helplessly awaiting the cloud of radioactive fallout that is drifting south after having already killed everyone in the northern hemisphere.[26]

As significant as these films were, what really characterized so much of Hollywood's output of the 1950s and early 1960s was its promotion of "American" ideals. The roots of this lay in the studios' often unconscious support for individuality, freedom of choice, material abundance, cultural vibrancy, and political moderation, dating back to the 1920s. Film executives were acutely aware of their role in selling what both they and official propagandists called "people's capitalism" at home and overseas, showing that the fruits of American free enterprise could be enjoyed by all, not just by the rich. In 1951, Motion Picture Association of America head Eric Johnston announced in the film press that Hollywood was on the front line in the Cold War. It was a role "that we can fill with credit and distinction as we have with every call in the past," he declared, "with ingenuity, with a large dash of daring and a large helping of the sauce of wholesome showmanship."[27]

Hollywood celebrated America's material prosperity like never before in the 1950s. There was a good reason for this: the nation's economic boom during that decade, partly driven by the defense industry, brought unprecedented growth and consumer spending power. Movies reveled in presenting the United States as a land of unbridled opportunity, fun, and get-ahead spirit in the 1950s. The musical—the quintessential American genre, offering utopian images of social harmony, affluence, and material well-being—thrived.[28] Walt Disney's films reverberated with tried-and-true Americanism even more than usual during this period. Having declared in 1947 that Hollywood's communists ought to be "smoked out," Disney, an FBI informant, proclaimed a year later that the time was ripe to "renew acquaintance with the American breed of robust, cheerful, energetic, and representative folk heroes." Hits like *Davy Crockett, King of the Wild Frontier* (Norman Foster, 1955), *Johnny Tremain* (Robert Stevenson, 1957), and *The Light in the Forest* (Herschel Daugherty, 1958) followed.[29]

Historical heroes, religion, and the Cold War came together in one of the defining genres of this era, the biblical epic. The very splendor of megabudget epics like *Quo Vadis* (Mervyn LeRoy, 1951) and *Ben-Hur* (William Wyler, 1959)—with their fantastic special effects, rich colors painted on spectacularly large canvases, and international stars—testified to America's capitalist-based creativity and advertised the superiority of democracy's freedom of spirit. At least one of these epics, Cecil B. DeMille's multimillion-dollar-grossing *The Ten Commandments* (1956), was designed to give scriptural authority to the ideology of America's Cold War.[30] On a separate note, Marilyn Monroe, one of the biggest female stars of the 1950s, came to symbolize American glamour, sexiness, and the pursuit of happiness—all things many Soviet propagandists rejected publicly as decadent but privately admired.[31]

Fueling so much of Hollywood's creativity during the 1950s was a relentless pursuit of the international box office. Hollywood had dominated the international film market since the 1920s, but after 1945 it found those areas under Communist control effectively closed off. American cinema attendance was in marked decline in the 1950s, which meant that it was vital to expand Hollywood's interests in regions such as Western Europe, Asia, and Latin America. If Hollywood could also offset the growing costs of filmmaking in the United States by making movies in these regions (so-called "runaway productions"), where labor and studio costs were far cheaper, so much the better. The State Department was more than happy, for commercial and diplomatic purposes, to help Hollywood in this respect by breaking down tariff and tax barriers. Put simply, Washington believed that the more people saw Hollywood movies, the more Americanized the world would become.[32]

The US government worked in other ways to bolster Hollywood's "Americanization" and Cold War programs in the 1950s. The CIA camouflaged its cinematic activities by secretly paying for a British animation company, Halas and Batchelor, to adapt one of the Cold War's greatest antitotalitarian fables, George Orwell's *Animal Farm*, for the big screen in 1954.[33] The United States Information Agency (USIA), coordinator of the American government's overt propaganda activities after 1953, sponsored documentaries extolling the virtues of "people's capitalism," celebrating America's racial "melting pot," and promoting the peaceful nature of nuclear weapons.[34]

Simultaneously, the State Department, the CIA, and USIA all worked to penetrate the Iron Curtain cinematically. In 1960, this bore fruit when, among other movies, William Wyler's 1953 romantic comedy *Roman Holiday*, a prime example of the feel-good, "runaway" Hollywood production of the early Cold War era, was exhibited in the Soviet Union.

FEAR AND LOATHING, 1962–1980

In contrast with its Soviet counterpart, the American government never had the power to ban films from the other side.[35] Nor could it entirely dictate to the nation's filmmakers how they should cover the Cold War. It never wanted that power, however, for all its occasional criticisms of Hollywood's disloyalty. After all, the US claim to have the freest media in the world lay at the heart of Washington's propaganda strategy during the Cold War, and it was one of the simplest and most powerful ways for Americans to distinguish democrats ("us") from communists ("them").

As it was, in the first decade and a half of the Cold War, very few filmmakers either desired or dared to challenge the super patriotic, pronuclear, anticommunist consensus in the United States. Once the 1960s got into full swing, however, this began to change. The subsequent shift in Hollywood's treatment of the Cold War can be attributed partly to Cold War events and partly to the wider political mood within the United States. The 1960s was arguably the most turbulent decade of the twentieth century for Americans (the 1962 Cuban

Missile Crisis, civil rights marches, political assassinations, Vietnam, the feminist movement, drugs, and rock 'n' roll), and it was quickly followed by one of the most dispiriting decades (Watergate, energy crises, economic recession, and international terrorism).

While the Cold War remained at the top of the geopolitical agenda during this period, to many Americans the conflict, which was now twenty to thirty years old, looked far less politically and morally clear-cut. If Moscow and Beijing really were the twin centers of evil, some asked, why was the US president going there? Could the US military ever be justified in burning a Vietnamese village in order to save it, as one officer notoriously stated on television? Did the existence of a "missile gap" really matter when the United States already had enough nuclear warheads to blow the world to kingdom come?

An equally important cause of greater Cold War dissent on screen was the structural changes Hollywood underwent in the 1960s and 1970s. These in fact started in the early 1950s, when anticartel legislation triggered the dismantling of the old studio system. Though most of the majors remained, their relative weakness created greater opportunities for independent filmmakers to make movies that were artistically avant-garde and politically experimental. Many of these filmmakers were liberals who, once blacklisting disappeared, felt more able to push for, among other things, a reconsideration of Cold War shibboleths.

In the late 1960s, the concept of a "New Hollywood" began to take shape, centered on a generation of younger directors who had cut their teeth in the faster-moving television industry and who were less beholden to both the old, conservative-minded studio chiefs and to many of the film industry's conventions. At the same time, Hollywood's old-fashioned censorship system was relaxed. This allowed for greater sexual, social, and political license on the big screen.[36]

Hollywood's treatment of the Cold War tracked these political and industry changes closely in the 1960s and 1970s. Anxieties and doubts about the direction in which US foreign policy was heading characterized the first decade's coverage, a sense of bewilderment and anger the second. Overall, movies gave a distinct if uncoordinated impression that America had lost its way in the Cold War, that the West and the East were playing a cynical game of power politics, and that peaceful coexistence was now essential.

Between 1962 and 1965, five movies were released that, together, heralded a sea change in Hollywood's attitude toward the Cold War. Two were political conspiracy thrillers directed by the thirtysomething John Frankenheimer, *The Manchurian Candidate* (1962) and *Seven Days in May* (1964). Two were nail-biting antinuclear dramas made, again, by young directors, *Fail Safe* (Sidney Lumet, 1964) and *The Bedford Incident* (James B. Harris, 1965). The fifth was a brilliant black comedy about the madness of nuclear deterrence, made, like *The Bedford Incident*, in Britain, by the thirty-five-year-old Hollywood exile Stanley Kubrick, *Dr. Strangelove or: How I Learned to Stop Worrying and Love the Bomb* (1964).

Each film, in its own way, took a scalpel to the Cold War consensus. Each also aroused deep controversy, thereby encouraging filmmakers, politicians, and the public to question received wisdom about the conflict. *The Manchurian Candidate* starred Laurence Harvey as Raymond Shaw, a brainwashed Korean War hero programmed as a Communist "mole" to assassinate an American presidential candidate. A complex, sophisticated movie, it launched a powerful assault on the American Right and on the media's role in fostering political paranoia.[37]

Seven Days in May depicted an attempted coup d'état by the US Joint Chiefs of Staff to prevent a dovish American president from signing a nuclear disarmament treaty.[38] *Fail Safe* was the first Hollywood movie to propose seriously that nuclear Armageddon could be brought about by accident due to the flaws within the machinery of deterrence. *The Bedford Incident*, focusing on a chase between a US Navy destroyer and a Soviet submarine, showed that World War III could result from fatigue and miscommunication.[39] *Dr. Strangelove*, a richly textured film now widely regarded as one of the finest of all Cold War movies, satirized the theory of mutually assured destruction by depicting America's political and military leaders as criminally insane sex maniacs.[40]

Another important movie of the era, though one far less well known today, is *The Russians Are Coming, the Russians Are Coming*. Directed by the forty-year-old Canadian-born Norman Jewison for United Artists and released in 1966, it told the story of a Soviet submarine crew that, after accidentally running aground in US waters off the coast of Massachusetts, causes a communist invasion scare when it goes ashore to look for help. The islanders and sailors eventually come together to save a young boy from falling from a church steeple. The movie humanizes the Russians by "decommunizing" them, rendering the enemy as just like us.

Jewison managed to enlist some minor help from Soviet film officials in making *The Russians Are Coming*, as part of his efforts to encourage peaceful coexistence. A gentle, slapstick satire on East–West relations, the movie tapped into a rich vein of US opinion in the mid-1960s, becoming the fifth-highest-grossing movie in the nation in 1966. The movie also enjoyed a series of special screenings in the Soviet Union, where audiences reportedly cried with joy and were amazed that the Americans were allowed to make such a funny and optimistic film about the Cold War.[41]

With one or two exceptions, the sunny optimism exhibited by Hollywood in *The Russians Are Coming* failed to last beyond the 1960s. The 1970s kicked off with several films evincing deep cynicism about the Cold War and particularly about America's role in it. Many of these were designed to appeal especially to Americans between the ages of fifteen and twenty-five, who had not been born when the Cold War started but now made up a disproportionately high percentage of filmgoers. In 1971, US cinema attendance reached an all-time low of 16 million patrons per week, after which it recovered slightly. By 1990, it stood at roughly 25 million patrons per week.[42]

Many of the anti–Cold War films of the early 1970s were, like some of their 1960s counterparts, complex dramas highlighting diplomatic intrigue and political skullduggery. Gone were the simple black-and-white images of the McCarthy era, with their easily identifiable, ugly "baddies" and well-dressed, honorable "goodies." Audiences had to work harder, both to follow the plots and to work out who was on whose side (or indeed if there were any clear-cut sides anymore).

John Huston's espionage thriller *The Kremlin Letter* (1970) was in this mold, centering on a proposal from the United States to the Soviet Union that the two superpowers collaborate in the annihilation of Mao Zedong's China.[43] Sydney Pollack's *Three Days of the Condor* (1975), based on a best-selling novel and suggesting that the CIA acted as a law unto itself within the United States and overseas, was equally challenging, both in its plot and politically. Hollywood quickly capitalized on the paranoia induced by press revelations of US Secret Service dirty tricks in the early 1970s, featured most prominently in the Watergate scandal. A flurry of taut, popular, liberal conspiracy thrillers was the result, including *Executive Action* (David Miller, 1973), *The Parallax View* (Alan J. Pakula, 1974), *All the President's Men* (Pakula, 1976), and *Twilight's Last Gleaming* (Robert Aldrich, 1977).[44]

This last film focused on the Vietnam War and was soon joined by others in the late 1970s that explored the ways in which that conflict had ripped apart Americans, physically and psychologically. Three of them—*Coming Home* (Hal Ashby, 1978), *The Deer Hunter* (Michael Cimino, 1978), and *Apocalypse Now* (Francis Ford Coppola, 1979)—attracted immense popular and critical acclaim.[45] Jane Fonda, who picked up an Oscar for her role in *Coming Home*, was one of the most creative and influential liberals working in Hollywood during this period. James Bridges's 1979 thriller *The China Syndrome*, which told the story of safety cover-ups in a nuclear power plant outside Los Angeles, was funded by her company, IPC Films, part of a long-running campaign Fonda had been conducting on-and offscreen to expose economic and corporate power elites in the United States.[46] Some commentators have since argued that such films represented an unprecedented liberal assault by Hollywood on the political and economic status quo, encouraging a short-term national shift to the left. Others claim the movies helped foster the New Right in the United States by depicting big government and large institutions as conspiratorial and dangerous to a free and libertarian community.[47]

Not everything was doom and gloom on the American Cold War screen in the 1970s, however. Nor was every film so didactic or straightforwardly propagandistic, either. Antidotes to this sort of material were movies that cast a skeptical eye on the Cold War but did so indirectly and humorously. One such film is Woody Allen's *Bananas*, the story of a New York nerd who gets caught up in Latin American politics to spice up his love life. Released in 1971, *Bananas* was part of a whole series of movies, many made on Hollywood's left-wing fringes, that played around with the idea that the CIA was the new American "enemy within."[48] More important, it also ridiculed the liberal Left. In sum, *Bananas* reflected and projected the view held by many Americans in the 1970s that the Cold War was an absurd anachronism.

BACK TO BASICS, 1980-1986

Ronald Reagan's sweeping victories in the 1980 and 1984 presidential elections marked a powerful reaction to the notion that the Cold War did not matter anymore. The Great Communicator's eight years in the Oval Office saw the United States take a decisive shift to the right, based in large part on a revitalization of the ideological and strategic conflict against the Communist Bloc. As a former movie actor and FBI informant within the film community, Reagan instinctively looked to the media, including Hollywood, to do his political bidding. This explains why he launched an impassioned assault on the cultural "liberal elite" that in his view had led the United States astray in the 1960s and 1970s, and why he appointed the former Hollywood impresario Charles Z. Wick to the directorship of the USIA. Movies (both old and new) played a key role in shaping Reagan's thoughts and actions in the White House. In turn, his rhetoric and policies had a significant influence on Hollywood output.[49]

American Cold War cinema of the 1980s was not as one-dimensionally anticommunist as some would have us believe. Though Reagan might have liked to see an informal blacklist initiated, there was no equivalent to that from the McCarthy era, nor any HUAC-style investigations designed to root out the corrosive "liberal elite" in the entertainment industry. Oppositional films of the type made in the 1970s continued to appear, albeit in smaller numbers, most of them plowing a similar "what's-it-all-about" furrow. Few of these attracted much attention.[50] Notable exceptions were Warren Beatty's Oscar-winning epic *Reds* (1981), about as even-handed an account of the Bolshevik Revolution as Hollywood was ever likely to produce during the Cold War, based on a book written by the legendary left-wing American journalist John Reed, and Costa-Gavras's *Missing* (1982), an Oscar-winning drama about the CIA's role in the 1973 Chilean coup that deposed socialist president Salvador Allende.[51]

Two other prominent films reflected the fears engendered in the early 1980s by Reagan officials speaking of a "winnable nuclear war." John Badham's *WarGames*, the fifth-highest-grossing movie of 1983, presented a new Cold War threat to world security—the possibility that unauthorized users might gain access to the computer systems controlling the superpowers' arsenals. Centered on a teenager who inadvertently gains access to the US nuclear defense system through his computer modem, *WarGames* soon acquired cult status among American youngsters.[52] Jayne Loader, Kevin Rafferty, and Pierce Rafferty's *The Atomic Café* (1982) was an independently produced feature-length documentary ridiculing civil defense information and training films from the 1950s. Distributed across the nation, and especially popular in colleges, the documentary drew attention to cinema's use as a government propaganda tool in the early phases of the Cold War. It also challenged the sort of claims ridiculed by Robert Scheer in his book *With Enough Shovels* (1982), including the assertion that most Americans could survive a nuclear attack.[53]

"His is a kind of 1952 world," one of Ronald Reagan's advisers told a journalist in 1980. "He sees the world in black and white terms."[54] Much the same could be said about Hollywood's rejuvenated attack on Soviet communism in the early to mid-1980s. During this period, virulently xenophobic movies once again appeared warning of communist landings on US soil: *Red Dawn* (John Milius, 1984) and *Invasion USA* (Joseph Zito, 1985). Films about Soviet defectors were back in vogue at the cinema and on television, including *Sakharov* (Jack Gold, 1984), *Moscow on the Hudson* (Paul Mazursky, 1984), and *White Nights* (Taylor Hackford, 1985).[55] The Soviet secret services were up to their old tricks in *KGB: The Secret War* (Dwight H. Little, 1986) and *No Way Out* (Roger Donaldson, 1987). US–Soviet relations were an ongoing battle between men (the Americans) and machines (the Russians) in *Firefox* (Clint Eastwood, 1982) and *Rocky IV* (Sylvester Stallone, 1985). And the Soviet Union was once again flexing its imperialist muscles, notably in Afghanistan, in *The Beast of War* (Kevin Reynolds, 1988).[56]

Of course, even the Hollywood Reaganites knew they could not simply erase a critical part of the Cold War by rewinding to the good old days of Dwight Eisenhower, Cecil B. DeMille, and John Wayne. The US military had to demonstrate that it had moved on since the 1950s and 1960s and that it was now capable of vanquishing its Soviet foe, as seen in *Top Gun* (Tony Scott, 1986). The American people had to rekindle their love affair with the US military, through *An Officer and a Gentleman* (Taylor Hackford, 1982), and with the nation's get-ahead spirit, seen in Philip Kaufman's *The Right Stuff* (1983), which focused on the early years of the East–West space race.[57] The shame and humiliation of Vietnam had to be exorcised, giving us *Missing in Action* (Joseph Zito, 1984), *Heartbreak Ridge* (Clint Eastwood, 1986), and *Good Morning, Vietnam* (Barry Levinson, 1987). Likewise, a scapegoat had to be found for the defeat in Southeast Asia: a pusillanimous government bureaucracy, as seen in *Uncommon Valor* (Ted Kotcheff, 1983).[58] One outstanding movie that fused all these themes was George P. Cosmatos's *Rambo: First Blood Part II* (1985). A gung ho action-adventure movie par excellence, *Rambo* represents the apotheosis of the politics of Reaganite entertainment.

PEACE AND VICTORY, 1986-1990

Hollywood's second Cold War reached its frenzied climax in 1985–1986, when *Rambo*, *Rocky IV*, and *Top Gun* headed the US and international box office charts. Had anyone predicted at this point that the Cold War would be over within a mere five years, and the Soviet Union consigned to history within six, they would have been given short shrift. Yet a careful look at Hollywood's output in the late 1980s does at least hint that a meaningful Soviet–American rapprochement was on the horizon.

Several filmmakers adjusted quickly and positively to the policies of glasnost (openness) and perestroika (restructuring) initiated by Mikhail Gorbachev, who became the Soviet leader in March 1985. Some of the resulting movies harkened back to the 1960s, demonstrating how few differences there really were between ordinary people on either side of the Iron Curtain. Thus, *Russkies* (Rick Rosenthal, 1987) told a touching tale, not dissimilar to *The Russians Are Coming, the Russians Are Coming*, about the friendship that develops between three American boys and a forlorn Soviet sailor washed up on the coast of Florida.[59] Other films depicted the longtime enemies now fighting as allies in new wars, against narcotics smugglers—Walter Hill's *Red Heat* (1988)—and Middle East terrorists—Sidney J. Furie's *Iron Eagle II* (1988). *Red Heat* was glasnost in action—the first entirely American-produced movie that incorporated scenes shot on location in the Soviet Union.[60]

The political climate was changing rapidly. In early 1988, Moscow hosted its first major American film festival. Among the movies screened in the Soviet Union for the first time were *Kings Row* (Sam Wood, 1942), starring Ronald Reagan, and Irvin Kershner's sci-fi blockbuster *The Empire Strikes Back* (1980).[61]

In 1989, two American films appeared, one at the cinema (Andrew Davis's *The Package*) and the other on television (Lawrence Gordon Clark's *Just Another Secret*), that depicted Americans preventing Gorbachev from being assassinated by renegade factions within his own spy establishment.[62]

Hollywood's last major contribution to the Cold War was John McTiernan's $30 million blockbuster *The Hunt for Red October*. Made with the assistance of the US Navy in 1989, the movie was the paradigmatic pro-détente American production: the story of a Soviet naval commander (played by Sean Connery, the original James Bond on screen) who defects with his country's latest high-tech nuclear submarine. His goal is to avert a first strike on the United States by the Communist old guard and to establish the grounds for a lasting peace between the Russian and American peoples. However, by the time *Red October* was released, in March 1990, it had become an instant period piece. The Eastern Bloc had disintegrated, Gorbachev had declared peace with the United States, and Americans could watch the movie knowing they had effectively won the Cold War.[63]

NOTES

This essay is an abridged version of chapter 1 of *Cinematic Cold War: The American and Soviet Struggle for Hearts and Minds*, by Tony Shaw and Denise J. Youngblood, published by the University Press of Kansas, © 2010. www.kansaspress.ku.edu. Used by permission of the publisher.

1. Kevin Brownlow, *Behind the Mask of Innocence: Sex, Violence, Prejudice, Crime—Films of Social Conscience in the Silent Era* (Berkeley: University of California Press, 1990), 443–447.

2. Tony Shaw, *Hollywood's Cold War* (Amherst: University of Massachusetts Press, 2007), 15–27.

3. Steven J. Ross, "The Rise of Hollywood: Movies, Ideology, and Audiences in the Roaring Twenties," in *Movies and American Society*, ed. Steven J. Ross (Oxford: Blackwell, 2002), 64–97; Richard Maltby, *Harmless Entertainment: Hollywood and the Ideology of Consensus* (London: Scarecrow, 1983).

4. Clayton R. Koppes and Gregory D. Black, *Hollywood Goes to War: How Politics, Profits and Propaganda Shaped World War II Movies* (New York: Free Press, 1987), 185–221. On Sam Goldwyn's role as producer of *The North Star*, see 209–215.

5. Daniel J. Leab, "*The Iron Curtain* (1948): Hollywood's First Cold War Movie," *Historical Journal of Film, Radio and Television* 8, no. 2 (1988): 153–188.

6. See, for example, Richard Fried, *Nightmare in Red: The McCarthy Era in Perspective* (Oxford: Oxford University Press, 1991); Thomas Doherty, "Hollywood Agit-Prop: The Anti-Communist

Cycle 1948–1954," *Journal of Film and Video* 40, no. 4 (1988): 15–27; Glen M. Johnson, "Sharper Than an Irish Serpent's Tooth: Leo McCarey's *My Son John*," *Journal of Popular Film and Television* 8, no. 1 (1980): 44–49.

7. Larry Ceplair and Steven Englund, *The Inquisition in Hollywood: Politics in the Film Community, 1930–1960* (Berkeley: University of California Press, 1979); Stephen J. Whitfield, *The Culture of the Cold War* (Baltimore: Johns Hopkins University Press, 1996), 127–151; Thomas Doherty, *Cold War, Cool Medium: Television, McCarthyism, and American Culture* (New York: Columbia University Press, 2003), 40–48, 251–258. The Hollywood Ten were an assorted group of screenwriters, directors, and producers imprisoned for contempt of Congress in 1950: Alvah Bessie, Herbert Biberman, Lester Cole, Edward Dmytryk, Ring Lardner Jr., John Howard Lawson, Albert Maltz, Samuel Ornitz, Adrian Scott, and Dalton Trumbo.

8. Frank Walsh, *Sin and Censorship: The Catholic Church and the Motion Picture Industry* (New Haven, CT: Yale University Press, 1996); Gregory D. Black, "Movies, Politics, and Censorship: The Production Code Administration and Political Censorship of Film Content," *Journal of Policy History* 3, no. 2 (1991): 95–129; Thomas Doherty, *Hollywood's Censor: Joseph I. Breen and the Production Code Administration* (New York: Columbia University Press, 2007).

9. Ceplair and Englund, *Inquisition in Hollywood*, 209–225, 258; Nora Sayre, *Running Time: Films of the Cold War* (New York: Dial, 1982), 18, 50; Lary May, *The Big Tomorrow: Hollywood and the Politics of the American Way* (Chicago: University of Chicago Press, 2000), 177, 191. Johnston was also president of the Motion Picture Export Association of America, a Motion Picture Association of America agency that dealt with foreign matters.

10. Ceplair and Englund, *Inquisition in Hollywood*, 204, 392; commentary by Peter Davis, director of the Oscar-winning documentary *Hearts and Minds* (1974), on *Hearts and Minds* DVD (Metrodome, 2005).

11. John A. Noakes, "Bankers and Common Men in Bedford Falls: How the FBI Determined That *It's a Wonderful Life* Was a Subversive Movie," *Film History* 10, no. 3 (1998): 311–319; Kenneth O'Reilly, *Hoover and the UnAmericans* (Philadelphia: Temple University Press, 1983), 82; Athan Theoharis, *Chasing Spies: How the FBI Failed in Counterintelligence but Promoted the Politics of McCarthyism in the Cold War Years* (Chicago: Ivan R. Dee, 2002), 155.

12. Shaw, *Hollywood's Cold War*, especially chapters 2, 4, and 6.

13. Richard Maltby, *Hollywood Cinema* (Oxford: Blackwell, 2003),124.

14. *Variety*, December 10, 1952.

15. *New York Times*, June 11, 1953.

16. Doherty, "Hollywood Agit-Prop."

17. Shaw, *Hollywood's Cold War*, chapter 2.

18. Ralph Stern, "*The Big Lift* (1950): Image and Identity in Blockaded Berlin," *Cinema Journal* 46, no. 2 (Winter 2007): 66–90. On the Pentagon–Hollywood axis, see Lawrence Suid, *Guts and Glory: The Making of the American Military Image in Film* (Lexington: University Press of Kentucky, 2002).

19. Daniel Leab, *I Was a Communist for the FBI* (University Park: Pennsylvania State University Press, 2000); *Time*, June 29, 1953.

20. David Eldridge, "'Dear Owen': The CIA, Luigi Luraschi and Hollywood, 1953," *Historical Journal of Film, Radio and Television* 20, no. 2 (June 2000): 182.

21. *Variety*, October 24, 1951.

22. *Hollywood Reporter*, November 28, 1952; *New York Times*, October 25, 1952; *Variety*, July 11, 1951; *Hollywood Reporter*, January 13, 1953.

23. James M. Skinner, "Cliché and Convention in Hollywood's Cold War Anti-Communist Films," *North Dakota Quarterly* (Summer 1978): 35–40; *New York Times*, June 27, 1949.

24. *Variety*, December 29, 1949; *Hollywood Reporter*, December 12, 1955.

25. *Storm Center* was based on a true story. See Louise S. Robbins, *The Dismissal of Miss Ruth Brown: Civil Rights, Censorship, and the American Library* (Norman: University of Oklahoma Press, 2000).

26. G. Tom Poe, "Historical Spectatorship around and about Stanley Kramer's *On the Beach*," in *Hollywood Spectatorship: Changing Perceptions of Cinema Audiences*, ed. Melvyn Stokes and Richard Maltby (London: BFI, 2001), 91–102.

27. The *Film Daily Year Book of Motion Pictures*, 33rd ed. (New York: Film Daily, 1951), 51.

28. The following musicals were among the top ten box office hits in the year of their release: *Annie Get Your Gun* (no. 5, 1950); *Showboat* (no. 2, 1951); *An American in Paris* (no. 3, 1951); *White Christmas* (no. 1, 1954); *The Glenn Miller Story* (no. 3, 1954); *Guys and Dolls* (no. 1, 1956); *The King and I* (no. 2, 1956); and *South Pacific* (no. 7, 1958). Cobbett Steinberg, *Reel Facts* (Harmondsworth: Penguin, 1981), 434–438.

29. Peter Filene, "'Cold War Culture' Doesn't Say It All," in *Rethinking Cold War Culture*, ed. Peter J. Kuznick and James Gilbert (Washington, DC: Smithsonian Institution Press, 2001), 164–166.

30. Shaw, *Hollywood's Cold War*, 114–128.

31. Vladislav M. Zubok, *A Failed Empire: The Soviet Union in the Cold War from Stalin to Gorbachev* (Chapel Hill: University of North Carolina Press, 2007), 173; Diane Neumaier, ed., *Beyond Memory: Soviet Nonconformist Photography and Photo-Related Works of Art* (New Brunswick, NJ: Rutgers University Press, 2004), 187.

32. Paul Swann, "The Little State Department: Hollywood and the State Department in the Postwar World," *American Studies International* 29, no. 1 (April 1991): 2–19; Kerry Segrave, *American Films Abroad: Hollywood's Domination of the World's Movie Screens from the 1890s to the Present* (Jefferson, NC: McFarland, 1997).

33. Daniel J. Leab, *Orwell Subverted: The CIA and the Filming of Animal Farm* (University Park: Pennsylvania State University Press, 2007).

34. Kenneth Osgood, *Total War: Eisenhower's Secret Propaganda Battle at Home and Abroad* (Lawrence: University Press of Kansas, 2006); Melinda Schwenk, "Reforming the Negative Through History: The US Information Agency and the 1957 Little Rock Integration Crisis," *Journal of Communication Inquiry* 23, no. 3 (July 1999): 288–306.

35. Soviet-made films were largely confined to art houses in New York and Los Angeles, where they played to niche audiences comprising left-wingers and/or lovers of Russian culture. James H. Krukones, "The Unspooling of Artkino: Soviet Film Distribution in America, 1940–1975," *Historical Journal of Film, Radio and Television* 29, no. 1 (March 2009): 91–112.

36. Peter Biskind, *Easy Riders, Raging Bulls: How the Sex 'n' Drugs 'n' Rock 'n' Roll Generation Saved Hollywood* (London: Bloomsbury, 1998).

37. Matthew Frye Jacobson and Gaspar Gonzalez, *What Have They Built You to Do? The Manchurian Candidate and Cold War America* (Minneapolis: University of Minnesota Press, 2006).

38. Michael Coyne, "*Seven Days in May*: History, Prophecy and Propaganda," in *Windows on the Sixties: Exploring Key Texts of Media and Culture*, ed. Anthony Aldgate, James Chapman, and Arthur Marwick (London: I. B. Tauris, 2000), 70–90.

39. Suid, *Guts and Glory*, 242–247.

40. James Naremore, *On Kubrick* (London: BFI, 2007), 119–137.

41. Norman Jewison, *This Terrible Business Has Been Good to Me: An Autobiography* (New York: Key Porter, 2004), 115–132; Walter M. Mirisch, interoffice memo to Norman Jewison, April 21, 1965, and letter from Jerry Ludwig (Mirisch Corporation) to David Zeitlin (*Life*), February 14, 1966, in David Zeitlin Collection, Academy of Motion Picture Arts and Sciences (AMPAS), Margaret Herrick Library, Los Angeles.

42. Maltby, *Hollywood Cinema*, 124.

43. John Huston, *An Open Book* (Cambridge, MA: Da Capo, 1994), 336–341; *Motion Picture Herald*, February 11, 1970.

44. Shaw, *Hollywood's Cold War*, 249–262.

45. Jeremy M. Devine, *Vietnam at 24 Frames a Second: A Critical and Thematic Analysis of Over 400 Films about the Vietnam War* (Jefferson, NC: McFarland, 1995), 130–197.

46. Wayne J. McMullen, "*The China Syndrome*: Corruption to the Core," *Literature Film Quarterly* 23, no. 1 (1995): 55–62.

47. Michael Ryan and Douglas Kellner, *Camera Politica: The Politics and Ideology of Contemporary Hollywood Film* (Bloomington: Indiana University Press, 1988), 95–98; Ian Scott, *American Politics in Hollywood Film* (Edinburgh: Edinburgh University Press, 2000), 119–124.

48. These include Ivan Dixon's *The Spook Who Sat by the Door* (1973), Saul Landau and Haskell Wexler's *CIA Case Officer* (1978), and Arthur Hiller's *The In-Laws* (1979).

49. Ronald Reagan, *An American Life* (London: Hutchinson, 1990), 104–125; Gary Wills, *Reagan's America: Innocents at Home* (New York: Doubleday, 1987), 246–258; Alvin Snyder, *Warriors of Disinformation: American Propaganda, Soviet Lies, and the Winning of the Cold War* (New York: Arcade, 1995).

50. See, for example, *The Osterman Weekend* (Sam Peckinpah, 1983), *The Falcon and the Snowman* (John Schlesinger, 1985), and *Spies Like Us* (John Landis, 1985), details of which can be found in William J. Palmer, *The Films of the Eighties: A Social History* (Carbondale: Southern Illinois University Press, 1993), 222–232.

51. Robert Rosenstone, *History on Film/Film on History* (London: Pearson, 2006), 97–110; Robert Brent Toplin, *History by Hollywood: The Use and Abuse of the American Past* (Chicago: University of Chicago Press, 1996), 104–124; *Los Angeles Herald-Examiner*, February 10, 1982.

52. Palmer, *Films of the Eighties*, 199–202.

53. *Films and Filming*, January 1983, 24–25; Robert Scheer, *With Enough Shovels: Reagan, Bush, and Nuclear War* (New York: Random House, 1982).

54. Frances Fitzgerald, *Way Out There in the Blue: Reagan, Star Wars and the End of the Cold War* (New York: Simon & Schuster, 2000), 74.

55. Shaw, *Hollywood's Cold War*, 9–11, 269–276; *Hollywood Reporter*, September 26, 1985; *Variety*, May 23, 1984; *Photoplay*, November 1984, 25–27.

56. *Hollywood Reporter*, April 3, 1984; *Variety*, August 12, 1987; *Photoplay*, August 1982; *Jump Cut*, April 1990; *Variety*, September 21, 1988.

57. Suid, *Guts and Glory*, 485–502; *American Film*, November 1983.

58. Devine, *Vietnam*, 219–223, 240, 266, 271–274.

59. *Variety*, November 4, 1987.

60. Shaw, *Hollywood's Cold War*, 285–292; *Variety*, November 16, 1988.

61. *Los Angeles Times*, February 10, 1988; Palmer, Films of the *Eighties*, 209.

62. *Variety*, August 23, 1989.

63. Suid, *Guts and Glory*, 570–578. *The Hunt for Red October* was the sixth-most-popular film in the United States in 1990.

TO CONDENSE A MOCKINGBIRD

Harper Lee, *Reader's Digest,* and the Cold War

KRISTEN POPHAM AND SIMON STOW

White Americans have long seen Harper Lee's 1960 novel *To Kill a Mockingbird* as a heuristic for racial politics. Indeed, its demand that readers metaphorically walk in another's skin has been seen as a democratic pedagogy for addressing the same. Nevertheless, even before the 2015 publication of *Go Set a Watchman,* a novel often understood as an early draft of *To Kill a Mockingbird*—one which featured a racially bigoted Atticus Finch—several critics had noted that the novel's dominant reading obscures a more complex, and more problematic, engagement with race than is generally ascribed to the text.

While there can be no definitive account of why one reading of a novel comes to predominate, this essay turns to an edition of *Mockingbird* published before *Watchman*—the 1960 *Reader's Digest* condensed version—to offer a possible explanation for the popularity of the anodyne understanding of Lee's most famous novel. The essay notes the widespread reach of the *Digest,* and the phenomenal success of its condensed book series, and shows how the *Digest*'s *Mockingbird* reflected the magazine's Cold War preoccupations, particularly with regard to race. Contrasting this version of the text with the full novel reveals how Cold War concerns shaped not only American politics but also the broader reception of American culture, and thus American politics—a feedback loop with ongoing resonance, as the popular uproar over *Watchman*'s racist Atticus suggests.

* * *

THE BIRTH OF A CONDENSATION

First published in February 1922 by DeWitt and Lila Bell Wallace, *Reader's Digest* was inspired by DeWitt's experience of reading American magazines in a French hospital. There, he hit upon the idea of condensing and anthologizing magazine articles and distributing them by mail. The *Digest* was phenomenally successful. In 1962, *Time* observed, "It dispenses more medical advice than the AMA Journal, more ribaldry than Boccaccio, more jokes than Joe Miller, more animal stories than Uncle Remus, more faith than Oral Roberts. It is published in 13 languages and 40 editions. . . . It goes to more than 100 countries and outsells all other monthly magazines in Argentina, Belgium, Canada, Colombia, Finland, Italy, Mexico, Peru, South Africa, Spain, Sweden, Uruguay, Venezuela—and, of course, the US."[1] By 1977, the magazine's monthly circulation was nearly 30 million copies across 170 countries. Its worldwide readership was estimated at 100 million.[2] Nevertheless, the *Digest's* impact cannot be captured by circulation alone. For, as Joanne Sharp notes, it played a significant role in creating the idea of America at both home and abroad.[3]

David Campbell argues, "If all states are 'imagined communities,' . . . then America is the imagined community par excellence."[4] From the very beginning, the *Digest* took its political role seriously, as a source of information about the world for its readers and as an instrument of moral and political pedagogy, with its ideology shaping the information received by consumers. John Heidenry notes that the politics of the magazine "were always conservative to reactionary."[5] Indeed, the *Digest's* worldview is suggested by its publication, in April 1945, of a condensed version of Friedrich Hayek's *Road to Serfdom*. So successful was it that the *Digest* received more than a million requests for reprints, many from politicians and corporations opposed to the New Deal.[6] Indeed, the *Digest* was "notable for its unrelenting attacks on the Roosevelt administration,"[7] presenting it as a "potential threat to American individualism," a "turn toward socialism,"[8] and a gateway to communism.

READER'S DIGEST, RACE, AND THE COLD WAR

"The Soviet threat," writes Sharp, "was necessary to the maintenance of US identity. The USSR offered a mirroring conceptual space to that occupied by

America; into this space were projected negative characteristics against which a positive image of American character could be reflected."[9] Accordingly, the *Digest* ran articles on the conditions facing Russian citizens and the problems of communism, contrasting them with American freedoms. Befitting its propagandist role in stirring up anticommunism at home to justify expansionism abroad, the *Digest* became "one of the most McCarthyite publications in the country."[10] It was, moreover, a powerful influence in nations that might be tempted by collectivism. The upbeat nature of the articles—one wag suggested the quintessential *Digest* article might be titled "New Hope for the Dead"— depicted an America in which anything was possible through a Puritan work ethic and unbridled individualism. Wallace believed the world would be a better place if people practiced what they read in his magazine.[11] What the *New Yorker* called the "rosier than anything heretofore known to optical science" glasses worn by *Digest* writers also provided the lenses through which the other great issue of the day—race—was viewed by foreign and domestic audiences.[12]

Gunnar Myrdal's *American Dilemma* (1944)—though deeply flawed— perfectly captured the problems facing a nation that saw itself as a beacon of democracy and proud defender of human rights. America, Myrdal argued, was torn between the "American creed"—a supposed commitment to the "ideals of the essential dignity of the individual human being . . . the fundamental equality of all men, and . . . certain inalienable rights to freedom, justice and a fair opportunity"—and anti-Black racism.[13] Myrdal believed that America's moral character would prevail, a position that the *Digest* could endorse, given Wallace's commitment to "the brotherhood of man, a utopian belief that men and women of all nationalities could live together in harmony."[14]

Nevertheless, the *Digest* perpetuated racial inequalities by, among other things, publishing "dialect humor" mocking Blacks. Likewise, an essay published in 1944 criticized the Black press for "attempts to indicate that the Negro gets unfair treatment." Indeed, the magazine embraced de facto segregation in an essay celebrating efforts to establish all-Black communities.[15] As the civil rights movement emerged, the *Digest* published several stories that were mildly supportive of the movement but wary of Black demands. They supported improved educational opportunities for Blacks but feared that too much progress, too quickly, would cause Blacks' "natural aggressiveness" to get out of hand.

Following the 1954 *Brown v. Board of Education* decision, the *Digest* sympathized with the white backlash. Following Eisenhower's decision to send the National Guard into Little Rock in 1957, the magazine asserted that "responsible Southerners" would oppose integration until "the moral standards of the white and Negroes, as groups" were "brought much nearer the same level"; and, in a remarkable attempt at political rehabilitation, the *Digest* said Orval Faubus, Arkansas's segregationist governor, "truly likes Negroes." In the late 1950s, Wallace invited Walter White, executive director of the National Association for the Advancement of Colored People, to a lunch where he declared that the *Digest* had carried more articles than any other magazine celebrating the achievements of nonwhites. White agreed but noted that the articles concerned fields like sports and entertainment with lower barriers to entry and achievement by Blacks. Wallace observed that he would gladly profile a successful Black businessman or doctor, if such a person existed.[16]

"For the *Digest*," observes Sharp, "it was not always what happened that was significant, but how it was described and explained." He also argues that "*Reader's Digest* might offer the single most important voice in the creation of popular geopolitics in America in the twentieth century."[17] For Sharp, a significant part of the magazine's power lay in telling America's story to the world. On race, the *Digest* purveyed America's preferred narrative to international audiences. The tension between America's professed values and its treatment of Black citizens was obviously something of a problem for its attempts to run the world: part of the fear of communism at both home and abroad was because race offered fertile ground for seeds of opposition to American values. The State Department sought to shape external perceptions of America's racial contradictions, offering a narrative of gradual progress focused less on what was happening at any given moment and more on how far the nation had come. America's trajectory was, it repeatedly suggested, clear, showing how constitutional democracy could resolve even the most intractable problems through reform.

"Rehabilitating the moral character of American democracy," writes Mary Dudziak, "would become an important focus of Cold War diplomacy."[18] In its aggressively pro-American outlook, its relentless positivity, its anticommunist, antistatist, and individualistic political philosophy, the *Digest* was the perfect weapon for the government to make the world safe for American democracy.

Indeed, Wallace often operated foreign editions at a loss, so committed was he to the *Digest*'s geopolitical role.[19]

CONDENSING THE BOOK AND MAKING THE READER

"Our magazines," declared President Eisenhower in June 1960, "are a leading force for moral and cultural growth in our country."[20] The *Digest* sought to achieve what Henry James called "making the reader," leading them through a text to a particular understanding of its meaning.[21] Where James sought an aesthetic effect, the *Digest*'s goal was moral and political: the reader should be led toward a definite understanding but experience it as coming to their own conclusion. It offered up expert opinions without jargon so that the reader might feel themselves informed on a particular issue, even as the relevant experts were carefully chosen by the magazine. Given Wallace's commitment to "making the reader" in his own image, and to a hegemonic expansionism that mirrored that of post–World War II America, he unsurprisingly sought to "make" even more readers by doing with books what he had done with magazines.

The first condensed book appeared in 1934, still as part of the magazine and not yet its own entity. It became so in 1950, when, as a direct mail subscription service, it was an instant hit. Oddly, sales figures for the books were closely guarded; nevertheless, many have suggested that the project was enormously profitable, with one editor asserting that the *Digest* became "one of the largest publishers of hard-bound books in the world."[22] As Evert Volkersz notes, part of the reason for its success was that it "combined several condensed titles in one volume," and because subscribers "lacked the negative option choice (although books could be returned)." Volkersz is on much shakier ground, however, when he asserts, "Unlike the Digest, which has a political and social agenda, the Condensed Books are published solely for their entertainment."[23] For, even if it could be argued that the choice of books was nonpolitical—and it is not clear that it can—Volkersz's own account of the process of condensing a book suggests how the values of the *Digest* came to permeate a text:

> Lacking a formal definition of *Reader's Digest*'s usage of the word "condensation," I propose the following . . . an extended hierarchical editorial process of

abridging and summarizing text by retaining both style and substance (known as "cutting"), omitting quotation marks from verbatim passages, replacing deletions with transitions made in the manner of the author, and toning down or excising excessive violence and explicit sex scenes, without changing vocabulary other than inserting dashes following the first letter of a profanity.[24]

Samuel Schreiner offers a more vivid account. "Rather than a slaughterhouse," he observed of the editing room, "the area seems more like a distillery . . . an operation in which the verbal water is boiled off over a series of editorial flames until there's nothing left but stuff of the highest proof." It was, he noted, "a perfectly logical operation that any literate person should be able to learn."[25]

Both accounts of the process overlook the ways in which the editorial process was shaped by editors chosen for their (mainly *male*) understanding of the *Digest*'s values. What counts as "excessive violence" or "explicit sex" is not an objective a category. The editors do not recognize the horizons of their own thought; as such, they miss how condensing a text is necessarily shaping it, and thus the reader, especially if that reader reads little else.[26] Furthermore, argues Daniel Baylon, the condensing process removes any hint of substantive critique or conflict, offering a sanitized product, "a vision of the world and a way of life" that "has lost the capacity to pose fundamental questions to . . . its readers."[27] Indeed, Volkersz's blindness to the manner in which the *Digest* seeks to make the reader is further suggested by his willingness to deny a social or political agenda while also observing that the *Digest* chooses "books that have clarity, simplicity, and drama, with characters who are respected by readers and aware of moral choices."[28] In this, the worldview of the *Digest*'s condensed books echoes that of the magazine, where, according to Sharp, "there is always a moral to the story."[29]

A MORAL TO THE STORY

To Kill a Mockingbird would seem to have been made for the condensed book program. Since publication, it has been widely understood as a tale of tolerance and liberal virtue in which a white Southern lawyer bucks the expectations of his racist neighbors by defending a wrongly accused Black man. Malcolm

Bradbury observes, "The good stands out from the bad at all levels."[30] The novel has, moreover, often been seen as a means of tackling the racism it depicts, by inspiring its readers to become more tolerant.

Moreover, a succession of writers and luminaries has borne witness to the transformative power of the text. Tom Brokaw declared of Lee, "She was in that pantheon . . . of people who helped us get liberated from racism in this country." Capturing much of what undoubtedly attracted the *Digest* to *Mockingbird*, Allan Gurganus observes, "Goodness is, I think, underestimated as a dramatic virtue in fiction. Except for the white-trash villains, everybody in the town is sort of good or trying to be. I think that's one of the enduring attractions of the book."[31] Much of the novel's appeal appears to lie in the character of Atticus Finch, a character whose apparent decency and commitment to principle has led many readers to compare him to Christ.[32]

It is unsurprising, then, that the *Digest* snapped up the novel four months before its July 1960 publication, despite its policy of only offering works by established authors. The novel's depiction of American racism appeared to be entirely congruent with the magazine's Cold War politics: its historical setting between 1932 and 1935 depicted racism as a past problem, not a present issue. For those concerned about America's racial politics in the present, it offered a set of solutions to racial intolerance reflective of the individualism and anticollectivist leanings of Wallace and the hegemony of his ideals. It depicts racism as a problem of individual intolerance and posits the individual imagination as a solution. "If you can learn a simple trick, Scout," Atticus observes to his daughter, "you'll get along a lot better with all kinds of folks. You never really understand a person until you consider things from his point of view . . . until you climb into his skin and walk around in it" (31). Readers are encouraged to imagine themselves in Tom Robinson's skin and thus to become more tolerant.

The conservatism of this position—and its appropriateness for Wallace's Cold War commitments—is twofold. First, it eschews collective action. It does not demand that readers join a political organization, simply that they think differently about themselves and their world. "The one thing that doesn't abide by majority rule," observes Atticus," is a person's conscience" (120). Second, Atticus's demand that his daughter, and by extension the reader, walk around in the skin of another is an approach that demands the reader understand the racist. It is possible to see this as a good thing; understanding the position of one with whom one disagrees might permit one to understand and better engage with them. Nevertheless, in its commitment to understanding over action, such an approach may promote political quietism. As Diane McWhorter observes, "One of the powerful and instructive things about the book is that even though it's such a classic indictment of racism, it's not really an indictment of the racist, because there's this recognition that those attitudes were 'normal' then."[33]

Nevertheless, what McWhorter sees as a positive might be seen as a negative, with her commitment to understanding negating the need for concerted action. The book appears to ask of its readers what Wallace offered to his: consideration of an alternative perspective without the expectation of anything beyond deference to American liberalism. Racism, *Mockingbird* seems to suggest, is something that *other* people do, which permits the reader to identify with the seemingly progressive Finch family and not with the bigoted townspeople.

It is, moreover, a commonplace among responses to the novel for readers to express how much they were moved by the text.[34] Such claims seem to serve as a testament to and a reconfirmation of the reader's own supposed moral decency—somebody so moved could not possibly be a bigot. Nevertheless, as James Baldwin observed, "People can cry much easier than they can change."[35] That which is seen as a marker of decency may become an obstacle to the critical self-reflection needed to overcome prejudice. This understanding seems to merely reaffirm the American values championed by Wallace's Cold War politics. It is a depiction in which the decency of the noble (white) individual sets an example for others, and in which the nation is moving inexorably toward the resolution of Myrdal's dilemma.

MOCKINGBIRD IN BLACK AND WHITE

In 2014, Alison Miller argued that *Mockingbird* "is about white people, it uplifts white people, it makes middle-class white people feel better about racism by projecting it onto 'common' white southerners." For this reason, it belongs in the "Cold War canon." It is teaching its readers to stand up to totalitarianism through individual action rather than by doing anything meaningful about race, and as Miller notes, this renders the novel's "race politics . . . utterly unworthy of reverence."[36]

Such criticism was not new. Since the early 1990s, there has been a steady stream of criticism of the novel, especially of Atticus Finch. Monroe Freedman identified the limitations on Finch's progressivism: "He goes to segregated restaurants, drinks from segregated water fountains, rides on segregated buses."[37] Likewise, Malcolm Gladwell observed, "If Finch were a civil-rights hero he would be brimming with rage at the unjust verdict. But he isn't."[38] Unsurprisingly, it was Black readers who most consistently took issue with characterizations of the novel as one of moral decency and overcoming prejudice.

Black readers' concerns range across a spectrum. James McBride observes, "The black characters . . . heroic as they are, . . . don't survive. The societal violence . . . [toward] Tom Robinson affects his family for generations, at least fictionally . . . That part of the story . . . has never been quite resolved in the manner that I would like to have seen it."[39] More common is criticism of the fetish of the "white savior." A long-standing trope in American culture, the white savior model presents an external actor as a force for liberation. The narrative denies Black agency, presenting Black people as waiting to be saved. As Ibram X. Kendi observes, "Though the novel was set in the 1930s, the teeming Black activism of that era was absent from *To Kill a Mockingbird*. African Americans come across as spectators, waiting and hoping and singing for a white savior, and thankful for the moral heroism of lawyer Atticus Finch.[40] Likewise, Isaac Saney notes that the novel takes place in the 1930s but written "as if the Scottsboro case—in which nine young black men travelling on a freight train . . . were wrongfully convicted of raping two white women who were riding the same freight train—never happened." In the wake of the trial, Saney notes, "a maelstrom of activity swept through African American communities, both North and South. They organized, agitated, petitioned, and marched in support of and to free the nine young men. *To Kill a Mockingbird* gives no inkling of this mass protest and instead creates the indelible impression that the entire Black community existed in a complete state of paralysis."[41] So completely is this narrative embraced, argues Randall Kennedy, that the standards for white heroism are extremely low. "In the mid-1930s," he writes, "when the events of *To Kill a Mockingbird* transpire, white dominance was so completely established that Finch could blithely disregard any political dissatisfactions Blacks felt and still get credit from his adoring daughter—and from millions of readers—for defending an innocent man."[42]

Without denying these Black critiques, it also is possible to say that they are predicated upon concerns of which the text it is acutely aware. Recent scholarship, much of it written in light of *Watchman*, suggests considerable continuities between the bigoted Atticus of the first-written but later-published novel and the supposedly saintlier Atticus of *Mockingbird*. Likewise, it suggests that *Mockingbird* is more complex than dominant readings indicate. Highlighting moments in which the text seems to demonstrate an awareness of that for which it is criticized—especially with regard its racial politics—and contrasting such moments with the corresponding depiction in, or erasure from, the *Digest* version suggests the ways in which the popularity and reach of the *Digest* version served to shape the reception of the original novel. Although there is no way to draw a direct causal arrow here, the frequency with which the novel's shades of gray become black and white in the condensed text might indicate the role that the *Digest* played in the history of the novel's reception.

TO CONDENSE A MOCKINGBIRD

In seeking to draw conclusions from what has been excised from or altered in the full text, it is important to acknowledge that elements of the text will have been rewritten or deleted for reasons of space. Nevertheless, it also should be noted that what the editors think is unimportant, problematic, or irrelevant to the narrative is very much a product of the lens through which they view it, which is focused on producing a particular image. Comparing the condensed edition to the complete novel shows not only how the *Digest* produced its desired reading but also how it may have come to dominate other readings of the novel. In many instances, the erasures from, and alterations to, the novel were driven by the *Digest*'s fundamental conservatism and the Cold War politics of DeWitt Wallace, especially on the issue of race.

Among the bowdlerized passages are the novel's sexual references. At the beginning of *Mockingbird*, the reader is informed that Atticus "liked Maycomb, he was Maycomb County born and bred; he knew his people, they knew him, and because of Simon Finch's industry, Atticus was related by blood or marriage to nearly every family in the town" (5). The sexual reference to Simon Finch's "industry" is subtle but sufficient for the *Digest* to remove it: "He liked Maycomb; he knew his people and they knew him: he was related by blood or marriage to nearly every family in town."[43] Likewise, while the novel describes the layout of Simon Finch's house: "The Daughters' Staircase was in the ground-floor bedroom of their parents, so Simon always knew the hours of his daughters' nocturnal comings and goings" (91)—a layout with incestuous overtones. This is omitted from the condensed text.

Lest this seem like overreading, note that while Atticus's joking suggestion about the Finches' incestuous streak survives, the more serious allusion to incest does not. Cross-examined by Atticus, Tom Robinson details his encounter with Mayella Ewell. "She reached up an' kissed me 'side of th' face. She says she never kissed a grown man before an' she might as well kiss a n——. She says what her papa do to her don't count" (222). The crucial last sentence is omitted in the *Digest*. Even the language of sexual violence is smoothed over. Bob Ewell's claim that "I seen that black n—— yonder ruttin' on my Mayella!" (197) becomes "I seen that black n—— yonder on my Mayella!" (523).

These and other such references are not the only changes in the condensed version. In keeping with Wallace's Cold War conservatism, the *Digest*'s version depicts a world with far greater moral clarity than the original. For instance, in his summation, Atticus declares, "There is not a person in this courtroom who has never told a lie, who has never done an immoral thing, and there is no man living who has never looked upon a woman without desire" (232). This sentence, which calls into question even Atticus's goodness, is missing from the condensed text.

Indeed, the popular understanding—especially among lawyers—of Atticus as a man committed to truth and decency is undermined by a close reading of his cross-examination of Sheriff Heck Tate. Atticus has established that Mayella Ewell's injuries are mainly on the right side of her face, and it has become apparent to Tate that her assailant must have been left-handed, and that, as Tom Robinson's left arm was paralyzed, he must be innocent. This is clear to both the lawman and the defendant: "Mr. Tate blinked again, as if something had suddenly been made plain to him. Then he turned his head and looked around at Tom Robinson. As if by instinct, Tom Robinson raised his head" (192–193). Moments later, an exchange occurs between Atticus and Heck Tate. It is notable for the moment when Atticus (speaking second) cuts off his witness:

> ". . . her arms were bruised, and she showed me her neck. There were definite finger marks on her gullet—"
> "All around her throat? At the back of her neck?"
> "I'd say they were all around, Mr. Finch."
> "You would?"
> "Yes sir, she had a small throat, anybody could'a reached around it with—"
> "Just answer the question yes or no, please, Sheriff," said Atticus dryly, and Mr. Tate fell silent. (193)

Atticus cuts Tate off before he can say "could'a reached around it with *one hand*," thereby undermining Finch's suggestion that Mayella's injuries were inconsistent with an attack by a one-armed man. While obviously good lawyering, it is inconsistent with the Atticus supposedly armed only with truth. The *Digest*'s version concludes with "gullet" (521). Likewise, while recent criticism has expressed concern about Atticus's cross-examination of a sexual assault survivor, there are moments in which such concerns seem anything but presentist, with both prosecutor and judge admonishing Atticus for his antagonistic engagement with Mayella (212).

While these changes may seem minor, their multiplicity makes them problematic. By removing ambiguities from the text, the *Digest* makes a reader with a Manichean worldview, a reader incapable of existing in the realm of uncertainty, where critical thought begins. The removal of nuance produces a reader who cannot see other ambiguities in the text or in life.

It is not clear, for example, what is to be thought about Atticus's refusal to hate Hitler. While some see this as an indication of the depth of his Christian love, others see sympathy with the fascist's views, if not his methods: Atticus was a member of a legislature whose eugenic policies were predicated upon reasoning similar to the Nazi's Nuremberg Laws, which took as their model American eugenics legislation.[44] Furthermore, Scout observes of her father, "I asked him once why he was impatient with Hitler and Atticus said, 'Because he's a maniac'" (282–283). Scout's choice of adjective is perhaps surprising, as is Atticus's choice of noun. "Impatience" would seem a remarkably mild response to one engaged in the ruthless persecution of a minority; likewise, "maniac" might be thought to imply a concern with Hitler's excessive zeal rather than an outright condemnation.[45] Certainly, it could be argued that Atticus's concern was not with discrimination *per se* but with the way it is pursued, as is suggested by his relationship to New South politics.

One of the *Digest*'s erasures is a reference to Atticus making Jem read the speeches of Henry W. Grady (166), one of the most articulate proponents of the New South ideology, which held that Blacks were naturally inferior but also stressed the need to protect their rights to avoid a violent uprising. Grady's removal from the text means that when Atticus observes, "I hope and pray I can get Jem and Scout through it without bitterness, and most of all, without catching Maycomb's usual disease. Why reasonable people go stark raving mad when anything involving a Negro comes up, is something I don't pretend to understand" (498–499). This can only be seen as a condemnation of racism itself rather than a concern about how white racism sometimes manifests itself in public life.

That this elision is more than mere coincidence is suggested by the excising from the condensed text of Atticus's articulation of Grady's worst fear: "Atticus was speaking so quietly his last word crashed on our ears. I looked up, and his face was vehement. 'There's nothing more sickening to me than a low-grade white man who'll take advantage of a Negro's ignorance. Don't fool yourselves—it's all adding up and one of these days we're going to pay the bill for it. I hope it's not in you children's time'" (253).

For Atticus, the town's failure to respect Tom Robinson's legal rights portends the apocalyptic outcome that his New South racism most fears. This is hardly the vision of racial progress suggested by the *Digest*'s Cold War commitments, and unsurprisingly it is cut from the condensed edition. A discussion of the problems of the American legal system (250–253) is similarly excised. It is, however, the depiction of race that marks the greatest divergence between the two versions of the novel.

* * *

SENTIMENTALIZING AND SANITIZING

In *Like One of the Family,* Alice Childress exposed the sentimentalization of Black–white relations in the domestic sphere, with her narrator, the Black maid Mildred, revealing the lie in the title of her book.[46] Generations of white critics, however, have described the relationship between the Finches' Black housekeeper, Calpurnia, and the Finches in romantic terms. As evidence, they point to Atticus's response to his sister's (mysteriously motivated) suggestion that he fire Calpurnia:

> Atticus's voice was even: "Alexandra, Calpurnia's not leaving this house until she wants to. You may think otherwise, but I couldn't have got along without her all these years. She's a faithful member of this family and you'll simply have to accept things the way they are. Besides, sister, I don't want you working your head off for us—you've no reason to do that. We still need Cal as much as we ever did." (156)

Atticus's justification undoes itself. Though Calpurnia is said to be a member of the family, Atticus's assertion that he does not want Alexandra to "work her head off" reveals the terms upon which Calpurnia is considered a family member—one who *is* expected to work her head off for the white family. His comment reveals the relationship to be like the one depicted in Childress's novel, an economic one that whites seek to obscure with the language of family and "faithfulness," a term whites often employed in discussing slaves, to mask forced servitude.

Tellingly, the *Digest* edition ends with Atticus's assertion that Calpurnia is a faithful member of the family; thus, Atticus's all-too-evident hypocrisy is erased. Also omitted is the indication that Calpurnia is, indeed, a biological member of the Finch family. In the original text, Calpurnia's ignorance of her birthday is one of multiple references to her likely descent from slavery on the Finch plantation, but all such references are absent from the *Digest* text.[47] Indeed, slavery all but disappears from this version.

Finch's Landing, we learn on page 2, was a plantation. The condensed text omits the reference, as well as the reference to "Finch Negroes" unloading goods at the Landing (91). Indeed, the only reference to slavery in the condensed version occurs when Calpurnia takes Jem and Scout to her church, the First Purchase African ME, so named "because it was paid for from the first earnings of free slaves" (504). The slaves referenced in the condensed novel are, as befits the *Digest*'s Cold War racial narrative, not only free but also on their way to becoming responsible citizens. In the full novel, however, we learn that "Negroes worshiped in it on Sundays and white men gambled in it on weekdays" (134). This suggestion of white disdain for Black Christians is absent from the *Digest*.

Calpurnia's church is the site of another significant race-related erasure. In *Mockingbird*, Calpurnia is accosted by Lula, a Black parishioner, who questions the housekeeper about bringing white children into a Black space: "You ain't got no business bringin' white chillun here—they got their church, we got our'n. It is our church, ain't it, Miss Cal?" The exchange is missing from the *Digest* version of the novel (136). Also missing is Lula's innuendo-laden retort to Calpurnia's assertion, "They's my comp'ny": "Yeah, an' I reckon you's comp'ny at the Finch house durin' the week" (135). Lula threatens the harmonious image of race relations that many critics see in the novel, and the image of the Black characters' deference and gratitude to the supposed sacrifice of the novel's white savior, Atticus Finch. Hence, Lula is absent from the *Digest*.

Even if some might consider it a stretch to see Lula's retort to Calpurnia as implying an intimate relationship between housekeeper and employer, its erasure from the condensed text is in keeping with the removal of all the novel's references to miscegenation, save for the crime of which Tom Robinson is accused. Miscegenation is, however, a persistent theme in the novel, embodied most obviously by Dolphus Raymond, a plantation owner who has a relationship with a Black woman that produces several mixed-race children (182). Likewise, as has been noted, the *Digest* replaces the suggestion that "Atticus was related by blood or marriage to nearly every family in the town" (5) with the less direct "he knew his people and they knew him: he was related by blood or marriage to nearly every family in town" (460). The original formulation suggests not only sexual impropriety but also cross-racial impropriety. As might be expected, the *Digest* also avoids discussion of the construction of race, entirely erasing Jem's observation that "around here once you have a drop of Negro blood, that makes you all black" (185).

There are several moments of idealized racial harmony in *Mockingbird*. Most obvious are the courtroom scenes, when Reverend Sykes welcomes Scout, Jem, and Dill into the segregated balcony, or when, at the trial's conclusion, the Black folk stand to show their gratitude and respect for Atticus. Such sentimental moments create the dominant understanding of the novel as one of tolerance, decency, and hope. Such readings must nevertheless ignore the aspects that unsettle this narrative. Little attention is given, for example, to the white children's acceptance of the seats: "Four Negroes rose and gave us their front-row seats" (187). Predictably, this display of white privilege is erased from the condensed text. Likewise, during the scene with the mad dog, when Calpurnia runs to warn the Radleys, putting herself at risk, Scout observes, "She went up to the front steps and banged on the door. . . . 'She's supposed to go around in back,' I said" (107). Her comment is omitted from the *Digest*.

Recounting Tom Robinson's death, Atticus observes, "The guards called to him to stop . . . They got him just as he went over the fence. . . . Seventeen bullet holes in him. They didn't have to shoot him that much" (269–270). Predictably, the *Digest* version omits the seventeen shots, and with it, the hate that put them in a Black body. Also missing from the condensed version's account of Robinson's death is his wife's reaction: "'Scout,' said Dill, 'she just fell down in the dirt. Just fell down in the dirt, like a giant with a big foot just came along and stepped on her. Just ump—' Dill's fat foot hit the ground. 'Like you'd step on an ant'" (275). The *Digest* depicts the disappointment of a white man who has lost a trial but not the despair of a Black woman who has lost a husband.

TO KILL A MOCKINGBIRD, READER'S DIGEST, AND THE COLD WAR

In 1958, Frank Leonard asserted, "In their significance in our culture, the *Digest* editions already have greater importance, in many respects, than [the] originals."[48] In this case, the *Digest* edition of *Mockingbird* may have served to shape the popular reception of the novel, flattening the wrinkles in its narrative and removing ambiguity and nuance from its depiction of racial issues. In keeping with its Cold War commitments, the *Digest* offered a text in which issues of miscegenation, sexual assault, Black refusal, and the history of slavery are simply absent. It is a version of history that America sought to present to the world: one of gradualism and the triumph of democratic institutions. It was, however, a story that it also chose to tell itself with damaging consequences.

In 2015, Harper Lee astonished the publishing world with *Go Set a Watchman*, a novel written prior to *Mockingbird* and featuring many characters and scenes from the later-written text. Many were shocked by the Atticus Finch of *Watchman:* a racial bigot, Citizen's Council member, and former Klansman. The many continuities between the two Atticus Finches should have been evident.[49] It may be, however, that the impact of the *Digest*'s condensed version was such that it obscured the details of this continuity, even from those who subsequently read the full text.[50] In this, *Mockingbird* shows how the Cold War influenced not just *what* was read during these years but also, more importantly, *how* it was read. Like the *Digest*, the Cold War served to make its readers, both at home and abroad.

NOTES

1. "The Press: The Magic Touch," *Time* 79, no. 5 (February 2, 1962).
2. Samuel A. Schreiner, *The Condensed World of the Reader's Digest* (New York: Stein and Day, 1977), 6.
3. Joanne Sharp, *Condensing the Cold War: "Reader's Digest" and American Identity* (Minneapolis: University of Minnesota Press, 2000).
4. David Campbell, *Writing Security: United States Foreign Policy and the Politics of Identity* (Minneapolis: University of Minnesota Press, 1998), 105.
5. John Heidenry, *Theirs Was the Kingdom: Lila and DeWitt Wallace and the Story of the Reader's Digest* (New York: W. W. Norton, 1995), 197.
6. Ned O'Gorman, *The Iconoclastic Imagination: Image, Catastrophe, and Economy in America from the Kennedy Assassination to September 11* (Chicago: University of Chicago Press, 2015), 29.
7. Heidenry, *Theirs Was the Kingdom*, 201.
8. Sharp, *Condensing the Cold War*, 78.
9. Ibid., xii.
10. Heidenry, *Theirs Was the Kingdom*, 249.
11. Schreiner, *Condensed World*, 18, 29.
12. Heidenry, *Theirs Was the Kingdom*, 205.
13. Gunnar Myrdal, *The American Dilemma: The Negro Problem and Modern American Democracy* (New York: Routledge, 2017), 4.
14. Heidenry, *Theirs Was the Kingdom*, 246.
15. Ibid., 210.

16. Ibid., 258–259.

17. Sharp, *Condensing the Cold War*, ix–x.

18. Mary Dudziak, *Cold War Civil Rights: Race, and the Image of American Democracy* (Princeton, NJ: Princeton University Press, 2000), 46.

19. Sharp, *Condensing the Cold War*, 42.

20. Ibid., 35.

21. Wayne C. Booth, *The Rhetoric of Fiction* (Chicago: University of Chicago Press, 1983), 302.

22. Schreiner, *Condensed World*, 84.

23. Evert Volkersz, "McBook: The Reader's Digest Condensed Books Franchise," *Publishing Research Quarterly* 11, no. 2 (1995): 55, 59.

24. Ibid., 58.

25. Schreiner, *Condensed World*, 49–50.

26. Volkersz, "McBook," 58.

27. Daniel Baylon, *L'Amerique mythifié. Le Reader's Digest de 1945 à 1970* (Paris: Presses de la Fondation, nationale des sciences politiques, 1989), 5, 279 (in French; author translation).

28. Volkersz, "McBook," 58.

29. Sharp, *Condensing the Cold War*, 38.

30. Malcolm Bradbury, *Punch*, October 26, 1960, 612.

31. Mary McDonagh Murphy, *Scout, Atticus, and Boo: A Celebration of Fifty Years of* To Kill a Mockingbird (New York: Harper Collins, 2010), 40, 98.

32. Lance McMillan, "Atticus Finch as Racial Accommodator: Answering Malcolm Gladwell," *Tennessee Law Review*, 77 (2009–2010): 703.

33. McDonagh, *Scout, Atticus, and Boo*, 145.

34. See Simon Stow, "American Skin: Bruce Springsteen, Danielle Allen, and the Politics of Interracial Friendship," *American Political Thought* 6 (Spring 2007): 294–316.

35. Robert Coles, "James Baldwin Back Home," *New York Times*, July 31, 1977.

36. Allison Miller, "Harper Lee and the Cold War Canon," *Perspectives on History*, August 4, 2015.

37. Monroe Freedman, "Atticus Finch, Esq., RIP," *Legal Times*, February 24, 1992, 20.

38. Malcolm Gladwell, "The Courthouse Ring. Atticus Finch and the Limits of Southern Liberalism," *New Yorker*, August 10 & 17, 2009.

39. McDonagh, *Scout, Atticus, and Boo*, 133.

40. Ibram X. Kendi, *Stamped from the Beginning: The Definitive History of Racist Ideas in America* (New York: Public Affairs, 2016), 369–370.

41. Isaac Saney, "The Case Against *To Kill a Mockingbird*," *Race & Class* 45, no. 1 (2003): 103.

42. Randall Kennedy, "Harper Lee's *Go Set a Watchman*," *New York Times*, July 14, 2015.

43. *Reader's Digest Condensed Books*, vol. 3 (Summer 1960), 460.

44. Simon Stow, "*To Kill a Mockingbird*: Why Can't the Finch Family Pronounce the Names of the Prospects for the 1935 Crimson Tide?," *ANQ* 33, no. 44 (2020): 347–348.

45. Simon Stow, "*To Kill a Mockingbird*: What Maycomb Knew About Hitler (and Why It Matters)," *ANQ* 34, no. 2 (2021): 162–165.

46. Alice Childress, *Like One of the Family: Conversations from a Domestic's Life* (Boston: Beacon Press, 1986).

47. Simon Stow, "The Other Finch Family: Atticus, Calpurnia, Zeebo, and Black Women's Agency in *To Kill a Mockingbird* and *Go Set a Watchman*," *Post45*, January 11, 2018, https://post45.research.yale.edu/2018/01/the-other-finch-family-atticus-calpurnia-zeebo-and-black-womens-agency-in-to-kill-a-mockingbird-and-go-set-a-watchman.

48. Frank G. Leonard, "Cozzens Without Sex; Steinbeck Without Sin," *Antioch Review* 18, no. 2 (1958): 218.

49. Laura Marsh, "Scholars Have Been Pointing Out Atticus Finch's Racism For Years," *New Republic*, July 14, 2015.

50. Part of the cultural matrix through which *Mockingbird* is now read is the 1962 movie starring Gregory Peck. It, too, removes or tones down many of the racial and political aspects of the novel. It is possible that the condensed version of the book—coming two years before the film—helped to shape the sensibility of the movie.

PLAYING BY NEW RULES

Board Games and Cold War American Culture, 1945–1965

MATT SPRENGELER

Games, like music, are common to most human societies, and board games have been a part of most known cultures going back thousands of years. People want—perhaps need—to play. The games they choose are a window to their hopes and fears. Domestic American culture from 1945 to 1965 shows us that people's games reflected how they saw their world. Several games became popular in the United States during the two decades after World War II, in part because they spoke to the anxieties of the time in a safe, controlled way. Games were a way to exert symbolic control over increasingly uncertain times. International nuclear tension was paired with a rapidly evolving American society. Alongside this came the rise of experts—scientists, politicians, home economics specialists, professors—promising guidance through the chaos.

Several of the period's popular games connect to this changing culture. They let players exert control over challenges that mirrored the real world. Scrabble mixed intellect with guesswork, similar to the newly popular game theory. Chess, often used as a stand-in for the Cold War today, was the ultimate game of expertise. Clue brought a friendly kind of terror into the country's living rooms. Risk offered a bloodless exercise in war, one without politics or nationalism. These four games show a changing nation.

SPELLING IT OUT: SCRABBLE AND GAME THEORY

Consider, if you will, the troubles of Ann and Andy. This imaginary couple, dreamed up by sociologist Jessie Bernard in 1959, had a problem shared by many real couples: Andy wanted to have sex more often than Ann did. Luckily for them, Bernard was ready with a solution, one that fit the mind-set of the early Cold War years. She applied game theory to their bedroom.[1]

Game theory was created by mathematicians for business and military research. Bernard found other uses for it. For her hypothetical couple with the troubled sex life—and for many other relationship problems—Bernard recommended using the mathematical techniques of game theory to find solutions. By listing all possible outcomes (in this case, one person wants sex, both do, or neither do) and assigning point values to them, Bernard claimed that one could find the best results for personal problems. In this case, if Andy wanted to have sex but did not know what Ann wanted, the suggested solution was for him to make advances 20 percent of the time and to accept his frustration 80 percent of the time.

Math, structure, order. This remedy for a sagging sex life was in step with the historical moment. In the words of historian Jackson Lears, "The post–World War II decades were the high point of the culture of control."[2] Game theory was one expression of that culture, and it was found in places besides Ann and Andy's bedroom. Businesses used it to try to gain competitive advantages in the marketplace; the military hoped it would give them an edge in nuclear wars. Ultimately, game theory is an attempt to control something unknowable—future human behavior. Americans tried to build formulas and rules to keep uncertainty out. Game theory was one form of this mind-set. Another, elsewhere on the game spectrum, was Scrabble.

This word game, invented by Alfred Butts in 1933, was an obscure pastime for almost twenty years. But in the summer of 1952, Scrabble became a national craze. Older popular board games like chess and Monopoly were "perfect information" games, in which all players have equal knowledge of the game's rules and can see every player's resources. Scrabble is an "imperfect information" activity, one of the first modern American games in which each player's resources (tiles with letters) are secret until they are used. Think of the game's board as a map that players compete to control by placing those tiles. Scrabble is also a game in which a player's vocabulary is essential and spatial skills make a difference—in other words, this is a game of education.

Scrabble was a board game suited to the early Cold War. It required a blend of logic and guesswork. Americans, after all, were dealing with what they saw as a shadowy international threat. Rivalry with the Soviet Union and worries about communism marked America's postwar actions. The rise of game theory and the popularity of Scrabble made sense against that backdrop. Both attempted to impose order on chaotic environments; both rewarded educated guesses in the face of imperfect information. This is a key underpinning of American's early Cold War culture: things that sustained the country through World War II were falling apart, and it was not certain that the new center would hold.

Many of the stories told about Scrabble's origin follow a standard course: the game's creation during the Great Depression is noted, its inventor's life as architect looking for extra income will be mentioned, the transfer of ownership to a social worker is described, and the sudden sales spike of 1952 is exclaimed over. Reports differ slightly on how dramatic this spike was—*Life* estimated that around 120 copies of the game were sold every week during early 1952, while the *New Yorker* reported weekly sales of 200 copies—but sources agree that weekly orders in the thousands were coming in by the end of that year, and they continued to climb. A similar theme was sounded in the *Saturday Review*, which instead of providing the standard biography, suggested that someone stood to make a large pile of money by marketing dictionaries alongside Scrabble.[3]

Interestingly, beyond the *Saturday Review* briefly describing Scrabble as something appealing to the "upper IQs of the nation," these articles made no effort to investigate the cause of this popularity. The closest they came was in *Life*, which repeated a rumor that a member of the family that owned the Macy's department store had played it and then demanded that Macy's carry it.[4]

Game theory, a more direct attempt to counter uncertainty with numbers and systems, was also discussed in the popular press of the day. A typical example can be found in a 1953 issue of *Popular Science Monthly*, which linked game theory to more casual game play. The article, which attempts to explain game theory to an audience of nonmathematicians, is also a window into mainstream perceptions during this time. When playing games that involve both luck and skill, according to the article, people behave the same way as they do in the fields of business and war. "In all these activities, there are good and bad broad, general courses of conduct, which can be mathematically proved to be such."[5] The article credits game theory with proving that there is always a single best strategy to follow in situations that mix skill with luck.

This relentlessly positive attitude, which used the power of calculation to banish human uncertainty, was often found in popular-market writings on game theory. For example, a similar tone was used in a 1955 article from *Scientific American*. An analysis of human satisfaction was embedded in its thorough summary of game theory. Satisfaction was described as something quantifiable: "Isn't satisfaction an inner psychological phenomenon that defies numerical measurement? It turns out that such measurement is possible if one is willing to postulate that the individual will always try to make his decision so as to maximize the expectation [of happiness]."[6]

Having postulated exactly that, and neatly removing uncertainty from human activity, the article explored strategies that decision-makers could use to tackle uncertainty head-on. In all cases—from two people gambling to Columbus sailing across the ocean—satisfaction was found if the proper columns were followed on appropriate charts for the selected strategies. This was the culture of control, an attempt to build cages from which uncertainty could not escape. From its opening paragraphs, this article was certain that human happiness could be managed by rational means.

Which leads us back to Ann and Andy. "Game theory demands a clear-cut statement of all possible alternatives in any given situation; it demands a prediction of the possible outcomes of these alternatives; it demands an evaluation of all these possible outcomes," Bernard said.[7] This article then applied that mind-set to all manner of domestic problems—sex life, household budgets, whether to divorce, and so on. Again, relentless faith was shown in the human ability to control the unknown.

In this light, it is interesting to note an article of the period that connected game theory back to board games in general, and to Scrabble in particular. Writing for *American Economic Review* in 1955, J. J. Polak attempted to apply economic principles to Scrabble to find strategies for winning.[8] He described his efforts as "diametrically opposite" to game theory. Rather than using simple games to create plans for economic actions, as game theorists did, Polak tried applying economic theory to produce good Scrabble actions. The bulk of his short, lighthearted article is a dissection of the probabilities generated by the game's rules, with no further reference to game theory, but it still indicates the degree to which both were present in the consciousness of the times.

A battle against uncertainty was being waged in America during this period. The prominence of game theory directly attests to it, as does the sudden and sustained popularity of Scrabble. A society's games reflect on its larger concerns. Observers at the time were aware of this connection. The bridge editor of the *New York Times*, Albert Morehead, acknowledged that people often played games for deeper reasons: "A player's selection of a game depends on his purpose in playing. . . . He nearly always has at least one unconscious motive, which can best be expressed in the psychologist's jargon: a card player uses a mock struggle as a substitute for the real struggle."[9]

The truth can still be found in the artifacts of the time, both physical and cultural. Games are a useful source for this kind of insight. Although games are found nearly everywhere, people underestimate their impact compared to newer forms of entertainment. Millions of people suddenly turned to Scrabble for recreation; it makes sense to try to figure out why this happened. Similarly, this was the period when game theory blossomed. Although not as blatant as a black-and-white monster movie, game theory provides an allegorical commentary on the culture it inhabited.

Scrabble did not cause a major change in American life, but it points to major characteristics in society. While game theory never caught on as a solution in the bedroom, it did have some effect in boardrooms and war rooms. People sought rational answers to uncertain situations. Through their play, both casual and serious, Americans were pretending to control things that seemed beyond their reach.

BLACK, WHITE, AND RED ALL OVER: COLD WAR CHESS

For a few years, the weight of the United States seemed to rest on the thin shoulders of a finicky, overdressed, tantrum-throwing young man whose only apparent skill was playing chess. Bobby Fischer canceled matches if they started too early, walked out if he didn't like how spectators were looking at him, and publicly accused Russian grandmasters of cheating at tournaments. He was also a prodigy who almost single-handedly turned back decades of Soviet Bloc chess domination. Fischer was an important symbol to Cold War America, one who was (and still is) imperfectly understood.

Chess forms the foundation of a powerful Cold War narrative. The game lends itself to the idea of a strategic struggle between similar contestants. In chess, each kind of piece moves across the board differently to do its job. In the same fashion, the years from 1945 to 1965 saw an explosion of new technology, notably the evolution of nuclear weapons and their delivery systems. And military hardware represented only some of the pieces in any player's arsenal. Economic influence, the power of persuasion, religion, or the lack of these—all kinds of things were in play during the Cold War game.

The chessboard itself was a convenient analogue to the post-atomic world. With its grid of black and white squares, the board is divided into specific territories, just like any real-world political map. The object of chess is to capture an opponent's king, an important but slow-moving piece. While victory might not be possible in a nuclear war, the competitors would be sure to target each other's capitals and other immobile targets.

Indeed, people at the time used chess to describe their experiences. Leon Volkov, a former Soviet military officer who defected to the United States and became a writer for mainstream magazines, visited a United States Chess Federation event in New York City in 1954. The federation was hosting a team from the USSR, and Volkov reported being repeatedly rebuffed by Russian "chaperones" when he tried to talk with his former compatriots. "The visitor to the New York tournament," he said, "will realize that for the Soviets even a chess game becomes a struggle between Communism and capitalism."[10]

Chess was more than a symbol during the early Cold War. The game itself was seen as a chance for the free world's finest minds to face off against their communist counterparts. These intellectual battles were important. As World War II ended, science and knowledge came to prominence in a new way. "Postwar America was the era of the expert," says historian Elaine Tyler May. "Armed with scientific techniques and presumably inhabiting a world that was beyond popular passions, the experts had brought us into the atomic age. Physicists developed the bomb, strategists created the Cold War, and scientific managers built the military-industrial complex. It was now up to the experts to make the unmanageable manageable."[11] The work of experts transformed the world in a fundamental way. Nuclear weapons—the province of highly trained specialists, beyond the control of the common person—were replacing rifles and cannons as the measure of a nation's military might. The United States struggled to maintain nuclear supremacy over the USSR and then over a growing list of other countries.

On a more abstract level, the symbolic overlay of chess on top of the Cold War gave Americans another way to direct the global struggle. Chess—a game that can be *won*, a pastime that does not end in doom—rapidly became a metaphor for the times. "It requires very little perception," wrote Edward L. Katzenbach Jr. in 1963, "to see the relevance of chess to the strategic problems of our time—to raising standards of living, to guerilla actions, and to the resolution of the Cold War."[12] In this context, chess was seen as serious business. It was an area where citizens of the United States matched themselves against Soviet representatives in meaningful yet nonlethal combat.[13]

These proxy fights grabbed the attention of American audiences. Magazines had regular stories and photo spreads covering the chess clashes; even *Sports Illustrated* followed these matches. This put a human face on the Cold War, as in a 1954 *Life* magazine story about a series of games between American champion Larry Evans and Soviet player Mark Taimanov: "Communism's rigid visage relaxed long enough to show Russian officials grimacing, fidgeting on their chairs and chewing their nails, like anyone else under tension."[14] A series of photographs showed various Soviet officials gnawing on their knuckles and making wry faces at the action on the chessboard. This echoes an observation made by Volkov at the US Chess Federation event. He asked a Soviet attendee whether chess had anything to do with politics and got the reply, "Of course it does! Remember, we are Marxists and Communists. For us, everything is political. Including chess."[15] This formed the backdrop for one of the greatest Cold War clashes, Bobby Fischer against the world.

Fischer was an American chess genius. Over the course of the postwar years, his aggressive style of play and headstrong behavior made him a hero to the nation. At a time when a long string of bland Russian grandmasters represented the menace of collectivism, Fischer defiantly followed his own path. His ongoing battle with his Soviet counterparts helped Fischer's compatriots turn their Cold War anxieties into a game.

Bobby Fischer changed the American view of international chess. In early 1958, the fourteen-year-old Fischer won the US Chess Championship, becoming the youngest national champion in American history. He began playing in international tournaments, defeating experienced opponents, and he was declared a grandmaster at the age of fifteen. Thereafter, he was on several

American teams competing in the international Chess Olympiad, helping the teams to several top-four finishes.

Nonetheless, Fischer was not a team player. He was a solitary person who did things his own way, on the chessboard as well as in his personal life. "Fischer's win-every-game approach is unique among post–Second World War players," wrote chess analyst Raymond Keene. "Even [Anatoly] Karpov, the only player to rival Fischer's supremacy in that era, is still often content to draw with black against strong players."[16]

As Fischer's career continued, the American interest in chess changed. The narrative, which had followed a US-versus-USSR pattern, evolved into Fischer's struggle to become the world's greatest chess player. Fischer's creative style of chess—always striving for the win when other players would draw, engaging in brash behavior unlike that of his restrained grandmaster peers—fed into the idea of the independent American character. Bobby Fischer became a human face of the Cold War.

He was not shy about clashing with his Russian rivals. His chessboard confrontations were headline news, and Fischer also involved himself in the larger politics surrounding the game. Most notably, in 1962 he accused Russians of conspiring to unfairly win a tournament in Curaçao, affecting the quest for the world chess championship. "By agreeing in advance to throw draws, or games, to each other after a few perfunctory moves, Soviet players, Fischer said, manipulate their scores, and make it impossible for a non-communist to break through to victory unless he wins almost every game he plays," explained contemporary writer Robert O'Brien. "American and English players have been muttering about this for the last ten years. But Fischer had the nerve to drop the bomb."[17]

In fact, Fischer went so far as to complain about it in the pages of *Sports Illustrated*. "The Russians have substituted propaganda for money as the incentive for holding on to the title," he wrote.[18] Fischer's argument was that the Soviets manipulated tournaments so that only players from Communist countries would end up in championship games. Fischer vowed to stop competing in these events unless the rules were changed. While the Soviets denied collusion, many chess authorities found Fischer's accusation plausible, and tournaments were changed to make it harder for teams to block out other possible winners.

Several months before the Cuban Missile Crisis, Bobby Fischer provoked a stare down with the USSR and emerged the winner.

Over the course of Fischer's career, the public picture of chess changed as people were drawn into the game as a symbol of the Cold War struggle. During the 1950s, before Fischer's rise to fame, chess was already a broad lens used to view the struggle between nations. This abstract us-and-them perspective gave way to tales of Bobby Fischer, the eccentric prodigy who single-handedly battled the Soviet chess machine. Fischer would be a symbol of American intellect into the 1970s, when he went into a period of retirement that would outlast the Cold War.

Fischer's mercurial behavior helped drive the enthusiasm for chess. He was not only an unpredictable genius at the chessboard but also a riveting spectacle away from it, openly accusing the Soviet players of conspiring to fix games, refusing to play matches before noon, observing a mysterious "holy day" every week, during which he would not even discuss chess. "He has gotten religion," noted teammate Larry Evans, "though no one has been able to find out which religion it is, or whether it has a brand name."[19] Fischer's behavior during the early Cold War years was flamboyant, perhaps unsportsmanlike, and definitely individual.

Chess was, in many ways, an idealized version of the situation that Americans faced during the early Cold War. It reflected a reality they wished to be true: a two-player game, tightly governed by understandable rules, that could be mastered by the mind. This same desire for control showed up as game theory, as the hunt for domestic communists, as a reluctance to name exactly what activity was producing the baby boom. The structure of chess itself, combined with the ongoing US–USSR rivalry for dominance at it, seemed to reflect the Cold War in a harmless and controllable way.

However, a close reading of chess shows that things were more complicated. It may have been a version of the Cold War that Americans wanted to see, but several basic characteristics of chess didn't line up with the times. Chess is a two-player game, for example, which fit the us-versus-them attitude that we have observed. However, more than two actors were present on the world stage—the actual Cold War was a game with many players, and they did not neatly sort themselves into two sides. Cultural analyst Steven Belletto suggests that the contemporary popularity of game theory, with its bias toward two players, influenced Americans to view their situation as a dual-player conflict even as they struggled to influence a "third world," the very name of which shows that multiple players were at the geopolitical table.[20] Poker, he suggested, was a game more suited to the world as it existed.

Another problem with the chess metaphor is that it has three possible outcomes: win, loss, or draw. Two players can agree to simply end the game rather than play it out. In the real world, though, the ongoing nuclear game has continued to the present day, with an expanding number of players and no sign of a draw.

The final problem with chess as a metaphor: it is a game of perfect information. Life lacks the clarity of chess. Using it as a lens to view the Cold War was (and is) inaccurate. The achievements of the New Deal, victory in World War II, the rise of experts and intellectuals with solutions for the world's problems— all of these were now in the shadow of a mushroom cloud. A two-player game with no secrets, one that could be mastered by the human mind, may have been more appealing than a direct reflection of the world as it was.

MURDER AT HOME: CLUE

Mass market board games were popular during the postwar years because they fit into America's new domestic life. Many of them were short-lived. Various cultural preoccupations provided the themes for these mayfly games (television shows were especially common), but they did not have lasting appeal. Connection to a popular pastime like TV was not enough to guarantee a game's place in broader society.

Often, board games from this time reflected the Cold War. For example, Uranium Rush was one of several mid-1950s games that capitalized on the public fascination with nuclear materials. The game was driven by a set of random mechanics, involving the use of a spinner to determine the movement of pieces around the board and the collection of cards that affected the player's supply of game money; many of the cards had a national security theme. Like Monopoly, it offered wealth on a random basis, making it easy for a less-skilled player to beat their competitors. Playing Uranium Rush put people in control of this dangerous substance for a little while, if only in their own minds.

Games of this nature did not last. They might have connected with short-term fears, but when those fears failed to become real, the pastimes reflecting them were sent to the trash. This disposable culture did, however, produce some enduring games. The familiar Clue is one of them, and it sheds light on the deeper concerns of the people who played it.

Clue is not technically a product of the Cold War—it was invented in England during World War II under the name Cluedo—but this postwar period is when it first came to the United States. Like Scrabble, it was a natural fit for the intellectual atmosphere of this period. Clue is a game of imperfect information and problem solving. The action centers on what each player knows about a murder that has been committed. Cards with locations, weapons, and murder suspects are dealt to everyone at the start of the game; each player also takes the role of one of these suspects. Everyone tries to figure out which suspect used which weapon to commit the murder, and in which location. The first player to announce the correct combination is the winner, but a false accusation removes the accuser from the game. Interestingly, the person playing the role of the murderer does not know that they are the guilty party. They must deduce it along with everyone else.

The rules for Clue were created in the mid-1940s by English legal clerk Anthony Pratt; the board was designed by his wife, Elva, an amateur painter.[21] Wartime material shortages prevented the game from being produced in large quantities until around 1950. It was not history's first detective-themed board game but it has been the most successful over the past seven decades, largely defining its category. Created by a British couple in need of diversion from the World War II air raids thundering outside their home, Clue was suited to American families spending the Cold War in their own homes.

It is significant that Clue's game board is the floor plan of a house. The traditional version is a mansion, with more conservatories and ballrooms than a typical suburban three-bedroom ranch home. But it is still a house, and the game's action takes place entirely within its walls. This was bound to appeal to postwar American domesticity. Changes like suburbanization and the baby boom were creating a new set of concerns, some positive and some negative. Clue was remarkably positioned to address them.

"When we talk specifically about what has happened to American families," Robert Foster wrote in 1949, "we are concerned with divorce, delinquency, illegitimacy, crime, prostitution, child failure and maladjustment, mental illnesses, marriage rates, birth rates, sickness, unemployment, poverty, and other major items."[22] This list of calamities was hardly unique to Foster's imagination. Writers in the popular press worried about how "the US family, deep in the millrace of social and technological change, is itself deep in trouble,"[23] and they considered how these families would confront the "bewildering choices and opportunities" of the times.[24] Looking back on the times, historian K. A. Cuordileone noted that "fears of being . . . less than *normal* could strike deep emotional chords in a way that fears of materialism or secularism or perhaps even the bomb could not."[25]

Games like Clue were seen as an antidote to the troubles of home and family. In 1952, Marguerite Kohl wrote, "Your children will learn good sportsmanship. They'll discover how to lose quietly and win gracefully. They'll find out how to get along with people. But, best of all, you will all have a share in that intangible something which makes a happy family." Kohl specifically cited Clue as a family game that was "a whale of a lot of fun" and then went on to say "people everywhere are playing indoor games again."[26]

Interest in games was obvious at the time, and it was often linked to home and family. Writing in *House Beautiful* magazine, Albert Ostrow spent several pages contrasting families that shared pastimes with families that had no common interests. Recounting a friend's memorable childhood game of checkers, Ostrow concluded that "nothing has shaken this central fact: Sharing good times can do more for the morale and unity of the family and parent–child understanding than any scientific rigamarole."[27]

Family life was a matter of concern in this period, and games were something that observers saw as helpful to families. In a sense, Clue itself was a symbolic solution to social worries. Some of the writers mentioned here expressed concern with violence, particularly when it was committed by (or affected) children and teenagers. These family-centered worries were often put into a larger Cold War context. "A and H bombs, rockets, chemicals, biological and radiological warfare are realities of our times. . . . Entertainment seems to exaggerate rather than mirror this world. It is replete with physical assault," wrote psychotherapist and scholar Emanuel Schwartz in 1961.[28]

Clue, by contrast, is a friendly game that draws on the clear and cerebral detective tradition of Sherlock Holmes. Any violence in Clue is always in the past, information is constantly shared among participants, and players win by using their heads rather than their fists.

Observers used this contrast in styles to make sense of the early Cold War world as it happened. In an article published in the *Saturday Review* in 1953—only a few pages from an article on the growing cultural presence of Scrabble—John Paterson outlined the differences he saw between Holmes and more gritty detective characters. He wrote that "two worlds, two notions of society are represented in the detective fiction of our day . . . To understand them is to understand something of the social and cultural climate of our period." The distinction Paterson drew followed the lines above—an earlier Holmesian school, with its order and its gentility, followed by a tough, hard-boiled style of "disintegrated values where evil cannot be isolated and destroyed as it could be in the fairy-tale world of the transcendent sleuth."[29] The postwar America which made Clue popular was going through a similar reordering. After a world war with decisive winners and losers, the USA and the USSR were in a battle where isolating and destroying each other was much less certain. It follows that this would be reflected in popular entertainment.

However, this reflection shows more than one thing. Just as the popularity of a tough guy style of detective demonstrated cultural anxiety, the attempts to cope with that anxiety showed in the popularity of old-fashioned Clue. The game addressed many common preoccupations, starting with matters of family and home life. Clue—like other common games—was an activity that families could do together. Game nights have long been considered a way for families to strengthen their bonds, and Clue was not only a potential answer to family problems but also a microcosm of the domestic worries being expressed. As noted, it is set inside a house. Each player is specific character, all of whom are linked by a common bond, not unlike family members. Strains develop as players pursue their individual interests—in this case, winning the game before anyone else. Similarly, postwar American families found themselves pulled in new individual directions. Just as Clue players chased a solitary victory on a house-themed board, many Cold War families felt that contemporary life was changing their basic nature.

We have already noted concerns about matters like juvenile delinquency and the rising divorce rate. Here we find some of the cultural elements that helped Clue become (and remain) popular. Its American release brought it into a country that was dealing with turmoil in its homes. The themes and conflicts of Clue created a controlled version of this tension. Clue benefited from its timing; it was invented just as its ideal moment began.

It was also fun. This point is easy to overlook, but it is crucial to explaining the success of any game. People play games because they enjoy them, not just to make some point in a history book. Clue, like the other games discussed here, allowed groups of people to spend time with each other. Parents, children, siblings could sit at a table, competing in a friendly fashion. This togetherness was an important part of postwar domesticity. Faced with an outside world that seemed to change rapidly, individual families treated their homes as "spheres of influence," as described by May: "Within [the home's] walls, potentially dangerous social forces of the new age might be tamed, where they could contribute to the secure and fulfilling life to which postwar women and men aspired."[30]

At this point, it is interesting to contrast Clue and a similar game called Mr. Ree. Mr. Ree came first, being published in 1937, and it also takes place inside a house wherein one of the players commits a murder. However, Mr. Ree is a footnote known primarily to game historians and collectors, while Clue rapidly became a success and has remained so for decades. One key difference between the games is how they portray subversion. Clue makes the murderer's identity a mystery—until the very end of the game, nobody knows who the guilty party is, even if it is one of the players. Everyone works toward the same goal; everyone wants to figure out who betrayed the group.

Mr. Ree, in contrast, gives its players control of the murder. They can collect items and play cards that let them "kill" other players, eliminating them from the game. Thus, the difference is agency. In Clue, everyone tries to figure out who has turned against the housebound group. In Mr. Ree, players win by working against each other and secretly arranging for their competitors' deaths. Clue never asked its Cold War players to turn against their group or to harbor dangerous secrets. During this time when subversion was a worry, the game that endured was the one that reinforced group identity and problem solving, not the one that encouraged players to betray each other for victory.

* * *

WAR WITHOUT BLOOD: RISK

In a different fashion, concerns about war and subversion can be seen in Risk, perhaps the most well-known war game in the United States. Created in France in 1957, it was first sold in the United States in 1959. Its tagline has been "The game of global conquest" or "The world conquest game" in various printings, and its board bears that out. Risk is played on a map of the world, players compete to control continents with their armies, and victory goes to whoever eliminates all other players' forces. Viewed broadly, it resembles Cold War tensions, with the battle over the game board standing in for the ongoing geopolitical struggle.

From a closer view, though, Risk's design and popularity push back against the idea of a nation locked in an existential struggle with the Soviet Union. One key element is the way in which Risk's board is designed. It divides the world into six habitable continents, each broken down into several territories. Instead of setting up these territories along political lines—NATO powers opposing the Warsaw Pact, or historic rivals Japan and China competing for Asia—Risk is heavily geographic. Players receive bonuses for controlling predefined areas of land, which were drawn without obvious reference to the struggles of the day. In fact, one of the territories in the European continent is called Russia (some editions of the game instead name it Ukraine), making it part of the same power bloc as many of its Cold War antagonists. The game of Risk is entirely about the physical control of space, with no ideological elements involved; even references to real-world political and cultural structures are limited.[31]

Chance, not control, is at the heart of Risk. When armies clash, for example, players roll dice to determine the outcome, and the outcome of the dice has a much larger impact than the number of troops involved. Randomness usually favors the underdog in games, and Risk's rules give small forces a disproportionate chance of holding off large ones. More tellingly, the reward for capturing an enemy-held territory is getting to draw a random card marked with a territory name and a special symbol. Matching sets of these cards can be traded in for ever-increasing numbers of new armies. Careful use of the cards is a key to victory in a typical game of Risk—they can radically change the balance of power by adding dozens of unexpected armies to the board. Hence, victory in Risk often comes down to chance. A player who randomly draws the right cards can upend the careful strategies of any number of opponents; the reverse is much less likely.

Another interesting element in Risk is the generic nature of its combat. The players use pieces called "armies," but these units are not distinct from each other in any way. Many other war games use pieces that differ in some way, such as the familiar Battleship with its ships of assorted sizes. A similar example from the early Cold War period is a game called Armchair General. Played on a Battleship-style grid, Armchair General incorporated two diverse kinds of terrain and five separate unit types, each of which had different rules for movement and firing.[32] Such distinctions are common to wargames. Risk avoids them. Combat in this game is indistinct and impersonal, with no significant differences beyond whether one is attacking or defending. Risk is also unconcerned with the nuclear arms race, despite being invented during a peak period of that race. The original game had no special rules governing weapons of mass destruction, although later versions have had official variants that incorporate such ideas.

This depersonalized warfare and lack of emphasis on nuclear arms are another element of Risk's success. As noted earlier, Emanuel Schwartz worried that the "age of anxiety" was turning into an "age of violence" as families lived under the shadow of war. Risk was created while worries about nuclear weapons were rampant. In Risk, this war becomes abstract. Soldiers are not fighting—"armies" are. The only weapons being deployed are a set of six-sided dice, and because no player can roll more than three of them at a time, the casualties come slowly. This picture of warfare would appeal to people who were preoccupied with the specter of actual war. Risk helped its players, at least symbolically, manage chance.

Chance, after all, is what Risk is built on; even the name implies it.[33] Playing the game would not only pass time enjoyably but also help manage the idea of danger. Winning Risk would be a shadow of real-world victory, while losing would be free of war's horrendous consequences. Brian Sutton-Smith, a scholar of play, has said that "the kind of existential threats that are most valued in society find expression in the appropriate forms of play."[34] Risk has offered one expression of such a threat for more than fifty years.

Contrast this with the nature of game theory. Its use during the early Cold War has been considered, but it is also worth remembering how faith in game theory was far from universal at the time. Belletto critiqued the idea that game theory was the precise, rational, statistical model that some people said it was. Instead of being a semiscientific set of rules operating outside human perceptions, Belletto argued, game theory was a narrative that fit into a Cold War that was "chiefly a conflict of competing ideologies and their attendant narratives."[35]

Drawing on many examples of Cold War writers, directors, and other cultural figures who attacked or satirized game theory, Belletto demonstrated that concerns about it were widespread during the postwar period. Novels like Kurt Vonnegut's *Player Piano* (1952) and Philip K. Dick's *Solar Lottery* (1955) satirized game theory's tenets and proponents. The Stanley Kubrick film *Dr. Strangelove, or: How I Learned to Stop Worrying and Love the Bomb* (1964) undermined the idea of controlling nuclear irrationality with supposedly rational policies. In its quiet way, Risk contributed to this counternarrative. It made war seem less terrible while also portraying it as a matter of chance.

The early Cold War years were uneasy ones. Games are a window into the ways that people deal with that kind of anxiety. Sutton-Smith observed that "the history of the human species, whether *homo erectus* or otherwise, is a history of considerable anxiety . . . [which] makes it not improbable that play and its variabilities have been selected over time to model and mollify this ever-present chaos."[36] Although board games have not received the same scholarly attention as other media, they do provide a window into the lives of the people who played them.

The four games examined here shared some important characteristics, notably the fact that each became popular in the United States during these postwar decades. And all of them remained popular while fad games like Uranium Rush never caught hold, and similar games like Mr. Ree failed to align with the interests of the mass audience. The scholar Stephen J. Whitfield observed that "the culture of the Cold War was by no means synonymous with the culture of the 1950s . . . [but] the Cold War also narrowed and altered American culture."[37] The artifacts that succeeded in this altered culture can add new dimensions to our interpretations. What people do for fun, how they spend their spare time—these help us understand who they were.

NOTES

1. Jessie Bernard, "Counseling Techniques for Arriving at Optimum Compromises: Game-and Decision Theory," *Marriage and Family Living* 21, no. 3: 264.
2. Jackson Lears, *Something for Nothing: Luck in America* (New York: Viking, 2003), 19.
3. L. Z. Hobson, "Speaking of Scrabble," *Saturday Review* 36 (August 22, 1953): 5.
4. Robert Wallace, "A Man Makes a Best-Selling Game—Scrabble—and Achieves His Ambition (Spelled Out Above)," *Life* 35 (December 14, 1953): 101–112.
5. Bruce Bliven, "Games Disclose Secrets of Success: Scientists Are Determining the Best Strategy in War and Business by Watching Their Students Play Cards," *Popular Science Monthly* 163 (December 1953): 125–128, 246, quote at 126. The article describes the use of card games, but some of them are clearly analogues of common board games like Monopoly.
6. Leonid Hurwicz, "Game Theory and Decisions: In Which Smith Plays a Game with Jones and Columbus Plays a Game with Nature to Illustrate How This Comparatively New Mathematical Tool Can Be Used to Grapple with Problems Involving Uncertainties," *Scientific American* 192, no. 2 (February 1955): 78–83, at 80.
7. Bernard, "Counseling Techniques," 274.
8. J. J. Polak, "The Economics of Scrabble," *American Economic Review* 45, no. 4 (September 1955): 648–652.
9. Albert Morehead, "Games: Who Plays What and Why," *New York Times Magazine*, October 13, 1957, 54–58.
10. Leon Volkov, "Russia's Captive Chessmen," *Newsweek* 43, no. 26 (June 28, 1954): 38.
11. Elaine Tyler May, *Homeward Bound: American Families in the Cold War Era* (New York: Basic Books, 1988), 26.
12. Edward L. Katzenbach Jr., "Poker, Pawns, and Power," *Saturday Review* 46, no. 12 (March 23, 1963): 25.
13. "Bernard Cafferty," in *World Chess Champions*, ed. E. G. Winter (New York: Pergamon, 1981), 89.
14. "Stress over Chess: Risky Play against US Alarms Soviet Boss," *Life* 37, no. 2 (July 12, 1954): 39.
15. Volkov, "Russia's Captive Chessmen," 38.
16. "Raymond Keene," in Winter, *World Chess Champions*, 120.
17. Robert O'Brien, "Bobby Fischer: Best in Chess?," *Saturday Review* 46, no. 17 (April 27, 1963): 22.
18. Bobby Fischer, "The Russians Have Fixed World Chess," *Sports Illustrated* 17, no. 8 (August 20, 1962): 18.
19. Larry Evans, "Bobby Would Rather Fight," *Sports Illustrated* 25, no. 23 (December 5, 1966): 91.
20. Steven Belletto, "The Game Theory Narrative and the Myth of the National Security State," *American Quarterly* 61, no. 2 (June 2009): 354.

21. David Parlett, *The Oxford History of Board Games* (Oxford: Oxford University Press, 1999), 356. Mrs. Pratt's first name is not documented in any of the standard sources but was given as Elva at www.theartofmurder.com, a Clue website maintained by Michael Akers.

22. Robert Foster, "Social Trends and Family Life," *Journal of Home Economics* 41, no. 7 (September 1949): 358.

23. "The American Family in Trouble," *Life* 25, no. 4 (July 26, 1948): 83.

24. Lawrence K. Frank, "American Family," *National Parent-Teacher* 53, no. 2 (October 1958): 15.

25. K. A. Cuordileone, "Politics in an Age of Anxiety: Cold War Political Culture and the Crisis in American Masculinity, 1949–1960," *Journal of American History* 87, no. 2 (September 2000): 539.

26. Marguerite Kohl, "Games Are Good for You," *American Magazine* 153, no. 4 (April 1952): 31, 117. It should be noted that in this article Kohl also presents an inaccurate recounting of Monopoly's origin.

27. Albert Ostrow, "Keeping the Fun in the Family," *House Beautiful* 94, no. 12 (December 1952): 214.

28. Emanuel Schwartz, "The Family in an 'Age of Violence,'" *New York Times*, January 22, 1961.

29. John Paterson, "A Cosmic View of the Private Eye," *Saturday Review* 36 (August 22, 1953): 7, 31.

30. May, *Homeward Bound*, 14.

31. The most obvious political references are the territories named Eastern United States, Western United States, and perhaps Northwest Territory. Interestingly, the region that incorporates Vietnam, an area of ongoing interest to both France and the United States during this time, is called Siam.

32. W. H. Fulker, "Game Calls for Land-Sea-Air Strategy," *Popular Science* 153, no. 6 (December 1948): 196.

33. A story often repeated is that when the game was licensed for sale in the United States, an American salesman suggested naming it RISK because those were the initials of his grandchildren. Although charming, the source of this tale is not reliably documented.

34. Brian Sutton-Smith, "Evolving a Consilience of Play Definitions: Playfully," *Play & Culture Studies*, vol. 2, ed. Stuart Reifel (Stamford, CT: Ablex, 1999), 249.

35. Belletto, "Game Theory Narrative," 333.

36. Sutton-Smith, "Evolving a Consilience," 244.

37. Stephen J. Whitfield, *The Culture of the Cold War*, 2nd ed. (Baltimore: Johns Hopkins University Press, 1996): 12.

THE COPS VERSUS THE COMMIES

Cold War Cuba and Chile in US Folk Music

EUNICE ROJAS

The involvement of US folk artists in the Vietnam War protests of the 1960s and 1970s is well known. What is less known is that a number of these artists also included in their repertoire songs critical of the US government's Cold War tactics in Latin America. Post–World War II US fears about the expansion of Soviet Communist influence led to the adoption of the Truman Doctrine, which was the name for the US foreign policy promise of military, political, and economic assistance to nations under threat of Communist influence. The Truman Doctrine offered the United States either a reason or an excuse to intervene in the political affairs of Latin American countries to "contain" the spread of communism.

This policy of containment ultimately had profound effects on several Latin American countries. Notably, the United States' unsuccessful attempts first to prevent the Cuban Revolution and later to topple Fidel Castro's Soviet-supported government resulted in a blockade that to date has lasted well over half a century and has survived multiple presidencies in both countries. Much more fruitful were the US efforts in Chile, where in 1973 the covert political and economic influence of the United States was mobilized to destabilize the country and bring about a coup d'état that toppled Salvador Allende's democratically elected socialist government. This essay analyzes songs about US Cold War exploits in Cuba and Chile penned and performed by US folksingers, and these artists' efforts to bring the consequences of the Cold War in Latin America to a place of prominence in US popular culture.

In the decades after World War II, while the United States and the Soviet Union were engaged in an ideological geopolitical standoff that involved exercising their military and economic might against each other in proxy wars around the globe, the Cold War was also being fought on a more subtle cultural front. In *Who Paid the Piper? The CIA and the Cultural Cold War*, British journalist Frances Stonor Saunders examines the covert Cold War efforts of the CIA to infiltrate the worlds of arts and letters, mainly in Europe. According to Saunders, the agency's aim in this was to "build a 'consortium' whose double task it was to inoculate the world against the contagion of Communism, and to ease the passage of American foreign policy interests abroad." This consortium, organized in large part by the Congress for Cultural Freedom, an anticommunist advocacy group run and funded by the CIA from 1950 to 1967, "was the hidden weapon in America's Cold War struggle, a weapon which, in the cultural field, had extensive fall-out."[1]

Following Saunders's groundbreaking investigation of the CIA's influence on the European cultural front of the Cold War, US historian Hugh Wilford, in *The Mighty Wurlitzer: How the CIA Played America*, examined the cultural Cold War efforts of the intelligence agency on the domestic front. Wilford describes how "the CIA attempted to mobilize a cross-section of American society in the Cold War struggle of hearts and minds—to 'play' America as if it were a giant musical instrument."[2] The musical references in both the Saunders and the Wilford studies hint that music was a central element in the cultural battle of the Cold War.

The cultural Cold War was by no means a one-sided battle. Saunders describes the Soviets as "experts in the use of culture as a tool of political persuasion."[3] In fact, the psychological warfare of propaganda and the funding of ideological cultural production was another proxy war waged between the two nuclear powers. In the United States, alongside this covert cultural war was an influential counterculture with a substantial musical component. The soundtrack to the Cold War–era counterculture included a revival of folk music, with lyrics often dedicated to social justice causes. Because the musicians of this movement shared a Leftist ideology, the US government viewed their music as suspicious and subversive, and it gathered voluminous files tracking the publications, activities, and performances of many of the artists.

In 1946, when folksinger Pete Seeger cofounded People's Songs, an organization created to promote and share socially conscious folk music, particularly labor songs, the FBI quickly took notice. After the first national convention for People's Songs took place, in 1947, an agent reported to FBI director J. Edgar Hoover that Seeger's organization played folk songs in places "where the hoity-toity red intellectuals gather."[4] Seeger himself was called to testify before the House Un-American Activities Committee (HUAC) in 1955 about whether he had ever sung for an organization of the Communist Party.[5] Seeger's refusal to answer the HUAC's questions directly resulted in a prison sentence, although his conviction was overturned years later. His defiant testimony before the HUAC also cemented his place on the infamous entertainment industry blacklist that denied employment to individuals with suspected communist sympathies. Accused of being "Moscow's canary," Seeger found himself banned from traditional commercial media. Undaunted, he resorted to what he termed "guerrilla cultural tactics" by calling up local radio stations to announce his concerts live on air before radio executives had time to silence him.[6] Seeger viewed left-leaning folksingers like himself as guerrilla fighters against the US intelligence forces on the domestic front of the cultural Cold War.

Despite his blacklisted status, Seeger helped foster a new generation of left-leaning folk music artists that burst on the scene in the early 1960s. Among these young troubadours was Phil Ochs, who was a journalism student at Ohio State University when the 1960s began. In January 1959, when Fidel Castro's rebel forces marched triumphantly into Havana after having ousted US-backed dictator Fulgencio Batista, Ochs immediately took notice of the extensive media coverage. The Cuban Revolution had begun in 1953, after Batista seized power by force following his election defeat in 1952.

US companies had significant business interests in Cuba in the 1950s, and the Batista regime and "his military and secret police received US aid." Nevertheless, although US intelligence agencies suspected Communist cooperation with Castro's rebellion throughout the 1950s, the Cuban Revolution did not become a true Cold War battle until after the triumph of the revolutionary forces.[7] Between 1959 and 1961, Castro's regime "took on the tone and shape of a Communist revolution," in part through massive expropriations of land that benefited the rural poor and angered wealthy Cubans and US investors.

At the same time, Castro also began to build an alliance with the Soviet Union, and by the end of 1961 Castro had declared himself a Marxist-Leninist for life.[8]

When Phil Ochs started as a first-year student at Ohio State, he was a relatively apolitical fan of Elvis Presley who was altogether unfamiliar with the folk music revival movement, but in the fall of 1959, he became roommates with Jim Glover, a guitar-and banjo-playing local student whose father was a Marxist. While the younger Glover introduced Ochs to the music of Pete Seeger and Woody Guthrie, the elder Glover spoke to Phil about the House Un-American Activities Committee, McCarthyism, Fidel Castro, and the exploitation of Cuban workers by US corporations.[9]

Castro, the underdog David struggling against the Goliath of the United States, proved to be an inspirational figure for Ochs. His friend Bruce Pollock quotes him as saying, "Castro got me into serious politics, socialism, and anti-imperialism. He became [my] teacher of anti-imperialism." As a journalism major, Ochs began writing for the Ohio State *Lantern* and aspired to become the editor, but his controversial political pieces full of admiration for Fidel Castro caused the editorial staff to remove him from political assignments.[10] As a result, Ochs created his own purely political newspaper. In addition, he frequently published political commentary as letters to the editor to both a local Cleveland paper and to the *Lantern*.

Ochs and his roommate, Glover, began playing as a folk duo under the name The Singing Socialists, though they soon changed their name to The Sundowners. Ochs's experience with journalism and his passionate political views made him a natural topical singer-songwriter. The first serious song that he wrote was in response to the news of the failed US invasion of the Cuban Bay of Pigs in April 1961. The approximately 1,400 counterrevolutionary forces seeking to overthrow Castro were mostly Cuban exiles living in the United States, trained, armed, and funded by the CIA, and they were quickly defeated by Castro's military. Although President Kennedy initially distanced the United States from having played any role in the attack, it was later revealed that he and his Joint Chiefs of Staff had approved the plan. According to historian Jim Rasenberger, "The Bay of Pigs had been a US operation and its failure ... was a distinctly American embarrassment.... The government had been caught bullying and prevaricating."[11]

Prior to the Bay of Pigs invasion, Ochs had published a letter to the editor of the Ohio State *Lantern*, condemning his country's harsh stance toward Castro while it ignored other repressive dictators around the world. For Ochs, this double standard toward dictators was an indication of the United States' imperialist attitude toward Cuba. His editorial continued with his prediction of the consequences of a US invasion of Castro's Cuba. "Had we attacked Cuba . . . Russia's screaming of 'Yankee Imperialism' would have a strong ring of truth throughout the world."[12] The Bay of Pigs invasion, though small and unsuccessful, ultimately confirmed Ochs's stated fears of US imperialism and the Soviet reaction.

In an interview with *Boston Globe* columnist Gregory McDonald, Ochs explained that the Bay of Pigs invasion not only inspired him creatively but also marked a turning point for him politically. "Up until the Cuban invasion I had been sort of moderate left. . . . It was that incident, the Bay of Pigs, that convinced me there was a lot of political fraud going on. So I sat down and wrote 'The Ballad of the Cuban Invasion.'"[13] Never recorded on an album, the song survives as a live recording uploaded to YouTube of a performance by Ochs at an unknown date and location.[14] In addition, recordings exist of a version of "Ballad of the Cuban Invasion" sung by Jim Glover at the Phil Ochs Memorial Concert, held shortly after Ochs's death in 1976.[15]

With just three verses and a somber tone, Ochs's first song lacks the caustic humor that is characteristic of some of his later topical songs. The first verse alludes to the doomed nature of the Bay of Pigs operation by comparing the chances of the thousand men who went to take the island to mere broken twigs. The second verse condemns the intelligence failure of the mission, noting the CIA's miscalculation of support for an overthrow within the Cuban population. Finally, the third verse questions the reasons for the US military involvement and funding of the invasion as well as the media portrayal of the conflict:

> Why were they wearing my country clothes?
> Why were they spending my country's gold?
> Who were the friends and who were the foes?
> The headlines were lying, why wasn't I told?

In addition to confirming the Soviets' accusations of Yankee imperialism, the botched Bay of Pigs invasion acted as a catalyst, launching the tensions between the United States and Cuba into the decidedly Cold War battle of the 1962 Cuban Missile Crisis. According to James Blight and Janet Lang's critical oral history analysis of the event, "the connection between the Bay of Pigs invasion and the crisis of October 1962 is fundamentally *psychological*," because Kennedy, Nikita Khrushchev, and Castro, the leaders of the three countries involved, subscribed to conflicting narratives and understandings of what had transpired at the Bay of Pigs. While Kennedy had sworn off any thought of a proper military invasion of Cuba after the intelligence failures surrounding the Bay of Pigs operation, Khrushchev was convinced that "the Bay of Pigs was simply stage one . . . of an all-out military effort . . . to attack and occupy the island," and he therefore acted to help protect the much smaller ally nation. Castro, meanwhile, firmly believed that the US failure at the Bay of Pigs made a massive military attack on Cuba inevitable and that Cuba stood no chance in such a fight.[16] For this reason, Castro understood that his country's only hope to ward off a US invasion was to involve the threat of Soviet nuclear power.

Among the worldwide public, the tense thirteen-day standoff between the United States and the Soviet Union over the ballistic missiles the Soviets had deployed to Cuba provoked very real fears of nuclear war, until Kennedy and Khrushchev came to an agreement and deescalated the conflict. The Soviets agreed to remove the missiles if the United States pledged not to invade Cuba and lifted the blockade preventing Soviet ships from reaching the island nation. In the wake of the crisis, Phil Ochs penned a fast-tempo and acerbic talking blues song entitled "Talkin' Cuban Crisis," relating from a first-person perspective the poetic voice's response to and attitude toward nuclear standoff. Ochs performed the song frequently in the years following the international crisis and included it in his first official album, *All the News That's Fit to Sing*.

The first verse of "Talkin' Cuban Crisis" describes hearing the news of the crisis on the radio, and the poetic voice alludes to a fear for his personal safety. In the second verse, he admits to a degree of uninformed ambivalence about the situation, but before the president addresses the nation, the radio announcer depicted in the song inserts a toothpaste commercial, cynically rhyming "cleaner breath" with "nuclear death." The sardonic inclusion of a commercial advertisement both during the critical news hour and within the song itself constitutes a critical commentary on the pervasive nature of capitalist culture. The song implies that even the threat of imminent nuclear war is a commercial opportunity not to be squandered.

The next verse turns to the president's address, and the poetic voice's depiction of it mockingly describes the Soviet missile bases as land reform taken to extremes, suggesting that the Cuban government expropriated property from the Cuban people only to hand it directly over to the Soviets for missile facilities. The agrarian reform in Cuba, in which the government expropriated large properties held by wealthy landowners to redistribute wealth among government cooperatives and peasant workers, was already a contentious ideological issue in the United States, and many of these former landowners had already left Cuba for the United States in protest. The hyperbolic implication that the very land taken by the Cuban government was now holding nuclear weapons aimed at the United States exemplifies both the very real and the very exaggerated tensions of the moment.

In the subsequent verses, the poetic voice again references the Cold War, describing Kennedy's blockade as a measure to hold back the "Russian bear" and to rally US forces stationed around the world "to teach the Russians a lesson / for trying to upset the balance of power." These lines constitute a clearly ironic reference to the perceived "missile gap," or the mistaken belief propagated by US intelligence officials that the United States lagged behind the Soviet Union in missile capabilities.

Near the end of the song, the poetic voice sarcastically sums up the view of many Republicans as wanting to "sink Cuba into the sea" to return the island to a democracy, albeit under water. In effect, the song accuses Republicans of desiring to save Cuba by destroying it. The final verse of the song references the Cold War by name, noting the heated intensity of the crisis within the context of a supposedly "cold" war.

The heavy use of irony throughout the song denotes a harsh criticism of the Kennedy administration's handling of the situation. While many Americans credited the president with having expertly maneuvered the country away from the possibility of nuclear war, the poetic voice of "Talkin' Cuban

Crisis" decidedly distances himself from those who supported Kennedy and his intelligence officials with respect to the Cuban Missile Crisis. While the song presents Kennedy escalating the crisis in an effort to appear strong, the final verse appears to credit Khrushchev with averting the nuclear showdown by backing down to the US demands.

Also included on the album *All the News That's Fit to Sing* is "Ballad of William Worthy," which tells the story of the title character, a real-life US journalist and activist who was convicted of illegally entering the United States after returning from a trip to Cuba to report on Castro's revolution in 1961.[17] Several years before those events, Worthy had defied US travel restrictions in order to report from Communist-led China, and US authorities had seized his passport upon his return. Although he filed a lawsuit against the US government to contest the government's actions, Worthy found himself unable to reobtain a valid passport. Despite his lack of legal travel documents, he jumped the travel ban yet again to go to Cuba without one when the opportunity arose to report on the revolution. Worthy's conviction for entering the United States illegally upon his return from Cuba was overturned in 1964.[18]

The chorus of Ochs's song, which is repeated several times, plays on Worthy's name to highlight the way in which the reporter's visits to Communist nations had stripped him of his rights as a US citizen. In effect, the poetic voice alleges that according to the US government, Worthy's travel to Cuba made him unworthy to return to his home country, rendering him no longer an American. The second half of the chorus exposes the duplicitous nature of the United States government's attitude in the matter by stating with mock perplexity, "But somehow it is strange to hear the State Department say / You are living in the free world, in the free world you must stay." The use here of "free world," the common Cold War propaganda term with which the Western Bloc nations referred to themselves, implies a hypocritical attitude on the part of the United States in prohibiting travel to and from countries that were not considered part of that world.

The second verse of "Ballad of William Worthy" sarcastically exposes the US double standard of prohibiting travel to Cuba because of its dictatorial rule while freely allowing travel to places such as Spain. Implicit but not mentioned in the song is the fact that Spain was at the time governed by the dictatorship of Francisco Franco. In the next verse, the poetic voice invites the listener to travel the world and wishes to be able to join in on the journey, but he laments that he might be subject to the same fate as Worthy. The implication here is that the voice's sympathetic stance toward the Cuban government is likely to result in his rights as a citizen being stripped away.

Although Ochs was never denied a passport or the right to reenter the United States after his trips abroad, by 1964, when *All the News That's Fit to Sing* was released, the FBI had already opened what would eventually become a robust file on the singer. Nevertheless, that year, the US government concluded that Ochs did not fit the criteria for placement on the security index, and in 1965 his FBI file was closed, though it would later be reopened.[19] Ochs, of course, had no direct knowledge of the extent or the limits of the intelligence scrutiny that he was receiving and merely suspected that the government was monitoring him because of his political views. Comments about being watched by the FBI made their way into his engagement with the audiences at his concerts as well as into his song lyrics, as is the case in the 1967 song "Miranda," which states, "The FBI is watching / They are tape recording every other word."

In the final verse of "Ballad of William Worthy," the poetic voice reverses his stance, suggesting that the listener avoid traveling to the "evil lands" on an ever-growing list of countries to be avoided. The list is lengthening at such a rate, according to the poetic voice, that it would be no surprise if soon all countries were forbidden. In such a case, the voice continues, the government would suggest visiting Disneyland instead.

The mention of Disney here works not merely as a local option for tourism to counter the foreign locations complicated by communism. Instead, Ochs is making an oblique reference to the Walt Disney Company's complicity with the US government in producing propaganda films during the 1940s. Although it is no longer financed by the government, during the Cold War Disney produced a series of films that asserted an ideological defense of the "American way of life."[20] Hence, the poetic voice's theory that the United States might one day forbid travel to all other countries and encourage listeners to visit Disneyland implies that those listeners would be traveling to the symbolic heart of US consumer capitalist propaganda.

In 1966, Ochs released *Phil Ochs in Concert,* a live album of recordings from recent performances in Boston and New York. In addition to some of his best-known ballads, such as "There but for Fortune" and "When I'm Gone," the LP includes the track "Cops of the World," which is an indictment of the United States' interventionist foreign policy. The poetic voice of the song takes on the persona of a chauvinist bully zealously going about the task of ravaging foreign lands. The final verse references the US pattern of involvement in regime change with the lines "We'll find you a leader that you can't elect / . . . / 'Cause we're the cops of the world, boys."

Directly following the general condemnation of US interventionism in "Cops of the World" is a track that delves into a specific example of US Cold War foreign policy in Latin America. "The Marines Have Landed on the Shores of Santo Domingo" is a descriptively titled song critical of the 1965 US military intervention in the Dominican Republic. It contrasts singing US Marines with fearful Dominican civilians. While President Lyndon Johnson's official reasoning for the military offensive offered at the time was to protect US citizens caught in the cross-fire of the Dominican Civil War, White House tapes and transcripts confirm that Johnson's true motivation was to forestall what he believed to be a Communist takeover aided by Cuba's Fidel Castro.[21]

Almost concurrently with his suicide in 1976, Ochs released an album of songs he had sung for *Broadside* magazine between 1965 and 1973, entitled *Phil Ochs Sings for Broadside*. In addition to his song about the US military intervention in the Dominican Republic, this album includes a track entitled "United Fruit," which criticizes the exploitative nature of the monopolistic US fruit corporation that operated in the Caribbean and Central America. In the song, Cuba is presented as the only nation hindering the United Fruit Company's efforts to profit off the labor of the local workers while working with the "hot-blooded leaders" of the military juntas to keep them oppressed.

Ochs had previously included a reference to United Fruit in the title song on his *I Ain't Marching Any More* (1965) album. While the rest of the song gives the poetic voice's weary account of having participated in major US military operations since the War of 1812, the final verse turns to the topic of Cuba. The lines "When they close the missile plants / United Fruit screams at the Cuban shore" reference the fruit company's involvement in the 1961 US Bay of Pigs invasion of Cuba and its reaction to the invasion's failure. When United

Fruit holdings in Cuba were expropriated by the government under Castro, the company offered up part of its fleet of ships to the CIA for the planned invasion at the Bay of Pigs.[22] After the botched invasion and the subsequent missile crisis referenced in the song, United Fruit found itself still barred from business in Cuba.

By the end of the 1960s, the triumph of the Cuban Revolution in defending its ideals against the behemoth of the United States had not gone unnoticed among left-leaning political groups in other parts of Latin America. In Chile in particular, Salvador Allende's Popular Unity party was strongly influenced by Castro's success in establishing a socialist government in Cuba. In 1970, Allende's election ushered in the first democratically elected socialist government in the world, despite heavy-handed CIA efforts to prevent the Leftist coalition from winning the election. After Allende's inauguration, covert operations on the part of the United States intensified under President Richard Nixon's instructions to the CIA to "make the [Chilean] economy scream" in order to create a climate in which a coup was likely to take place.[23]

Allende's presidency and his enactment of socialist policies in Chile also caught the interest of Phil Ochs. According to biographer Michael Schumacher, "To Phil, Allende was the most compelling political story since the Castro-led revolution in Cuba—not to mention the kind of peaceful revolution he had dreamed about for the United States." In August of 1971, Ochs traveled to Chile with friends Jerry Rubin and Stew Albert and managed to meet with a wide assortment of Chileans on both sides of the political aisle and from very varied backgrounds, but Ochs's most profound encounter was with Chilean singer-songwriter and activist, Victor Jara. As a cultural ambassador of the Allende administration, Jara had traveled widely throughout Latin America to sing the praises of Allende's government, but neither Ochs nor his friends had ever heard of Jara when they chanced upon him on the streets of Santiago. According to Stew Albert, who accompanied him on the trip to Chile, "Victor Jara was a role model for Phil. He *did* what Phil wanted to do." Ochs was mesmerized by Jara and by what he had helped to accomplish in Chile. The serendipitous encounter between the two artists led to several performances together and even a guided tour of a copper mine led by Jara, during which Ochs and his friends were able to see and speak to the miners at work.[24]

President Nixon's orders for the CIA to take action to help create a coup climate in Chile were successful, and on September 11, 1973, a military coup led by General Augusto Pinochet overthrew the Allende government. Salvador Allende died by his own hand that day as the military forces bombed and then stormed the presidential palace while thousands of his supporters were detained in makeshift prisons around the city. Among those detained in the immediate aftermath of the coup was Victor Jara, who spent several days with thousands of other political prisoners in a Santiago stadium before he was tortured both publicly and privately and ultimately shot to death.[25]

During the fall of 1973, Phil Ochs had been traveling in Africa and had not been aware of the news of either the toppling of the political movement he so admired or the death of his Chilean musician friend. Upon hearing of the death of Allende and Jara during the military coup, Ochs reacted at first with disbelief and anger. According to biographer Marc Eliot, "he took it personally, as if *he'd* been overthrown."[26]

Ochs immediately began channeling his anger into organizing and fundraising for a benefit concert at New York's Madison Square Garden in May 1974 to raise awareness of what had taken place in Chile. Despite Ochs's impassioned and frenetic efforts to drum up interest in the event, "potential concertgoers failed to share his enthusiasm for the project, and ticket sales moved at a crawl." In addition, the political nature of the event made promotion somewhat problematic, given the US government's stance toward Chile and the high-profile Chileans Ochs had managed to secure in the audience, including the daughters of both Victor Jara and Salvador Allende. According to Deni Frand, whom Ochs had hired to help organize and promote the concert, "There was a sense of vulnerability . . . because you knew you had the FBI around, or the CIA around." Instead of being deterred, Ochs reveled in the knowledge that his activities were attracting the interest of the same US intelligence agencies that were now being exposed as having helped to force the coup in Chile and to support General Pinochet.[27]

To attract a large audience, Ochs hoped to enlist Bob Dylan to perform at the concert, but the notoriously reclusive Dylan was reluctant to commit. In order to convince him, Ochs met with Dylan and "delivered an impassioned plea, capped by a shattering, verbatim reading of Allende's inaugural address."

Ochs and Dylan, just one year apart in age, were friends, but although Ochs admired Dylan's talent, he was also envious of his enormous success. Dylan ultimately agreed to perform just the day before the show, but by the time he took the stage, near the end of the event, he was audibly drunk, as were the majority of the other performers, including Ochs himself. The final four songs of the night featuring Dylan and an assortment of others "sounded like a tavern singalong at closing time."[28]

Earlier in the night, however, the event had taken on a more serious tone. Victor Jara's wife, Joan, gave a speech detailing the grisly scene in which she had walked past piles of corpses to identify her husband's body. Pete Seeger recited Victor Jara's final song, a poem written while he was imprisoned, which another detainee had managed to smuggle out. Finally, Woody Guthrie's son Arlo performed several songs, including a new one based on a poem written by British author Adrian Mitchell in honor of Jara. Two years later, Arlo Guthrie included his musicalized version of Mitchell's "Victor Jara" on his album *Amigo* (1976).

Guthrie and Mitchell's "Victor Jara" tells the life story of the folksinger, from his hardworking roots as a peasant child to his brutal death at the hands of Pinochet's military henchmen. The middle verses of the song describe Jara's efforts to sing for the people, to support copper miners and the factory workers' rights, and to lend his voice to Allende's political campaign. Each verse ends with the refrain "His hands were gentle, his hands were strong." According to music scholar Ian Peddie, the refrain's focus on the artist's hands references two of Jara's own songs ("Angelita Huenumán" and "Plegaria a un Labrador"), which "also had centered on the hands: those of a skilled rural artisan, and those of workers called to unite."

This image of gentle and strong hands used productively for art, work, and community building contrasts with the brutality of the final verse in the song, in which the stadium guards break Jara's hands as part of the torture they force him to endure prior to killing him. Peddie also points out that the structure of Mitchell's poem replicates the arch form of many of Jara's songs, in which "the first quatrain, together with its refrain, is repeated at the poem's conclusion."[29]

The detail given in the verse describing Jara's imprisonment, "caged in a stadium with five thousand other men," references the title and the first line of Jara's final poem, "Estadio Chile" (Chile Stadium), which begins "Somos cinco mil aquí" (We are five thousand here).³⁰ The penultimate verse presents Jara, undeterred by his imprisonment, continuing to sing for his fellow prisoners until he is tortured and killed by his captors.

Another folksinger-songwriter from the same generation as Phil Ochs and Bob Dylan to take up the topic of the US involvement in Chile's 1973 coup was Tom Paxton. Paxton, along with Dylan and Ochs, had formed part of the Greenwich Village folk music scene of the early to mid-1960s. In fact, according to fellow Greenwich Village musician Dave Van Ronk, "Dylan is usually cited as the founder of the new song movement, and he certainly became its most visible standard-bearer, but the person who started the whole thing was Tom Paxton."³¹ Known for his prolific production of songs, Paxton set himself a goal of writing a song a day, and during the first fifteen years of his career, beginning in 1962, he released approximately one album per year, excluding compilations. His live album *New Songs from the Briarpatch* (1977) includes, as its tenth track, a combination of two separate songs, "Mister Blue" and "White Bones of Allende," performed consecutively as one in the live concert.

"White Bones of Allende" features a poetic voice addressing Secretary of State Henry Kissinger, who had served both in that capacity and as national security advisor under Presidents Richard Nixon and Gerald Ford from 1969 to 1977. The three verses of the song begin with descriptions of the opulence, fame, and statesmanship surrounding the figure of Kissinger. In the first half of each verse, the poetic voice paints a picture of a Kissinger who lives in luxury, banters with reporters, dances with royalty, and travels on diplomatic missions around the world, but the following two lines of the verses depict his darker and more sinister side. This other side of Kissinger is a man who plays with innocent lives like pieces on a chessboard and is haunted by the ghosts and the bones of those killed because of his policies. The refrain, which follows each of the three verses and is sung with a heightened sense of urgency and emotion, states that the titular white bones of Allende and those of the other Chileans killed as a result of the coup and the dictatorship "are not silent, they are screaming, they're your peace prize, Doctor K."

The award mentioned in the refrain refers to the Nobel Peace Prize that Kissinger was conferred, along with Vietnam's Le Duc Tho, in December 1973 for helping to negotiate the Paris Peace Accords to end the war in Vietnam.

The Vietnamese leader rejected the award outright, and Kissinger donated the money to charity, did not attend the ceremony, and later attempted to return the medal.³² Nevertheless, for the poetic voice of Paxton's song, the timing of the peace award, coming on the heels of the violent military takeover in Chile—which had, in turn, been facilitated by the Nixon administration's machinations—made Kissinger's Nobel Prize for Peace terribly ironic. The sorrowful widows, unmarked graves, and scattered bones of the victims of the coup described in the song contrast with Kissinger's peace prize and the depiction of his opulent lifestyle.

One additional folk song to document the Chilean coup was recorded by Pete Seeger's half sister Peggy Seeger and her British husband, Ewan MacColl, on their 1977 Folkways Records album *Cold Snap*. "Allende's Song," written by Don Lange, a singer-songwriting truck driver from Iowa, presents a poetic voice who is driving a truck through the US heartland, thinking about the contrast between the peaceful life on the US roads and the violent coup that the United States had helped to finance in Chile. In the refrain that repeats four times throughout the song, Allende is described as "the good doctor," who is lying apparently dead, with blood pooled in his eyes, "and the bullets read U. S. of A." The line regarding the bullets, referencing the US economic aid to the supporters of the overthrow of Allende, is repeated twice in the refrain for heightened emphasis of this point.

The penultimate verse includes another reference to US financing with a line about Uncle Sam footing the bill for Allende's killing. The subsequent line notes that after Allende's death, "the truckers are rolling again." This mention of truckers refers to the Chilean truckers' strike in the weeks just prior to the 1973 coup, which had a catastrophic effect on the nation's economy. According to a *New York Times* article from August 1973, "Left-wing newspapers have accused the United States of financing the truckers' strike and the anti-Government campaign in the opposition news media in an attempt to carry out an 'economic coup d'état.'"³³

Another *New York Times* article, published in September 1974, shows that as little as a year after the Allende government was overthrown, the US funding support of events in Chile that would create a coup climate was becoming public knowledge. According to the *Times*, "At its peak, the 1973 [US-funded] strikes involved more than 250,000 truck drivers, shopkeepers and professionals who banded together in a middle-class movement that, many analysts have concluded, made a violent overthrow inevitable."[34] The successful takeover of the government by a regime with economic policies favorable to the United States, of course, put an end to clandestine US financing of strikes, and the truckers returned to business as usual.

The final lines of "Allende's Song" reference a pacifist and defiant poet who lies dead with nobody to mourn him. The poet in these lines could either be either Victor Jara or Pablo Neruda, the Chilean Nobel literature laureate who died, allegedly of cancer, less than two weeks after the military takeover. In 2017, though, medical experts called into question his cause of death, fueling rumors that he was murdered by the Pinochet regime.[35] Whether it is a reference to Jara, to Neruda, or to both, the defiance of the dead poet in "Allende's Song" contrasts in this final verse with people in the houses that the trucker sees as he drives down the road, who "do what they're told." In this way, the song serves as a criticism not just of the US government actions in helping to topple the Allende presidency but also of the complacency of the US public, which enjoys the bountiful and beautiful land, and the peaceful conditions described throughout the song, without pausing to consider the actions of their government abroad.

As with all of the songs examined here, the topical nature of "Allende's Song" meant that whatever popularity it might have had would be short-lived. Furthermore, the passion that the authors and performers poured into their art and artistry contrasts with the tepid public reception of these pieces about US involvement in Chilean and Cuban foreign affairs. Peggy Seeger has only ever enjoyed a fraction of the notoriety of her brother Pete. Tom Paxton's song about Allende is far from one of his most well known. Phil Ochs had to scramble and beg to sell out his benefit concert for Allende, and his songs about Cuba are far from the ones for which he is best remembered. In addition, Bob Dylan's drunken performance helped to make Ochs's Chile benefit concert not releasable as an album. Nevertheless, the fact that all of these artists took up musical arms in the cultural Cold War of the 1960s and 1970s by putting to music the topic of US actions in Cuba and Chile demonstrates that it was a matter of some concern to at least a select type of US audience at the time.

NOTES

1. Frances Stonor Saunders, *Who Paid the Piper? The CIA and the Cultural Cold War* (London: Gratna, 1999), 2.
2. Hugh Wilford, *The Mighty Wurlitzer: How the CIA Played America* (Cambridge, MA: Harvard University Press, 2008), 10.
3. Saunders, *Who Paid the Piper?*, 17.
4. David King Dunaway and Molly Beer, *Singing Out: An Oral History of America's Folk Music Revivals* (Oxford: Oxford University Press, 2010), 73.
5. Dahlia Lithwick, "When Pete Seeger Faced Down the House Un-American Activities Committee," *Slate*, January 28, 2014, http://www.slate.com/blogs/browbeat/2014/01/28/pete_seeger_huac_transcript_full_text_of_anti_communist_hearing_courtesy.html.
6. Alec Wilkinson, *The Protest Singer: An Intimate Portrait of Pete Seeger* (New York: Vintage, 2009), 4.
7. Thomas G. Paterson, *Contesting Castro: The United States and the Triumph of the Cuban Revolution* (Oxford: Oxford University Press, 1994), 16, 21.
8. Stephen Rabe, *The Killing Zone: The United States Wages Cold War in Latin America* (Oxford: Oxford University Press, 2012), 63.
9. Marc Eliot, *Death of a Rebel: A Biography of Phil Ochs* (New York: Carol Publishing Group, 1989), 23–24.
10. Bruce Pollock, *In Their Own Words* (New York: Macmillan Publishing, 1985), 26, 48.
11. Jim Rasenberger, *The Brilliant Disaster: JFK, Castro, and the USA's Doomed Invasion of Cuba's Bay of Pigs* (New York: Scribner, 2011), xiii–xiv.
12. Eliot, *Death of a Rebel*, 28.
13. Gregory McDonald, Souvenirs of a Blown World: Sketches from the Sixties Writings about America: 1966–1973 (New York: Seven Stories, 1985), 188.
14. Krutponken, "Phil Ochs—Ballad of the Cuban Invasion," YouTube video, 1:31, July 17, 2012, https://www.youtube.com/watch?v=yorR5VostsA.
15. Boot Leg, "Jim Glover—Ballad of the Cuban Invasion (Live at the Phil Ochs Memorial Concert, 1976)," YouTube video, 2:45, September 1, 2018, https://www.youtube.com/watch?v=g4nVNgvtQIc.
16. James G. Blight and Janet M. Lang, *The Armageddon Letters: Kennedy, Khrushchev, Castro in the Cuban Missile Crisis* (Lanham, MD: Rowman and Littlefield, 2012), 21, 25, 27.
17. Emily Langer, "William Worthy, Defiant Journalist, Dies at 92," *Washington Post*, May 12, 2014.
18. Margalit Fox, "William Worthy, a Reporter Drawn to Forbidden Datelines, Dies at 92," *New York Times*, May 17, 2014.
19. Eric Blair, *Folk Singer for the FBI: The Phil Ochs File* (Morrisville, NC: Lulu Press, 2009), 8–9.
20. Steven Watts, "Walt Disney: Art and Politics in the American Century," *Journal of American History* 82, no. 1 (1995): 105.

21. David Coleman, ed., "National Security Archive Electronic Briefing Book No. 513," *National Security Archive,* April 28, 2015, https://nsarchive2.gwu.edu/NSAEBB/NSAEBB513.

22. Peter Chapman, "Rotten Fruit," *Financial Times,* May 15, 2007.

23. Peter Kornbluh, *The Pinochet File: A Declassified Dossier on Atrocity and Accountability* (New York: New Press, 2003), 36.

24. Michael Schumacher, *There but for Fortune: The Life of Phil Ochs* (New York: Hyperion, 1996), 239–241.

25. Joan Jara, *An Unfinished Song: The Life of Victor Jara* (New York: Ticknor & Fields, 1984), 247–250.

26. Eliot, *Death of a Rebel,* 246.

27. Schumaker, *There but for Fortune,* 291, 294–295.

28. Ibid., 105, 293, 297.

29. Ian Peddie, *Popular Music and Human Rights: World Music* (Farnham: Ashgate, 2011), 115.

30. Graciela Jorge and Eleuterio Fernández Huidobro, *Chile Roto: Uruguayos el Día del Golpe de Chile* (Santiago: LOM Ediciones, 1983), 184.

31. Dave Van Ronk, *The Mayor of MacDougal Street: A Memoir* (Boston: Da Capo, 2005), 197.

32. Jessica Contrera, "Bob Dylan, Bill Murray and Henry Kissinger: When honorees don't want their prize," *Washington Post,* October 23, 2016.

33. Marvine Howe, "Chile Calls Truck Strike 'Catastrophic,'" *New York Times,* August 18, 1973, 1.

34. Seymour M. Hersch, "CIA Is Linked to Strikes in Chile That Beset Allende," *New York Times,* September 20, 1974, 1.

35. Pascale Bonnefoy, "Cancer Didn't Kill Pablo Neruda, Panel Finds. Was It Murder?," *New York Times,* October 21, 2017.

US AND THEM

The Eagle versus the Hammer and Sickle
in the Cold War Sporting Arena

KURT W. JEFFERSON

The devastation of the twentieth century's two world wars, combined with the awesome destructive power unleashed with the dawning of the atomic age, made conflict between the United States and its Cold War adversary the Soviet Union something that both sides sought to avoid. Consequently, the United States found many ways of conducting a "war by other means" to assert its ideological and material superiority over its Communist foes. Sport became one of the many arenas in which this struggle was played out.

This essay reviews the role of sports on the American home front during the Cold War. It highlights the importance of sport not only as a commercial endeavor but also as a sociocultural factor in American life that became a political tool in the fight against global communism. Certain sporting competitions and athletic events helped to change the American perspective on Russians and the associated nations of the Soviet Bloc and reinforced the bifurcation of the Cold War's ideological struggle between liberal capitalist democracy and communism.

SPORTS AS A POLITICAL TOOL

Sporting endeavor has been an integral part of American society since the early years of the republic. Sport embodies principles fundamental to the nation's identity, such as individual effort and reward and the democratic-capitalist notion of competition.¹ The historical linkage of sports to prowess and leadership qualities is best reflected by the fact that many US presidents were athletes and built much of their early development and growth around sporting activities and accomplishments. Indeed, many presidents continued to engage in sports after entering the White House.

Teddy Roosevelt was a rugged individualist who participated in multiple safaris and outdoor shooting and trophy-hunting activities prior to and after his presidency. His emphasis on the outdoor life set the stage for other presidents who championed the virtues of physical and outdoor activity. President Woodrow Wilson, although afflicted with poor eyesight and physical frailties, played football and baseball in college, golfed frequently as governor and president, and remained an avid fan of Princeton Tigers football. President Franklin Roosevelt was a cheerleader at Harvard. President Dwight Eisenhower was an accomplished football and baseball player in high school in Abilene, Kansas, and played early on in his time at West Point, until he was injured.² President John F. Kennedy was on the swim team at Harvard and later became an accomplished weekend golfer. President Richard Nixon played football at Whittier College and President Gerald Ford was a star lineman at Michigan. President Ronald Reagan was a four-year letter winner as a lineman on the Eureka College Red Devils football team in his home state of Illinois. He had been a lifeguard on the Rock River, near his hometown of Dixon, Illinois, and claimed to have saved seventy-seven swimmers from drowning during his high school and college years.³ President George H. W. Bush was a starting baseball player at Yale in the late 1940s, and both Bill Clinton and Barack Obama were golf addicts who played frequently during their tenures in the Oval Office. Obama also was a high school basketball star in Hawaii. President George W. Bush played baseball in prep school and played on Yale's rugby union team in college. President Donald J. Trump was on his high school's varsity soccer team and captained the varsity baseball team as a senior in 1964.

These presidents helped to solidify sporting achievement as a defining characteristic of red-blooded Americanism. It is no surprise, therefore, that sporting prowess became a key component of the image of themselves and their society that Americans wanted to project abroad. The Cold War was not, however, the first time that sport took on geopolitical ramifications.

The 1936 Berlin Olympics had already foreshadowed the potential of sport on a global scale to be an arena where ideological battles were fought. For most Americans, the 1936 games are remembered for the brilliance of one athlete: Jesse Owens. The African American star sprinter from Alabama was already a multiple world record holder in track and field, but his four golds at the Olympic Games remain an ongoing source of pride in American sporting lore. The dominance of a Black athlete in the crucible of anti-Semitism and fascism exposed the abhorrent racial politics that lay at heart of Hitler's Germany.

The Nazi Olympics set the stage for a familiar set of ideals, and after the Cold War began, Americans grew to not only appreciate these ideals but also to expect their athletes to reflect them. Those ideals involved individuals who stood up to a dictatorial state that restricted people's freedoms but also had the audacity to claim moral and political superiority over liberal Western democracies. It was a pitting of freedom against authoritarianism. Sport transcended being a mere pastime, leisure activity, or form of mass entertainment during the Cold War and gained enormous political significance. After 1952, rivalries between the East and West emerged in a range of Summer and Winter Olympics sports, including gymnastics, basketball, swimming, boxing, track and field, skiing, ice skating, and hockey. Russians engaged Americans in several important battles in multiple competitions, and in occasional noncompetitive one-time events. Each victory became an act of what Hans J. Morgenthau has called the "politics of diplomatic prestige" and Joseph S. Nye Jr. has called "soft power."[4]

The United States had the chance to flex its rhetorical muscles at the 1952 Helsinki Summer Olympic Games—the first time that the Soviet Union entered the competition. The Soviets had joined the International Olympic Committee in 1951. According to Erin Redihan, "The United States Olympic Association reminded its athletes before London [in 1948] that sportsmanship should come first. That sentiment vanished once the Soviet Union joined the IOC in 1951 and announced its intention to compete at Helsinki." The entry of the Soviets into international competition took the propaganda battle to new heights. The Russians told their citizens that the American military had taken over all aspects of Olympic sports and that the "militarization of the country" was at hand. Because America's main sports—football and baseball, for example—were limited in international scope, it was perhaps inevitable that the Olympics would attain such a high profile in Cold War sporting battles. Consequently, both countries' Olympians were pressed to work harder to defeat the other. As one notable piece of agitprop said at the time, and would be echoed for the next forty years, "Every victory in international contests, graphically demonstrates to the whole world the advantages and strength of the Soviet system."[5]

Bob Mathias, the 1948 and 1952 American champion in the Olympic decathlon—a discipline that claims to bestow the title of "world's greatest athlete"—said, "They [the Soviets] were in a sense the real enemy. You just loved to beat 'em. You just had to beat 'em. It wasn't like beating a friendly country like Australia." The Americans just barely prevailed in the medal count in the Helsinki games: seventy-six to the Soviets' seventy-one. Americans won forty gold medals to the Soviets twenty-two. The Soviets won thirty silver medals while the United States took home nineteen. Following these games, Redihan argues, "both came to view the Olympics as a highly visible yet low-stakes battleground in their cultural Cold War."

The Helsinki games had taken place in the waning months of the Truman administration. The Eisenhower administration then took a somewhat more confrontational approach to the Soviets than had its predecessors. Prior to Ike's election as president in November 1952, Republicans had blamed Franklin Roosevelt and his administration for "enslaving Eastern Europeans at Yalta and pilloried the Truman administration for 'losing' China to the Communists."[6] The threat of "massive retaliation" as a nuclear arms doctrine, outlined by Ike's secretary of state John Foster Dulles, upped the ante in terms of high-stakes foreign policy. The Eisenhower administration even considered using tactical nuclear weapons as potential military tools to aid both Chiang Kai-Shek's Nationalist China and the French in Vietnam.[7]

Thus, the stage was set for heightened concern over geopolitical rivalry and confrontation as well as for an ever-expanding economic and cultural battle. The Khrushchevian thaw of 1957 to 1964 failed to produce the harmony that the Americans or Soviets may have hoped for. Paradoxically, however, the intense sporting competition, which is by definition a zero-sum, winner-take-all endeavor, helped regenerate both sides and may have contributed to a kind of easing of relations during the 1960s and 1970s.

US policymakers' decision to prop up an unpopular regime in South Vietnam drew the nation deeper into the kind of war of colonial succession they previously had sought to avoid. The Vietnam conflict brought about several layers of political, economic, and social developments that spurred further need for the politics of sports not only to impact the American homeland in new and profound ways but also to broaden the "war by other means" motif to other Communist states, such as China. After Richard Nixon's February 1971 visit to China to meet Premier Zhou Enlai and China's state leader, Mao Zedong, China's continued growth and prestige on the cultural, economic, and social stage of global affairs began. The country was still developing slowly due to Mao's economically destabilizing and socially catastrophic Cultural Revolution (1966–1976), and it would be many years before the United States and China would square off in international competitions in a competitive manner that mirrored the Soviet and American sporting confrontations. In April 1971, however, the Chinese government invited the American table tennis team, which was competing at the world championships in Japan, to a friendly matchup in the People's Republic of China.

Mao issued an invitation to the Americans to come to China immediately after the competition ended in Japan. Mao had enthusiastically followed the PRC team's fortunes in the Japanese tournament. Appreciating the potential public relations benefit of an American team being welcomed on Chinese soil, he noted "the small ping-pong ball could be used to move the large ball of the earth." According to Margaret MacMillan, in *Nixon and Mao: The Week That Changed the World*, "The decision to initiate what became known as 'ping-pong' diplomacy had been made at the highest levels, indeed by Mao himself, after chance encounters brought Chinese and American table tennis players together. Chinese athletic teams, which had been condemned during the wildest days of the Cultural Revolution as 'sprouts of revisionism,' were only just starting to take part in international events again."[8]

The event was more diplomatic than sporting or political. It was a mere tool in the broader strategy of American and Chinese international relations under Nixon and Mao. The few days the American table tennis team spent in Beijing in early April 1971 were received well in both countries. The role of sports as a cultural unifier and tool of state diplomacy became an increasing expectation in both the West and the Communist Bloc.

The other cultural change in the West in the 1960s was attitudinal. The political balance in liberal democracies was changing. The Vietnam War had brought about cultural and political division in the United States and Western Europe. The civil rights movement, an ongoing struggle both on the ground and in the courts of law, as well as other civil liberties movements of the 1960s, necessitated an active response from the Kennedy and Johnson administrations. Following John F. Kennedy's assassination in November 1963, President Lyndon B. Johnson's escalation of the Vietnam War in 1966 and 1967 led to sustained and violent protests on college campuses around the nation.

The year 1968 also saw global challenges to existing power structures in Western nations. France saw the resignation of President Charles de Gaulle in early 1969, after he had served as that nation's first constitutional president since 1959, when protests over inadequate access to classes for students combined with workers' strikes focused on other labor-related issues. Thus, the Cold War battles fought in sporting arenas began to take on a new character. Not only were they a struggle of liberal capitalist democracy versus the totalitarian Soviet state, but also they now were seen as a struggle within a broader struggle—one tied to race and gender. While these domestic iterations of sporting struggle played out, the Olympic Games and other international competitions continued into arenas in which the East and West renewed their "war by other means."

In the area of men's basketball, the Americans had long been dominant. The game was invented in the United States in Springfield, Massachusetts, in 1891 by James Naismith, a Canadian by birth, who would go on to coach at the University of Kansas. The Americans won gold medals at the first seven Summer Olympic basketball competitions (1936–1968). They also won the gold at the first five Pan-American games, and ultimately eight of the first nine men's basketball competitions at the games (1951–1983). This American dominance was particularly impressive given that American players were amateurs and had not signed professional contracts, unlike some players in other countries.

This changed for the Americans in 1992 with the advent of professional basketball players playing in international men's basketball competitions. The one global competition in which the Americans had less men's basketball success was the FIBA World Championship (known today as the Basketball World Cup). Since 1950, the Americans had won the Fédération internationale de basket-ball's gold medal five times. Although the Soviets were more successful, winning silver and bronze medals in the tournament in the 1960s and 1970s, their erstwhile Communist Bloc ally Yugoslavia had bettered the Soviets by winning the competition five times (1970, 1978, 1990, 1998, and 2002), although the latter two golds were earned as a rump Yugoslav state after the socialist republic's splintering due to internal conflict and collapse.

Thus, by the 1970s and 1980s, the rise of both other Communist powers and other Western powers served as another layer of intrigue and complication with regard to the importance of sports in the Cold War period. Now the Americans and the Russians had to fend off not only each other but also ideological and geopolitical allies. Although men's basketball had taken root in the Soviet Bloc and Southern Europe, US allies in the Western Hemisphere, such as Brazil, had been steadily improving since the early 1960s, and even Brazil's old nemesis, Argentina, started to take off as an improving national team in basketball by 2000, after a fifty-year wait—it had won the first-ever FIBA cup in 1950. After the collapse of the USSR in 1991, the Spanish and French teams also became forces to reckon with in European basketball.

All of this was a challenge to American and Russian hegemony in the sporting realm. What's more, when the Soviet Union's teams ceased to exist, many of its basketball stars began playing for its near neighbors, especially Lithuania, and when the rump Yugoslavia ended in 2003, many of its great players now hailed from the newly independent state of Croatia.

The 1968 American men's basketball team at the Mexico City Summer Olympics will be remembered more for who did *not* play than for who did. Many of the more talented college stars, such as the seven-foot-one Lew Alcindor (soon to call himself Kareem Abdul-Jabbar), declined to play as an act of protest related to civil rights protests over the treatment of African Americans in the United States (part of Dr. Martin Luther King Jr.'s broader work of economic and political boycott prior to his assassination in April 1968). Spencer Haywood, a six-foot-eight center from a Colorado community college, started at center. The nineteen-year-old Haywood and twenty-one-year-old University of Kansas guard Jo Jo White would lead the Americans against the Soviets and the Yugoslavs. The Americans had beaten the Russians by fourteen points in the 1964 Olympics in Tokyo.

The Americans were coached by the sixty-four-year-old veteran NCAA- and

Olympics-winning head coach Henry "Hank" Iba. Mr. Iba, as he was called, was the antithesis of the spirit of the age. He was a grizzled, defense-minded coach who had a rigid system of basketball. He represented the "old school" that had started coaching at the collegiate level when jump balls were held after every basket and there was no centerline or ten-second rule in bringing the ball up the court. The game was quite different in 1929, when Iba started coaching at Northwest Missouri State Teacher's College, where his win/loss record was 93–15.[9]

In the qualifying round in Mexico City, the Americans soundly beat their opponents, including besting the eventual runners-up, Yugoslavia, by fifteen points. The long-anticipated matchup with the Soviets in the knockout rounds never materialized. The Americans dispatched Brazil 75–63, but Yugoslavia upset the Soviets 63–62 in the semifinals. The Americans earned their seventh straight gold medal in Olympic competition by beating the Yugoslavs 65–50. The Soviets won the bronze over the Brazilians. It would be the end of an incredible streak for the United States; four years later, controversy struck in Munich, West Germany.

MUNICH: THE END OF OLYMPIC INNOCENCE AND THE REALITY OF COLD WAR MAYHEM

The 1972 Summer Olympics were in many ways the end of an era in sports. The deaths of nine Israeli athletes and staff at the hands of the Palestinian Black September terrorist organization on the grounds of the Olympic village in Munich brought home the realization that sports were no longer the innocent domain of a world that was looking for escape and the putting aside of politics during international sporting competitions. The Olympics came to symbolize a new era of postcolonial conflict that came out of the Vietnam era, during which the Soviet Union and the United States would fight proxy wars in the name of democracy and communism. These conflicts were found in various corners of the world, from Panama in 1965 to Yemen in 1970 to Palestine and Israel after 1948, and a few years later, in Lebanon in 1975. The anger over 1 million displaced Palestinians, housed in squalid United Nations Relief and Works Agency camps in the areas surrounding Israel, had led, by the 1960s, to several Palestinian terrorist and liberation groups, such as Fatah, the military arm of Yasser Arafat's Palestinian Liberation Organization. Other groups, like Dr. George Habash's communist Popular Front for the Liberation of Palestine were more militant.[10] Sadly, a Cold War identity conflict bled over into the Olympics in Munich, and the actions of the militants maligned the Olympics and, more importantly, cost athletes their lives.

On September 5, 1972, less than a week before the competition was to end, the Black September terrorists made their way into the Munich Olympic Village and took as hostages eleven Israeli coaches and athletes and a West German policeman. The Israeli government attempted to work with the German government and local police, but an ill-fated rescue attempt by an insufficient number of German paramilitary forces ended in disaster. Having already killed two of their victims, Black September operatives murdered the nine remaining Israeli athletes as the terrorists tried to flee with the hostages. Thus, the 1972 Olympics would forever be remembered as a bleak event in which politics impacted sports in the most gruesome of ways.

On the sporting field, the most controversial moment came in the basketball gold medal game, when the United States, the seven-time defending Olympic champions, lost on several controversial calls at the game's end. Prior to this, the United States and the USSR were both 7–0. The Americans had decimated their competition, including the eventual bronze medal winners, Cuba. Having previously won sixty-three straight games in all Olympic basketball competitions, the United States was favored, but the Soviets took the Americans to the wire.

The controversies began in the final seconds, as the referees allowed a Soviet time-out and the horn sounded in the middle of a free throw by American guard Doug Collins, who nonetheless made the free throw and gave the Americans a one-point lead at 50–49. Then a failed attempt by the Soviets to get a shot off on the ensuing inbound ball led to what fans in the arena and the Americans thought was the end of the game. However, the secretary-general and cofounder of FIBA, Renato William Jones, ran onto the court to force the officials to award an additional three seconds to give the Soviets another chance. The Soviet bench made further frantic cries, claiming problems with the clock. This resulted in the Russians being awarded further replays of the inbounding of the ball. Eventually, on the third try at an inbound pass, the

Soviets scored, when their star, Alexander Belov, laid the ball in the net, after the referees had admonished the seven-foot American center (and later US congressman from Maryland), Tom McMillan, to play less aggressively against Belov. The United States refused the silver medal, and FIBA counted the game as a gold medal for the Soviets, although the officials missed a technical foul on the Soviets for calling a time-out during a free throw. The United States protested the game, but to no avail, as the International Olympic Committee claimed the game fell under FIBA control.[11]

By the time of the 1972 Olympics, the preponderance of amateurs in sport was increasingly challenged. Although it would not be until 1992 that an American team largely comprised professional players, the Soviets had players from CSKA Moscow, a reputable professional team, and the Russian players on the 1972 Olympic team had played a total 739 international contests, compared to only seven for the Americans.[12]

The commercial appeal of global sport took on greater importance with the growth of media corporations and the global public's obsession with sports. The 1976 Olympics saw the continued use of corporate endorsements, and stars like Bruce (now Caitlyn) Jenner, who won the decathlon for the Americans in Montreal in 1976, benefited from support that allowed athletes to train year-round in the run-up to major international sporting competitions.

The 1972 Olympics did have stars, including the Belarussian gymnast Olga Korbut of the USSR and the American swimmer from Modesto, California, Mark Spitz, who took home seven gold medals. That year also marked President Nixon's attempt at accomplishing détente with both the People's Republic of China and the Soviet Union. Despite the easing of tensions between the West and the Communist Bloc nations, however, the rivalry between the United States and the Soviet Union continued, and the 1972 Olympics (with the American support of Israel and the Soviet support of Palestinian Arabs, including providing arms for them) continued to be a source of tension in the Cold War.

INTERNATIONAL SPORTING FRIENDSHIP DURING THE COLD WAR: THE HARLEM GLOBETROTTERS AS CULTURAL ICONS AND DIPLOMATS

Despite the major Cold War sporting rivalries between the United States, Russia, and other Communist and socialist nations, the use of sports for diplomatic ends was also a tool for improved relations between Communist Bloc nations and the United States. One American sports team, the Harlem Globetrotters, became one of the few American teams to engage in overt diplomacy during the era.

The Globetrotters were founded by impresario Abe Saperstein in Chicago in the late 1920s. Like professional baseball teams, the Globetrotters were a barnstorming team that played both fun exhibitions and more serious professional tournament basketball. The Globetrotters won the 1940 World Professional Basketball Tournament. The tournament was played yearly in Chicago (from 1939 to 1948) and included several teams that went on to play in the coming National Basketball Association. In February 1948, the Globetrotters twice beat the eventual 1947/48 National Basketball League (predecessor to the NBA) champions, the Minneapolis Lakers, and their all-star center, George Mikan, 61–59. The Globetrotters repeated the feat against the Lakers one year later, winning 49–45 at the Chicago Stadium in front of more than twenty thousand spectators.[13]

Indeed, the Globetrotters were becoming one of professional basketball's top teams. However, in an era of racial segregation in the United States, the African American team faced repeated discrimination. It was not until the professional baseball teams of the late 1940s and early 1950s began integration that things started to change. The Brooklyn Dodgers signed Jackie Robinson in 1947 and the Cleveland Indians signed Larry Doby in 1947, and as a result, the era of segregation in professional sports in the United States began to come to an end.

The Globetrotters have represented the United States in scores of countries since the early 1950s. By 2013, the franchise had played nearly 25,000 basketball games since 1926, some four hundred contests a year. Most interesting was that while American sporting teams were in zero-sum, politically tinged competition with the Soviets and other Communist states, the Globetrotters represented an olive branch to the Communist world. For instance, the Globetrotters were the first American basketball team to play in the Soviet Union. After seeking to visit for eight years, they finally were given the OK by the Kremlin in July 1959. The owner of the St. Louis Browns, the mercurial Bill Veeck (who had put vines on the Wrigley Field walls in Chicago in the 1930s and would bring exploding scoreboards to baseball with the White Sox in the late 1950s), had contacted the Soviet embassy in 1952 in hopes of getting the Globetrotters visas to visit Moscow. The Trotters were allowed to tour Russia for six days that summer. They were not allowed to play any Soviet competition and had to bring their opposition, the "San Francisco Chinese," with them. Also traveling with them were ten individuals providing halftime acts. The Russians claimed that their universities were free and open to all races, unlike many American institutions of higher learning. Wilt Chamberlain, the future Hall of Fame center and the tallest Globetrotter, at seven foot one, said, "Did you ever hear of a slave owning thirty suits, twenty pairs of shoes, a Cadillac, and a ranch house?" The tour, although politically tinged, was successful, as 135,000 people saw the Trotters play in their nine contests. The final night was broadcast across the Soviet Union to 1.35 million people.[14]

The Globetrotters would go on to represent America in multiple countries during the Cold War, and they brought smiles to all who were entertained by them. By the end of the Cold War, the team was aging and largely a staged show, with some basketball talent but not the talent that was displayed in the 1940s and 1950s. Nonetheless, the Harlem Globetrotters represented an important legacy for international goodwill and sports diplomacy in the Cold War era (1945–1991). They not only helped to counter the "ugly American" stereotypes but also showed Russians, Cubans, and Eastern Europeans a side of American life that most in the Communist world never saw, namely high-quality basketball and entertainment, and the ethnic melting pot that is the United States. The Trotters actively sought goodwill and to bring friendship and peace via sport to a world that had gone to the brink in power politics by the early 1950s. Due to heightened political tensions over atomic weapons and other geopolitical fault lines, realpolitik in Washington and Moscow was difficult to reconcile with the other side's ideologies and goals. Thankfully, Saperstein's players, many from poor, rural backgrounds in the segregated American South, were able to do what few politicians could do: bring smiles to the faces of citizens in Communist nations.

MIRACLE ON ICE: THE END OF THE COLD WAR SPORTS RIVALRY BETWEEN THE UNITED STATES AND USSR

The election of former California governor Ronald Reagan as the fortieth president of the United States on November 6, 1980, ushered in a new conservative regime in Washington and new era of rivalry between the Russians and the

Americans. By the end of Jimmy Carter's presidency (1977–1981), the rivalry had become further strained. In light of the hostage crisis in Iran and despite signing a strategic arms agreement in 1979, the Americans boycotted the 1980 Summer Olympics in Moscow following the Soviet invasion of Afghanistan on December 24, 1979. The Russians would retaliate in 1984 by refusing to participate in the Los Angeles Summer Olympics. However, the decade started with what some Americans viewed as the most unlikely triumph in their sporting history: the Winter Olympics upset of the Russians in hockey at Lake Placid, New York on February 22, 1980. The Russian national hockey squad had won five of the previous six Olympics and were heavily favored.

The stunning victory by coach Herb Brooks's American team in 1980 was a true David versus Goliath battle, similar to the 1972 men's basketball gold medal game but with the script reversed. The Soviets had lost only one Olympic match since the 1960 games, where they won the third-place bronze medal. In a twenty-year period, they had outscored their opponents 175–44 in goals, and they had previously outscored the United States 28–7. The Russians had not lost in Olympic competition since 1968.

The heroics of the Americans, as seen in captain Mike Eruzione and goalie Jim Craig, both of whom had played at Boston University, served to get the Americans to the medal round. The team of amateur college players was, on paper, no match for the year-round military personnel employed as full-time hockey players by the Soviets. The Americans had already upset the Czechs, who were predicted to finish strong in the competition, and they had held their own in drawing co-division-leader Sweden. After upsetting the Soviets 4–3, the Americans beat Finland 4–2, which was enough to give them the gold medal with a one-point advantage over the Soviets. The "Miracle on Ice," now the stuff of legend in the post–Cold War United States, was voted in 1999 the greatest American sporting moment of the twentieth century by *Sports Illustrated*.[15]

THE AMERICAN-SOVIET COLD WAR SPORTS RIVALRY COMES TO AN END

The Americans and the Russians had a bitter rivalry in the sports arena throughout the duration of the Cold War. Contrary to the American perspective on the nature of this relationship, the Soviets came out on top in terms of Olympic competition, winning more medals in the aggregate from 1952 to 1988 (when the USSR competed at the Olympic Games as a nation-state). James Riordan notes:

> The USSR has gone on to dominate the Olympic Games, summer and winter, challenged only by the German Democratic Republic which gained more medals than the USA in the 1976 and 1988 summer Games, and more medals than the USA in 1980 and 1984 winter Olympics. The only interruption to communist victory was 1968, when the USSR took second place to Norway in winter and the USA in summer, and in the summer 1984 when major communist sporting nations did not compete.[16]

Americans frequently explain away Communist East Germany (a state from 1949 to 1990) and its success by noting the use of illegal performance enhancing drugs by East German athletes. However, the Americans were smitten with Katarina Witt, the famous East German figure skating gold medalist of the 1984 and 1988 Winter Olympics, and Witt eventually turned media star by acting in movies and on television. She remained in a unified Germany as a citizen of the post-1990 reunified state. The total Cold War Olympic medal count (from 1952 to 1988) was 1,009 medals for the Soviets and 774 medals for the Americans.[17]

While sporting victories may seem inconsequential compared to the wider geopolitical battles of the Cold War, they were enormously important to those who witnessed them. In those moments of triumph, sporting achievements became a reflection of the strength and vitality of an entire society. They truly became a war by other means. And while similarly intense international rivalries have yet to emerge in the post–Cold War world, at least for the United States, the inevitability of global competition and antagonism will likely result in a future iteration of something similar. And if, in some small way, these symbolic victories continue to provide a safe alternative to the horrors of actual war, then they are anything but inconsequential.

NOTES

1. Alan Brainer, John Kelly, and Jung Woo Lee, eds., *Routledge Handbook of Sport and Politics* (Milton Park: Routledge, 2020).

2. Evan Thomas, *Ike's Bluff: President Eisenhower's Secret Battle to Save the World* (New York: Back Bay, 2012), 32.

3. James Rosebush, *True Religion: What Made Ronald Reagan Great and Why It Matters* (New York: Center Street, 2016), 7.

4. Hans J. Morgenthau and Kenneth W. Thompson, *Politics among Nations: The Struggle for Power and Peace*, 7th ed. (New York: McGraw-Hill Education, 2005); Joseph S. Nye Jr., *Soft Power: The Means to Success in World Politics* (New York: Public Affairs, 2004).

5. Erin Redihan, "The 1952 Olympic Games, the US, and the USSR," *Process: A Blog for American History*, February 8, 2018, http://www.processhistory.org/redihan-1952-olympics.

6. Thomas, *Ike's Bluff*, 53.

7. Stephen E. Ambrose, *Eisenhower: Soldier and President* (New York: Simon and Schuster, 1990), 382–383.

8. Margaret McMillan, *Nixon and Mao* (New York: Random House, 2007), 176, 178.

9. Iba grew up on a farm in rural Missouri and graduated from Westminster College in Fulton, Missouri, in 1928, where he played football, basketball, and baseball. The campus's Henry P. Iba Court is named in his honor—it is the same gym that was home to Winston Churchill's Iron Curtain clarion call of the Cold War.

10. Kurt W. Jefferson, *Christianity's Impact on World Politics: Not by Might, Nor by Power* (New York: Peter Lang, 2002).

11. Neil Amdur, "The Three Seconds That Never Seem to Run Out," *New York Times*, July 28, 2012.

12. Ibid.

13. Ben Green, *Spinning the Globe: The Rise, Fall, and Return to Greatness of the Harlem Globetrotters* (New York: Amistad, 2006), 200–225.

14. Green, *Spinning the Globe*, 283–286.

15. John Healy, "Remembering the 1980 'Miracle on Ice' US Team: 5 Interesting Facts," Audacy (February 21, 2020), https://www.audacy.com/national/sports/gallery/the-1980-miracle-on-ice-u-s-team-5-interesting-facts.

16. James Riordan, *Sports, Politics, and Communism* (Manchester: Manchester University Press, 1991), 142.

17. "Olympic Analytics—All Results, Medals, Statistics, Analytics," http://olympanalyt.com/OlympAnalytics.php.

CONTRIBUTORS

RANDI BARNES-COX is associate professor of history at Stephen F. Austin State University, where she teaches courses on Russian history, popular culture, and comparative Cold War cultures. She holds a PhD in history from Indiana University and has published articles on consumption and consumerism in early Soviet culture. Her current research interests include American perceptions of the Soviet Union and civil defense activities in Texas during the Cold War.

MARK BOULTON is the Harry S. Truman Fellow and professor of history at Westminster College in Fulton, Missouri, where he serves as the department chair and as the director of the Museum Studies program. He is the author of *Failing Our Veterans: The GI Bill and the Vietnam Generation* (2014). He is also a member of the Royal Historical Society.

FRANCESCO BUSCEMI earned his PhD on television and food at Queen Margaret University, Edinburgh. He currently teaches media history and media writing at the Catholic University of Milan, after working at the Universities of Stirling, Bournemouth, Como, and Venice. Buscemi researches the ways in which the media and society have helped each other to innovate over the years. His most recent books are *From Body Fuel to Universal Poison: Cultural History of Meat, 1900–the Present* (2018), and *Pasta, Pizza and Propaganda: A Political History of Italian Food TV* (2022).

MARY ELIZABETH BASILE CHOPAS is a lawyer of the Massachusetts Bar and an adjunct law professor at Boston College. Chopas has been a lecturer on law at Harvard Law School. She earned her PhD in history from the University of North Carolina at Chapel Hill and her JD from Boston College Law School. Chopas is the author of *Searching for Subversives: The Story of Italian Internment in Wartime America* (2017), which analyzes the legal process of selective internment and its lasting effect on Italian communities.

ANN V. COLLINS is professor of political science at McKendree University in Lebanon, Illinois. She is the author of *All Hell Broke Loose: American Race Riots from the Progressive Era through World War II* (2012) and *The Dawn Broke Hot and Somber: US Race Riots of 1964* (2018). Her research centers on racial violence, political history, and American politics.

TOBIAS T. GIBSON is the Dr. John Langton Professor of Legal Studies and Political Science and the Security Studies program director at Westminster College, in Fulton, Missouri. He is the coeditor of *Contextualizing Security: A Reader* (2022). Gibson is also an adjunct with the Missouri State Defense and Strategic Studies graduate program.

KURT W. JEFFERSON is dean of graduate education and professor at Spalding University in Louisville, Kentucky. He is the coeditor of *Contextualizing Security: A Reader* (2022) and the author of *Celtic Politics: Politics in Scotland, Ireland, and Wales* (2011). His political analysis has appeared on BBC World Service (Arabic Service), the Voice of America, BBC Radio 4, Wisconsin Public Radio, and Jamaican Public Radio (Kingston).

ERIC T. KASPER is professor of political science at the University of Wisconsin–Eau Claire, where he also serves as the director of the Menard Center for Constitutional Studies. He has authored, coauthored, or coedited six books and authored or coauthored numerous academic journal articles, including several on the freedom of expression. His books include *The United States Constitution in Film: Part of Our National Culture* (2018; with Quentin D. Vieregge) and *Don't Stop Thinking About the Music: The Politics of Songs and Musicians in Presidential Campaigns* (2012; with Benjamin S. Schoening).

ANGELA F. KEATON is professor of history at Tusculum University in Greeneville, Tennessee. Her article "Backyard Desperadoes: American Attitudes concerning Toy Guns in the Cold War Era," earned the Carl Bode Award for best *Journal of American Culture* article in 2010. She also writes about pedagogy. Her article "Professionalism Isn't Just for the Workplace" was published in *The Teaching Professor* in 2017. She is currently at work on a monograph about post–World War II gun culture.

KURT EDWARD KEMPER is professor of history and director of the General Beadle Honors Program at Dakota State University. He is the author of *College Football and American Culture in the Cold War* (2009), *Before March Madness: The Wars for the Soul of College Basketball* (2020), and the textbook *American Sports History, 1607–Present* (2021).

ELAINE TYLER MAY is Regents Professor Emerita of American Studies and History at the University of Minnesota. She is a past president of both the Organization of American Historians and the American Studies Association. Her books include *Homeward Bound: American Families in the Cold War Era* (1988), *Pushing the Limits: American Women, 1940–1961* (1994), *Barren in the Promised Land: Childless Americans and the Pursuit of Happiness* (1997), and *Fortress America: How We Embraced Fear and Abandoned Democracy* (2017).

KRISTEN POPHAM graduated from the College of William & Mary in 2020 with a BA in government and French and francophone studies. She completed a Fulbright scholarship to France from 2021 to 2022. She is currently a JD candidate and Hamilton Fellow at Columbia University School of Law.

CHARITY RAKESTRAW leads the development of the social sciences and humanities curriculum at Western Governors University. She earned her PhD in history from the University of Alabama and is the author of *Ministers and Masters: Methodism, Manhood, and Honor in the Old South* (2014). Her current research interest is popular religious culture in the United States with an emphasis on the history of megachurches.

EUNICE ROJAS is the Herman N. Hipp Professor of Modern Languages and Literatures at Furman University, where she also serves as chair of the Interdisciplinary Minor in Latin American and Latinx Studies. She is the coeditor of *Sounds of Resistance: The Role of Music in Multicultural Activism* (2013) and the author of *Spaces of Madness: Insane Asylums in Argentine Narrative* (2014) and *Gringos Get Rich: Anti-Americanism in Chilean Music* (2023).

TONY SHAW is professor of contemporary history at the University of Hertfordshire. He has authored numerous books on film history, including *Hollywood's Cold War* (2007), *Cinematic Cold War: The American and Soviet Struggle for Hearts and Minds* (2010; with Denise J. Youngblood), *Cinematic Terror: A Global History of Terrorism on Film* (2014), and *Hollywood and Israel: A History* (2022; with Giora Goodman).

MATT SPRENGELER is an academic adviser and adjunct professor at Des Moines Area Community College. His research interests include board and card games, American comic strips, the early years of television, and other pop culture topics.

SIMON STOW is the John Marshall Professor of Government and American Studies at the College of William & Mary. A political theorist, he works at the intersection of theory, American politics, literature, and culture, paying particular attention to issues of race. He is the author of *American Mourning: Tragedy, Democracy, Resilience* (2017) and *Republic of Readers? The Literary Turn in Political Thought and Analysis* (2007), and coeditor of *A Political Companion to John Steinbeck* (2014).

PETER J. VEROVŠEK is assistant professor in the history and theory of European integration at the University of Groningen and the author of *Memory and the Future of Europe: Rupture and Integration in the Wake of Total War* (2020). He is currently working on a biography of Jürgen Habermas as a public intellectual.

LINDA WEISS is a Fellow of the Academy of the Social Sciences, professor emeritus in government and international relations at the University of Sydney, and honorary professor of political science at Aarhus University. Her research focuses on state capacity and public–private sector relations, with an emphasis on high technology and national security. Her most recent book, *America Inc? Innovation and Enterprise in the National Security State* (2014), is available in Chinese and Korean translations.

INDEX

ABA. *See* American Bar Association (ABA)
Abdul-Jabbar, Kareem, 310
Abrams, Nathan, 204
Academy Awards, 230
Acheson, Dean, 136
ACLU. *See* American Civil Liberties Union (ACLU)
Advanced Research Projects Agency. *See* Defense Advanced Research Projects Agency (DARPA)
advertising, 126–127; abundance of, 203; and alcohol and tobacco, 126; and color, 204–205; and food, 202; and guns, 147; weaponization of, 204
Afghanistan, invasion by Soviet Union, 7, 316
Aid, Matthew, 203
Ailing Industrial Base, The (report), 94, 95
Air Force, US: expansion of bases, 11–12; in film, 230
Alcindor, Lew. *See* Abdul-Jabbar, Kareem
Allende, Salvador, 241, 286; influenced by Castro, 296; overthrown, 297; in protest songs, 299, 300
Althern, Gary, 171
American Bar Association (ABA), 64, 66, 68–69; Assembly and House of Delegates, 68–69, 70, 71; Canons of Ethics, 65; Special Committee on Communist Tactics, Strategy and Objectives, 73
American Cancer Society, 83
American Civil Liberties Union (ACLU), 64

American Committee for the Protection of Foreign Born, 67
American Communications Association v. Douds (1950), 50, 52
American exceptionalism, 8; football and, 166, 169, 175, 178; religion as, 187
American Legion, 110; influence on Hollywood, 228–229, 233
American male, 127–128; and domesticity, 151; football as training, 168–169; and guns, 150–151; and hunting, 146; and postwar affluence, 163–164, 170; and sports, 305–306
American Meat Institute, 207
American Medical Association, 165–166, 208, 210
Americanism, 125–126, 164–165; and athletic prowess, 305–306; and Bobby Fischer, 273–274; and the frontier, 221; and idealism, 226, 233; of *Reader's Digest*, 249–250
Anders, Władysław, 112
Andersen, George R., 66–67
Anderson, Robert, 155–156
Anti-Bolshevik Bloc of Nations, 114
anticommunism, 23–24, 26; attorney loyalty oaths, 64–68; and Billy Graham, 183–184; Christian, 183–184, 187–189, 194–195, 220; CIA, 287; and ethnic lobbies, 101, 103; and film, 225, 226–247; and football, 166–170, 174–175; and hunting, 148; and immigration fears, 99; and individual film artists, 229; and magazines, 203; and migrants, 102; and

325

anticommunism (*continued*)
 modernism, 203; and oaths, 50, 62–63; and prosperity gospel, 194–195; public opinion and free speech, 48, 53; of *Reader's Digest*, 249–250; Supreme Court decisions and, 45, 50, 51, 53; Taft-Hartley Act, 62; and television, 203
antiwar movement, 26
apartheid, 131
apocalypse, as rhetoric of television evangelists, 185, 189–193, 197, 221, 312
Apocalypse Now, 239
Arendt, Hannah, 100
Armageddon, 191, 193, 197
Army Health Services Command, 83
Army Medical Research and Development Command, 92
Arness, James, 52
ARPA. *See* Defense Advanced Research Projects Agency (DARPA)
association, freedom of, 54
Atomic Energy Commission, 82, 83
Auerbach, Jerold, 64, 65, 68
Avon ladies, 204

Babcock, Havilah, 149, 156–157
Bakker, Jim, 193, 196, 197
Bakker, Tammy Faye, 196
Baldwin, James, 255
Baltimore Afro-American, 134
Barenblatt, Lloyd, 52
Barenblatt v. United States (1959), 52, 53
Barnhisel, Greg, 203
basketball, 309–311, 312–313; and diplomacy, 313–315; professionals in the Olympics, 313
Batchelor, Bob, 203
Batista, Fulgencio, 288
Baudrillard, Jean, 204–205, 213, 214
Bayh-Dole Act, 91
Baylon, Daniel, 253
Bay of Pigs, 53, 139, 289; catalyst for Cuban Missile Crisis, 291; United Fruit Company and, 295–296; US imperialism and, 290
Beatty, Warren, 240

Bedford Incident, The, 237
Bella, Ben, 140
Bellah, Robert, 187
Belletto, Steven, 275–276, 283
Belmonte García, Juan, 153
Bennett, Charles, 187–188
Berlin Airlift, 6, 230
Berlin Blockade, 6, 81, 106
Berlin Olympics (1936), 306
Berlin Wall, 7, 53; fall of, 9, 56
Bernard, Jessie, 267–268, 270
Bernhard, Nancy, 203
Bernstein, Barton, 82
Big Jim McLain, 52
Big Lift, The, 230
Biological and Toxin Weapons Convention, 90–91
Biological Warfare Committee, 82–83
biological weapons, 90–91
biotechnology, 90–92
Birmingham, Alabama, attacks on Blacks, 140–141, 142–143; global response to, 141, 143
Black, Hugo, 51, 53
Black militant, 30
Black Panthers, 29
Black Power, 26, 29
Black September, 311–312
Blackboard Jungle, 164
Blaik, Red, 169
board games, 267; Armchair General, 282; Battleship, 282; chess, 269, 271–276; Clue, 276–280; family, 278, 279; and game theory, 270–271, 277; Monopoly, 269, 276; Mr. Ree, 280, 283; Risk, 281–282; Scrabble, 268–271, 279; Uranium Rush, 148, 276, 283
Bolshevik Revolution, 225, 240
Boone, Pat, 193
Borges, Jorge Louis, 205
Boston Bar Association, 71–72
Boston Marathon bombings, 115
Bowler, Kate, 194
Bowles, Chester, 140
Bradbury, Malcolm, 253–254
Brandenburg v. Ohio (1969), 55, 57

INDEX 327

Brazil, 310, 311
Brennan, William, 54, 56
Brewer, Roy, 228
Brokaw, Tom, 254
Bronson, Charles, 31
Brooks, Harvey, 89
Brown, Harold, 94
Brown v. Board of Education (1954), 136–137, 251
Bryant, Paul "Bear," 166
Brzezinski, Zbigniew, 116
Buckley, William F., 174
Bureau of Justice Statistics, 31
Bureau of the Budget, 81
Burnett, Leo, 207–210
Bush, George H. W., 9, 305; and Willie Horton ad, 32
Butts, Alfred, 268

Campbell, David, 249
capitalism, 20, 38, 126, 291–292; Christian, 183; combined with religion, 193–196; and consumption, 126, 194–196; and consumption and physical fitness, 164, 170; Disneyland as heart of US capitalism, 294; impact on society, 163; as patriotism, 226; and prosperity gospel, 194–195; and Robert Schuller, 195
Carafano, James, 115
Carhart, Arthur Hawthorne, 146, 148, 149
Carlyle, John, 155
Carruthers, Susan L., 113
Carter, Jimmy, 8, 316
Carter administration, 93
Castro, Fidel, 286, 288, 290; alliance with Soviet Union, 289, 291; influence on Allende, 296; impact on Ochs, 289
Catholic Hour, The, 183
CBN. *See* Christian Broadcasting Network (CBN)
Central High School (Little Rock), 137–138
Central Intelligence Agency (CIA), 6, 80–81, 89, 106; acquiescence to foreign interests, 103; and Bay of Pigs, 289, 290, 295–296; depicted in film, 230, 238, 239, 240; domestic activities, 287; interference in Chile, 296, 297;

involvement in Central and South America, 8; and Ochs, 297; and soft power, 219–220, 235, 297
Chafee, Zechariah, Jr., 64, 76n30
Chamberlain, Wilt, 315
Charles, Nickie, 204
Chemical Warfare Service, 82–83
Chemical-Biological Coordination Center, 83
Chiang Kai-Shek, 307
Chicago Defender, 133, 134
children: targeted advertising, 203–204; used in advertising, 212–213
Childress, Alice, 261
Chile, 296; CIA involvement in, 8, 240, 286, 297; in protest folk music, 297, 299–300, 301
China, 151; and détente, 8, 313; in film, 238, 239; lack of free expression, 58; and table tennis, 308; and Truman, 81, 307
China Syndrome, The, 239
Christian anticommunism: and movies, 220, 234; revivalism of, 184–185, 188, 189–190, 194–195; and television, 183, 194–196
Christian Broadcasting Network (CBN), 182, 183, 196, 197
Churchill, Winston: "Iron Curtain" speech, 5, 48, 125; criticism of, 134
CIA. *See* Central Intelligence Agency (CIA)
civil rights movement, 26, 29, 53, 132, 309, 310; backlash against, 30–31, 168; and *Reader's Digest*, 250–251
Civil War, 44
Clark, Tom, 49
clear and present danger (test), 46, 51
Clinton, Bill, 129, 305
Cohen, Lizabeth: *A Consumers' Republic*, 126
Cohen v. California (1971), 55, 57
Cohn, Harry, 229
Cold War: advertising, 202–215; and American ambivalence, 235; and apocalypse, 185, 189–193; and athletic prowess, 163; and celebrity chefs, 204; and chess, 271–276; and Christian ministries, 194–196; and communication, 202–204; and culture, 184, 185–187, 195, 219, 264, 269, 280, 283; and cynicism, 238–239;

Cold War (*continued*)
  and domesticity, 20, 26, 146, 151, 152, 277, 280; and food, 148, 202, 204; and food advertising, 205; and football, 175–176; and games, 148, 267–283; as Holy War, 188–189; ideology, 219, 220, 304–311; and magazines, 148; and movies, 220–223, 226–247; and music, 286–301; Ochs critiques, 290–292, 293; and Olympic Games, 222–223; and nuclear arms race, 189–193, 220, 282; and race, 32, 131–143, 248, 263–264; and sports, 304–313; and television, 148, 194–196, 221
colonization, 131; racism and, 132–133
color: as propaganda tool, 204–205, 234; symbolism, 208–209
Coming Home, 239
Committee on the International Geophysical Year, 175
communism: atheistic nature, 188–189; created by Satan, 183; depiction of domestic fears of, 1, 14, 20, 23, 24, 26, 45, 46, 128, 162, 171; fears of global, 2, 6, 7, 8, 15, 106, 107, 111, 113; and film industry, 13, 52, 230–232; and Supreme Court cases, 46, 52–55; and US government, 16, 24
Communist Party, 50, 52, 54, 288; campus membership, 162; depiction in film, 231–232; lawyers' membership in, 62, 64, 66–67, 68–69, 70
Conant, James B., 176
Conference of Independent African Heads of State and Government, 141
Conference on International Organization, 133
Congress, US: and desegregation, 139; and European immigration, 107, 110–111, 116; lobbying of, 100, 103, 104, 113, 115, 116; and race and segregation, 135–136, 142; and religion and policy, 187–188; Subcommittee on Juvenile Delinquency, 164
Congress for Cultural Freedom, 203, 219, 297
Congress of Racial Equality, 139
Congressional Budget Office, 95
Congressional Prayer Room, 188
Connery, Sean, 243

containment, 6, 14, 163, 286. *See also* Truman, Harry S.; Truman Doctrine
Cooper, John Sherman, 169
CORE, 139
Cosmopolitan, 165
Coughlin, Charles Father, 183
Counter Intelligence Corps, 109
counterculture, 26, 125–126, 221–222; music of, 287
Cox v. Louisiana (1965), 54
Craig, Jim, 316
crime, 22; firearms as protection from, 23, 37; and General Telephone and Electronics, 25; Hollywood, fears and, 31, 37; and home security, 25; juveniles committing, 33, 34, 164
crime rates, 28–31, 33
Crouch, Paul, 196
Cuba, 286–296; Bay of Pigs, 53, 139, 289; revolution, 289, 296; travel to, 293; US business interests in, 289, 295–296; US invasion of, 290, 291
Cuban Missile Crisis, 8, 53, 140, 291
culture: American, 176, 268–269; and color, 204; games, 267; football, 166–171, 174; symbols, 204; of toughness, 164–166, 170
Cuordileone, K. A., 278

"Daisy Girl" ad, 27
Darby, John Nelson, 185; and the Rapture, 191–192
DARPA. *See* Defense Advanced Research Projects Agency (DARPA)
Daughters of the American Revolution, 229
Davis, Bette, 233
de Gaulle, Charles, 309
death penalty, 30
Death Wish, 31–32, 33
decolonization, 7, 133
Deer Hunter, The, 239
Defense Advanced Research Projects Agency (DARPA), 87, 88–89; Offset Strategy, 94; university research, 92
Defense Industrial Base Panel, 94
Defense Procurement Authorization Act, 92

INDEX

Defense Reorganization Act, 88
Defense Science Board, 203
DeMille, Cecil B., 229, 234, 241
democracy: and faith, 186–187; guns culture, 150; and race, 135; and security, 19–21, 38, 220
Dennis v. United States (1951), 50–51, 52, 53, 56, 67
Department of Agriculture, US, 82
Department of Defense, US, 80–81, 83, 86, 88–89; deputy director of research and engineering, 87; and Hollywood, 230; and university research, 92
Department of Energy, US, 82, 83–84
Department of Health, Education, and Welfare, US, 91
Department of Justice, US, 102, 136; Civil Rights Division, 140
Department of State, US, 107, 109, 113, 136, 251; and Hollywood, 230, 234–235; and McCarthy claims, 2, 14, 52, 64, 172; reservations about recruiting escapees, 113
desegregation: and Birmingham, 140; and *Brown*, 136–137, 139; and Congress, 142; at University of Mississippi, 139
détente, 55, 102, 143, 243, 313; end of, 93, 94
Dick, Philip K., 283
Diem, Ngo Dinh, 187
DiIulio, John, 34
director of defense research and engineering, 88, 94
Disney, Walt, 229, 234
Disneyland, 196, 294
Displaced Persons Act, 107, 108–109
Displaced Persons Commission, 109, 110
Doby, Larry, 314
Dole, Bob, 33
domino theory, 26
Douglas, William, 50, 56, 58
Dr. Strangelove or: How I Learned to Stop Worrying and Love the Bomb, 237, 283
Dr. Zhivago, 219–220
Draper Laboratory, 93
drugs: fears of, 33

Du Bois, W. E. B, 132, 133
"duck and cover," 12, 148
Dudziak, Mary, 251
Dukakis, Michael, 32
Dulles, Allen W., 112
Dulles, John Foster, 106, 113, 137–138, 307; use of religion, 186–187
Dylan, Bob, 297–298, 299, 301

East Germany, 113, 317
Eastern bloc, 99–101, 102; agents of, 110; defectors, 105
Eastwood, Clint, 223, 241, 242
Easy Rider, 127
Eisenhower, Dwight D., 81, 88, 153, 241; American story, 219, 252; antihomosexuality, 129, 173–174; and Central High School (Little Rock), 137–138, 140, 251; and football, 166–67, 169, 305; immigration policy, 111, 112; and military-industrial complex, 86; religion and policy, 187–188; rollback of communism, 106; and Soviet repatriation, 105
Eisenhower administration: immigration policy, 105–106; nuclear policy, 189; and Olympics, 307; and religion, 186–187
Elfbrandt v. Russell (1966), 54
Empire Strikes Back, The, 242
Encounter (magazine), 203
Equal Credit Opportunity Act, 128
Equal Rights Amendment, 129
Eruzione, Mike, 316
escapees, 108, 111–112, 113
Espionage Act, 46
Eternity (magazine), 195
ethnic lobbies, 100–101; anticommunism of, 101
Ex parte Garland, 69, 76n35
executive orders, 13, 129, 136, 173–174
expression, freedom of, 56, 57

Fail Safe, 237
Fairchild Semiconductor, 95
Falwell, Jerry, 190, 191; and Reagan, 193; shift in theology, 192–193
Faubus, Orval, 137, 251

INDEX

FBI. *See* Federal Bureau of Investigation (FBI)
Federal Bureau of Investigation (FBI), 26, 63, 66–67; and counterculture, 288, 294; and Hollywood, 229, 230; and immigration, 109; and Ochs, 294, 297
Federal Civil Defense Administration, 13; backlash against, 30–31; feminist movement, 29
Federal Republic of Germany. *See* West Germany
Federally Funded Research and Development Centers, 84
FIBA, 309, 312, 323
Field & Stream, 147, 148, 149, 151–152, 154
Fifth Amendment, 72–74; protections against self-incrimination, 69, 73
Finney, Charles Grandison, 184–185
First Amendment, 44–45, 69; flag burning, 45, 56
Fischer, Bobby, 271, 273–274
Fonda, Jane, 239
food: and emotion, 205; Jewish, 204; meat, 204, 207–210, 214; in shelters, 13, 148, 189, 197
football: attacks on, 170–172; Ivy League, 169, 171–175; and national security, 170–172; presidential advocacy of, 166–169; as prevention of communism, 163, 167, 169, 170, 174–175; in Space Age, 175–176; and toughness, 166–172, 174
Ford, Gerald, 299, 305
Ford, John, 229
Fort Detrick, 91
Foster, Robert, 277–278
Fountain, Lawrence, 200n44
Fourteenth Amendment, 53, 54, 69
Franco, Francisco, 293–294
Frankfurter, Felix, 49, 50, 51
Frankl, Razelle, 185
Frederick National Laboratory for Cancer Research, 91
Free French Forces, 111–112
Freedman, Monroe, 256
Freedom Rides, 139
Freedoms Foundation, 23
Freund, Paul A., 72

Friedan, Betty, 128
Friedberg, Aaron L., 80, 88

Gable, Clark, 153
game theory, 267–271, 275–276; application in games, 268, 270–271; featured in *Popular Science Monthly*, 269; featured in *Scientific American*, 270; satirized, 283
Gardner, George K., 71
gated communities, 35–36
gender roles, 128–129, 150–151, 204
GI Bills, 15–16
Gibson v. Florida Legislative Investigation Committee (1963), 53–54
Gladstein, Andersen, and Leonard (law firm), 66
Gladstein, Richard, 66–67
Gladwell, Malcolm, 256
Glazer, Nathan, 100
Glover, Jim, 289, 290
Go Set a Watchman, 248, 257, 264
Goetz, Bernhard, 31
Goldberg, Arthur, 53
Goldwater, Barry, 171; presidential campaign of, 26–27
Good Morning, Vietnam, 242
Gorbachev, Mikhail, 9, 242; in film, 243
Gordon, Elizabeth, 24
Graham, Billy, 165; "Communism's Public Enemy Number One," 183–184; nuclear attack message, 192
Great Society, 38
Greece, 134
Greenwich Village, 299
Griffin, Tracy E., 73
Griswold, Erwin N., 72–74
gun control, 157–158, 160n34
gun culture, 148, 150, 158; and democracy, 150; and language, 153–155
guns, 149–150, 152; feminization of, 154–155; relationships with, 154–157, 161n45, 161n47
Gurganus, Allan, 254
Guthrie, Arlo, 298
Guthrie, Woody, 289, 298

INDEX

Hagie, C. E., 150
Hague v. Committee for Industrial Organization (1939), 47
Haley, Bill, 164
Halvorsen, Gail, 203
Hamilton, Andrew, 162–163
Harding, Susan Friend, 192–193
Harlem Globetrotters, 313–315
Harley-Davidson, 127
Harris, Reed, 172
Hart, David, 80
Hayek, Friedrich, 249
Hays, William E., 70–71
Haywood, Spencer, 310
HBO, 196
Healy v. James (1972), 55
Heartbreak Ridge, 242
Heidenry, John, 249
Hellman, Lillian, 65
Hells Angels, 127
Henry VIII, 65
Heritage USA, 196
Herzog, Jonathan, 188
Highland Superstores, 127
Hiss, Alger, 125
Hitler, Adolf, 259–260
Hobson, Julius, 30, 139
hockey, 316
Hoey, Clyde R., 129
Hoffman, David, 86
Hollywood: and anticommunism, 226–232, 235–247; and communism, 226, 232–235; and international markets, 234–235; nascent film industry, 225–226; and Office of War Information, 226; outside influence on, 228–229, 232; stoking fears of crime, 31
Hollywood Ten, 13, 63, 227–228
Holmes, Oliver Wendell, 46
homeowners' associations, 35
homophobia, 173
homosexuality, 129; and communism, 171, 172
Hoover, J. Edgar, 229, 288
Hopkins, Ernest, 165
Horton, Willie, 32

Hour of Power, 195
House Armed Services Committee, 94
House Beautiful (magazine), 24–25
House Un-American Activities Committee (HUAC), 13, 52, 62, 64, 65, 66, 125, 227–228, 229, 232, 288, 289
Howe, Mark DeWolfe, 72
Howland, Joseph, 24–25
HUAC. *See* House Un-American Activities Committee (HUAC)
Humbard, Rex, 195, 200n46
Hummer H2, 37
Humphrey, Hubert, 28, 164
Humvee, 37
Hungary, 106
Hunt for Red October, The, 243
hunting, American culture of, 148–149; and African Americans, 159n11; and books and magazines, 147–149; and consumerism, 147; and masculinity, 146, 151–152, 161n44, 161n47; and patriotism, 149, 152; to prevent the spread of communism, 148, 153; and soldiers, 147; and women, 159n11
Hunting North American Deer, 146
Huttunen, Martti, 204
hyperreality, 205

Iba, Henry "Hank," 311
Immigration and Naturalization Service, 109
incarceration rates, 34
Internal Security Act (1950). *See* McCarran Act
International Longshoreman's and Warehouseman's Union, 66
International Refugee Organization, 105, 109
Interstate Highway System, 12
Invasion USA (1952), 230
Invasion USA (1985), 241
Iran, 7, 316
Iron Curtain, 101, 106, 107, 113, 124n94, 137, 220, 232, 235, 242; and Churchill, 5, 48, 125, 134, 318
Iron Curtain, The (film), 227
Israel, 190, 191; athletes, 311–312
Israel lobby, 102, 115

Isserman, Abraham, 67–68
Ivy League: football, 171–175

Jackson, C. D., 106, 112
Jackson, Robert H., 47, 56, 57; Nuremberg trials, 48, 50
Jacobs, Seth, 187
James, Henry, 252
James Bond films, 220, 243
Janus v. AFSCME (2018), 57
Japan: innovation and, 93
Jara, Joan, 298
Jara, Victor, 296–297, 298–299, 301
Jenner, Bruce (Caitlyn), 313
Jewitt, Carey, 206
Jim Bakker Show, The, 197
Johnson, B. K., 31
Johnson, Lyndon (B.), 8, 26–27, 177, 309; "Daisy Girl" ad, 27; and Kennedy civil rights legacy, 143
Johnston, Eric, 228, 233
Joint Chiefs of Staff, 81, 88; Bay of Pigs, 289; in film, 235
Jones, Renato William, 312
judicial restraint, 49, 51
juvenile delinquency, 33, 34, 164; board games as counter to, 279–280; sports as counter to, 165

Kaplan, Joseph, 175, 177–178
Kasenkina, Oksana, 106
Katzenbach, Edward L., Jr., 273
Kellogg's Sugar Frosted Flakes, 210–211
Kendi, Ibram X., 256
Kennan, George F., 101; "Long Telegram," 5
Kennedy, John F.: advocating fallout shelters, 12; assassination of, 15, 143, 309; assassination of and gun control, 157; as athlete, 305; and Bay of Pigs, 289, 291; and Birmingham, 140, 142–143; and Congress, 142; and Cuban Missile Crisis, 291, 292, 293; and deterrence, 189; and football, 167–168, 177; and freedom rides, 139; inaugural address, 166; and James Meredith, 139–140, 168; and Khrushchev, 139, 291; and Little Rock, 140; race relations and foreign policy, 138, 140, 141, 168; and space race, 168–169
Kennedy, Randall, 256–257
Kennedy, Robert, 169
Kerr, Marion, 204
Kersten, Charles J., 112
Khrushchev, Nikita: and Cuban Missile Crisis, 291, 293; and Kennedy, 139, 291; and Kitchen Debate, 20, 126, 128, 194; "Secret Speech," 232; and thaw, 307
Killian, James, 87
King, Martin Luther, Jr., 15, 140, 141, 310; and March on Washington, 142
King Football, 172
Kings Row, 242
Kissinger, Henry, 102, 299–300
Kohl, Marguerite, 278
Korbut, Olga, 313
Korean War, 80, 184; and interrogation, 164
Koslowski, Rey, 115
Kovacs v. Cooper (1949), 49
Kremlin Letter, The, 238
Ku Klux Klan, 55
Kubrick, Stanley, 237, 283

Ladies Home Journal, 25, 165
Lahr, Angela, 190
Laird, Melvin, 78
Lange, Don, 300
LaRoche, Chester, 171, 177
Late Great Planet Earth, The, 190–191; and Reagan, 193
Lattimore, Owen J., 64
Lavender Scare, 129
law and order, 26; heightened sentencing, 30; in presidential campaigns, 27–28
Law of the Soviet State, The, 52
Lawson, Marjorie McKenzie, 135
Le Duc Tho, 299–300
Lears, Jackson, 268
Lee, Harper, 248, 254, 264
Legion of Decency, 228
Lenin, Vladimir, 4

INDEX

Leonard, Frank, 263
Leonard, Norman, 66–67
Life (magazine), 147, 148
Life Is Worth Living, 183, 184
Lincoln Laboratory, 84, 85
Lindsey, Hal, 190–191, 193
List of Subversive Organizations, 62
Lodge, Henry Cabot, 138
Loeb, Philip, 228
"Long Telegram" (George F. Kennan), 5
Los Angeles Examiner, 162
Los Angeles Times, 21
loyalty oaths, 54, 62, 174–175; attorney oaths, 17, 64–68, 70, 125; and Fifth Amendment, 69, 72–74; states requiring, 70; workplace, 62–63
Lucas, George, 220
Lucas, Louis F., 149–150
Lumumba, Patrice, 7
Luraschi, Luigi, 229

MacColl, Ewan, 300
MacMillan, Margaret, 308
Malcolm X, 131, 141, 143
Man from U.N.C.L.E., The, 149
Manchurian Candidate, The, 237
Manhattan Project, 83–84, 86, 89
Mao Zedong, 6, 238, 308; Cultural Revolution, 308
March on Washington, 142
Marines, US, 12
Marlboro Man, 127
Marshall, Burke, 140
Marshall, George Preston, 172
Marshall Plan, 6, 126
Marx, Groucho, 210–211, 213
Marx, Karl, 4
Marxism, 71, 227
masculinity, 146, 165; and domesticity, 151; and guns, 150–154; and football, 166; history of, 159–160n22; postwar affluence and, 163–164, 165; and sentimentality and guns, 154–155, 160n34
Massachusetts Bar Association, 71–72, 73
material consumption, 165–166

Mathias, Bob, 307
May, Elaine Tyler, 272, 280
Mayer, Louis B., 226
Mays, Benjamin, 135
McBride, James, 256
McCarey, Leo, 229
McCarran Act, 14, 173–174
McCarthy, Joseph, 52, 64, 73, 232; and football, 172–173; homophobia, 173; and red scare, 14; West Virginia speech of, 2, 14
McCarthyism, 25, 26, 65, 125, 238, 289; critiques of, 223, 233; of *Reader's Digest*, 250
McDougall, Walter, 87
McGovern, George, 28
McNair, Brian, 202–203
McNamara, Robert, 8
McPhail, Thomas, 203
McPherson, Aimee Semple, 185, 194
McWhorter, Diane, 255
Medhurst, Martin, 203
Meredith, James, 139, 168
military-industrial complex, 86, 89
Miller, Alison, 255–256
Milling, Chapman J., 154
Mindszenty, József, 232
minivans, 36
Minneapolis Lakers, 314
Minton, Sherman, 49
"Miracle on Ice," 316
Missing in Action, 241–242
MIT, 84, 85–86
Mitchell, Adrian, 298
Mobutu, Joseph-Désiré, 8
Monroe, Marilyn, 234
Moody, Dwight, 185
Morehead, Albert, 271
Mosinee, Wisconsin: Communist takeover of, 1–3
Moskin, J. Robert, 151
Motion Picture Alliance for the Preservation of American Ideals, 228
movies, 220–221, 225–247; based on literature, 221–222, 239, 240; Cold War phases, 226–227
Moynihan, Daniel Patrick, 100

Mrozek, Donald, 164–165
multimodal analysis, 206
Munich Olympics, 311–313
Munn, Clarence, 169
Murphy, Frank, 47, 49
Murray, Susan, 204
muscle cars, 127
Mutual Security Agency, 106–107, 112
mutually assured destruction, 7, 189, 220
Myrdal, Gunnar, 132, 250

NAACP, 53, 251; and international racial equality, 132, 135, 137
Naismith, James, 309
NASA. See National Aeronautics and Space Administration (NASA)
Nasser, Gamal Abdel, 7
National Aeronautics and Space Administration (NASA), 82, 87, 88; Apollo program, 89; Crystal Cathedral, 195
National Association for the Advancement of Colored People. See NAACP
National Basketball Association, 314
National Cancer Institute, 83, 91
National Defense Appropriation Act, 85
National Defense Education Act of 1958, 16
National Football Foundation, 170–171, 176
National Guard, 137, 139, 140, 251
National Highway Traffic Safety Administration, 36
National Institute for Allergy and Infectious Diseases, 91
National Institutes of Health, 82, 83, 87, 88, 91–92
National Lawyers Guild, 66
National Prayer Breakfast, 188
National Rifle Association (NRA), 147, 149–150
National Science Foundation, 82, 88, 92, 97n24
National Security Act of 1947, 6, 11, 80–81
National Security Agency, 81
National Security Council, 81, 193
National Security Council Memorandum 68. See NSC-68
NATO, 6, 112

Nazi Germany, 4–5; and Berlin Olympics, 306; and intelligence networks, 116; records of, 110; refugees from, 105
Nazis: immigration to US, 110–111; safe haven for, 102
NBC, 210–211, 214
Neruda, Pablo, 301
Never Let Me Go, 230
New York City Bar Association, 69
New York Times v. Sullivan (1964), 54, 58
Newell, David, 147
Newsweek, 23, 32
9/11, 197, 203; antidemocratic response, 19; and fears of migrants, 99, 115
Nixon, Richard, 90, 143, 299; accusing Hiss, 125; as athlete, 305; and Chile, 296, 297, 300; and China, 8, 308, 313; and Kitchen Debate, 20, 126, 128, 193–194, 200n44; and law and order in presidential campaigns, 27–28; race relations and foreign policy, 138
Nixon administration: biological warfare program, 83, 93; and Chile, 300
Norfolk and Western Railway: and public anxiety, 23
North Atlantic Treaty Organization (NATO), 6, 112
North Korea, 6
Northwest Missouri State Teacher's College, 311
NRA. See National Rifle Association (NRA)
NSC-68, 6, 11, 81, 87
nuclear fallout shelters, 12–13, 148, 189; and *Life* magazine, 13, 21
nuclear family, 21; demise, 277–278; and games, 280; guns compared to marriage, 154–155; and television, 221
nuclear war, 148; anxiety about, 26–27, 291–292; as apocalypse, 185, 189–193, 221; and capitalism, 291–292; Cuban Missile Crisis, 291; in film, 233, 240–241; and God's plan, 190–192; prophecy, 190–191
nuclear weapons, 6–7, 21, 278, 282, 292; arms race, 21, 163, 189–193, 272; as deterrence, 237; and Dr. Suess, 222; in film, 237; missile gap, 235, 292; mutually assured destruction, 7, 189, 220; nuclear triad, 7

INDEX 335

Obama, Barack, 305
Obote, Milton, 141
Ochs, Phil, 288–289, 299, 301; and Allende, 297; "The Ballad of the Cuban Invasion," 290; "Ballad of William Worthy," 293–294; benefit concert, 297; and capitalism and nuclear war, 291–292; Castro's impact on, 289; and Chile, 296; "Cops of the World," 295; and Dylan, 297–298; "The Marines Have Landed on the Shores of Santo Domingo," 295; "Talkin' Cuban Crisis," 291–293; "United Fruit," 295; and Victor Jara, 296–297; views on US imperialism, 290
O'Connor, Jack, 149, 153, 154–156
Office of Scientific Research and Development Committee on Medical Research, 82
Office of the Director of National Intelligence, 83
Office of War Information, 226
Officer and a Gentleman, An, 241
Offset Strategy, 94, 95
Ohio State *Lantern*, 288, 289
oil crisis, 93
Olympic Games, 222–223, 306–307, 316–317; boycotts, 316; medal count, 316–317; in Munich, 311–313
On the Beach, 233
One Man's Wilderness, 149
Organization for Ukrainian Nationalists, 114
Organization of African Unity, 131, 141
Orwell, George, 48, 235
Outdoor Life, 148, 153
Owens, Jesse, 306

Page, Warren, 148
Palestinian Liberation Organization, 312
parenting, 165–166
Parenting (magazine), 148
Paterson, John, 279
Patterson v. Colorado (1907), 45–46
Paxton, Tom, 299, 301
Peddie, Ian, 298
People's Songs, 288
Perry, William, 94

Perspectives USA (magazine), 203
Petit, Michael, 34
Phil Donahue (show), 196
physical fitness, 163–166; Kraus-Weber tests, 164; national security concern, 164, 168
Pierce, Charles, 168
Pinochet, Augusto, 297, 298, 301
Pipes, Richard, 116
Pittsburgh Courier, 134, 135, 137
Plato, 56
Playboy, 161n47
Pledge of Allegiance, 47, 187
Polak, J. J., 270
Pollitt, Daniel H., 65–66, 68
Pollock, Bruce, 289
popular culture, 203; board games, 268–283, 219–224; comic books, 222; Congress for Cultural Freedom, 203, 219; protest songs, 223, 286–301; video games, 223
Popular Front for the Liberation of Palestine, 312
Popular Science Monthly, 269
Post Office, US, 187
Praise the Lord (show), 196
Pratt, Anthony, 277
Pratt, Elva, 277
President's Committee on Civil Rights, 135
prisons, 34
privacy, and anticommunism, 24–25
Production Code Administration, 228, 233
propaganda, 104–105, 106, 111, 137; and color, 204–205; Congress for Cultural Freedom, 203; food as means of, 205; "free world" as, 293; and modernism, 203; and movies, 220, 222–227; as strategic communication, 202, 213
prophecy, 190, 191, 193
protests, 26, 27, 57; against US intervention in Chile, 286, 296–301; against US intervention in Cuba, 286–296; civil rights, 53, 54, 139; music of, 290, 291–292; Tiananmen Square, 56; Vietnam War, 53, 127
Psychological Strategy Board, 230
PTL, 196

Public Health Service, 82
Puffin biscuits, 212–213
Puhalla, Dennis, 204
Putin, Vladimir, 197

"quantum sleeper," 25

race relations, 131–132, 248; in *Mockingbird*, 256–257; and *Reader's Digest*, 250–251
racism: as depicted in *Mockingbird*, 253–257, 260; as foreign relations issue, 131–132, 135, 136–139, 140–141, 251–252; of Nazi Germany, 306; versus democracy at home, 250
Radio Free Europe, 107
Rambo: First Blood Part II, 242
Rand, Ayn, 228
Ranlett, Charles A., 147
Reader's Digest, 248; anticommunism of, 249–250; condensed books, 249, 252–253, 257–260; impact, 249, 251–252, 263–264; racism of, 250–251; values, 252–253, 257–260
Reagan, Ronald: anticommunism of, 8–9, 16–17, 220, 240–241, 242; as athlete, 305; and General Electric, 16; and Gorbachev, 9; House Un-American Activities Committee testimony, 13; and nuclear war, 193; presidential election of, 30–31, 103, 240; rivalry with Soviet Union, 315–316
Reagan era: violent films, 31
Red Dawn, 241
Red Heat, 242
Red Menace, The, 232
Red Scare, 45, 46, 58, 125; in films, 52, 63; and lawyers, 63, 73
Redihan, Erin, 306, 307
Reeves, Richard, 140
Refugee Act, 116
refugees, 105, 107–108
religion, 165; and apocalypse, 189–193; Christianity and (anti-)communism, 183, 186–187; Christianity and patriotism, 187–189, 234; and political rhetoric, 186–187; and radio and television, 183
Reserve Officers' Training Corps (ROTC), 16

Right Stuff, The, 241
rights revolution, 19
Riordan, James, 317
Roberts, Oral, 191
Robertson, Pat, 182, 184, 191, 197; and the Bakkers, 196
Robinson, Jackie, 314
Rolling Stones, 127–128
Roman Holiday, 235
Roosevelt, Franklin, 39, 85, 249, 305, 307
Roosevelt, Theodore ("Teddy"), 305
Rose Bowl, 169–170
Rosenberg, Julius and Ethel, 6, 125, 204, 231
Ruark, Robert, 152–153
Rusk, Dean, 138–139, 141; and Senate Commerce Committee, 142
Russian studies, 16
Russians Are Coming, the Russians Are Coming, The, 237–238
Rutledge, Archibald, 149, 154, 159n15
Rutledge, Wiley, 48, 49

Sabu, 231
Sacher, Harry, 67–68
Saney, Isaac, 256
Saperstein, Abe, 314–315
Sartre, Jean Paul, 203
Saturday Evening Post, 152, 162
Saturday Review, 269, 279
Saunders, Frances Stonor, 203, 287
Schenck, Charles, 46
Schenck, Joseph, 226
Schenck v. United States (1919), 46
Schlafly, Phyllis, 128–129
Schlesinger, Arthur, 151
Schreiner, Samuel, 253
Schuller, Robert, 195
Schumacher, Michael, 296
Schwartz, Emanuel, 282
Schwarzenegger, Arnold, 37, 220–221
Schweinler, Francis F., 3
Schwoch, James, 203
Scientific American, 270
Secret Service, US, 238–239

INDEX   337

security: Americans and firearms, 21, 31, 39; and democracy, 19–21, 29, 38–39; and gated communities, 35; as self-defense, 20–21, 33
Sedition Act of 1798, 44
seditious libel, 45
Seeger, Peggy, 300, 301
Seeger, Pete, 288, 289, 298, 300, 301
segregation, 131, 132; antidemocratic, 135; and Globetrotters, 314
Senate, US, 14, 107, 169; Commerce Committee, 142; Foreign Relations Committee, 113
Seven Days in May, 237
700 Club, The, 182, 197
sexual revolution, 26
Shain, Yossi, 102
Sharp, Joanne, 249–250, 251
Sheen, Fulton, 183, 184
Shelley v. Kraemer (1948), 136
Sherry, Michael, 20, 62
Small Business Investment Corporation, 87
Smith, Tony, 102
Smith, Walter Bendell, 108
Smith Act, 50, 52, 66, 67, 71
social semiotics, 206
South Vietnam, 15, 53, 187, 307
Soviet Union: alliance with Cuba, 289, 291; and atomic bomb, 81, 83, 84, 125; and basketball, 310–311, 312–313; Birmingham response, 140–141; and chess, 271–276; collapse, 307; and détente, 55, 313; fear of Reagan, 193; film in, 235, 238; Globetrotters visit, 314–315; and "Grand Alliance" of World War II, 5; and hockey, 316; ideological competition with the US, 3–9, 106, 151, 163, 185, 193–196, 219, 272–273, 279, 287, 304–311; immigration from, 104, 272; invasion of Afghanistan, 94; and Israel, 190, 191, 193; and nuclear weapons, 189–193, 272, 291; and Olympics, 306–307, 310–313, 316–317; and postwar repatriation, 105; and poverty, 203; propaganda war with US, 104; proxy wars, 311–312; and Robert Schuller, 195; and space race, 8, 87–89, 212, 213; and spies, 99, 108–109; and sports, 306–311; support of Palestinian Arabs, 313; and technological advancement, 93–94, 95, 222; and US imperialism, 290
Sow, Malick, 139
Space Age, 175–176; food, 212–213
speech, 44, 66, 69; as preferred freedom, 48, 51; prior restraints of, 44; and viewpoint discrimination, 50
Spence, Brent, 200n44
spiritual-industrial complex, 194–195
Spitz, Mark, 313
sports: and diplomacy, 308, 313–315; and leadership traits, 305; and race and gender, 309
Sports Afield, 148
Sports Illustrated, 273, 274, 316
Sputnik, 8, 16, 80, 212, 222; Sputnik effect, 86–89
SRI International, 93
Stalin, Joseph, 4; death of, 113; speech to Soviet Party Congress, 5
Stallone, Sylvester, 220–221, 241
Stanford Research Institute, 93
Stanford University, 85–86
State Department. *See* Department of State, US
Stern, Bill, 171
Stevenson–Wydler Technology Innovation Act, 91
Stewart, James, 229
Stimson, Henry L., 82–83
Stone, Harlan Fiske, 46, 48–49
Stonewall riots, 129
Storm Center, 233
Stromberg v. California (1931), 46
Student Nonviolent Coordinating Committee, 139
Students for a Democratic Society, 55
Subcommittee on Juvenile Delinquency, 164
Subversive Activities Act of 1949, 70, 76n41
Sullivan, L. B., 54
Sunday, Billy, 185, 194
superpredators, 34
Supreme Court, US: anticommunist decisions, 45, 50, 51, 53; and First Amendment, 44–45; and protection of rights, 15; and public opinion, 54–55, 57–58; and Second Amendment, 38

survival biscuits, 148
Sutton, Matthew Avery, 185
Sutton-Smith, Brian, 282, 283
SUVs, 36–37
Swaggart, Jimmy, 191
Sydney Morning Herald, 137
Syse, Karen, 204

table tennis, 308
Taft-Hartley Act, 62
Tarrow, Sidney, 104
Terminiello v. Chicago (1949), 49, 50
terrorism, 115, 116, 311–312
Texas Instruments, 95
Texas v. Johnson (1989), 56, 57
"This Is Life" (advertising campaign), 207–210
Thomas, J. Parnell, 227
Thomas v. Collins (1945), 47, 49
Thompson, Hunter S., 127
Thompson, J. Walter, 204
Thompson, Wade, 171
Thornhill v. Alabama (1940), 47, 49
Three Days of the Condor, 239
Tiananmen Square, 45, 56
Time (magazine), 22; crime fears and, 29–30
To Kill a Mockingbird, 248; Black readers' views, 256–257; condensed version, 257–260; conservatism of Atticus, 254–255, 256, 259–260, 261; and eugenics, 259–260; miscegenation in, 262; New South ideology, 259–260; racism and interpretation of, 253–257, 261; and slavery, 261–262; and white privilege, 263
Tony the Tiger, 210–211, 214
Top Gun, 241
totalitarianism, 24, 55, 100, 221, 255
Touré, Sékou, 140
Treaty of Yalta, 105
Trinity Broadcasting Network, 196
Truman, Harry S., 5, 81, 106; and Conference on International Organization, 134; and "containment," 6; Executive Order 9835, 13; Executive Order 9980, 136; Executive Order 9981, 136; and importance of faith, 186, 187; "losing" China, 307; and President's Committee on Civil Rights, 135–136; relations with the Vatican, 187; veto of McCarran Act, 15
Truman administration, 80–81; and fall of China, 81; immigration policy, 105–106, 111; and Olympics, 307
Truman Doctrine, 134, 227, 286
Trump, Donald J., 305
Turkey, 134
Turner Broadcasting System, 196

U-2 (spy plane), 53
UCLA: communists on campus, 162
United Fruit Company, 295–296
United Nations, 112–113; charter and racial equality, 138; failure to support racial equality, 135; Work and Relief Agency camps, 311–312
United Nations Relief and Rehabilitation Administration, 105
United States: and basketball, 309–311, 312–313; business interest in Cuba, 289; and chess, 271–276; and Chile, 300–301; and China, 308; and color TV, 204–205; and Cuba, 290–296; and education, 15–16, 163; "Grand Alliance" of World War II, 5; and hockey, 316; ideological competition with the Soviet Union, 3–9, 106, 134, 137–139, 163, 185, 193–196, 203, 219, 272–273, 279, 287, 304–311; immigration policy, 104, 106–111, 115; involvement in Latin America, 286–301; involvement in Russian civil war, 4; and nuclear weapons, 272; and Olympics, 306–307, 310–313, 316–317; propaganda war with Soviet Union, 104; and proxy wars, 311–312; and soft power, 219; and space race, 8, 87–89, 168–169, 212; and specialization, 175–176; sports, 304–313; support of Israel, 313; travel policy, 293; Truman Doctrine, 134
universities: anti-Soviet, 116; dropping football, 170–171; as part of NSS, 85–86, 92; and protests, 90, 309; "un-American," 174–175
University of Chicago, 171
University of Mississippi, 139
United States Information Agency (USIA), 139, 140–141, 235, 240

United States Supreme Court. *See* Supreme Court, US
United States v. Carolene Products (1938), 46
United States v. Robel (1967), 54
urban riots, 26
US News and World Report, 32; heightened crime fears and, 29; versus socialist government, 23
USIA. See United States Information Agency (USIA)
USSR. *See* Soviet Union

Van Leeuwen, Theo, 206, 210
Van Ronk, Dave, 299
Veeck, Bill, 314
Vietnam War, 26, 86, 92, 93, 184, 235, 308, 311; and international sports, 308; and Paris Peace Accords, 299; protests against, 53, 90, 127; pushback against in film, 221, 229, 239; pushback against in song, 223, 286; and racial politics, 143
viewpoint discrimination, 50
vigilante justice, 30–31, 38
Vinson, Fred, 49, 50, 51
Vishinsky, Andrey, 52
Voice of America, 220
Volkersz, Evert, 252–253
Volkov, Leon, 272
Volunteer Freedom Corps, 101–102, 111–114, 115
Vonnegut, Kurt, 283

Walk East on Beacon, 230
Wallace, DeWitt, 249–252, 254–255, 257
Wallace, George: law and order of, 27, 28
Wallace, Lila Bell, 249
Walsh, William C., 76n34
war on drugs, 33, 34
War Powers Act, 85
Ward v. Rock Against Racism (1989), 56
WarGames, 240–241

Warsaw Pact, 6
Washington Post, 22
Watergate, 22, 236; impact in Hollywood, 239
Watson v. Memphis (1963), 54
Watterson, John, 172
Wayne, John, 52, 220, 229, 241
Weissmuller, Johnny, 231
welfare program, 33
Wendy's, 127
West Germany, 113
West Virginia v. Barnette (1943), 47, 56, 57
Westminster College: and Churchill speech, 48; hosts Churchill and Truman, 5
White, Jo Jo, 310
White, Walter, 132, 251
Whitfield, Stephen J., 283
Wick, Charles Z., 240
Wiebes, Cees, 203
Wigger, John, 197
Wilford, Hugh, 287
Wilkins, Roy, 135
Wilson, Woodrow, 305
Winchester (gun company), 152
Winthrop, John, 194
Witt, Katarina, 317
Wofford, Harris, 139
Wojcik, Daniel, 190
women: as portrayed in media, 30; and targeted advertising, 203–204
Woodwell, Douglas, 100
World War I: speech rights, 44
World War II: US rise of technology, 79–80, 85
Worthy, William, 293–294
Wright, Richard, 132
Wylie, Philip, 165–166

Yugoslavia: basketball, 310–311

Zhou Enlai, 308

www.ingramcontent.com/pod-product-compliance
Lightning Source LLC
Chambersburg PA
CBHW051207300426
44116CB00006B/456